# ENGLAND'S POSTAL HISTORY
## to 1840

with notes on Scotland
Wales and Ireland

by

# R. M. WILLCOCKS

*Cover design by*
Michael J. Southall.

*Additional illustrations by*
Michael Southall and A. Bruce Auckland.

Published by the Author.

## THE GB SERIES

This is the second book in the series, the first being a priced catalogue of the types of handstamp used in Great Britain and Ireland. This is still available from Vale Stamps, the selling agents, at £3.50, and it is doubtful if it will be possible to publish a revised edition for a few years yet.

THE COUNTY CATALOGUES: it is hoped to begin preparation of the first of these catalogues as soon as possible, covering broadly the area of East Anglia and a strip down the Midlands. It should include most (or all) of Beds, Birmingham, Bucks, Cambs, Derby, Essex, Herts, Hunts, Leics, Lincs, Middlesex, Norfolk, Northants, Notts, Oxon, Rutland, Staffs, Suffolk, Warwick and Wilts. These will list and price all known stamps of every town and village up to 1840 - 43, from the research of specialist editors. Volumes of other areas will follow as soon as possible, and orders for all or any of the series are now being booked by Vale Stamps, 21 Tranquil Vale, Blackheath, London S.E.3 OBU.

Please note that recent changes in county names and boundaries are ignored as beneath contempt.

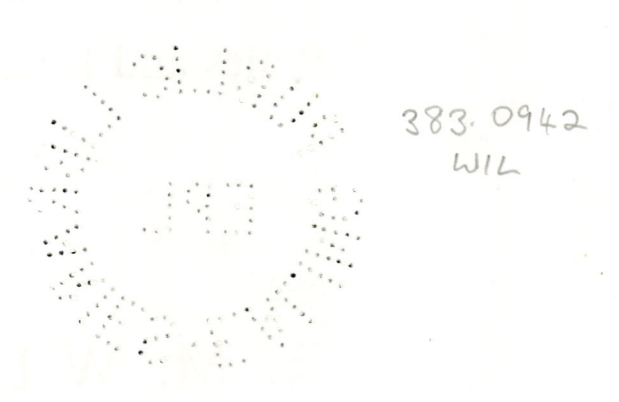

© Copyright 1975

ISBN O 9502797 1 4

*Printed in Scotland by Woods of Perth (Printers) Ltd., 3/5 Mill Street, Perth, Scotland.*

# Contents

|  |  | Page |
|---|---|---|
| Preface | ... | VI |
| Chapter 1 | Early Letters: Cuneiform Tablets | 1 |
|  | Papyrus, Paper, and Parchment | 2 |
|  | The Merchant Posts | 2 |
|  | The Carriers | 3 |
|  | The Royal Mail | 4 |
|  | The First Public Post | 6 |
|  | Two Calendars: A warning | 8 |
| Chapter 2 | The Post of 1635 to 1660: Witherings | 9 |
|  | The Civil War, 1642 | 11 |
|  | The Reorganised Parliamentary Post of 1653 | 14 |
| Chapter 3 | The Restoration Post Office: Henry Bishop and O'Neale | 16 |
|  | Early Rates and Charges | 20 |
|  | The General Post | 21 |
|  | Gardiner's Survey | 25 |
| Chapter 4 | The London Local Post: Dockwra | 27 |
|  | The London Penny Post | 28 |
|  | London Receiving Houses | 29 |
|  | Charles Povey's Halfpenny Post | 31 |
| Chapter 5 | Cross and By-Posts: Early Farmers | 32 |
|  | Exeter to Bristol and Chester | 35 |
|  | Ralph Allen | 39 |
| Chapter 6 | Provincial Town Stamps: Early | 46 |
|  | Mileage Stamps | 49 |
|  | Later Town Stamps | 52 |
| Chapter 7 | The Franking System | 54 |
| Chapter 8 | John Palmer and Mail Coaches | 63 |
|  | Inns and Coffee Houses | 67 |
|  | Decline: Coaches and Sir Francis Freeling | 70 |

| | | | |
|---|---|---|---|
| Chapter 9 | London, The 1794 Reforms and Later: Edward Johnson | ... | 72 |
| | Later ... | ... | 74 |
| | London Cross Post | ... | 77 |
| Chapter 10 | Provincial Local Delivery: Early Penny Posts | ... | 80 |
| | Ireland | ... | 81 |
| | Scotland | ... | 82 |
| | Manchester | ... | 85 |
| | Bristol | ... | 86 |
| | Birmingham | ... | 87 |
| | The Fifth Clause Post of 1801 | ... | 89 |
| | Charing, and Maidstone to Tonbridge | ... | 93 |
| | Later Provincial Penny Posts | ... | 96 |
| | Guaranteed Posts | ... | 99 |
| | The Illegal Twopenny Post | ... | 100 |
| Chapter 11 | Instructional Stamps: More to Pay, Charge Marks | ... | 102 |
| | Crowns | ... | 103 |
| | Too Late, Late Fee | ... | 104 |
| | Examiners Marks, Houses of Parliament | ... | 105 |
| | Sunday Post | ... | 106 |
| | Money Letters and Registration | ... | 109 |
| | Soldiers and Sailors Letters | ... | 110 |
| | Additional Halfpenny Tax | ... | 114 |
| Chapter 12 | The Reforms of 1839-40: The Growth of Agitation and Wallace | ... | 117 |
| | The Hill Family | ... | 122 |
| | The Select Committee on Postage, 1837 | ... | 126 |
| | Uniform Fourpenny and Penny Postage | ... | 128 |
| | The Adhesive Label | ... | 133 |
| Chapter 13 | Maritime Postal History, contributed by Alan W. Robertson, M.B.E. | ... | 139 |
| | Ship Letters ... | ... | 140 |
| | Packet Services | ... | 143 |
| Appendix | Rural Distribution | ... | 149 |
| | Free Delivery to Every House | ... | 155 |
| ——— | General Rates of Postage — England | ... | 156 |
| | Scotland, by A. Bruce Auckland | ... | 156 |
| | Ireland, by F. E. Dixon | ... | 157 |
| ——— | The Perpetual Calendar, taken from Whitakers Almanack | ... | 158 |

iv

## Illustrations

*Following page*

| Plate | | |
|---|---|---|
| 1 | Papyrus, heiroglyphic writing on wood, and unopened papyrus letters. A Venetian merchant's letter of 1459, with his mark ... ... ... ... | 8 |
| 2 | A Sumerian clay tablet of 2045 BC with its envelope | |
| 3 | Haste Post Haste letter from Deal to Oliver Cromwell, endorsed down the Kent road at Canterbury, Sittingborn, Rochester, Dartford and Southwark | |
| 4 | 1649, a Royalist smuggled letter from Calais with 4d charge and a parliamentary navy letter from William Robinson with endorsement and 6d | |
| 5 | Letter from the Earl of Warwick, Tilbury Hope, 1642, saying that he has lost the battle for the Letter Office and talking about Witherings ... ... ... | 24 |
| 6 | 1653 Broadside announcing the resumption of the public post | |
| 7 | The Kent Post slogan of 1661, with a Bishop mark | |
| 8 | Part of Hollar's map of London after the fire, showing the three possible sites of the Letter Office | |
| 9 | A leaflet advertising the Dockwra Penny Post, 1680 ... ... ... ... | 40 |
| 10 | Letter of May 1680 before stamps were used in this post, and another of January 1681 with P stamp of St. Pauls office | |
| 11 | Shooters Hill, a panorama of 1805, and a map showing the rides and boundaries of the London Twopenny Post | |
| 12 | A 'strip' road map, the Dover end of the Kent road | |
| 13 | A selection of unusual East Grinstead town stamps ... ... ... ... | 56 |
| 14 | 1839 propaganda for Penny Postage: a very large sheet and two very small ones which would be twice the postage of the large sheet | |
| 15 | Post Office notice that the penny postage would start on 10 Jan 1840 | |
| 16 | A letter posted 9 Jan at 4d, and forwarded next day at 1d: another posted at Leeds on 10 Jan with a first day handstruck 1d | |
| 17 | A notice giving instructions for cancelling ink for the 1840 1d black, sent with the Maltese Cross handstamp ... ... ... ... ... ... ... ... | 72 |
| 18 | The courtyard of a coaching inn, probably the Bull and Mouth, London | |
| 19 | 1807 notice of times of closing the mails at Birmingham | |
| 20 | 1837, the daily statement of dispatches from Birmingham | |
| 21 | The Bath-London coach handing over mails in early morning ... ... | 88 |
| 22 | Bill listing mail coaches from the Swan with Two Necks, Lad Lane, and part of a parcel wrapper with the Swan label | |
| 23 | Reward notice for robbery of the Dover Foreign Mail Cart, 1814 | |
| 24 | The Pandora, a Post Office Naval Packet from Falmouth, under full sail | |

# Preface

HERE at last is the book that started it all. Six years ago, with no experience, it seemed so easy to write a potted history of the Post Office as an introduction to a new catalogue.

Like Topsy, it just grew and grew until a fresh start had to be made in separate volumes. Then the catalogue developed by itself into separate studies of the counties, each by the leading specialist in that area, and finally the delay caused by continual rewriting and the amount of research made essential the summarized catalogue published last year, as an interim measure. Its reception has been very good indeed, although sales have not been as large as had been hoped. Still, it is early days yet, and there is no doubt it has had a great effect. When this book is published, it is hoped to begin the preparation of the first county catalogue, comprising East Anglia and much of the Midlands, and this should not take too long. I am very conscious that many editors have been ready for a year or more, and can only apologize. A great deal of extra work has come to me through taking this book away from the contracted publisher; I was sorry to do so but I could not believe that fitting every book into a standard layout and size would be satisfactory — these should be tailored to suit the book. I felt sure they would want to cut the size considerably, and there were other points of disagreement.

Only two detailed studies have been written since about 1900, and both are excellent. Alcock and Holland is a collector's book, and I am amazed at the enormous knowledge that went into it before 1939, but it contains little of the history which I am sure is necessary to proper enjoyment of the hobby, and it has been out of print for twenty five years. Adhesive stamps can be stuck into the album in catalogue order, filling spaces, but postal history should be so much more than this. The study by Howard Robinson is a fine example of studious research, but is written by a historian for historians, and not for collectors. Thus, many of the points a collector needs to know are not dealt with. I have tried to strike a balance between the postmark book and the history book, and should acknowledge here the great amount of information I have obtained from both. An example of the difference of outlook is the Civil War period 1642-52. Alcock and Holland begins twenty years later, for before 1661 there were no postmarks. Robinson and nearly all other books deal at length with the battle for control of the Letter Office, but the practical side of how a letter was carried (which is of much more importance to the collector) has been ignored. Nobody has stated that a post as we understand it could not have run in this period, yet this is clear. At the other end of my period, the 1839-40 story is very shortened, and emphasis again is on things that other writers do not say. Much is omitted that is repeated in every book.

For reasons of time and space most of Ireland and Scotland had to be left out, but generally the story is much the same as England. It is a pity, but no doubt they will be covered by others. Wales was always administered from London. The first chapter, on letters from 3,000 BC, is no more than a summary to give a working knowledge, and those interested can go to specialized books. In the same way, the vast European post of Thurn and Taxis can have no place in a book on the English post office: it seems there is no good study in English — please will someone write one, it is a wonderful subject. The bibliography has been kept short, for so many books are completely outdated and are interesting but not much help. The Government reports that are valuable for information are unobtainable, and need a large amount of reading for each fact that emerges, so these are not worth listing. Further, when I see a vast bibliography I always feel that the author is showing off, trying to impress the reader with the number of books he has studied. I believe some authors list every book they can trace, however remote the connection and whether they have read it or not.

Of the sources available for study, first must come the Records Room in the GPO Headquarters, St Martins le Grand, and perhaps long friendship here allows a blunt word without offence. Source material is superb, detailed, accurate and vast in quantity, and within the limits allowed them the staff do a very fine job — my thanks to them for the trouble they take. However, a change in policy seems to have downgraded it into just another job in the normal promotion ladder, and this is a great pity. Use of these records will increase greatly, and postal historians can do a lot to help the Post Office (not least in support to keep their records under GPO control) but facilities could be improved. In particular, there should always be a knowledgeable postal historian on the staff who does not have to leave when promotion is due, and if necessary they must take one from outside. If it can be done in the National Postal Museum and the British Museum, so it can in Records, and it is time the Post Office was proud of them.

Bruce Castle museum at Tottenham (Rowland Hill's old school) has some very fine material, always has an interesting exhibition, and is well worth a visit. However, for some of us the tragedy of the H. G. Fletcher collection still hangs over Bruce Castle. The British Museum and the Public Records Office both have enormous quantities of letters of all periods, much of which has probably not been examined. As the postal angle has never been considered, it has to be searched for but can be most rewarding. The same applies to most County Record Offices, and these are the best source for most students who cannot work in London, but another blunt word of warning here. Trained archivists at present have an inbuilt suspicion of collectors, and it is up to collectors to overcome this for everyone's good. An archivist's job is to preserve the archive in good condition for future generations, so do handle it with care and respect: a bad student is talked about and gives all collectors a bad name, which harms everybody. We are trying to interest them in the postal side, so help us in this, tell your archivist about interesting postal covers he has, point out really valuable letters which should have special protection, and try to persuade him to start a register of unusual postal marks so that others will not have to search. Try to persuade him to put on postal exhibitions. It is hoped that archivists, historians, and autograph collectors will realise how much help they can get from the postal side of the letters they study.

The Foreign Branch has been omitted because frankly we know little about it, and much more work is needed. In this connection, may I thank Alan Robertson for providing such an interesting maritime section for this book: after twenty years work Alan knows so much more that it would be sheer impertinence for me to attempt it. I hope I have been consistent in use of the word stamp in its original meaning of handstamp. If I mean the nasty sticky things whose price goes up every day, I have said 'adhesive stamp' or the original term 'adhesive label'. Illustrations are reduced by 20% in size to use the blocks made for the catalogue. I am sure I shall be castigated for putting so few footnotes and references, but this is after considerable thought. I want this book to be read as well as studied, and you can't read a book with continuous references to notes (it is worse if they are all at the back). Suffice it to say that I have been as careful as possible in accepting statements, and can justify most of them. The condition factor I refuse to go into here, and no two people agree, but you are always wise to buy the best condition you can afford (or in many cases, obtain). At the same time, I have no sympathy for those who collect in a purely visual way, as one collects paintings. The story behind an item and the information it gives are vastly more important, and as postal history is now so scarce it would be to everyone's benefit if these people changed their hobby to paintings.

Many people are thanked in the text for the help they have given, but in addition the Local Delivery chapter owes a lot to the researches of G. F. Oxley and J. A. Dennett, and extensive use has been made of the copious notes for a book on this subject by the late W. G. Stitt Dibden. The London sections, especially the cross post, owe a lot to the work of Barrie Jay, and his editing and support of the entire project have been invaluable. My thanks go to Mrs Turnham for six years typing and retyping of the manuscript with great accuracy, deciphering must have been a horrible job at times: also for the valiant efforts of Harry Cumming and the staff of Messrs Woods of Perth, it is pleasant to work with a firm who still take a pride in their job. A hundred others have had a hand in some way, even if only an idea put forward in conversation, but it is impossible to mention them all.

Finally, I would like to stress a point I mentioned in the catalogue, the debt we all owe to the pioneers. It is so easy for us today to look down our long noses at the writings of Hendy, Brumell, Graveson, and Stitt Dibden, to sit in judgement and point out their mistakes (I would have included Frank Holland and Foster Bond but I don't think they made mistakes). We forget that each little statement, accepted glibly and without thought as a fact, had to be discovered and proved and might have taken weeks of work. A fact is no longer thought about—it is just there, like Everest. In twenty years time probably the Free/O stamp will be dismissed in three lines in the books, with a bare statement of its purpose. There will be no clue that for about four years, Jim Lovegrove has lived with and dreamed about this handstamp, and still we have no answer. Postal History now is growing up, which is why I am so certain that the background to a postmark is just as important as the item itself. How it was used, or why it was used, gives an extra dimension. Frequently these can be supplied only by a knowledge of how the Post Office worked at the time, and often it is necessary to deny a bright theory because it was not done in that way. Administration in general was logical but conservative, and when one finds a problem which appears to break all the rules (as we have now with the Maidstone to Tunbridge post) difficulties really begin. The future is bright if we work on these lines.

*Blackheath*,
1974.

---

NOTE:

Unfortunately a few blocks were made full size; these are marked †. They are figs. 30, 31, 32, 39, 41, 42, 47 (Bath and Coventry), 61a, 67, 75, 86, 97, 107, 109, 116.

**Chapter 1**

# EARLY LETTERS

THE earliest surviving writing is hieroglyphic or pictographic, a series of signs or little pictures to convey an idea or message, carved in stone and dating well before 3,000 BC. This became quite standardized, a sign or picture conveying the same meaning to all scribes, and was widely used in Egypt and the Levant. It is possible that the earliest were on wood, but none of these has survived. Development from this is almost entirely due to the Sumerians, who inhabited the southern half of Babylonia between the Tigris and Euphrates (part of Iraq), but recognition of the vital importance of Sumer to civilization is quite recent. Babylonia, one of the two great civilizations 2,000 years before the Greek and Roman ages, was divided into two tribes, Akkad in the north and Sumer in the south, and from the latter came the first practical writing system — the cuneiform script which probably developed from some pictographic form of writing. Before 3,000 BC Sumerians were using signs with a definite meaning and then began inscribing them on moist clay; when used for messages these are the first letters.

Cuneiform script developed gradually, losing all connection with the pictures from which it had arisen, reducing the characters from 1,000 to about 300, and before 2,000 BC it had become functional and the scribes widespread. From the small land of Sumer, cuneiform spread and was used for various languages and can clearly be called the ancestor of modern writing. The scribe fashioned an elongated 'cushion' of moist clay, inscribed his messages in wedge-shaped characters with a reed stylus, and baked it in the sun. A later development was the covering with a layer of brittle clay which could be cracked away on arrival — the first envelopes. Some envelopes have an address inscribed on one side, and the seal of the sender on the reverse. The tablet was dried a little, then covered with the envelope, so both dried together — if opened unofficially it was impossible to put another envelope around the dry tablet.

Many tablets have the sender's seal, and again Sumerians invented the cylinder seal which could roll in a charming design, was easier to suspend when carried, and (the larger area giving more flexibility and variety) was a big advance on the stamped seal. If their enormous advances in mathematics, and their realism in sculpture, architecture, and astronomy are added to their invention of the first practical and portable system of writing, Sumer can be considered the cradle of civilization, and wielded an enormous influence throughout the cultured world at a period when we in Britain had hardly begun to run round in woad. Understanding of the zodiac, the knowledge to forecast eclipses and measure time accurately with only the most elementary instruments, bear out their fantastic lead over the rest of the world. Their year was 12 months of 29 or 30 days; each day was 12 double hours of 60 minutes. Babylon, Nineveh, Ur, Umma, and Nippur are names that should speak for themselves. The earliest tablets are around 3,000 BC, the majority between 2,000 and 400 BC, and although the Hittites on the Anatolian plateau seem the only other people to use them, numbers surviving are very large — the British Museum obtained 26,000 from the Royal Library at Nineveh alone. Carriage of these letters must have been widespread, as many Babylonian tablets are found in Egypt, but are not of Egyptian origin. Unfortunately, nearly all are safely buried again in museums and institutes, and very few are available on the market.

The Babylonian cuneiform language was deciphered about 1847 by Sir Henry Rawlinson from a text carved in three languages on an inaccessible cliff near Baghdad, listing the achievements of Darius, King of Persia. Decipherment of Sumerian and other cuneiform texts followed, but some are still not understood. A word of warning is needed on these cuneiform tablets, for tourist reproductions were widely made in Egypt in the 1930s, but are easily recognizable with a little practice; of reddish colour and sandy consistency, the granules rub off easily and they do not look old. It seems that they are all reproductions of the same tablet.

**Papyrus**

Papyrus was the earliest type of paper (before 2,000 BC) and was made from the stem of the papyrus reed which grows on the banks of the Nile. Fuel and utensils were made from the papyrus root; boats, sails, cloth, and paper from the stem, whilst the pith gave a nourishing food. The famous use was paper, for which the stem was split longitudinally in suitable lengths, and, after prolonged soaking in the Nile, two layers of stems were laid across each other; these were pounded with stones until the fibres adhered, and then were baked in the sun. Though widely used in Egypt, Greece, Assyria, and elsewhere as far as Italy, the fragility means that little survives outside museums. Normally a brush was used to write, and the first recognizable alphabet comes about 1,500 BC on papyrus from Palestine.

Both clay tablets and papyrus are difficult and expensive to purchase, but they can be studied and enjoyed in most of the larger museums. The British Museum has a wonderful display of both, fully explained, yet few but students examine them. They have some of the tablets describing the Flood (from which it is probable the legends grew of the Biblical Flood) and one on show could have been written yesterday, from a civil official complaining that his last three letters had not been answered. A papyrus to catch the eye of a postal historian was by far the earliest campaign letter seen: a dispatch from Nubia to the Commander in Chief in Thebes reporting they had found the tracks of thirty two Nubians and three asses, which they were following and might need assistance (an early Haste Post Haste letter!). Letters can also be seen, written in ink on potsherds about 500-600 BC.

**Paper**

Paper was invented about AD 105 in China or Korea, but the oldest dated piece is in the British Museum, AD 406. It was made from rags or bark, and Egypt was making it in the eighth century, Spain and Italy in the twelfth century. The earliest English paper was made about 1490 by John Tate at Hertford, but he ceased in 1507 having supplied it for a few books during those years. His watermark (in case you should see it) was an eight-pointed star enclosed in a double circle. The first paper mill to be successful in this country was begun by Sir John Spilman at Dartford, when in 1588 he was given the monopoly of papermaking and collecting rags by Queen Elizabeth. Paper made by Tate was used mainly for pamphlets, but was used for Wynkyn de Worde's *de Proprietatibus Resum*.

**Parchment**

Parchment was first made by a satisfactory treatment of animal skins in about 160 BC though a poor quality was used earlier. Vellum (the finest quality parchment made from young kids, lambs, and calves only) really became known in the second century AD. Parchment was used universally for letters and documents until gradually paper took over as it became more widely available — in England after 1500. Letters written in English before 1500 are very rare indeed — anything apart from Venetian merchant's correspondence is pretty rare anyway, and the Court or anyone who could write used French or Latin. English was very infra dig. The carriage of early letters would have been by servants sent on horseback, for those who had need to send letters would certainly have plenty of servants available to carry them. Anyway, the need for letters was small, life was very local and even for the aristocracy a journey from the north to London was much further than Australia today, entailing weeks of planning.

**The Merchant Posts**

To the merchants communication was vital, and fortunately quantities of Venetian letters of the 1400-1520 period have come on the market, so are available addressed to Venice, Genoa, etc., from the known world. It is interesting that only about one in fifty seems to be from London, a fair guide to our importance: most are from other Italian towns and the Middle East. Their organized relays must have been excellent, but little is known of the letter carriage. Probably London to Dover was the only English route, but in Europe it is thought that each city post carried the letters to its boundary with the next city post, and handed them over for conveyance. Ship owners carried them across the seas and it is likely that a complete network of these merchants' couriers covered Europe and many parts of the Middle East. They would have tried to run to a fixed schedule, for early intelligence of the happenings and prices in other countries was vital to trade, and could make the difference between large profits and losses. This was in no sense a public post, but was restricted to the merchants who paid for it, and most letters have attractive Merchants' Marks drawn on the front, near the address. Designs of these marks vary, but nearly all have a long vertical line, most with cross lines (probably the sign of the Cross) and suspended at the bottom of this line an oval, circle or pear shaped object enclosing various designs or monograms. The seal (if present) incorporates the same design and usually an additional safeguard was tying through the flap and the letter with string (under the seal). Those letters with the original string and seal are very desirable, and for British collectors those from London (recognizable by the superscription "da Londra" or "in Londra") are the best. Very occasionally letters of this period have the albino impression of the family seal of the sender on the front, about the size of a sixpence. They seem to be of certain families — Sforza, Ferdinand of Aragon, Farnese, Este, Borghese, or in some cases the City Arms — Papal State, Bologna, Milan, etc. A hundred years later, the Counts of Thurn and Taxis developed from their German headquarters a European post for the various rulers on similar lines. A thorough study of the Thurn and Taxis post is needed badly.

As stated above, the Venetian merchants' post had to be paid for, probably on a basis of the number of letters sent, or a charge according to numbers and the distance carried, and this implies some system of charging the sender or the receiver (no charges are marked on them). Each post would presumably debit letters of the other posts against credits of their own, which would entail book-keeping, but no accounts have been found. Thus merchants' marks could have been:

(a) confirmation that the sender was a member of a post, and authorization for it to be carried in other posts,

(b) the sign of the sender, against whom it could be debited in each post. His mark was used on his merchandise, household goods, seals, etc, and was hereditary.

No reason is known why so many of these letters have no merchants' mark, or how they were carried. This courier service (the Merchant Strangers' post) had an interesting survival in special treatment and rates granted to the Dover Road postmasters 100 years later for hire of horses. When it was suppressed by Elizabeth about 1584, the Merchant Strangers' post was continued by the Merchant Adventurers (British merchants) and there is little doubt that both were more efficient than the Royal Mail. The Merchant Venturers' post was stopped in 1627, but probably continued unofficially for many years, and may well have been used for smuggling home letters from Royalists exiled in France between 1647 and 1660. Examples seen of these smuggled letters bear initials only for the sender and addressee and no address, but a 4d or 8d charge (2d less than the Post Office). Names were dangerous to use in case they fell into Cromwellian hands.

**The Carriers**

The carriers have a most important place in the story, much greater than is realized. There is little doubt that they carried the majority of early private letters addressed beyond easy reach of a servant, and that a wonderful network existed from early times, centred on London. Their carts rumbling along the rutted tracks called roads must have been a common sight for three hundred years. From the one-horse man to the large Common carriers owning hundreds, they filled a need for contact when adjacent counties were more remote than countries are today, and their influence was such that until 1711 postal acts granted Common carriers the right to carry letters freely on their route. Letters surviving today prove that a century later they still carried them, and it is quite possible that their early carriage was co-ordinated. A series of letters in 1649 and 1650 from Cromer to Manchester illustrates the problem — one is endorsed to be delivered in London and forwarded, the others are simply addressed to Manchester. Presumably in this case the Norwich carrier took them to London, and handed them to the Manchester carrier so payment could have been made at both ends, but if three carriers were involved who paid the second one? It seems probable that arrangements for sharing charges were evolved for cases of total payment at one end, or where three carriers were used.

The Common carrier was the large firm who ran a regular scheduled service and charged higher rates, but if the goods were lost he was responsible by law for their value. With the frequency of highwaymen this was quite a big risk which no small man could chance. Very little research has been done on the influence of the carrier on the postal service, but it was very large. In 1637 John Taylor (the Water Poet) published *the Carriers Cosmography*, and listed some hundreds under the towns from which they worked. He gave the inns in London at which they lodged but did not give their names, probably from fear because most were small unlicensed men. A few 'foot posts' are included, one being from York which seems a long walk. If this really was a foot post, it would presumably be done by a series of men and may have given a regular service to all the towns between.

Stitt Dibden* reprints a most interesting memorial of 1680 from the Gentry of the County of Bedford, saying that there is no post to Bedford or any places adjacent, they can only use carriers, and consider a post would show £200 above its cost. 'Tuesday last a gentleman coming from Bedford in the Stage Coach lay that night at St. Albans. There was that Night Two Stage Coaches that came thither from Bedford Towne. Three more from other parts of that County, and also 7 Waggon Carryers from those parts. All these had great store of letters, Each putt his letters into his owne Bagg and Sealed them up. Then all their Baggs with many Baggs more belonging to other Carriers then in that Towne were put into a great Male. And sent up by Horseman to London that Night so that they were delivered by the Carryers Severall Porters Wensday morning before the Post letters went abroad.' This speaks of a pretty good organization, and it is twenty years after Bishop: in the next year these porters attacked and broke up some of the Dockwra receiving houses.

Jason Grover was a very big carrier based on Ipswich, and covering the East Anglian coast to London. Research by Mrs. G. Driver has already shown that Grover was the pioneer in his area, and seems to have combined various postmasterships with carrying the letters himself. Witherings decided to make an example of Grover, and had him put in goal, but so great was his influence that the merchants came to his London prison to arrange carriage of their goods. Mrs. Driver mentions two petitions to the Privy Council in 1637, one from the Norwich merchants stated 'we always had our letters safely and speedily carried by a horseman for little or no charge to us . . . of late Mr. Witherings has intercepted our letters and molested our carriers.' The other, signed by Sir Nathaniel Bacon and five others, asked for confirmation of Grover as Postmaster of Ipswich, Norwich, and Yarmouth 'which he has held for nearly 40 years, though confined by the usurped powers to Ipswich, Saxmundham, Scole and Colchester.' Doubtless, other areas will show similar figures of great power when the research has been done.

Even as late as 1843, in *The State and Prospects of Penny Postage*† (three years after the adhesive stamps), Rowland Hill was forced to admit that 'There are districts considerably larger than the county of Middlesex into which a Postman never enters' and a little later 'in some places quasi Post Offices have been established by Carriers and others, whose charges add to the cost of a letter in some instances as much as 6d. A penny for every mile from the Post Office is customary'. It will be seen that they still played an important part in rural delivery in 1843, but more of this later. In general, the Post Office only took action against private carriage of any kind if they were providing a service themselves, and in many cases where it was not economical they were pleased for private enterprise (frequently the Postmasters themselves) to supplement their service.

### The Royal Mail

The Royal Mail was carried chiefly by couriers who rode delivering a number of letters to widely scattered addresses, and when Sir Brian Tuke (the first known 'Master of the Post', who probably copied the special relay posts of 1482 for the Scottish War) laid regular posts along a

---

\* *The Post Office 1635-1720*, Special Series No. 10 of The Postal History Society, which reprints a number of most useful acts and documents not seen elsewhere.

† Published by Charles Knight and Co., who wrote and published so much in favour of Penny Postage.

few main roads from London as need arose for Henry VIII, the courier system was continued for more urgent letters. We also have the very rare 'Haste Post Haste': letters of extreme urgency which could be authorized by a few top officials only, were carried without a break, and were signed by each postmaster or innkeeper with the time of arrival when the courier changed horses. There were thus three methods of carrying the Royal Mail in the sixteenth century:

(1) If the destination happened to be near a road so important that a regular post was laid, and the letter was not urgent, it was sent by the laid post. This was a regular series of post-boys carrying the post on a recognized route (the post in its early meaning being the packet of letters in a portmanteau). Their stages were 10-20 miles, and owing to their slackness, poor horses, and delivery of private letters en route, it was liable to be slow. Incidentally, the term Postmaster comes from the fact that in the earliest period of the laid post the man designated Postmaster had to convey the post (packet of letters) himself, and could not appoint a deputy to carry it. Literally, therefore, he was Master of the Post. In the time of Tuke, and much later, it is probable that only the Dover and Edinburgh roads had constant laid posts, with others as need arose.

(2) Letters off these routes were conveyed by the Messengers, who were paid a retainer plus a salary for every day they were out, uniform, etc., and went round (normally on their own horse) delivering letters all over the country. On their return they put in a claim for expenses and these warrants for payment, signed by the Secretary of State or Lord Treasurer, are Elizabethan (or later) postal documents of considerable interest. They give full details; a typical one signed by William Cecil, Lord Burghley in 1596 reads (in normal English):

Mense November 1596

Edward Carpenter, one of her Majesty's ordinary messengers, prayeth to have allowance for his charges and travel riding in her Highness's service with letters from the right honorable the Lord Keeper of the Great Seal of England and the right honorable the Lord Treasurer of England with other Lords of her Majesty's most honorable Privy Council, to divers Lords and Ladies of honour touching the last payment of the third subsidy of three entire subsidies granted to her Majesty at the Parliament holden at Westminster in the 35th year of her Majesty's reign, viz. one letter to Lady Sheffield, one other to Lady Burgaveny at her house in the county of Kent, one other to the Lady Katherine Brough at her house in the county of Surrey, one other to the Lady Anne Compton at her house in the county of Sussex, near Etonbridge, one other to the Lady Bacon at Gorambury in the county of Hertford, one other to the Lord Compton, one other to the Lady Countess of Bedford at Cheyneys in the county of Bedford, one other to the Lord Mordant at Drayton in Northamptonshire, one other to Lady Wentworth the second dowager in Oxfordshire near Oxford, one other to the Lady Countess of Derby, and one other to the Lady St. John of Bletsoe at Broome Hall in the county of Warwick, and from thence returned to London, for the which service the said Edward Carpenter most humbly prayeth to have allowance. To be allowed by the right honorable the Lord Treasurer of England. To be paid by one of the Tellers of her Majesty's Receipt at Westminster.

W. BURGHLEY.

Mr. Taylor I pray you pay the sum of six pounds in discharge hereof.

VIN. SKYNNER.

Endorsed over "Edward Carpenter his Bill for £6.13.4d."

(3) Letters of great urgency were carried by a messenger 'post haste' without stopping to rest, demanding a fresh horse and a guide (who brought back the horse from the next change) when necessary, and these letters are endorsed with his times of arrival to ensure no time was lost. A typical example of 1652 bringing news to Cromwell of a big naval battle off the North Foreland left Deal after 9 p.m., reaching Whitehall after 3 p.m., 18 hours for 75 miles. It is endorsed Canterbury 1 a.m., Sittingbourne 5 a.m., Rochester 8 a.m., Dartford 12 noon and Southwark 3 p.m.

The cost of hiring horses grew so large that Elizabeth gave postmasters the sole right to supply horses for travellers at 2½d a mile, on condition that they always had horses fresh for her couriers at a special rate of one penny a mile. Only if none was available from him within thirty minutes could the traveller hire from other people. There were not many postmasters, they were usually large innkeepers and their main official function was to keep horses in readiness. Royal couriers had the right to demand the best horses from any mayor or individual in case of need. Although not allowed officially, a blind eye was turned on postboys carrying private letters with the Packet in increasing numbers to augment their low pay. Delay became so bad, however, that in the last years of her reign Queen Elizabeth had to order that they must not diverge from their route to deliver private letters, nor make special journeys without a Government Packet.

There are many references for students to these early postmasters and their activities and troubles in the State Papers (Domestic) in the Public Records Office, many of which were extracted and published in the 1950s by A. E. Trout in *The Philatelist* (a monthly journal published by Robson Lowe Ltd., 50 Pall Mall, London S.W.1.). They were always in trouble, their salaries in arrears, and many had to keep twelve to twenty horses in their stables. Frequently arrears of pay seem to have been five to seven years, and Howard Robinson* quotes a petition of 1628 from all the Postmasters of England 'being in number 99 poore men, some of whom bye now in prison, and many of the rest daily threatened to be arrested by reason of their great debts.' Evidently there were ninety-nine Postmasters in England in 1628. They claimed that their arrears of pay, unpaid since 1621, were £22,000, rising to £25,535 in 1630 and to the staggering sum of £60,000 in 1637. Under these conditions, who can blame them if they took all the opportunities offered to increase their income by private carriage of letters and hire of horses?

At this time, many city councils ran their own posts to London which, though primarily for civic mail, were probably open to the inhabitants to use if they had an influential friend. Little is known about them, but it seems certain that they were not public as we understand it.

**The First Public Post**

The first public post was probably on the West Road to Plymouth, run by Samuel Jude (much information in this section was provided by David Cornelius)†. It had always been the practice for ships from Spain and the Levant to put ashore messengers at Plymouth, who posted to London with news and letters, and saved several days. Jude, a London merchant, kept horses for posting at various places on this road and by 1626 had two servants travelling weekly to Plymouth carrying private letters as well as his own and those of other merchants. This was, of course, a potential threat to the postmasters' monopoly of the hire of horses and carriage of letters on which they relied for a reasonable income, and brings to our notice the Hutchins family. It is possible that when more research has been done they and Samuel Jude will provide one of the most interesting stories of all. Thomas Hutchins was Postmaster at Crewkerne, a stage on the West Road, and seems to have been a man of forceful character. He and his family had been the postmasters of Litchfield for many years, but probably moved to Crewkerne when the stages of the West Road reopened in 1620. He first comes to notice with petitions in 1617 for payment of arrears of his wages, and in 1621, when Charles, Lord Stanhope succeeded his father as Master of the Post, Hutchins mounted a campaign to improve the conditions of service of the postmasters.

Since Elizabethan days, when they were given a monopoly of hiring post horses, postmasters' finances had grown steadily worse. Their position had to be purchased originally (normally a year's pay) and they then had to pay 'poundage' (two shillings in the pound on their salary which went to the Paymaster), forty shillings a year for a mysterious Treasury charge called Orders, and a half crown on every acquittance. With occasional 'douceurs' to the Master of the Post, and the delay of many years in payment of their salaries it is not surprising that despite their own methods of securing unofficial income, things were tight and they provided a fertile field for agitation. Remember that no part of the postmaster's income at this time came from post letters; he was paid to provide horses for the Royal Mail and for travellers, frequently to provide a guide and, as he normally combined innkeeping with the postmastership, it was the means of filling his

---

\* *The British Post Office, A History* by Howard Robinson, Princeton University Press, 1948.

† *Devon and Cornwall, a Postal Survey 1500-1791* by David B. Cornelius, The Postal History Society, 1973.

inn with travellers. Letters carried unofficially helped, and so did the payments made by farmers and other innkeepers to prevent their horses (and those of their guests) from being requisitioned at an awkward moment.

Hutchins and others, it seems, built up an early form of Trade Union on the Western Road (probably very much wider in extent) with postmasters making payments to his central fund, and he had considerable success. The injustice which started the movement seems to have been a demand that postmasters who had purchased their position from his father should repurchase it from Lord John Stanhope on his succession as Master of the Posts in 1621. Hutchins succeeded in having this annulled by the Privy Council in 1623, and got the existing fees halved or abolished, but made such a nuisance of himself that the Privy Council ordered the posts not to 'employ as their Solicitor Thomas Hutchins, who has so importuned the Council by his clamours that he is ordered to be committed if he appears before them again'. Apparently little notice was taken, for when Samuel Jude began carrying letters openly in 1626 Hutchins was strong enough to counter this threat to a profitable sideline. The position was difficult, for postmasters were excluded specifically from making special journeys with private letters, but by 1629 Hutchins had interested the Privy Council in the prospect of an income to replace the considerable drain on the Royal Purse, and received permission to 'undertake the speedy dispatch of all private letters weekly from London to Plymouth, and from Plymouth to London' and the delivery of letters 'upon the road, and 20 miles out of the road if need shall require'. Thus was laid the foundation of the public post, probably run as a postmasters' co-operative, and the remarkable thing is that for six years Stanhope did nothing but try to raise the purchase price of a postmasters' place on the West Road from twenty to one hundred pounds.

Thomas Witherings (see later), with the example of Hutchins and his own experience running the Dover Road to France, saw the possibilities of a profitable national post and submitted his proposals successfully in 1634-5 despite the scepticism of Stanhope and the Government. An interesting sidelight on the Hutchins post of 1629-35 is that in the 1635 Proclamation establishing the official post, Witherings is ordered on the West Road 'to take the like port that nowe is paid as neare as possibly he can'. As the other roads (except Dover) had charges specified, it is fair to assume that Hutchins charged 2d under 80 miles, 4d from 80 to 140 miles and 6d beyond, and that the entire postal system copied his pioneer scheme. One big advantage of the public post which may not be appreciated is that it overcame the big drawback of the Courier system — at the time of greatest need, good horses were liable not to be available for government dispatches. With news of a big victory or the sighting of the enemy fleet, private hire paid very much better, and so many couriers would carry news, instructions etc. that unless government messengers could keep ahead, they were liable to get the only horse left.

Fortunately a record has been preserved of a private post developed from the Hutchins post. This was a foot-post from Barnstaple to Exeter in 1633 run by the Mayor and Aldermen of Barnstaple. The post left at 7 a.m. each Tuesday, arriving at the Postmaster's house at Exeter on Wednesday morning, in time for the London post. He stayed in Exeter to await the mail from London, and had a walk of over 40 miles each way. It states that the charge from London was 6d a single letter, 8d double (Hutchins' charge), and a footnote adds that letters from Barnstaple to Exeter were 2d to include delivery. It is probable that for through letters to London a special rate of 5d was agreed, with the other penny going to the foot-post. Probably a number of postmasters on the West Road ran similar posts to link with the London post.

Thomas Hutchins probably died in 1632, for in 1633 his two sons petitioned the Privy Council against the great injustice of having to pay £100 for the Postmastership of Crewkerne, against the valuation of £20 'anciently given'. They said that their father and grandfather had held the office for seventy years, and one feels this may have been the pattern of the post at this period — as one family was the cobbler, another the saddler, so the post was often kept in the family. It is probable that Robert carried on at Crewkerne, for the brothers made it obvious that they were willing to pay the increase from twenty to one hundred pounds if they could have the carriage of private letters, as their father had, but Edward went to make his fortune in London. He appears a few years later as 'Postmaster at the White Hart near Charing Cross', and will be dealt with under Receiving Houses.

**Two Calendars: A Warning**

The Julian calendar (after Julius Caesar) was very slightly inaccurate, so that in 1582 Pope Gregory XIII ordered the 5th October to be the 15th, losing ten days, but Britain did not adopt the Gregorian calendar until 1752, when the 3rd September was called the 14th. Thus, letters can be found from France which seem to have arrived here before they were posted. In 1752 we also standardized the year to end on 31 December, for before this many people dated their letters to end the year on 24 March, the 25th being New Year's Day. For letters before 1752, it is impossible to be sure which year is meant if written between 1st January and 24 March, unless the writer puts both years. If he put 1665/6, it is 1666 in our present Gregorian style. Thus, the execution of Charles I was the 30th January 1648, but an Italian would have called it 9th February 1649. Reference books compromise, and consider it 30th January 1649, adjusting only the year ending. There seems to have been a gradual change-over in usage, so it is probably fair to say that the majority of letters before 1700 have to be adjusted, the majority after 1700 do not, and the more extreme the date, the greater the chance of this applying. To be certain, though, one must prove which type the individual used. This is usually possible in a correspondence, but not often with a single letter. To prevent confusion, dates in this book are given the double year: thus 1715/16 is now 1716. A perpetual calendar is printed as an appendix.

*Papyrus with (at upper right) the horizontal layer bent down to show the vertical layer beneath; a strip of wood with funerary inscription in heiroglyphic writing, and two unopened papyrus letters, one tied with original string.*

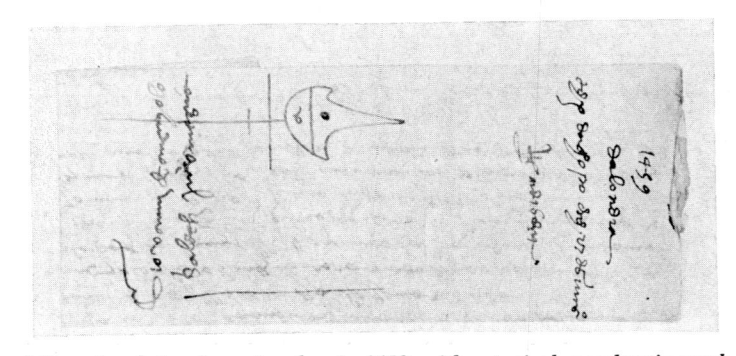

*A Venetian letter from London in 1459, with a typical merchant's mark.*

**Plate 1**

*A Sumerian clay tablet of 2045 BC with cuneiform writing and, on the right, the envelope in which it was sent. Note the cylinder seal impressions rolled into the wet clay (page 1).*

*The reverse showing the inside of the envelope, the back having been broken away.*

**Plate 2**

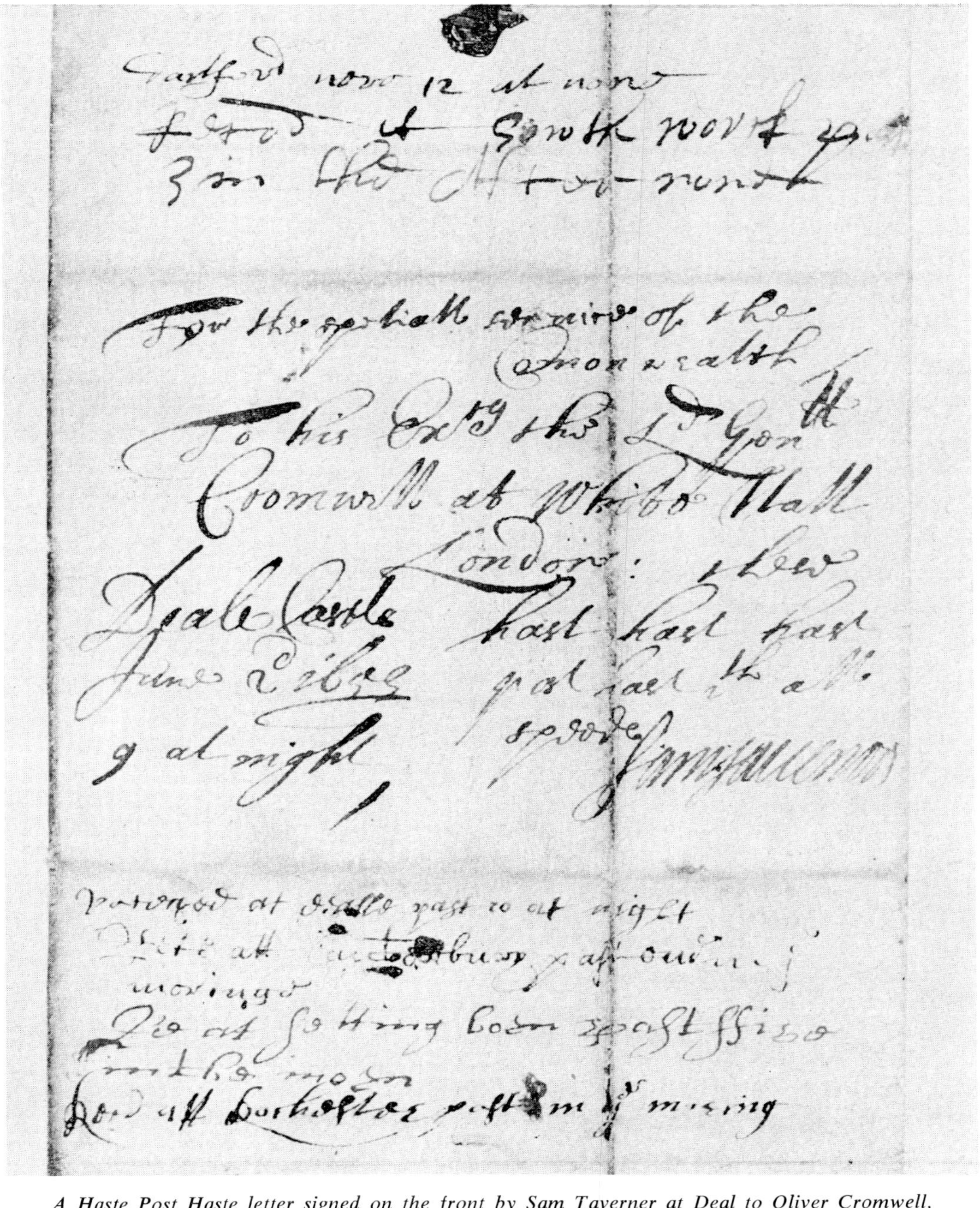

*A Haste Post Haste letter signed on the front by Sam Taverner at Deal to Oliver Cromwell, 2 June 1653. Endorsed at Dealle, Canterbury, Sittingborn, Rochester, Dartford, and Southwark, it gives news of a great naval battle against the Dutch (page 5).*

**Plate 3**

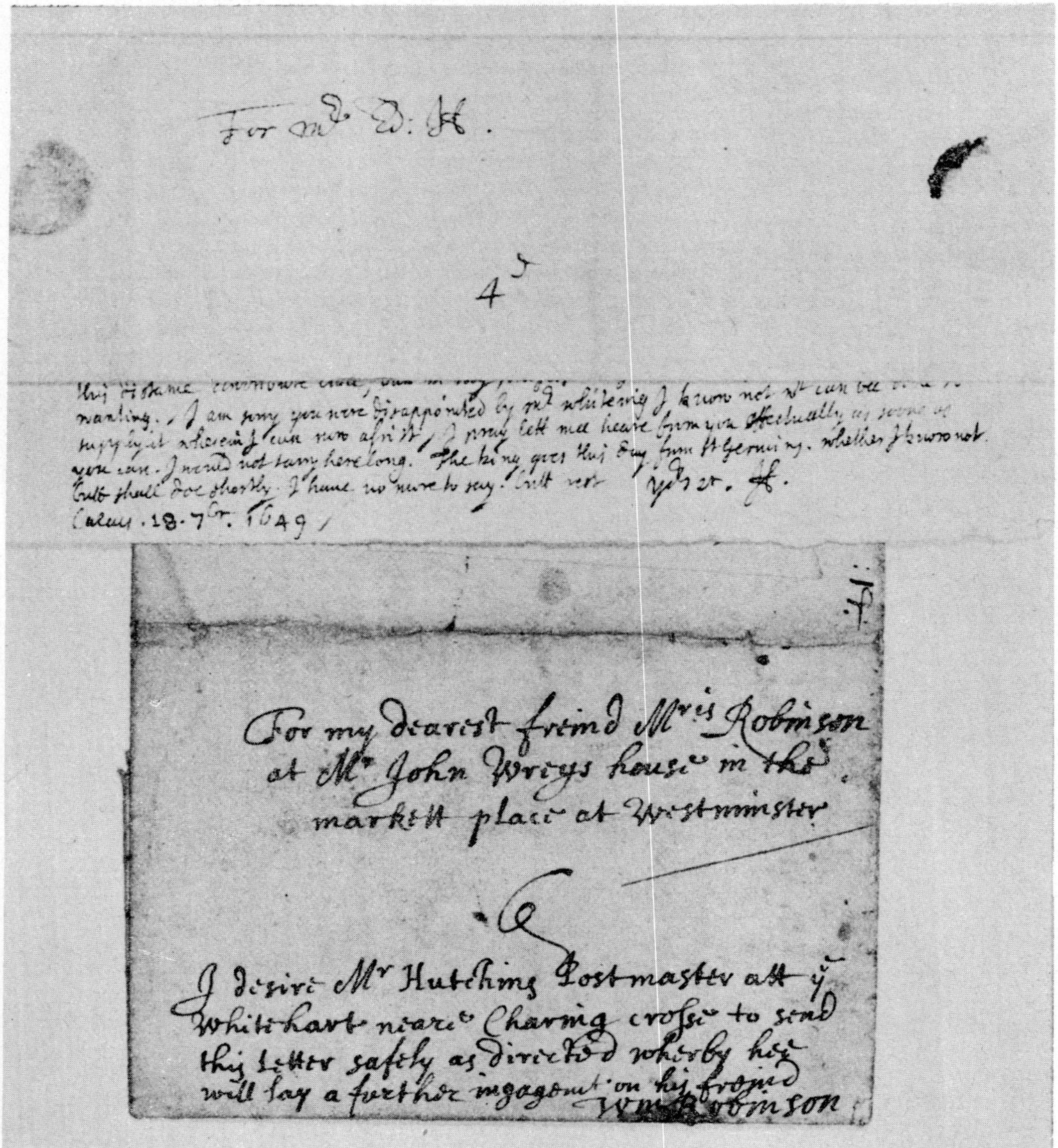

For Mr Ed: H.

4d

wanting. I am sorry you were disappointed by Mr Whitering I know not wt can bee ... supply it wherein I can serve as in it, I pray lett mee heare from you effectually as soone as you can. I need not tarry here long. The king goes this day from St Germains. whether I know not. but shall doe shortly. I have no more to say, but rest Yrs &c. J. H.

Calais. 18. 7ber. 1649.

For my dearest friend Mris Robinson at Mr John Wreys house in the markett place at Westminster

6

I desire Mr Hutchins Postmaster att ye White hart neare Charing crosse to send this letter safely as directed whereby hee will lay a further ingagemt on his friend Wm Robinson

*1649, a letter from Calais smuggled by the Royalist underground post, James Heath to his brother Edward. No names or address, but a 4d. charge. Below is a letter of the same year from William Robinson of the Parliamentary navy at Plymouth, with a charming endorsement and a 6d. charge (pages 12-13).*

**Plate 4**

**Chapter 2**

# THE POST OF 1635 TO 1660

BEFORE 1635 quantities of private letters had been carried in the post, for salaries were so low that it was recognized as a perquisite of the postmaster and postboy, but officially it was for Government and Royal mail, and private letters were not accepted. We have already seen that salaries of Postmasters were seven years or more overdue, yet the post was a considerable drain which the Royal purse could ill afford. Charles must have known that their positions gave them large perquisites apart from the monopoly of hiring post horses, for despite the arrears innkeepers and others were willing to pay the Inland Postmaster for the position, but this could not continue indefinitely. There is a divergence of opinion as to who deserves the credit for opening the post to private letters, but there seems little doubt that the main drive came from Charles himself to remove a considerable financial burden, and to enable him to control (and open where necessary) the letters then circulating. Sir John Coke, Principal Secretary of State, was probably more than the government official who handled the appointments, for in so doing he made the man appointed responsible to him, and took a personal interest. It will be seen later that the author feels strongly, however, that Witherings was nominee of the Earl of Warwick, was in his employ, and was there primarily to further Warwick's interests.

There were two Postmasters — Inland and the Dominions Overseas held by the Stanhopes, and Foreign Parts held by the de Questers until in 1632 the Foreign patent was given to Frizell and Witherings, soon held solely by Witherings. An extremely able man, said to have been a London mercer, Thomas Witherings was appointed five years after the official suppression of the Merchant Adventurers' post on the death of their Postmaster, Edward Quarles. At a time of considerable mercantile unrest, he made great improvements in the service. His regulations make it clear that to replace the Merchants' post he carried private letters overseas as well as the Royal Mail, and his improvements were so successful that even the merchants' criticisms were quieted. The first outstandingly able postal reformer in this country, he came of a good Staffordshire family closely connected with the Court and had been Harbinger to Queen Henrietta Maria, a post which gave him plenty of experience of overseas communications. He concerned himself with conveyance on the Continent as well as to it, and so speeded things by use of 'staffeto' posts, travelling day and night, that letters from London to Antwerp took three days where they had taken eight days before.

With the Foreign Posts running smoothly, he turned his attention to the Inland Post. The Dover Road already came under his rule, and conditions, rates for postboys, and quality of the horses were very much better than any other road — they were the elite. A Royal Patent of 1396 shows that before this date it was divided into stages, and fixed the rates at 12d. a stage for hire of horses from the hackneymen — probably it was the only good road in the Kingdom at this time. This reputation and the quality of the horses were maintained so well that in 1511, the year after Sir Brian Tuke was made Master of the Posts, the hackneymen were appointed 'extraordinary posts' at a rate of half a crown a stage, whereas on every other road horses were hired at a rate per mile. It is estimated that this gave the Dover Road hackneymen 1d. a mile more than those on other roads. It is noteworthy that most of the *Haste Post Haste* letters surviving are on the Dover Road, and that the Warden of the Cinque Ports ranked in precedence with the Earl Marshal.

Witherings, therefore, was in control of *the* road, and had the model of the Jude/Hutchins West road to Plymouth when in 1635 he made his 'proposition for settling of Staffets or Pacquet posts betwixt London and all parts of His Majesty's Dominions, for the carrying and recarrying of His Subjects' letters. The cleere proffitt whereof to goe towards the payment of the Postmrs of the Roades of England, for which His majesty is now charged £3,400 per annum'. This was accepted by Charles, and on 31 July 1635 the *Proclamation for the settling of the Letter office of England and Scotland*' was issued, giving Witherings sole rights to carry private letters, with the exceptions of the Common Carrier, on or near his regular route, and personal servants. Stanhope, the existing Inland Postmaster, was retained until 1637 to convey the State Papers only.

Witherings was commanded to lay posts from London on the Essex Road via Colchester to Norwich; Edinburgh with byposts to Lincoln, Hull and elsewhere; Chester and Holyhead to Dublin for the whole of Ireland; Exeter on to Plymouth; and Oxford to Bristol. The Kent Road was omitted, as it was already under his control. They were to be conveyed day and night, substituting horse posts for existing footposts, so that an answer could be received in London within six days. Witherings issued broadsheets advertising the posts, and giving instructions that from the commencement on 3 November 1635, letters should be left at his house in Sherborne Lane, near Lombard Street. For the first time a regular scale of charges was laid down, 2d a letter below 80 miles, 4d below 140 miles, 6d elsewhere in England or Wales, 8d to Scotland and 9d to Ireland for the single sheet letter. Letters of two or more sheets were two or more times the rate, an enormous charge, but in 1637/8 the letter over 1 oz was reduced to treble (under 80 miles) or double (over 80 miles) the single rate. From 1637 to 1839, letters under 1 oz were charged by the number of sheets, over 1 oz by weight.

Despite his monopoly (which it was most difficult to enforce) Witherings met considerable opposition on all sides, and only a man of the highest calibre could have overcome it. The dual harness with Stanhope, both using the same postmasters and the latter most resentful of the intruder Witherings, must have caused endless friction. Merchants had a new cause for complaint at the further inroads into the liberty of the subject (one feels they had more grounds for complaint against Elizabeth, a genius but completely dictatorial in her relations with her subjects as with her Officers of State and other Monarchs). The postmasters resented the loss of many of their perquisites, and the direction that all letters were to be sent via London on these six roads must have added appreciably to the cost in many cases. Thus, taking Charles Clear's estimate in *Penny Postage Centenary* that in 1630 private letters into or out of London averaged 25,600 a week (and this seems very high when compared with numbers surviving) and that this number stayed constant, it is doubtful if more than a small fraction of these passed through the Post. The greatness of Witherings is that in the face of this opposition, he established on a solid foundation the first organized system for the carriage of private letters within the state system.

Howard Robinson states that Royal orders of June and July 1637 deprived Witherings of the Inland Office, and limited the postal service to letters connected with Government. This appears to be a misreading, probably caused by obscure drafting of the Orders, but does not detract from his scholarly study *The British Post Office*. The Proclamation of 11 February 1637/8 (seven months later) is absolutely clear that Witherings is still in charge of the Inland Office and changes the rates slightly for private letters, so it is apparent that Witherings accepted private letters in 1638. However, Stanhope was removed and Witherings was in sole charge, though he was brought more tightly under the control of Secretary of State Coke and his deputy Windebank. Witherings was thus in control of all private letters from 1635-40, and speculation on the background is interesting.

As has been stated, one reason for the King opening the post in 1635 was undoubtedly financial, but more important was to have control of private letters. The opening of letters from or to people suspected of disaffection was widely practised before and for many years after this period. The Secret Committee of the Commons, 1844, quotes extracts from the Commons Journal in 1640-41 which show that every mail overseas was stopped and the letters read openly. This was to try to discover the King's plans to obtain help from France. Secrecy was easier for Charles II when Sir Samuel Morland invented a remarkable machine which lifted and replaced seals or wafers without any sign of opening. He invented a wide range of other machines, including those which could reproduce a seal exactly, and imitate writing so that the writer could not distinguish it. A man of remarkable intellect, Morland was a diplomat drawn from the peace of Magdalene College who supported Cromwell but, like many others, switched to Charles at the right moment. His copying machines were destroyed in the Post Office in the Great Fire of 1666, but it is probable that Sir John Wildman (another remarkable man of whom more later) had a similar machine whilst he was Postmaster General in 1689.

Any mention of the post in Witherings' day must be coupled with an important warning. A map has been circulated very widely (on thick yellow paper) labelled 'Mail Routes and Post Towns organized by Thos Witherings, 1635-51'. This map, the roads or the towns shown have no connection whatsoever with the man or the period, and must be disregarded. The details have been picked out and used in reputable books, and from it false conclusions have been drawn, so any reference to towns 'on Witherings map' must also be disregarded. No map or details to construct one exist as early as this, and this map was based on Gardiner's survey of nearly fifty years later: in fact it is too advanced even for 1682. Disregard any reference to Witherings' map.

It is unlikely that Charles had reason to doubt the loyalty to the Crown of Stanhope, or he would not have been left in charge of State dispatches from 1635 to 1637 (a field more vulnerable than private correspondence), so the presence of a very influential backer is indicated to enable Witherings to take the Inland Letter Office from Stanhope in 1635. If his outstanding success in the Foreign Letter Office is given as a reason, how did he, a fairly minor official in the Queen's household, secure the Foreign Letter appointment? In 1640, on his removal from the Inland Postmastership, Witherings assigned his office to the Earl of Warwick, who had become so prominent on the Parliamentary side that he was arrested shortly after: Warwick raised large forces for Parliament in 1642 and in the next year became Lord High Admiral. A letter recently discovered from the Earl of Warwick in 1642 on the subject of his petition to the Lords for the Letter Offices speaks of Witherings as if he had intimate knowledge of the personal affairs of both Warwick and the Duke of Manchester. It seems very probable that Witherings was strongly backed from 1632 by the Earl of Warwick, that Warwick was the power behind him until his removal in 1640, and this removal was caused by Warwick's outspoken sympathy for Parliament as much as Witherings' views. It was a key position, for every postmaster was appointed by him, and he controlled a vast amount of patronage which produced support and information on the activities of friends and enemies. Warwick was just the type of man who would see the importance of the position, and have his nominee occupying it, and Witherings could never have secured the removal of Lord Stanhope. It was evident that a showdown between King and Parliament had to come, and power and knowledge were much more important than money. It is probable that up to 1700 (or later) the motive to control the Post Office was power, and probably many Postmasters General were acting for other people.

No doubt the King tried to ensure that his Postmaster was loyal, so in 1640 Witherings was removed, his replacement being Philip Burlamachi, a prominent merchant and staunch Royalist. Probably Witherings remained in charge of the Foreign Post Office for some time longer. Burlamachi, always insecure, appears to have hedged his bet in 1642 when disorders began, and assigned his office to Edmond Prideaux, chairman of the committee of Lords and Commons to investigate his appointment. A struggle between Warwick and Prideaux (a struggle between Lords and Commons) resulted in a victory for Prideaux, but it is not known what really happened to secure the assignment to Prideaux.

A statement by Burlamachi of 25 December 1641 in the State Papers gives money received from 4 August 1640 £8,363: money expended £4,867: balance in hand £3,496 of which £1,400 had been paid to the Secretary of State. 'Of the other £2,000 those that keep the Office are to be considered for their pains and attendance, which are great'. This seems to bear out Witherings' contention that Burlamachi increased the payments to postmasters and staff to secure their support unfairly, and the profit margin is remarkable considering that the total revenue was only £5,973 a year. The expenses of £3,476 a year are almost exactly the same as the cost of the post in the 1620s, before Witherings opened it to the public, and this gives some idea how restricted was the post in 1641.

Certainly from 1642, probably earlier, the rival posts must have carried only Royalist or Parliamentary dispatches. As no closure of the public post has been found, it is doubtful if it was needed. If it was made dangerous and difficult enough, people would not use the post, and anyway it would have been impossible to run during the war.

The Royal Standard was raised at Nottingham on 22 August 1642, but some fighting and much bickering had gone before, and it had been evident for more than a year that war would come. The removal of Witherings (and thus Warwick) in 1640 is probably one of the early precautions. Very generally, it was a war of isolated minor clashes between local levies with a few large armies jockeying for position, of adjoining estates or nearby towns declaring for opposing sides and skirmishing continually. There was no front line, so the entire postboys' route would be a hazard. Of many hundreds of letters of this period examined by the author, not one bearing an indication that it was carried in the post between August 1642 and 1648 has been seen, but in 1649 the Parliamentary victors revived some service for their own letters. Private letters from their own leaders and officials occasionally carry 'Post Paid' or a charge. The Calendar of State Papers has hardly any references to the Inland Letter Office in this period, but it records the laying of two special (Parliamentary) posts in November 1644.

A series of letters to his wife in Westminster from William Robinson, a Puritan officer who had raised a Troop at his own charge and was a close friend of Col. Fleetwood, in 1649 illustrates the difficulties well. From Shaftesbury on 12th May, en route to Plymouth 'if you send your letter to Mr. Coytmore to Derby House he will send it to me in the Admirals packet on Tuesday'. In two others from Plymouth in May, he cannot tell her where to send except through Mr. Coytmore and on 2nd June in Milford Haven 'I hear that our messenger hath disappointed me, for the letter that I writ by Capt. Ball to be delivered to Col. Popham's man for thee, was not delivered to him', and again 'My dearest life, thy deare letters are my greatest entertainments and delights in these parts and I wish dayly we could have better means of intercourse . . . in the meantime we must send often to one another by Heaven, which is the best and nimblest conveyance'. Later he adds 'I have divers letters writt to divers friends, but dare not trust this bearer with them'. On 4th June, still at Milford 'Since my departure I have received but two sheets of paper from you . . . but now I hope we shall have better convenience of intercourse for we have this week ordered a Post to go weekly hence to London and we shall send from the Irish coast to this place weekly for letters. . . . I writt to thee one letter since I came hither and sent it by a seaman who had leave to return home for London'.

Two days later he follows this with another which is one of the most important, and certainly the greatest enigma, 'I sent thee a pacquett of letters yesterday dated from Milford Haven, but this going by the Post I hope may come as soone to thee as that: if it doe, prithee send away those enclosed with speed' but this is written 'from aboard the Triumph neare the Isle of Lundee, June 6th 1649'. Later he says 'A lettr now would be dearely wellcome to mee from thee, for meethinkes it is an age since I receiv'd one'. The remainder is a charming example of a love letter showing the pious trust in God of the puritans, and emphasizes Robinson's position of friendship with Col. Fleetwood (who became Commander-in-Chief of the Parliamentary forces and married Cromwell's daughter) and Mr Speaker, and that his cousin Luke Robinson was a member of the Council of State. He speaks as if this letter was a 'first day cover' of the new post, which he expected would arrive before his letter of 4th June, yet he wrote it when out at sea. If the post ran from Milford, had they a supply ship just going in there? The address leaf has no charge, endorsement, or other clue.

On the 3rd July in Plymouth Sound he writes 'while I stay here I may have the happiness to hear twice a week from thee' but he has not received any more letters; her last would be sent to Kinsale. This has a normal address, but on the last of the series, also from Plymouth on 5th July, beneath the address he writes 'I desire Mr. Hutchins, Postmaster at the White Hart near Charing Cross, to send this letter safely as directed, whereby he will lay a further ingagement on his friend Wm. Robinson'. The same phrase is on the earliest letter, of 12th May, but on the letter of 5th July is a 6d charge — the only one showing postal carriage. If the Captain of a Parliamentary warship, a close friend of Admiral Deane and Fleetwood, could not get his letters through by post, there was no post, so 6th June could easily be the first day. Notice Edward Hutchins again (son of Thomas) and now Postmaster at the White Hart near Charing Cross. It is doubtful if this post was yet available to the public or anyway, doubtful if they dare use it.

All these letters are three or four years after the end of the Civil War, the King had been beheaded, and Cromwell was clearing up the remaining pockets of trouble. Robinson's ships had trapped Prince Rupert with three or four ships in Kinsale harbour, and were waiting for him to come out. Yet only the last letter has an indication of postal carriage, and letters were not getting through to him although Plymouth was the main base, and they were sent in the Admiral's 'packet'. It is highly probable that this severance of communication was planned by Parliament, which was very scared of a counter rising (which came in fact in 1651) and realized it could only be organized by continuous messengers which should be noticed and could be stopped. It shows the feeling of insecurity current at this time.

The Civil War period has been examined at some length because very little is known or has been written about it. Some students do not agree that there was no post available to the public, so evidence has been given from the Robinson letters. Additional pointers are:

(a) a complete absence of letters carried in the post from 1642 to 1648, and their great rarity before 1642. Many hundreds have been examined from various correspondences, and only one (1648) has a charge. This is most probably a carrier's charge for the first leg of the journey, as from thence it must have been free anyway. From 1649 to 1652 known postal letters still are all from parliamentary supporters.

(b) a report by Prideaux to the Commons in 1650 that the Common Council of London had sent 'a natural Scot' to lay a post to Edinburgh and on other roads, settle his own postmasters, and run a weekly post. Study at Guildhall produced nothing but the fact that in 1649 a petition about the post was presented three times to the Commons by a deputation from the Common Council, and each time the door was slammed in their faces. The petition cannot be traced at present, but it seems probable that it was asking for an efficient post to be organized for the business community, and when this was not received they were driven to run their own post. It is certain that the City Council, one of the strongest supporters of the Puritans, would never have set up a rival post if one had been available. Two Judges of Appeal had held in 1646 that whilst Witherings' patent to the Letter Office was good in law, his claim to exclusive rights to carry the mail was not good, so it is probable the City post used this as justification.

In the same report, Prideaux stated that he had erected postages for the service of the State, had published that there should be a weekly post, and with the benefits from the postage of letters he had taken from the State the charge of the postmasters of England (except the Dover road), amounting to £7,000 a year, and the Irish packet boats, an extra £600. Prideaux makes clear that the post was primarily for letters of State, and this was nine months after the Robinson letters tell us the post was opened again: £7,600 in nine months is equivalent to the £10,000 paid for the farm of the post three years later (see next section), and probably this allowed a fair margin of profit. It is definitely a considerable overestimate in his own favour. The historical summary published as a preface to the First Report of the Postmaster General, 1854, states that the gross revenue for the entire year 1649 was only £5,000, and this would include special payments made by postmasters for their position, and other people. There would be no check possible on Prideaux's figures, and this is a good example of the difficulty found with many official reports and documents. Those written by the man in charge (especially Army Commanders) naturally put his own actions in the best possible light: in this case Prideaux wanted his control to continue, so he shows how well he has done. What is a public post? It seems probable that even this was only for known Parliamentary supporters, or if it was open to all, the Royalists certainly dare not use it.

(c) In 1649 a half dozen letters are known from members of the Royalist Heath family exiled in France, to England, which bear no name or address—simply Mr. Ed. H and a 4d charge. Signed J.H., it is apparent that James Heath feared the results of these smuggled letters falling into the wrong hands and dared not use the post (if it existed). Cromwell of course was busy with a large part of the army in Ireland, then returned to oppose Charles II and the Scottish army at Worcester; in these turbulent conditions any post must have been very limited, used by well known puritans only.

(d) a charming letter seen from Sir Edward Dering, 15 December 1642 to the Governor of Warwick Castle (a parliamentary stronghold), protesting strongly at his arrest 'without reason' at

Henley-in-Arden and asking for the return of property stolen. Sir Edward admits that he had escaped from custody, was using an alias, had 'a false beard to disguise my self withall, but not used' yet is most indignant for he 'would not be so unwise as to have either letters or ought else that might render me subject to any danger upon search or enquiry.' This letter alone should convince anyone of the impossibility of a normal post running at this time: he had escaped from custody, used an alias, had a false beard, but took great umbrage that they considered him fool enough to carry a letter.

(e) a letter of 7 May 1653 from Bristol to the Commissioners of the Navy was endorsed 'per the New Post' in a different hand and ink. This can refer only to the opening of a post as we understand it, suggested below for 1652/3.

(f) When students talk about the post running at this time, whose post do they mean? Obviously they know nothing of the conditions. There were two authorities, the King and Parliament, locked in a death struggle. Each ran their own post for their own dispatches, and the last thing either would do is to carry letters from ordinary people who wanted to post one. If 'The Post' had run, every horse would have been requisitioned by the armies (even the carriers' old carthorses were pressed frequently) and every letter confiscated. Historians expert in this period advise the author that a post for public letters was quite out of the question for a dozen reasons.

**The reorganized Parliamentary post of 1653**

On 18 January 1652/3, when the rising which culminated in the battle of Worcester had ended and Charles II had fled back to the Continent, Parliament felt more secure and reopened the post for all private letters. A notice has survived (now in Guildhall, London) which has been widely reproduced, but only recently has its importance been realized. It is usually described as a list of letter receivers, but it is much more; a notice announcing that after a break of nine to eleven years, the post was now carrying the public letters again. Very few can have been carried in the first period (1635-42?) of the public post, but from 1652 a number of letters has survived bearing postal endorsements, so evidently it was now on a satisfactory basis. Even then, how satisfactory is open to doubt for in May 1653 the Council of State decreed 'That the carrying of all letters, public as well as private, be managed by such, and only such, as the State shall appoint. . . .' 'That Postmasters and others employed by Mr. Prideaux, being godly and well affected' be continued if approved by the Council of State and if they have given evidence of their good affection. Other paragraphs said:

(a) that the Committee settle the rates for private letters; maintain a weekly service to Ireland, one or more packet boats to be maintained for the Milford-Waterford route and the same for Chester-Dublin.

(b) that a post be settled between Dover and Portsmouth, Portsmouth and Salisbury, London and Yarmouth, and Lancaster and Carlisle.

(c) that propositions be received for the Farming of the Post.*

It is obvious that very close supervision was kept on the postmasters and the letters they carried, and this order is also important for the suggestion of the first Cross Post (a post from one post road to another, not passing through London) from Dover through Portsmouth to Salisbury, where it would link with the West Road. Another was from Lancaster to Carlisle (surprising, but some years later Gardiner gives a cross road from Carlisle to the Edinburgh road, so this may well have started at the same time. It is open to considerable doubt whether this intention was ever carried out, for no evidence of these cross posts has been found, and Post Office publications and other authorities state that no cross post existed before 1660.

The result of these orders was that the first farm of the Post, both Inland and Foreign, was granted to John Manley on 30 June 1653 on payment of a rent of £10,000 a year; after two years

---

* Farming the Post was a system by which the farmer paid to the Government (or Monarch after 1660) an agreed sum each year. He received the income, and was liable for the expenses of the post, but had to run it within the conditions laid down; these became more varied and the posts more widespread with each contract. It was an ideal system for the times, getting a rapid increase in the facilities with a guaranteed profit to the country. For more details, see Cross Posts and Ralph Allen. Although some books say that Prideaux farmed the post, all evidence is against this: it seems he ran it for the Commonwealth, and Manley was the first 'farmer'.

it was given to Mr Secretary Thurloe at the same rental. It seems probable that with the increasing volume of letters, profits, and power of the Letter Office, John Thurloe thought it wiser to control a department to which his personal supervision was necessary.

The first postage act in 1656-7 confirmed the rights of the 'Postmaster General' (the first use seen of this title) to carry letters, establish rates and supply horses on the post roads. Inland postage rates were the same as 1652, 2d under 80 miles, 3d over 80 miles in England, 4d to Scotland, 6d to Ireland and Foreign rates are set out in fair detail. One innovation which became standard was a warning that all letters brought by ships must be handed in at the first port of call, but no payment was made for letters handed in by ships crews. This act established beyond doubt the Post Office monopoly for carrying letters, although still with the usual exceptions for carriers. This first period of the post can thus be summarized:

Before 1635, no Inland post for private letters existed, though many were carried unofficially by the post boys. Letters to the Continent were first carried officially in 1632, but continued to be carried unofficially for some two hundred years.

From 1635 to about 1642 the Royal Mail was open for private letters, but few have survived showing postal carriage, which may indicate fear of opening and a very small use. No date of closure has been found, so it may have just fallen into disuse. If it was made too dangerous, or the service was too irregular, people would not use it.

From 1642 to 1648 or 1649 it is practically certain that no public post (as we understand it) existed. Parliament ran a post for its own dispatches, but even high officers had difficulty getting letters into it. Foster Bond states that James Hickes was appointed Royal Postmaster, and doubtless this loyal servant tried to organize some system in the areas held for the King, but again it would have been a system to speed Royal orders and news, not to carry the letters of His subjects. Hickes was ordered to live in Weymouth in 1644, presumably to maintain vital communications with France (from which country Charles still hoped to receive assistance) and possibly to provide an escape route if necessary. Hickes could not run a public post from Weymouth.

In May or June 1649, a new post was laid to Milford and Plymouth, and probably others were laid at the same time. It seems to have been used by influential government supporters only, but this could be because the Royalists found it too dangerous to use. Probably it was inefficient and irregular, and only to places of military importance.

On 18 January 1652 a reorganized post opened, which seems to have been the first return to normality. Letters with postal charges 1652-60 are still pretty rare, but one gets the feeling that at last it was usual to post a letter, for those few who needed to do so.

On 30 June 1653, Sir Edmond Prideaux having now made it a paying proposition, the post was farmed to John Manley for £10,000 a year, under the supervision of the Secretary of State, John Thurloe.

In August 1655 the farm was taken over by Thurloe at the same rent, probably to enable a closer examination of the mail of suspected persons.

**Chapter 3**

# THE RESTORATION POST OFFICE

ON the Restoration of 1660, Henry Bishop was made Postmaster General and was granted the farm of the post for £21,500 a year dating from 25 June. His name will always be known for his introduction of the date stamp now called the Bishop Mark, the first stamp in the world of any Government Post Office. Stamps had been used for Royal signatures on documents well before this date, so he did not invent the stamp. The Bishop Mark (Figs 1-5) was introduced in 1661 because it was thought desirable to have a check on the frequent complaints of delay in carriage, and the earliest example is 19 April in the Public Records Office. Letters a few days earlier show no trace of a stamp, so it is probable this is about the first day of use and Bishop Marks in January to March must be assumed to be 1661/2, or 1662 in modern terms. Originally used in London only (Fig 1) it spread to Dublin (Fig 5) and Edinburgh (Figs 3-4) and influenced stamps used later in other cities. Overseas, Canada and America used it quite extensively, Indian examples are known and now a West Indian copy has been found, probably from Jamaica.

Dublin and London were always black; Edinburgh used red consistently after the first few years in black, and until about 1725 Edinburgh used an upright oval, then the usual circle. The Bishop Mark showed no year, just a divided circle with two letters of the month at the top, the day of the month below. From 1713, with very rare exceptions in 1719-22, the London Inland Office Bishop had the day on top and the month below (Fig. 2), but Edinburgh, Dublin, and London Foreign Branch retained the original form. From 1661 to 1673 the month normally has serifs, but after this most have sanserif letters. FE, SE and DE of later years frequently have serifs, but all other months with serifs are rare, again occurring occasionally between 1719 and 1722. Dublin, and probably Edinburgh had the day fixed and the month movable, but London Bishops are thought to have been solid. The 365 may have been used for a number of years.

Letters which did not pass through one of the capital cities bore no stamp until 1697, when the first provincial town stamps started. The Bishop Mark was used in London for one hundred and twenty six years, unchanged apart from size, but from 18 January to 30 April 1787 the Inland

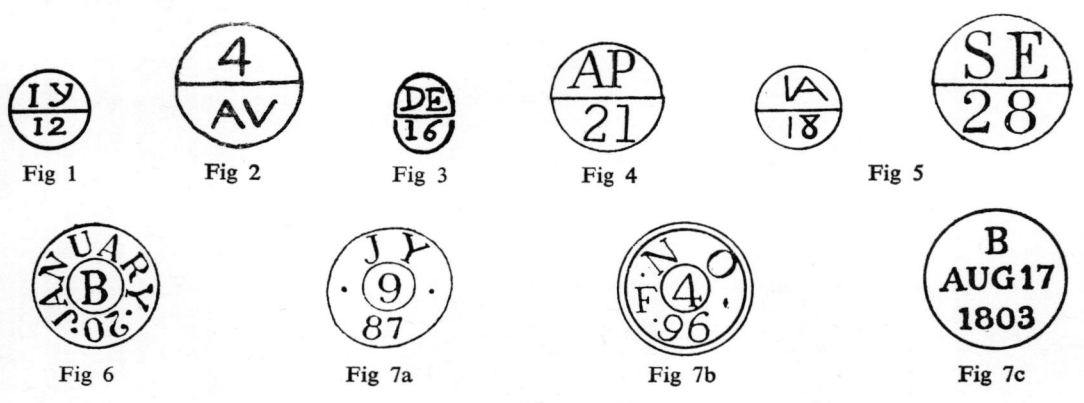

Fig 1　　Fig 2　　Fig 3　　Fig 4　　Fig 5

Fig 6　　Fig 7a　　Fig 7b　　Fig 7c

Office used both the Bishop Mark and an experimental design (Fig 6): on 1 May 1787 both ceased and the Inland Office settled down to Fig 7 and similar types. Edinburgh changed the design of its date stamps in 1803, Dublin in 1795 and the London Foreign Office in 1797. All these new designs included the year for the first time. Earliest years of the Bishop Mark are pretty rare, and it is not until after the Fire of London in 1666 that clear strikes are more easily available. This could be because a large proportion of letters were addressed to London, and were burned in the Fire of that year.

The early years of the Restoration were a period of turmoil; many postmasters were removed on the grounds of allegiance to the Puritan regime, and so it is probable that the grumbles about delays which gave rise to the dated postmark were frequently justified. It is remarkable, however, how many Puritan supporters were left as postmasters, and how well they worked with Royalists who had suffered heavily. It is even more remarkable that Henry Bishop was appointed Postmaster General. It would appear to be the same story we saw with Witherings in 1635: as Witherings acted as a very competent 'front' for the Earl of Warwick, so did Bishop act as a 'front' for Sir John Wildman.

Even now the influence of Sir John Wildman has not been properly assessed, but certainly it was larger than is realised: much of this note is extracted from one book only, which there has not been time to verify, but there is no reason to doubt it.* Superficially the only time that Wildman was in a position of power in the Post Office was his short term as Postmaster General, 1689-91, a period of only eighteen months, when William of Orange was grateful for his assistance in securing the Throne. This remarkable man is summed up by Ashley,

"A remarkable feature of our written history' observed Disraeli in the third chapter of his novel Sybil (1845), 'is the absence in its pages of some of its most influential persons. Not one man in a thousand, for instance, has ever heard of Major Wildman; yet he was the soul of English politics in the most eventful period of this kingdom and one of the most interesting to this age, from 1640 to 1688, and seemed more than once to hold the balance that was to decide the permanent form of our government. But he was the leader of an unsuccessful party'.

"Wildman's party was the republican party and his goal the establishment of a democratic English republic. For this he conspired for fifty years and through five reigns. With unusual discrimination he planned the murders both of Cromwell and of Charles II. He was imprisoned in turn by the Long Parliament of Charles I, by Cromwell and by Charles II. A fifth of his active political life was passed in prison. A warrant was made out for his arrest by James II and, if the hopes of his political opponents had been fulfilled, he would have died on the scaffold instead of full of years and honours, one of the richest aldermen of London." And later Ashley says, "Nothing is more curious in Wildman's career than the manner in which, whatever the blows of fate might be, he soon emerged smiling (that is, if he ever smiled) in a place of profit, interest, or importance. Although to the last moment he had struggled against the Restoration, within some six months of the King's return we find him a dominant figure in the reconstituted royal post office. On the other hand, such was his incorrigible gift for intrigue that no one can have expected that he would keep his position for long."

Wildman first comes to notice as the author of a pamphlet *The Case of the Army* published on 9 October 1647, for there is little evidence that he did much during the Civil War. At this time he worked with John Lilburne, leader of the Levellers, a republican group strongly supported in the Army. They believed that ultimate power should rest with the people, and not with their elected representatives in Parliament. In the confusing situation where the Army opposed Parliament, yet both hoped that an arrangement could be reached with King Charles to retain the monarchy as little more than a puppet, the Levellers were a strong fourth party opposed to the ideas of all three. Wildman was voted Member for Scarborough in the election of 1654, but like many more his election was set aside by Cromwell, exclusions which produced strong opposition outside Parliament. The first mention of Henry Bishop is 1654, when he tried to interest John

---

* *John Wildman, Plotter and Postmaster* by Maurice Ashley; Jonathan Cape 1947.

Bradshaw (who had presided at the trial of Charles) in a petition of the Army to Cromwell. He is described by Ashley as a crony of Wildman who acted as a link between the extremists led by Wildman (Lilburne had been banished by Cromwell to the Channel Islands) and orthodox Republicans such as Haselrigg and Bradshaw.

Although by 1657 the Royalists were suspicious of Wildman, they still continued scheming joint plots with the Levellers. Bishop probably had a hand in the Sussex section of the Overton, Hewitt, and other plots, and kept on the closest terms with Wildman, despite which he now had obtained with the Royalists 'a considerable reputation as a thoroughly dependable person'. However, when John Stapley (a nephew of Lord Goring) and others were arrested suspicion was very strong that Wildman (receiving the information from Bishop) had betrayed them to Thurloe. This, then, is the background to the acceptance of Bishop's offer to farm the post for £21,500 a year compared with the £10,000 paid at the time of the Restoration. It fits well, particularly the remainder of the story which explains the only two facts known heretofore: firstly that Bishop, a country squire of Parham in Sussex, could guarantee to pay £21,500 each year for a gamble. It might be a good bet, but must have been a big risk under the unknown conditions of a restored monarchy. Most country gentlemen did not have that sort of money — it was a massive sum in 1660. Secondly, that when the gamble was paying off, and with less than half his contract expired, he sold out to Daniel O'Neale at a pretty low price. With reference to the first point, it must be added that presumably Bishop's offer was the highest of quite a number, for the restored monarch was very hard-up and it was a desirable position. There can have been little guide, for the severely restricted farms of Manley and Thurloe would be no indication of the revenue from a post fairly free from fear. More important, there would be little guide to the total expenses of the post, all of which must be met by Bishop in addition to the £21,500. It may well be that the power was of more importance than the profit.

The Royalists must have accepted Bishop as 'a Sussex gentleman of unimpeachable political sympathies', and Ashley says that a Post Office clerk made a definite statement that Wildman provided Bishop with the capital. Wildman also outlined for the Government how Thurloe had gained his intelligence (and there is little doubt he was an expert, having been one of Thurloe's agents), under four heads:— to secure spies in all the reigning factions, to keep a close watch on mail passing through the General Letter Office, including that of Ambassadors and Ministers, and to disguise as messengers a few agents to follow strange messengers and footposts about the City of London, to sell them licenses and administer an oath of loyalty. He also advised that information should go not to the Secretaries of State direct but to a secret rendezvous by night, where it could be examined at leisure whilst keeping the victim in ignorance. Thus, to the fortune that Wildman had made by speculation in forfeited lands it seems he hoped to add another and greater one: with his paid nominee having complete power over the Post Office, and his own Royal license to bribe, subvert, or terrorise the London messengers and footposts his power would have been completely out of control.

Within a few months of Bishop's appointment rumours began to reach Sir Edward Nicholas of trouble and disaffection. In December 1660, Humphrey Cantell, Postmaster of Newbury, complained '. . . . Major Wildman, who puts in and out whom he pleases, and there is one Thompson, and Oxenbridge, Anabaptists who are employed as (his) agents to put in and out whom they please to the Office.' Petitions were received, one purporting to come from three hundred postmasters, that Bishop used his unfettered control to threaten them with loss of their jobs, forcing them to work under worse conditions than under Cromwell. In August 1661 Thomas Ibson, a London clerk discharged by Bishop, made sweeping accusations under strict examination about Wildman and others: 'This man hath the greatest share in the present post farm, solely rules, directs and governs all in it, and the Postmaster (an honest gentleman) is little better than the other's pupil . . . is so absolutely under the domination of Wildman (as well for purse as for conduct) that he cannot be accounted Master himself, much less of his office and that great trust thereby reposed in him, which sufficiently appears by Major Wildman's overacting and directing all things in that office, and that the good colonel does nothing, or rather can do nothing by himself without the other'. Allowing for a large amount of spite and bias in this last complaint, the sum of them leaves no doubt that Wildman at the least had very considerable power in the Post Office when officially he had no connection.

There were other complaints, and on 25 November 1661 came one which, although again from a tainted source, was evidence enough to act. After the Sussex plot of 1658, Major William Smith died in prison convinced that Bishop and Wildman had betrayed him, and his widow took 'The Sign of the Catherine Wheel' at Hounslow. Two of the clerks from the Post Office had ridden post haste to Hounslow, intercepted the Western mail there, and taken it into a private room at her inn. They examined it for two hours then returned it to the post boy with strict instructions to say nothing. On this Sir Edward Nicholas acted, and the ringleaders including Wildman were arrested. Although not brought to trial, he was detained in the Tower, then in St Mary's Castle, Isles of Scilly, and finally Pendennis Castle for nearly six years. Henry Bishop's reputation kept him out of the Tower, but he must have been under grave suspicion: probably it was thought that with Wildman's genius for trouble removed, Bishop would conform. In 1662 and 1663 other plots were discovered, real or imaginary. With effect from 25 March 1663 the farm was transferred to Daniel O'Neale for £8,000, although Bishop does not appear to have surrendered it until 6 April. Lord Arlington, who had replaced Sir Edward Nicholas as Chief Secretary of State, received from O'Neale £2,000 plus £1,000 for each year left of the farm. These guarantees total £105,000 over four years, in addition to the expenses of the Post Office. The Patent Roll states 'The King, for divers good causes and considerations, grants to Daniel O'Neile, esq., one of the grooms of the chamber . . . the office of Postmaster General . . . from the 25th of March last past for the term of four years and one quarter. . . .' This was dated 29 April 1663, and it would appear that Bishop's actions at last had overtaken his reputation for loyalty — note the wording of the patent above. It may have been in part because Wildman was in prison, his support was withdrawn, and he was not available to take decisions and use the Letter Office information for his own gain.

Daniel O'Neale (or O'Neill in the Dictionary of National Biography, O'Neile in his Patent) was the nephew of Owen Roe (Red) O'Neill, and an Irish Protestant by conversion. Born of a rebel and military family, he succeeded in being impeached for plotting and put in the Tower by the age of thirty, in 1642, from which he escaped: a fine beginning for an Irishman. Before this he had been a popular member of the Court, and in 1641 had been sent with William Legge to discover the intentions of the Scottish leaders. He fought as a Royalist at both battles of Newbury, and at Naseby, and commanded Prince Rupert's foot regiments at Marston Moor. Spending much of his time in Ireland and then on Royalist intrigues abroad, he achieved a considerable influence with Charles II and took part in the rising of 1651. On the Restoration he received a pension and some grants of land, so that when a real loyalist was needed to reorganise the Post Office in 1663 he would be a natural choice. Unfortunately, he died in the next year and his widow took over the remainder of the farm. The eldest daughter of Lord Wotton of Marley, she had been governess to Mary, daughter of Charles I, and married Henry Lord Stanhope, son and heir of the first Earl of Chesterfield. On his early death she married an eminent Dutchman, John Polyander à Kerckhoven, having refused Van Dyck. On the marriage of Mary to Prince William of Orange she was confidante and adviser to the Princess, was involved in the Royalist plots, and was even arrested in England in 1651 but acquitted. On the Restoration she was created Countess of Chesterfield in her own right, and on the death of Princess Mary she entered the service of the Duchess of York (wife of the future James II, on whom the Post Office revenue was settled). She married O'Neale in 1663, her second husband having died in 1660. Here is another talking point for the future — is it coincidence that within a few months James Duke of York was given the revenue and contol of the Post Office, his wife's friend of long standing was married to O'Neale, and the Post Office farm was transferred to O'Neale. There has not been time to consider yet which was cause and which was effect. Whether any or all of these three were responsible for the ousting of Bishop, or whether a suitable man happened to be available when Bishop had to be sacked, is not yet clear.

During the term of the Countess of Chesterfield, 1664-67, the running of the Post Office was in the hands of Colonel Sir Philip Frowde and his able assistant James Hickes, and included the horrifying period of the Plague and the Fire; it would be interesting to know if full rebate was given on the rental for these 'Acts of God', as it is clearly allowed in the terms of O'Neale's patent and would amount to some £35,000. From Midsummer 1667 the farm was taken over by Sir Henry Bennet, Lord Arlington, on a grant of ten years. The rental is unknown, but was said to be £43,000 by 1674. Arlington had become Secretary of State in 1662, and had a finger in every pie. Sir Joseph Williamson ran his affairs as Secretary of State, and the postal side was run by his brother Sir John Bennet and Andrew Ellis. Dispirited letters from poor James Hickes to Williamson (they were friends) show that postmasters were having to purchase their positions afresh at a year's salary, and that Bennet was cutting most salaries considerably. Bennet was most unpopular apart from that, for 'when he comes into the office it is with such deportment and carriage that no king can exceed'. Ellis died in 1672 and was succeeded by Colonel Roger Whitley, whose letter books (called the Peover Papers, now in G.P.O. Records) are a never ending source of information to students. On the expiry in 1677, no further farms of the entire Post Office were granted, it being taken into his own hands by the Duke of York and still run by Roger Whitley as Deputy Postmaster General.

When the revenue returned to the Crown on the accession of the Duke of York as James II in 1685, it was valued at £65,000. It was surrendered to the State by George III with the income from the Crown Lands, in return for an annual grant.

**Early Rates and Charges**

In the original proclamation of 1635 charges were based on the distance a letter was carried (this was continued until December 1839), 2d under eighty miles, 4d under one hundred and forty miles and 6d above this within England and Wales. To Scotland was 8d, Ireland 9d. These sums were for a single letter of one sheet, and were multiplied by the number of sheets in the letter. Evidently it was soon realized that this was unfair, taking no account of the size of the sheet, and from 1637 to 1839 a multiple per ounce was used on larger letters.

|  | *1635* per sheet | *1637* sheet | ounce | *1652* sheet | *1657* sheet | ounce |
|---|---|---|---|---|---|---|
| Under 80 miles | 2d | 2d | 6d | 2d | 2d | 8d |
| 80-140 miles | 4d | 4d | 9d | 3d | 3d | 1/- |
| Above 140 miles | 6d | 6d | 1/- | 3d | 3d | 1/- |
| To and from Scotland | 8d |  |  |  | 4d | 1/6 |
| To and from Ireland | 9d | 9d |  |  | 6d | 2/- |
|  |  | 6d per sheet over 2 ounces |  |  |  |  |

No further details of the 1652 rates are available at present. The Restoration in 1660 made no difference to English and Welsh rates, nor in the charge to Dublin. Scotland, however, was now rated from Berwick, with a surprising increase in the ounce charge (1/6d) when the single letter to Berwick was still 3d. Scotland from Berwick and Ireland from Dublin were 2d (8d per ounce) under 40 miles, 4d (1/- per ounce) above 40 miles. Edinburgh to London presumably was 7d single, 2/6d per ounce. Much remains to be discovered about postage rates for authorities seem to quote the same things, and leave other points unanswered. A large correspondence between Gifford (near Haddington) and London in the 1680-90 period has a variety of rates, some of which can not be explained.

There was no guarantee that a letter would arrive, and these charges were considerable compared with the value of money, so it is noticeable that from 1660 a reasonable but decreasing amount of the mail was prepaid. The explanation has now been found in a notice in the London Gazette of February 1686/7 (the Gazette always used old style, so that October 1686 is before February 1686). After stating that it has been the custom to receive payment to London or Dublin at the country stages for letters travelling beyond, it continues 'These are to give Notice that all Postmasters whatsoever, both of England and Ireland, are ordered not to demand the above-mentioned Postage any more: And also all Letter Receivers in and about London, and all Officers at the General Post Office in London, have the same directions given them'. It is not very clear what is meant, for a majority of letters before this are unpaid so it was not demanded. Equally, it does not seem to stop the sender prepaying to London if he desired, so it may have been that some had demanded it, and this is to make it clear that it is optional. The fact remains that London had its first PD stamp in 1713 (Fig 8) and before 1740 it is so rarely used inland that Col. G. R. Crouch stated (incorrectly) that before 1740 it was only used on Foreign letters. From this date, more were prepaid, and later the practice arose of writing paid charges in red, unpaid in black ink. Later paid stamps in red have the words in full (Fig 9).

A sobering thought is that from 1635 to 1840 there was not one case of the General Post rates being reduced, with the unimportant exception of the resumption of the post during the Commonwealth. This was not so much a reduction as an improved organization from the pioneer efforts of Witherings, combined with the private enterprise efforts of Oxenbridge at half the official rates which forced Manley to cut his charges. Once the Post Office monopoly of letter carriage was secure the rates rose steadily, until by 1812 many letters cost four times the 1657 rates. The development of cross posts from 1700 helped by reducing many milages: a letter from Bristol to Exeter was now charged for 80 miles whereas it had been over 300 via London. A list of the inland postal rates is given as an appendix for easy reference.

Fig 8    Fig 9    Fig 10    Fig 11

### The General Post

The general post, which in 1660 ran on the six main roads only, developed gradually, but most towns off these roads had to collect mail from them privately. Probably the system taken over by Bishop consisted of:

1. The Kent and Essex roads to Dover and Yarmouth, which ran every day. The Kent road had its own receiving office at the Round House, Love Lane, which was advertised in attractive slogans 1661-65 (Fig 10). Miss Bagust, in *Small Post Offices of London* pointed out that a token of 1657 bears a crowned head of Charles I (rather risky) and the legend 'Kings Head Post House, Love Lane', and suggested that the Round House (probably a disused lock-up), superseded the Kings Head as the Dover Post House. A notice in the London Gazette of 26 August 1667 announced its removal to the Grand office in Bishopsgate Street, which seems to have been the end of a separate post house for the Dover Road. The Essex post had two slogans a little later, but these just advertise that it went every day (Fig 11), so Miss Bagust may be correct in suggesting that the Kent slogans from 1661 were to tell people the Post House had moved from the Kings Head to the Round House. When re-established after the Fire in the house of John Dane, in a passage near the pump in Crutched Friars, it was called the Kent and Sussex Post Office, but more details are needed of this Sussex link. The Essex post was daily only to Colchester, and three days a week on to Yarmouth.* Harwich was one of the main packet ports at this time, yet no Government post ran there. In a letter in the Public Records Office (S.P. 29/303/35) of 15 February 1672, Silas Taylor, the Packet Agent, complains that the stage from Colchester to Harwich is very badly managed by one of the townsmen, who charges a penny above the postage for each letter. He complains bitterly of the vagaries of this management, and says that with this penny they pay more than any other town for an equal distance, and for a much poorer service. This is twelve years after Bishop. Taylor's letter had a good effect, for the Gazette announced on 2 May 1672 that the post would run between London and Harwich and London and Portsmouth every day except Sundays.

---

*A lesson many postal historians must learn is that at any period the post was more backward than they realise. Most started as stamp collectors and have worked backwards, and it may be that this tends to make them too advanced in their judgement. It needs a generation who started their serious study on postal history to assess it accurately.

2. The west or Plymouth road, Bristol road, Chester road via Holyhead to Ireland, and the North Road to Edinburgh, all ran on Tuesday, Thursday and Saturday nights from London, leaving at 2 a.m. Monday, Wednesday and Friday were called the by-nights.

From these six roads ran a few branches to important towns, and improvements came from the increase in towns served by these by-posts, not in the six Post Roads. It has already been seen that in 1628 there were ninety-nine postmasters; in December 1660 another petition reveals that there were nearly 300 but this is still a very small number considering that they were now dealing with the public letters.

In 1665, during the Plague, a rudimentary attempt was made to disinfect letters coming into London by toasting them over a fire and sprinkling them with vinegar, and between twenty and thirty of the Inland Office staff of fifty died. James Hickes records that with the heat and vinegar they could not see each other, but true to character he stuck to his post throughout that fearful scorching summer. Fortunately the volume of mail fell off very considerably. In early July 1665, the King moved the Court to Hampton Court, then to Salisbury, and in September to Oxford, a city to which he was most attached: here it stayed until early 1666. In mid-October special cross posts were established from Andover on the West Road and Towcester on the Chester Road for Ireland, to Oxford. The former went via Newbury, which was a stage on the Bristol Road, and if the branch from Maidenhead to Gloucester, South Wales, and Milford to Ireland was running at this time there would be a stage at Abingdon. In the State Papers Domestic are various letters from James Hickes, very rude about Mr Rathbone of Andover, who seems to have forgotten on occasions to turn this Plymouth bag on to the Oxford cross road, and allowed it to go through to London 'This should not be passed over, or he will never mend! On the Towcester cross road a stage was established at Brackley.

They must have been in poor shape to deal with the emergency when the Fire broke out just before 2 a.m. on Sunday morning, 2 September 1666. Hickes, who was Clerk of the Chester Road*, stayed in the office until 1 am next morning and saved all he could.

A problem that has always exercised postal historians is the position of the Letter Office at this time. It is partly the glamour of that famous happening, and partly the James Hickes letter, saying that Sir Philip and Lady Frowde fled at midnight but he stayed till 1 am when his wife could bear it no longer. One can just see him grabbing everything he could and rushing out with flames licking his coat tails. He states that he had considerable difficulty in getting away, and this is probably very true.

There is no proof of the position of the Letter Office at any time from 1635-7, when it was at Witherings' house in Sherborne Lane, to a day or two after the Great Fire in 1666 when the London Gazette, printed in a churchyard amidst the ruins, states 'The General Post Office is for the present held in the two Black Pillars in Bridges Street, over against the Fleece Tavern, Covent Garden, till a more convenient place can be found in London', with the exception of the 1652 (probably 1653) Guildhall Broadside. This begins 'All Gentlemen, Merchants, and other persons may please to take notice, that upon Tuesday night the eighteenth day of January 1652 the Letters were sent from the old Post-House (at the lower end of Thread-needle-street, by the Stocks, in London) at the Rates of twopence the single Letter within eighty miles of London, and threepence the single Letter above eighty miles within this Commonwealth'. The Stocks was the Stocks Market, one of the largest and earliest markets for food of most kinds, until its removal about 1739 for the building of the Mansion House. Before this date the Lord Mayor of London had no house in the City for his official residence. The Letter Office in 1652/3 then, occupied the west end of the present Bank of England site, and Princes Street, but note that it is called here the old Post-House, so must have been there for some years. It is very near indeed to Witherings' house in Sherborne Lane, and it likely that it was moved here by Burlamachi in 1640.

It may have been here in 1640 and reopened in 1652, but what happened between this date

---

* Each road was controlled by a Clerk with enormous power, responsible to the Comptroller only and stationed at the Chief Office. James Hickes we have noticed already as Charles I Postmaster during the Civil War and he must have been a tremendous character, loyal above all to the Post Office, his job and his life. Though nominally only the senior of the six Clerks at this time, his experience and position must have been much greater, and at times of crisis Hickes was always there to take control and reorganize.

and the Fire in 1666? All late Victorian books give a number of sites, as if it were a shuttlecock. J. W. Hyde, for example, in *The Post in Grant and Farm* 1894, states that it was in Sherborne Lane, then Bartholomew Lane, then Cloak Lane, Dowgate, and finally to the Black Swan, Bishopsgate Street, where it was at the time of the Fire. Others have a similar pattern, but Walter G. Bell in *The Great Fire of London*, the revised edition 1923, states that it was in Cloak Lane, Dowgate. This book is the standard authority, and Bell adds that he has committed himself on no evidence, only deduction, as the Bishopsgate Street site was never burned. Dowgate Hill would fit Hickes letter for time, so he considers it correct, and this site has been accepted unquestioned by subsequent authors, with one exception. Foster Bond, in most useful background chapters preceding *State Papers Domestic concerning the Post Office in the reign of Charles II* by T. H. Elliott (Postal History Society 1964) carefully lists the three possible sites and decides there is not enough evidence in favour of any one: he is the only person who even considers Threadneedle Street at all.

Recent research* has unearthed two very relevant papers which do not appear to have been seen by any of the writers, and which are considered conclusive that the Letter Office did not move at all. After a number of fruitless searches through the fire claims, assessments, and other records, Guildhall Library produced the fascinating map drawn by John Leake and engraved by Wenceslaus Hollar in 1667, prepared immediately after the Fire. It shows in fair detail the burned and surviving parts of the City, and amongst important features labelled is the Post House, exactly opposite the Stocks Market on Threadneedle Street, where it had been. This is not just any map, where one draughtsman copies the previous one, but 'An Exact Surveigh ... in December 1666, by the order of the Lord Mayor, Aldermen, and Common Councell of the said City' and was surveyed to be a guide and basis for the rebuilding. Another point that emerged from this map is that the two corners of Cloak Lane with Dowgate Hill appear to be occupied by St John Baptist Church and the Tallow Chandlers Hall — even if the latter is not exactly on the corner, certainly there was not room for a building of the size needed.

The second evidence is even more conclusive, for the editor of the new edition of Pepys' diary, Robert Latham, said that the late Professor Reddaway's placing of it in this position was founded largely on the Hearth Tax records, in the Public Records Office. These proved to have an entry under Broad Street Ward, St Christophers Precinct, for the Post Office, which was rated on 33 Hearths, £4-19-.† St Christophers Church was a few yards along Threadneedle Street, the other end of the Bank of England building, and apart from this Bishopsgate Street was in Bishopsgate Ward, and Cloak Lane/Dowgate Hill was either Dowgate or Vintry Ward. Although the tax book was undated, Professor Reddaway had written on it 'This must be pre-Fire' and this is confirmed as the site was not rebuilt. Princes Street, beside the Bank of England now, was cut through some years later. It can be accepted therefore, that the Letter Office remained at the site on 'Threadneedle Street, opposite the Stocks' from 1653-66, and being described as 'The Old Post-House' it had been there before this date, possibly in 1640-1.

There is one discrepancy: James Hickes letter is dated 3rd September, and at this time, Threadneedle Street was whole and safe for another day. The site marked was burned at about 1 am, but on the night of 3rd/4th and not 2nd/3rd. There are two possible explanations. Any reader of the story of the Fire is left with a feeling of horror at its speed in leaping through whole areas: this was not particularly because of the closeness of houses across a street, but because the enormous heat at its heart generated rising air currents which carried blazing brands for hundreds of yards to start a new blaze behind the gangs and trained-bands trying to restrict it. The air must have been full of flaming cinders, and if Hickes ran out on the 2nd/3rd, as he said, Cannon Street was an inferno as well as Dowgate Hill, only three hundred yards from Threadneedle Street, so it must have seemed that the Letter Office would go at any minute. By chance the flames went along Cannon Street, and not North, so the office was safe. The other explanation, which the author prefers, is human error. If the letter had been dated in full, Monday 3rd September, it would have been unarguable, but it is only 3rd September. Hickes had been at full stretch for at least thirty-six hours with no sleep, and under great pressure. Many people do not know the date

---

\* '*The Letter Office in the Fire of London*' by R. M. Willcocks (*The British Mailcoach* No 1, Spring 1974).
† P.R.O. E179/147/617 page 133.

under normal circumstances, so what is more likely than that he had missed a day and wrote it on the 4th dating it the 3rd. A small piece of confirming evidence is that Hickes says the Chester and Irish mail is in, and he sends Williamson his letters. If this was Monday 3rd, all six of the mails should be in, and if five were delayed he would say so. It is more probable it was written on Tuesday 4th (the Irish mail was always the one to be delayed), that Hickes had sent to Williamson letters from the other mails the previous day, and this was the balance that had been delayed.

Sir Joseph Williamson, to whom Hickes was writing, was Secretary to Lord Arlington, the Secretary of State and joint farmer of the Post Office with Lord Berkeley from 1667. He had been Secretary to Arlington's predecessor, Sir Edward Nicholas, and wielded considerable power. He was editor of the Oxford Gazette in 1665, and carried on with the London Gazette on its return to the capital. For his Gazettes rapid and accurate news was essential, and in this country this was provided by the postmasters at ports. In the State Papers are hundreds of letters addressed to Hickes or Williamson giving news of shipping and any local happenings, all sent free franked. There is little doubt that Williamson was gathering political intelligence in a big way, and this he extended overseas using Consuls etc. Hickes undoubtedly worked very closely with him. Over a thousand letters are addressed to Williamson or Hickes at the Letter Office, but only one has a clue to the location — near Cornhill. He succeeded Arlington as Secretary of State in 1674, but resigned in 1678.

After the General Letter Office in Threadneedle Street was burned down on 3rd or 4th September, a temporary Post Office was set up at the Two Black Pillars in Bridges Street, Covent Garden, according to the London Gazette of 3rd-10th September. It remained there for some weeks before finding an adequate home in Bishopsgate Street (letters in P.R.O. SP29/174 of October 1st and 3rd are to the letter Office in Bishopsgate Street) and in 1678 moved permanently to Lombard Street. A letter from Ireland of 11th September carried by the post to London still had no trace of a Bishop Mark, so new stamps apparently were not available for at least eleven days after the Fire. It would be interesting to hear of other letters arriving in London, or sent from London at this time.

A steady annual increase from 1667 is seen in letters available today, and it seems that letters became more usual amongst landowners, the legal profession and merchants. Doubtless this was helped by increases in the by-posts feeding letters into the six main roads to London. By 1677, when Thomas Gardiner delivered his first survey, by-posts had grown to a reasonable number and gave a fair coverage for much of the populous parts of England. Large areas, however, were left to make their own arrangements, some had posts run privately by the postmaster from their nearest Post Town (the Post Office did not object to postmasters improving the service). On 17 December 1668 the London Gazette carried a notice that all postmasters should deliver all letters within ten miles of their stage, charging twopence extra for this service but carrying back the answer free. It is not clear if the postboy was expected to wait whilst the letter was read and another letter was written, but it is very doubtful if this was carried out. Most by-posts ran only once a week, some less than this. Despite the efforts of men of the calibre of Hickes, little improvement is seen in the speed of the mail for many years, due mainly to the dreadful state of the roads, the ever-present danger from highwaymen, and poor quality of the postboys and horses supplied. The introduction of time-bills with the letter bags, to be signed by every postmaster, could not secure much improvement whilst the roads were mere tracks, some almost impassable in winter. The appointment of six Surveyors in 1715 gradually led to an improvement in the facilities provided, safety of the mails and tightening of the supervision. These Surveyors travelled the roads, acting as a link between the Clerks in London and the postmasters so remote from them, and were really responsible for the practical administration of their road. It was now possible to identify and remove if necessary the worst offenders, either in the running of the postal service or defrauding the revenue, and their personal knowledge of the men and offices would be of great value in improving efficiency. Their power grew steadily over a span of two hundred and thirty years, as a link between Post Office, postmaster and the public. From a notice in the London Gazette of 17 December 1768 (reproduced in the Postal History Society Bulletin No. 25, April 1943) it would appear that slightly before this date the post on all major post roads had been made a six-day post.

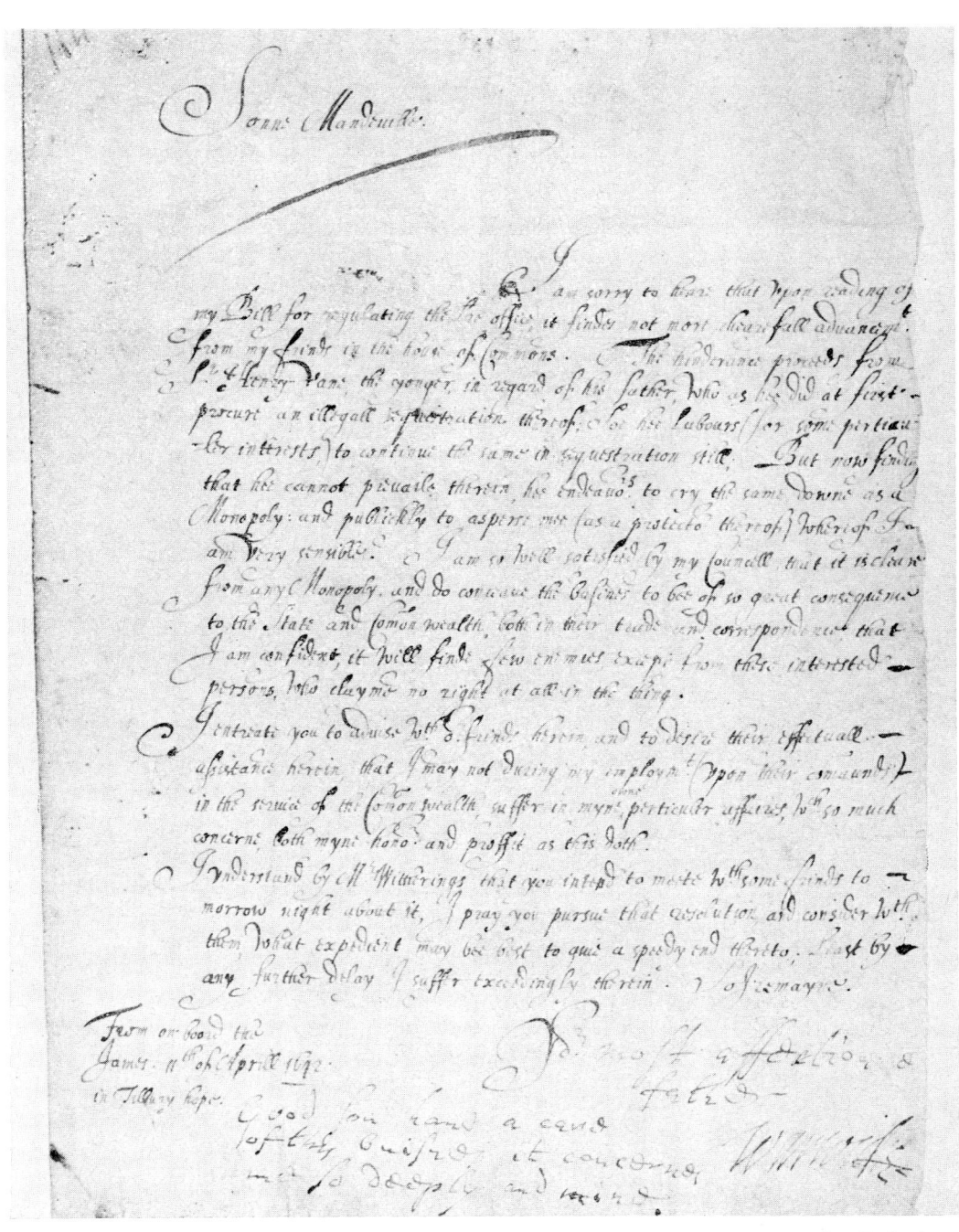

*1642 letter from the Earl of Warwick on board the James, Tillbury Hope, to the Earl of Manchester saying that he has lost the battle for the Letter Office. The last paragraph shows that Witherings was still very close to them both (page 11).*

**Plate 5**

ALL Gentlemen Merchants, and other Persons may please to take notice, that upon Tuseday night the eighteenth day of *January* 1652. the Letters were sent from the old Post-house (at the lower end of Threedneedle-street, by the Stocks, in *London*) at the Rates of twopence the single Letter within eighty miles of *London*, and threepence the single Letter above eighty miles within this Common-wealth (usually sent unto) and so proportionably for double Letters and Packets, and Packets of printed Books, or two shillings the pound, and the State Packets and Letters carried free: And so to continue going forth Tusedays and Saturday nights, and Answers expected Mundays and Fryday mornings, as formerly accustomed.

And Letters may be received in for conveyance by the old Post at those Rates at the several places accustomed. *VIZ.*

At Mr. *Bartholmew Haggets*, at the Sarizans Head in *Westminster*.
At Mr. *Robert Genns*, the Rose in King-street.
At Mr. *Edward Huchins*, Post-master, at the white hart at Charing Cross
At Mr. *Adams*, the Porter of the Gate at the Savoy.
At Mr. *Ralph Oldhams*, at the Gun in the Strand.
At Mr. *William Leakes*, at the Crown at Temple Bar.
At Mr. *Lawrance Blacklocks*, at Temple Bar, Stationer.
At Mr. *Abell Ropers*, over against Dunstones Church in Fleet-street.
At Mr. *Charles Adams*, the Marygold against Fetter lane end.
At Mr. *John Allins*, the white Horse in Fleet-street.
At Mr. *Thomas Taylor*, in the inner Temple lane.
At Mr. *Lawrances*.
At *Matthew Days*, a Porter belonging to Lyons Inn.
At Mr. *Richard Best* Stationer in Graise-Inn Gate.
At Mr. *William Atkins*, Stationer at staple Inn.
At Mr. *John Places*, Stationer at Furnifalls Inn.
At Mr. *Thomas Simms*, at the sign of the Angel at Riddriff stayers.
At Capt. *Grigsons* next the white Lyon, by the new stayers at *Wapping*.
At Mrs. *Staltinborgh*, Tower-hill next the Navy Office.
At Mrs. *Smith* next the Cock in *Ratlef*.
At Mrs. *Ivy* over against the Gun in Woodstreet.

*The Persons that leave Letters at any of these places, are desired to bring them in thither before ten of the clock, Tusedays and Saturday nights; and at the Post-house by the Stocks by twelve a clock.*

*1652/3 Broadside announcing the reopening of the public post, and a list of Receivers Reproduced by courtesy of the Guildhall Library (pages 14, 22).*

**Plate 6**

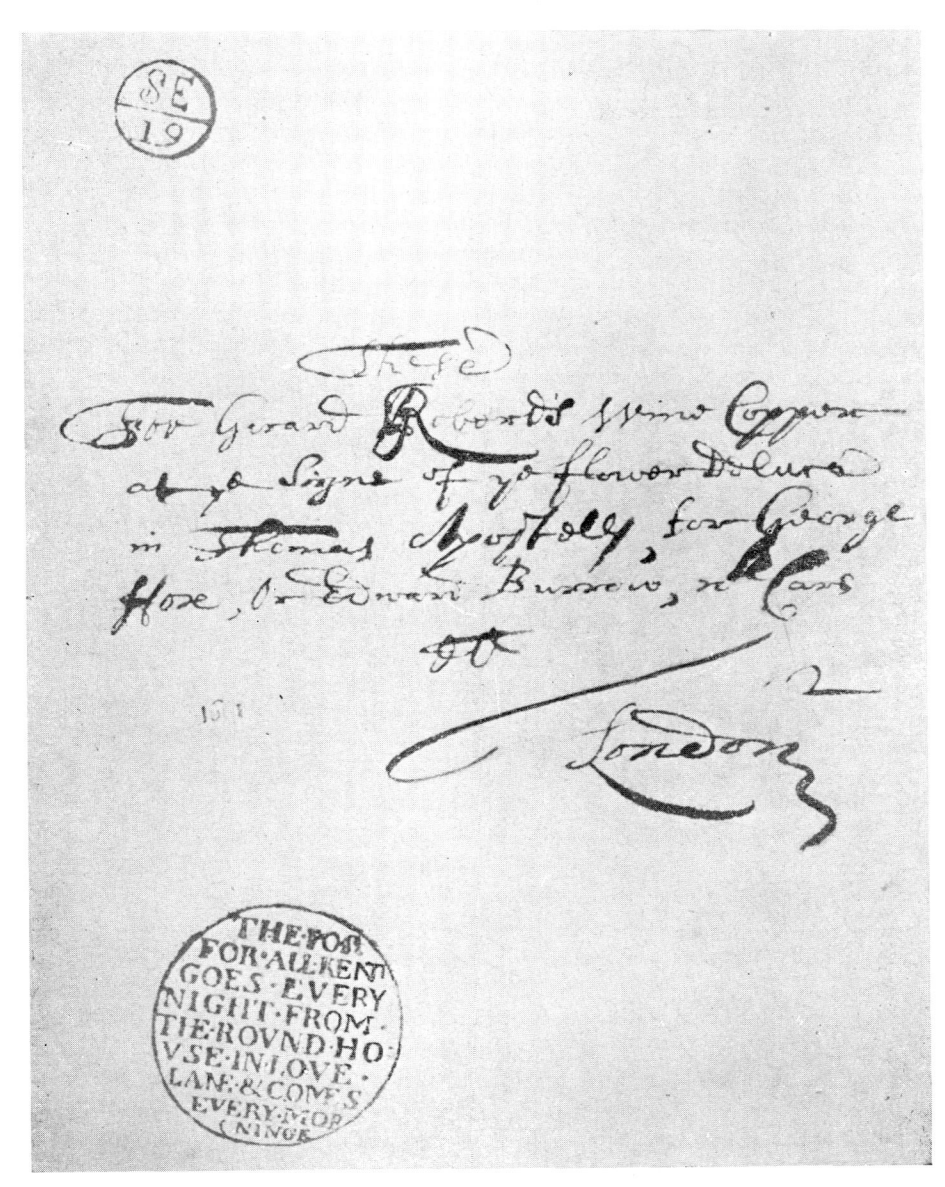

*A letter of 1661 with a superb example of the slogan for the Kent Road (page 21).*

---

*Note to Plate 8 overleaf: the three possible sites of the Letter Office are 1) Cloak Lane, which runs in from the left margin of the map, low central. 2) The Posthouse on Threadneedle St. (rather high left of centre). 165 marked is the Stocks Market, 48 is St. Christophers Church. 3) Bishopgate St. runs to the top right corner of the map from Cornhill, and shows only the first four houses burned.*

**Plate 7**

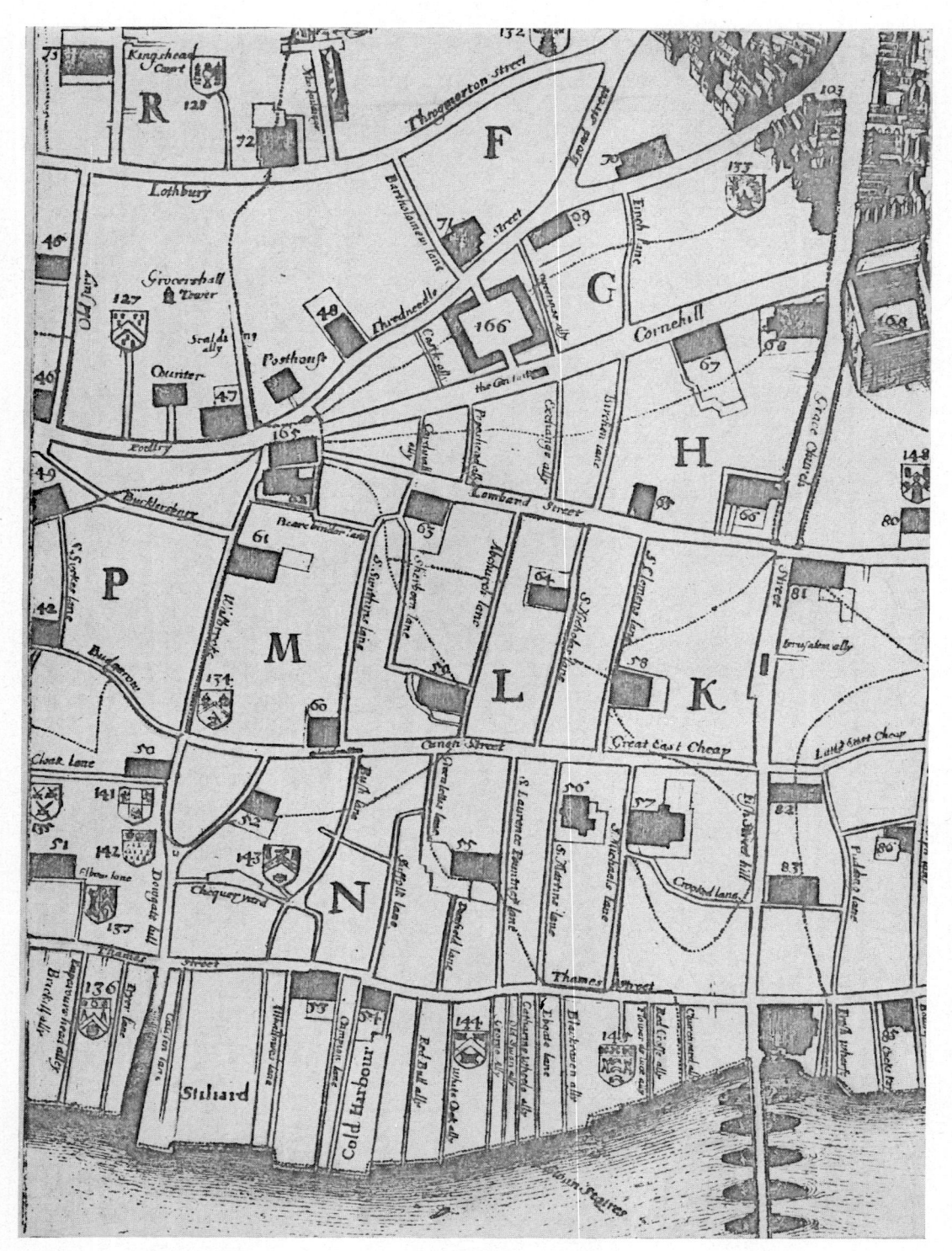

*Part of Wenceslaus Hollar's map of London after the Fire 1666-67 (page 23).   See note below plate 7.*

**Plate 8**

**Gardiner's Surveys**

In 1677 and 1682 Thomas Gardiner, Controller of the Inland office, compiled two surveys of the working of the Post Office, and these are probably the earliest detailed accounts of the internal organisation. They were edited (with valuable background comments) by Foster Bond and published by the Postal History Society in 1958, and the book is invaluable to an understanding of the background to postal history. It must be realized that the postal history of 1660 to 1800 cannot be judged in terms of 1970; each must be considered in the context of the times, and the explanation of many postmarks lies in the organization. Though the Farming system of leasing the Post Office to an individual for a fixed revenue may seem repugnant to our present long-haired intellectuals, at that time it worked; and probably it worked more for the benefit of those writing letters than does our present bureaucratic system.

The six post roads are given in full detail by Gardiner, showing that by 1682 considerable advances had been made in by-posts to feed in letters. At the end of 'notes on Postmasters' he states that with other perquisites they receive 'a reciprocal benefit with the Clarkes in the General office by receiving Gazettes free of postage, wherewith they advantage themselves in their common trade of selling drink and they have their single letters free to and from London'. This right of postmasters to receive newspapers free by post became a considerable source of income to them, and when it was reduced (and finally stopped) they and the Clerks of the Road were compensated heavily. A good study is written by Jeremy Greenwood in *Newspapers and the Post Office, 1635-1834* (Postal History Society, 1971). The Inland office staff was 8 clerks, 3 windowmen, 3 sorters and 32 letter carriers; all officers had to appear by 6 in the evening and the office gates were shut at 12 at night to make up the mails (the office surrounded a courtyard).

The General Post Receivers and their salaries in 1677 were:

| | |
|---|---|
| Mrs Grone between the Temple Gates | £27 |
| W. Nott in the Pall Mall | £10 |
| Geo. Luce in King St., Westminster | £20 |
| Lloyd by Bedford House | £12 |
| Nicholas Thatcher at Graies Inn Gate | £16 |
| John Place at Furnivalls Inn Gate | £ 6 |
| Magnes in Russell St. Covent Garden | £13 |
| Mrs Roberts by York Buildings, Strand | £ 6 |

Each Receiver had a stamp so their letters could be identified, and as they received salaries they were forbidden to receive any gratuity 'as other Receivers do (having no salaries) bringing letters from Grinwich, Deptford, Blackwall, Southwark and such like'. This was the time of change from Receivers office numbers, Fig 12, to stamps with their initials (Fig 13). In the 1682 list, the only changes are that Mrs Grone is now Grove, Magnes is now James Maynes and his salary has increased by 6/8d. Town Receivers sent letters twice a night, at 9 pm and 11 pm.

Fig 12                    Fig 13

The Window Men (receiving the letters at the Chief Office) had separate boxes for letters paid and unpaid, from which the sorters took them to stamp and sort into the six roads. Finally the Clerk of the Road entered them (with sums due from and credited to each postmaster) in the Road Book, put the letters into bags for each town and the bags together in a 'large Mayle'. Incoming mail was the reverse process. The 1682 report has a more querulous tone, and complains of the small unofficial receivers and people receiving letters in the streets, which brings a glut at unseasonable times: frequently they destroy them for the sake of the money received. He also complains that the King's letters (Government letters) often come very late, which delays the mail.

The Irish office in Dublin was managed with four clerks and five letter carriers (probably a clerk for the Munster, Ulster, and Connaught roads and a Clerk in Charge) and had only two mails a week inwards (Monday and Friday, called Post Mornings) and two outwards (Tuesday and Saturday, called Post Nights). It had been farmed by George Warburton from about 1667, at a rental of £2,500 year in 1673, but Gardiner says in the 1682 report it had been taken over by the farmers of the Irish Customs, paying £3,600 a year. They also had responsibility for the three packet boats from Dublin to Holyhead, and their upkeep and crew. He recommended a three-day post from London (which does not appear to have been accepted by 1682) adding that the post was inconsiderable without the English letters. These farmers are quoted by T. V. Jackson as 'the arrantest jugglers in Christendom'* and indeed Gardiner's comment 'this office is very ill managed in comparison with ours in London' was confirmed when the Irish farm was ended a year later, and George Warburton was reinstated as a salaried Deputy Postmaster General.

On Ship Letters (letters given to the Captain of a ship sailing to or from Britain on which he was paid one penny a letter when handed in at a post office) Gardiner suggests that as nearly all come from places where there is a Governor or Consul, the appropriate official should put all letters in a sealed bag on which the Captain would be paid his pence on handing in. He would then send by a different route a letter stating the contents of the bag. This early attempt to harness the revenue on Ship Letters was never carried out, and the Post Office could never collect the dues satisfactorily.

On the London Penny Post of Dockwra (see Chapter 4), which should have been the most important section, the 1682 report reads poorly, and makes one realize that the Post Office had no reason to suppress Dockwra but the loss in revenue. Gardiner's personality emerges from these reports as a very loyal servant, in some respects a brilliant mind who could see what should be done and was a hundred years ahead of his time, but he descends here to petty squabbling. With his imaginary bogeys of what might happen, and his ignorance of the needs of the public who wrote letters, he shows that there was no genuine reason to suppress Dockwra. 'The Penny Post brings a multitude of letters into our Grand Office at a late time of night of which few or none are with money. Which, besides the great hindrance of our despatches, is an argument that they imbezle money.... They may, if continuing, corrupt our Postmasters in the Country to send them a good part of such letters as should come by post to us, to be sent by flying coaches, heglers, etc, allowing them a share with themselves'. Gardiner must have had a very thin case to write so far below his usual standard.

---

*Postal History Society Bulletin nos. 100 and 164*, quoting from unnamed papers.

**Chapter 4**

# THE LONDON LOCAL POST

WILLIAM DOCKWRA was a London merchant who saw opportunity in the fact that no post was provided inside cities — one could send a letter to Edinburgh by post, but not inside London. In 1680 he started his own London post with a group of associates, based on a large number of Receiving Houses (possibly in the hundreds) and covering the area of the Bills of Mortality. He guaranteed rapid delivery (at least within four hours) and though it seems that a second penny was charged for delivery to the country area, the basic charge of one penny prepaid carried up to a pound weight, and included compensation for loss (an early form of registration).

Collectors interested in Dockwra are advised to read *William Dockwra and the rest of the Undertakers* by T. Todd, a wonderful study of the man and his works. Since this book was written, two letters were unearthed in the West Sussex Records Office, Chichester, which were carried in the penny post before stamps were used. Dockwra's London Penny Post apparently opened on 27th March 1680, although a notice of 6th April said that as the Receiving Houses were not yet ready, letters could be left at any Coffee House. The earliest triangular stamp is in the British Museum, 13 December 1680, but the two Chichester letters are of 18 May and 11 June 1680, to St Martins Lane. Both are endorsed in different hands 'penny letter house pd' and in a corner of the reverse $T/7\frac{1}{2}$ and $W/5$. respectively. It seems probable that this records their posting at the Temple Office at 7.30 and Westminster Office at 5 pm, but more evidence is needed.

Although it is always called Dockwra's post, it was started with other associates, including William Murray and Dr. Hugh Chamberlen, and when Murray was arrested for distributing a seditious pamphlet in May Dockwra carried on alone. On his release, Murray started a rival post of his own, and as the postmarks fall into two distinct types it is probable that the first type of triangular stamp (Figs 14-16, and known from 13th December 1680 to 22nd March 1680/81),

| Fig 14 | Fig 15 | Fig 16 | Fig 17 |

was Murray's post and Dockwra copied the idea with similar but less ornate stamps (Fig 17, known from 18th July 1681 to 27th June 1682). The Chichester letters would therefore be the only letters known from the original post of Dockwra, Murray, and Chamberlen. Nothing more is known of Murray's post, but so successful was the Dockwra post that the Post Office suppressed it in 1682, and continued it practically unchanged.

Todd goes fully into the known facts of Dockwra's later life. In 1685, when the Duke of York (in whose name the action was brought) became James II, Dockwra lay low. On the accession of William three years later he petitioned again and was granted a pension of £500 a year for seven years from June 1689. After a year in America he returned, and was made Master of the

Armourer's Company: there are various inventions in his name. In 1697 Nathaniel Castleton was removed from his position as Comptroller of the Penny Post office, and Dockwra was given the post at a salary of £200 in addition to his pension, which was extended for a further three years. In June 1700 Dockwra was removed and Castleton reinstated — the whole business seems rather smelly. Little is known of his three years as the head of the Penny Post, but a letter in the British Museum of 25 April 1698 says that many outlying places were taken out of the Penny Post area to increase the revenue of the General Post, and implies that he was meeting a lot of opposition. His death is recorded on 25 September 1716 'at near a hundred years of age': in fact, on his own statements he was a little less than eighty, but a good age for the time.

**The London Penny Post**

There were now three distinct posts in London: the General Post, Local Post and Foreign Branch, each with separate letter carriers, and this cumbersome system continued from 1682 until well into the nineteenth century. Letters with Dockwra's original stamps are very rare indeed, as are the earliest Government stamps with a single letter in the centre triangle to denote the sending office (Fig 18). The former group are the most expensive stampless letters, and would probably sell anywhere between £3,000 and £5,000 today. The Dockwra Chief Office at his house in Lyme Street was moved to Crosby House, Bishopsgate, but otherwise the Government Offices remained the same at Hermitage, Temple, Southwark, Westminster, and St. Pauls (letters L or B/CH, H, T, S, W, and P in the centre). In 1685 the Chief Office became B and much later G for General Office.

It is doubtful if Dockwra set any boundaries as such, for if anyone in outlying villages would act as agent and bring in the letters, he would accept them. There is evidence that from 1683 the Post Office continued with a very large area, for it made no difference to them. As Dockwra had done, so did they charge a penny extra for the country districts, and as the General Post rate below eighty miles was twopence they received the same money in either post. In 1711, however, the minimum General Post charge was raised to threepence so it became important to specify which areas were one penny, which were twopence, and which must travel in the General Post at threepence. The limit was fixed at ten miles, which Joyce says excluded such towns as Walton-on-Thames, Cheshunt, and Tilbury, which had long been served by the Penny Post 'without exciting a murmur'.

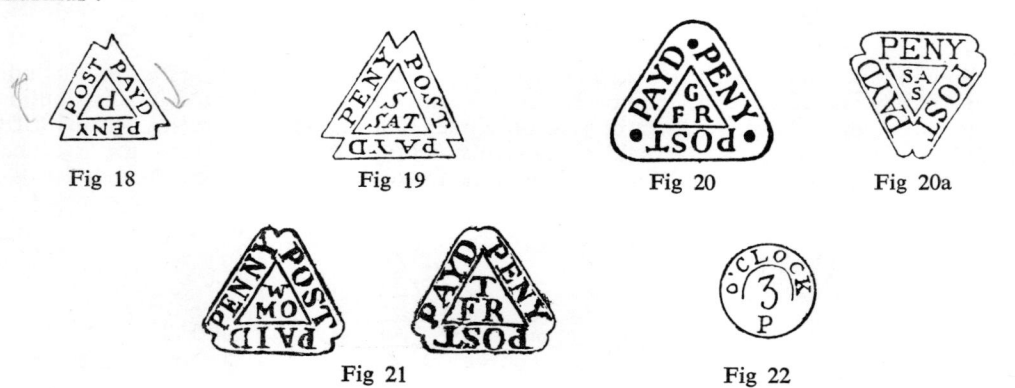

Fig 18    Fig 19    Fig 20    Fig 20a

Fig 21    Fig 22

The London Penny Post (or 'Dockwra type') stamps are a fascinating field, and much study is being done (Figs 19-21). To standardize references they are described by turning the triangle until the office letter, and day letters beneath it, are upright, then reading the words at left, right, and bottom in that order. Up till now all classification has been based on the order in which the words 'Penny Post Paid' come in the triangle, but this is now known to be unimportant, and research is directed to classifying them under the relevant office. In this way, it will be known when changes occurred, and which stamps were in use at a given time. Some most surprising gaps occur, and the type of information that is emerging is that Westminster Office used two sets of stamps (W/MO to W/SA) from 1784, and that no Hermitage stamps have been seen between

1703 and 1754. The order of words was obviously not considered important — it seems that the triangle was already cut and the engraver added the office and day when needed, as he picked it up. Important varieties exist, such as the very large size stamps, the reversed N of PENY, inverted centre Fig 20a (with line above, not below the day letters), a distinctive narrow type for Southwark and a G stamp with large dots in the three rounded corners (Fig 20). The last is very distinctive, and only three are known, one very poor. The three primary classifications of types of the Government penny post stamps are:

1. 1683-85, Fig 18, very similar to Dockwra's original stamps, with only a large office letter inside the triangle. They can always be separated, however, for while all Government types have the three words reading inwards, Dockwra's stamps have PAID reading outwards.
2. 1685-1711 or later, Fig 19, with the day below the office in three letters except TU and TH; a thin, finely cut stamp, probably metal and with an italic S in POST.
3. 1703-94, Figs 21 etc., normal types, heavier and probably cut in box-wood.

Stamps giving the time at which the letter was sent out for delivery (Fig 22) were used (except between 1709 and 1763), and from 1740 many Receivers used stamps with their name (Fig 23) or wrote them on the back of letters. These stamped names of the Penny Post receivers are a very interesting group, and quite difficult to find. Some are framed, Grape and Allen both added 'Stationer' in a circular format. It is now known that a few were receivers for both General Post and Penny Post letters, and used their stamps on both. Walter had different stamps, the Penny Post name being enclosed in a dotted rectangular frame. In 1794, when the Penny Post was entirely reorganized by Edward Johnson (adding a second Chief Office in Westminster), Receiving Houses were issued with their own name stamps. The reforms are discussed later.

## London Receiving Houses

London Receiving Houses of the General Post were twenty in 1652, as can be seen from the Guildhall broadside illustrated. In addition, Edward Hutchins is described as Postmaster at Charing Cross, as he was described on the Civil War letters of 1649 and is known to have been in 1642. Thanks to the Westminster Reference Library, attention was drawn to *A Survey of London* edited by G. H. Gater and Walter H. Godfrey, which could be a mine of information. The White Hart occupied the present-day 21-24 Cockspur Street and the site of another inn, 'The Two Chairmen', for most of the seventeenth century and was one of the most important inns of the area. Thomas Sparks or Parkes was licensee 1628-41, Richard Sparks 1644-5, and his widow in 1652-7. John Howard was the occupier 1659-68 and his widow until 1672. Three more people carried it on until 1685, when it disappears. It was granted by Thomas Viscount Falconbridge on a building lease at this time to Samuel Aubery, was pulled down and replaced by eight houses built around White Hart Court. In the State Papers Domestic is a petition of Thomas Parkes 1637-8, Postmaster from London to Barnet, that he has executed the office about six years without neglect, and has received but two years pay at 20d per diem. There is also a request from John Howard 1667-8 to have the post kept at his house as before, and the rate books of 1659 have 'Postmaster' against Howard's name.

It would seem probable that when Edward Hutchins left his brother as postmaster of Crewkerne and came to London in 1633 or later, he was taken on by Thomas Parkes to run the postal side of the White Hart. It would have been post horses, of course, but there might have been quite a number of state packages and letters to be sent. This work he continued through the Civil War under the brother Richard Sparks and Richard's widow, and he must have been pretty well known to have letters addressed to his care. The status of this Post Office is not yet known, but apparently it was the office for the Barnet (and Chester?) Road. The Round House in Love Lane was for the Kent (and later the Sussex) Road, and one or two more are emerging. The Dog and Bear in Southwark may have been for the West Road, and the Golden Lion, Red Cross Street Posthouse where Hickes wrote his letter after the Fire, could have been for the North Road. It seems likely that each road had its inn posthouse, but it is surprising that only the White Hart at Charing Cross was listed in the 1652/3 broadside. It may have served the Bristol Road as well, for in late 1665 Philip Frowde reproved the postmasters of Charing Cross, Hounslow, Maidenhead and Reading for neglect. All these would be on the same road. Apart from these, of course, there was only the one Post Office in London, all others being just Receivers.

The receivers were mainly innkeepers and shopkeepers, plus the porters at the gates of the Savoy and Lyons Inn — people to be found at well known places, and it is fair to assume that at fixed times the letters were taken from the Receiving Houses to the General Post Office without extra charge. A broadside of 1661 says that several people calling themselves receivers have exacted an extra penny, and lists only five official salaried receivers (a surprising reduction from twenty receivers and a Postmaster listed in 1652), but it was possibly to save expense:—

Westminster, Mr Parker at Mr Grincells shop, a grocer next Sanctuary Gate;
Strand, Mr Roberts, a grocer at the Bay Tree over against Yorke House;
Covent Garden, Mr Magnes, Stationer, in Russel Street;
Holborn, Mr Place, Stationer at Grays Inn Gate;
Fleet Street, Mr Eales at his shop in St. Dunstans Churchard.

An advertisement of 1664 lists six receivers, Magnes and Parker being replaced by John Place at Furnivals Inn (probably a branch of his father's business at Grays Inn, a good area for stationers), Humphrey Greensell at the Sanctuary, Westminster, and Anthony Lissen at the Blew Bore in Bow Street. It also adds 'after 10 at night from our Lady till Michaelmas, and after 9 from Michaelmas to our Lady, none of these shall take in letters, but with those he hath, come and deliver them to the Grand Office where for the accomodation of Gentlemen they may be received until 11, and no longer'. A list of 1677 has been quoted (see Gardiners survey), from which it appears that Mr Magnes (or his son) had returned, and eight were now employed. Although Gardiner repeated the same eight receiving houses in his 1682 report, the London Gazette of 2 November 1682 gave notice that a post went to Bristol every day via Hounslow and Bath. There followed a list of fifteen receivers, adding Partridge, next door to the Rummer, Charing Cross; Leasham, against Northumberland House; Dormer, at the Golden Cock in Panton St.; Kunholt, at the King's Head by Charing Cross; Harrison, at Lincolns Inn Gate; Games, in Charterhouse Yard; and Powl, at the Three Tobacco Rolls, King St., Bloomsbury. Magnes was replaced in Russel Street by Mr Bentley. This notice bears out the author's view that the reduction from twenty receivers listed in 1653 to five in 1661 should not be taken literally. It may be that there were two grades, and only senior receivers were normally listed and issued with handstamps, but there can be no other explanation of two official lists within a few months, one nearly twice the size of the other.

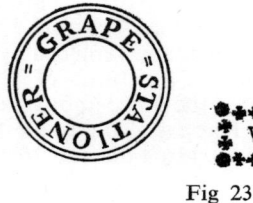

Fig 23

Fig 24 Partington

Fig 25 THE HALFPENNY CARRIAGE

Gardiner says that each had a stamp, and from 1670 a series is known, some resembling Bishop Marks and others being numbers in a circle (Fig 12). Numbers 1-5 were known, but recently two examples of 7/Off were found on letters of 1670, now in the Bodleian Library, Oxford. It is not certain if the eighth had a numbered stamp. In 1670 initial stamps are known for the General Post receivers (Fig 13), and these continue for about a hundred years. Some were obviously very large offices (a good proportion of those known before 1700 and many shortly after are GC), but many are very rare, some probably are still unknown. Penny Post receivers, a separate body, normally used their full name if they employed a stamp, and the few General Post letters bearing a receiver's name in full seem to have been struck by receivers serving the Penny Post as well. Partington is an exception, being much more common on General Post letters than Penny Post letters (Fig 24). It is interesting that so many stationers' shops were receivers, a natural extension of their business.

**Charles Povey's Halfpenny Post**

From October 1709 to May 1710 ran the second London private post. Doubtless the organizer, Charles Povey (who imagined himself a second Dockwra), was a remarkable man, yet he appears to have been a copier rather than an innovator. The importance of his post seems minor in itself, although greater in its effect. Povey's main claim to fame is that amongst innumerable things to which he turned his attention was fire insurance, but even here he copied existing organizations and the Exchange House Fire Office, which he founded between 1706 and 1708 and which developed into the Sun Fire Office, seems to have grown much faster after Povey ceased to attend Board Meetings.

Shortly after his disagreement with the Sun Insurance, he started 'The Halfpenny Carriage' for conveying letters inside the Cities of London and Westminster, and Southwark. It was modelled on the Dockwra post but with more reliance on the collection of letters by 'ringers of bells' than Receiving Houses in shops, inns and coffee houses. Numerous men (and women) walked the streets with bells to collect and deliver letters, but it is doubtful if the run of eight months was long enough to worry the Post Office, and there could have been little doubt of the results of a test case.

In 1682 Dockwra had provided a most efficient service, supplementing but not in opposition to the Post Office, and the Postmaster General was quite happy to leave him until it was running well enough to expropriate. Thirty years later the London local post was probably still quite efficient and, as far as is known, Povey simply undercut by serving only the paying central area. He claimed that two eminent Counsel gave their opinion that 'no Act of Parliament then in force hindered any subject from taking in or delivering out letters within the Bills of Mortality', but this was not really the point. The Post Office had succeeded in claims to a complete monopoly, and until this could be set aside it was begging the question whether delivery in London (or anywhere else) was specifically excluded by the Postal Acts in force.

Povey replied to the notice to cease operations with bombastic claims and hair-splitting (he said that as he called it a carriage, and not a post, there was no infringement) and threats more suited to the circus ring. He put every possible obstacle in the way of the collection of evidence against him, and his threats descended by stages to an equally loud whine. Joyce goes into the case in detail, and links it fully with relevant circumstances in the Post Office. The authority of the Postmasters General still came from the 1660 Restoration Act, and doubtless the changed conditions over a period of fifty years had called for a new comprehensive act many years before 1711 — in fact it is very doubtful if anybody, including the Post Office, was really authorized to run a local post. Certainly the English Postmasters General were not legally empowered to run the Scottish Post Office from London, as they had done for the three years since the Act of Union. These unsatisfactory circumstances led to the Consolidating Act of 1711, which included an increase in charges of one penny a single letter inside England, fourpence the ounce. Letters between London and Edinburgh had been fivepence single in Scottish Law from 1660, but the English rate was threepence to Berwick and fourpence on, Edinburgh being above the forty mile limit for twopence. In practice, the usual charge was fivepence in either direction and this was corrected in 1711 when both Edinburgh and Dublin became sixpence single from London.

To the postal historian, the main interest of Charles Povey is the discovery in 1960 of a letter in the Public Records Office* carried in his post. Dated 24 January 1710 from a Frenchman in the Savoy Prison, Mattheas Ebelinge Bonnasse, to 'M. Boyle, Secretaire d'Etat de la grand Bretagne, a Londres', it bears a three-line stamp THE/HALFPENNY/CARRIAGE in serif capitals (Fig 25). It seems doubtful if any examples will come on the market now, although further copies may easily be lying in archives which would be helpful for information. If one should be sold, it might become the most valuable stampless cover, and possibly the most valuable cover of Great Britain, but postal history prices would have to increase considerably for it to exceed some overseas stamped envelopes or autograph letters.

---

* P.R.O. reference SP 34/14/83.

**Chapter 5**

# CROSS AND BY-POSTS

UNTIL recently, little research had been done into one of the most important postal subjects — the means by which the Post Office broke out of its self-imposed straight-jacket and began a postal service to the country, not just to those parts adjacent to the six roads. At present when one thinks of Cross Posts one thinks of Ralph Allen, but the subject goes very much deeper. A fine book by Professor Boyce* deals with Allen as a literary figure, and another reprints Allen's *'Narrative'* sent to the Post Office in 1761, three years before his death, together with a study of the man by Adrian Hopkins. Whilst it was due to Hopkins' work and enthusiasm that interest in Ralph Allen was aroused, his studies of Hong Kong, Afghanistan, and particularly wreck covers left little time for English postal history: study of Allen must be in the context of the whole cross post, and preferably wider than that. Boyce's interest is literary, so that although he too made most helpful discoveries, Allen's postal career (which was his life's work and main source of income) is little more than an introduction.

It is astonishing that until Hopkins, and an article by Boyce in The Postal History Bulletin No. 122, 1962 (where Quash is described as 'probably an important, but still shadowy figure'), no research of merit had been done. From the recent fine research of Mrs. Emonet but still unpublished, and with the assistance of Miss Philbrick and David Cornelius, it appears that Quash may prove one of the most important figures in Postal History. Part of this section is only deduction, and a little is even guesswork (it must be said that Mrs Emonet does not agree with all of it), but at least it will serve as a basis for further study. One curious result is a feeling that the memorial commemorating Allen's birth, erected by the Postal History Society at St. Blazey Gate, Cornwall in 1955, is in the wrong place: it should be at St. Columb.

In Post Office terminology of the period, a cross post was one which ran from a town on one of the six main post roads from London to a town on another of these roads. A by-post ran either from one of these roads to a town away from the post roads, or from one town to another on the same road (the latter sometimes being called a Way Letter). The important thing is that letters in neither of these posts passed through London, and London was the centre of the post. A country letter in England was one passing through London, to and from other towns; in early days these were treated (very unfairly) as separate journeys, each rate being computed from London. Many letters of the Pengelly correspondence (approximately 1660-1720) were from Exeter to Yarmouth or the reverse, and although any distance in England above eighty miles was threepence, these were charged sixpence, for both towns were more than eighty miles from London. In Ireland a country letter was one coming into Dublin, and in Scotland to Edinburgh.

This method of charging letters was a major handicap to the development of the early post, for one of the main concerns was to keep up the revenue and any major improvement would involve cutting out London and the double rates that were charged. The six main post roads remained constant, therefore, and all developments went into bringing letters into these roads by extending the by-posts. Any improvement liable to cause a temporary fall in revenue was frowned upon, and it has already been seen that the Warwick-Stratford area had to suffer its letters to be

---

* *'The Benevolent Man, a life of Ralph Allen'* by Professor B. Boyce, Harvard University Press and Oxford University Press: and *'Ralph Allen's own narrative, 1720-1761'*, edited by Adrian E. Hopkins, Postal History Society 1960.

sent via Coventry until 1697, despite innumerable protests, as the postage was reduced by a penny a letter if they were routed on the by-post to Banbury.

Unfortunately, all administration was centred on London and the development of by-posts normally involved the Post Office in heavy losses. A system of checking receipts from letters not passing through London was obviously beyond it and postmasters, being no more honest than they had to be, pocketed a proportion of the revenue. Thus, we have the peculiar state of affairs where the Post Office was much in favour of by-posts in theory, providing somebody else ran them, incurred the risks and took the profits, but gave a guaranteed income irrespective of the total receipts. Some larger postmasters in the 1680s were encouraged to farm by-posts from the Postmaster General, either their town and satellite villages or a small area, and the more successful ones grew to cover quite large areas. The logical development was for an individual to farm a complete branch road, and thus came 'the contract farmers', always clearly separated from the 'renters of the by and way letters' in Post Office accounts. The former had a definite legal contract, but it seems likely that the latter just paid an agreed rent, some only £2 or £5 a year. This arrangement suited all concerned, if suitable farmers could be found, and most important it gave the public a much better service, for profits came only from increasing the revenue.

Well before this, in 1653 the Council of State had ordered that a cross post be established from Dover through Portsmouth to Salisbury and the West Road, but it is extremely doubtful if this carried private letters, if indeed it ran at all. In all the early period, care has to be taken to distinguish between intention and successful completion, and (before 1660) between State and Public posts. In 1665 when King Charles moved the Court to Oxford to avoid the plague, letters survive in the Public Records Office showing that a cross post was set up from Andover (West Road) across the Bristol road to Oxford, and another from Towcester on the Chester Road. A letter from James Hickes to Joseph Williamson of 8 January 1666 (P.R.O. ref. 29/144/70) complains that Mr Rathbone, postmaster of Andover, has again let the Plymouth bag for Oxford go on to London; this should not be passed over or he will never mend his ways. On 14 January (29/145/33) John Clarke at Plymouth apologized for Mr Rathbone's negligence, and added there is neglect elsewhere, too, 'for on post days the mail which used to come at 6 a.m. or 7 a.m. does not arrive till noon or 1 p.m. Lord Bath is much displeased, and the King's affairs in the West are obstructed', and when he sent to examine the Post Labels it was found that mail was received at Exeter ten hours before it reached Ashburton. This for a distance of nineteen miles! This cross post picked up a bag of Royal mail on the Bristol road at Newbury, and a similar post ran across to Oxford from the Chester Road, but were they used to carry private letters? It is doubtful, but certainly possible.

The 'renters of the by-letters' are recorded from 1686/7, but it is notable from the letter books of Col. Roger Whitley, deputy Postmaster-General 1672 to 1677 (called the Peover Papers, in G.P.O. records) that despite his encouragements few were willing to take the risk. A revealing letter quoted from these letter books by Brig. G. A. Viner* is illustrative of Whitley's sense of humour, the inability of the Post Office to collect the postage on by-letters, and the postmaster's reluctance to take the responsibility of a farm. Writing to Robert Tayer, postmaster of Chichester, in December 1673 he says

> '.... Examininge my bookes, I am in admiracon to finde Noe acco't of By-Letters from Chichester, a considerable towne, a place of Trade, an Episcopale sease (Chanclrs Proctrs & men of Business) and the Stage managed by soe ingenious a p'son as Mr. Tayer, and yett noe acco't from yo'r owne or Neighbour Stage.... I am not of a litigious Nature, yet cannnot bee so wanting ... as to pass by Injurys of this Nature, I expect reparacon for the tyme past ... and a just acco't for the future, or if you would rather bee att a Certeinty, & avoyd ye trouble of accompting, I will farme ye By-letters of yo'r Stage (as i doe in severall others) if you like this way make a faire proposeall ... choose wch way you please, to Acco't or farme them. But I must receive satisfacon....'

Apparently Whitley had secured some small farms already, but no details have been found until the accounts ending 25 March 1688 which list a number £50 or less, and John Stukeley of

---

* *The Postal History of Chichester, 1635-1900*, published by Chichester City Council 1965.

Plymouth at £250. The previous year though, entries start for 'Farmers yearly rent per contract' which is the phrase used for the large farmers of areas or branch roads. The largest by far was Robert Tayer of Chichester, and it may be that his brilliance at avoiding all payment for by-letters was harnessed to administration for his own profit or loss. This was one of the only two branch roads running directly from London: the other to Hastings and Rye was farmed by Robert Hall for £75.10.0. but Tayer undertook to pay a rental of £620 a year. The two others in the 1686/7 accounts are Gilbert Staughton of Bedford, £300, and Crispin Osborne of Thetford, £100. There is a possibility that Thetford and Chichester were farmed by 1682 for £90 and £500 respectively. During the next twenty five years rentals increased steadily at first, and then were fairly constant but in number the farmers on a yearly contract (the large farms) never exceeded ten. Renters of the by-letters were much more numerous. The Chichester branch was Kingston, Guildford, dividing at Petersfield into the Chichester and Arundel forks. It was soon overtaken in size by the Ferrybridge and Wellingborough partnerships, the former covering large areas of Yorkshire (which had only the one Post Road), the latter a branch from Towcester through Leicester and Derby to Sheffield. Gilbert Staughton for many years was a partner in both of these enterprises, and the Ferrybridge rent exceeded £2,000 in 1696/7, whilst Wellingborough stayed around £1,500 for many years. Chichester under John Barnes grew to about the same figure, and the total rents reached their peak in 1700/01 at £8,000.

A few years after the first farms, the brothers Bigg began a postal career which would probably repay further research. Ralph Allen has attracted erudite authors for his literary friendships, but the influence of the Biggs, Francis Stanley, the Ferrybridge partners, Gilbert Staughton, and Joseph Quash above all was very important to the development of communications over the whole country; it is doubtful if Allen would have succeeded as he did without their pioneer example and the foundations they laid. Stephen and Richard Bigg first appear in the accounts for the year ending 25 March 1693 for one quarter's rent, £75, from 25 December 1692 for the Buckingham branch. Buckingham was a branch from the Chester and Holyhead road at Stoney Stratford (Brickhill) and their rental (which soon became £900 to £1,150 a year) was for the posts in parts of Middlesex, Herts, Bucks to Banbury, and Warwick. It may well have stretched at times along the by-road to Shrewsbury and central Wales. In 1698/99 the Biggs were released from accounting for their overseas and Scottish letters via London in a document curious because it seems doubtful if there would have been many of them, yet 'if obliged thereto shall be unavoidably ruined'. Secondly, it admits that this inclusion was a mistake in the contract, and thirdly Mrs Emonet has discovered that the date in the Calendar of Treasury Papers for the contract of '3 years from 1687 Lady Day' is an error which has been copied in many books. It should have been 1697, as confirmed by the rents paid. Finally, this document raises the question of administration of the farms at this period, for it states specifically a release for the Scottish and overseas letters through London to towns in their area. It was always assumed that postage paid at the receiving end belonged to the farmers if carried entirely within their area, and was accounted proportionately if carried partly outside the area, but here they are released from accounting for the postage collected when most of the journey was outside. If its inclusion was a mistake, the same must apply to other farms. Much more information is needed here, for some of this revenue would have to be paid to other countries by the Foreign Branch.

Having secured their midland revenue satisfactorily, in September 1700 Stephen Bigg appears to have left Richard to manage whilst he and Benjamin (probably a brother) went North with a contract daunting in size to farm most of Lancashire and Westmorland at a rent of £2,526. The contract preamble states that this is because of their diligence, satisfaction to the people, and encouragement to the revenue at Buckingham. Prospects must have been enormous, for Liverpool had just completed its first dock and both it and Manchester were thriving and expanding fast, but probably the task was beyond their powers of organization. On 4 June 1701 they were released, and the accounts for the year ending 25 March 1701 show payment by Stephen and Richard Bigg of £1,000 for Buckingham, and Stephen and Benjamin Bigg for one half year to Lady Day — £1,250.8.8d. for Lancaster. It is proof of the standing of the Biggs, and how necessary good farmers were to the post office, that they were released without penalty. The reason given was that the new Chester road was 'very prejudicial', but it is difficult to see how it could have made much difference unless terms of farms were very different from our present understanding, and this may well have been mutual face-saving. One would have expected it to help by bringing in more letters. The next year they appear amongst the small renters under 'Chester by-letters, £112.10.0'. Brother Richard carried on at Buckingham, and more will be heard of him later, but the post office does not appear to have trusted Stephen and Benjamin again in any large venture.

The new Chester road mentioned above introduces another major character who was stretched beyond his capabilities and crashed — Joseph Quash. As postmaster of Exeter, the accounting centre for all the South West, Quash held a very responsible position when in 1696 he was empowered to set up and manage the first satisfactory cross post for public letters, from Exeter to Bristol; in the same year he appears as a renter of by-letters (the small farmers) for £140 a year. An attempt had been made by Col. Roger Whitley in 1674 to link the Bristol and the Western roads in Somerset, but it lasted only two months; the volume of mail carried must have been extremely small, and it cannot be called a success. The need for a link between the Bristol and Exeter roads remained, however, and in October 1696 Quash started his post on a completely new route to leave Exeter on Saturday and Wednesday at 4 pm, and from Bristol on Monday and Friday at 10 am. Each journey took 24 hours, and the stages and salaries allowed were Exeter £50, Tiverton £38, Wellington £29, Taunton £22.10.0, Bridgwater £36, Wells £54 and Bristol £30. Salaries covered riding work for four journeys a week except the two termini (two journeys each) and Quash of Exeter managed the post, whilst Henry Pine of Bristol was to check the accounting. By 1700 the road produced a net profit of £255 per annum, and a year earlier it had been extended to Wotton-under-Edge for the convenience of the clothing trade. Shrewsbury petitioned in June 1699 for an extension, and authority to lay the post to Chester was given by Treasury Warrant on 10 July 1700, nine days after the Warrant for Stephen Bigg and his Lancashire post. The announcement of this post was in the Gazette of 26 September 1700, that it will go thrice weekly between Exeter and West Chester via Tiverton, Wellington, Taunton, Bridgewater, Wells, Bristol, Wooton under Edge, Gloucester, Tewksbury, Worcester, Kidderminster, Bridgworth, Shrewsbury and Whitchurch. Letters sent from Exeter on Wednesday will be in Chester on Sunday morning. Quash was paid £65 for settling the road and Mr Jenner £26 for measuring it. Quash was thus manager of a road from Exeter through Bristol to Chester in addition to his position as postmaster of Exeter, but he had very able assistants in Henry Pine of Bristol and Thomas Reynell of Chester so in 1706 he farmed this 'Exon Road' for £600 a year. Research is badly needed into the Chester office, for Thomas Reynell was very capable and in addition to his postmaster's position on the cross road (which he held from the opening in 1700 until his death in 1712) he was Chester postmaster, and probably by-postmaster for the last four years; contemporary reports in G.P.O. records speak of him very highly. Having established his position as farmer of the Exon road, in 1707/8 Quash settled another cross road from Bristol through Bath to Oxford, and may have run the South Wales road too; his influence over the whole area must have been very great. It is interesting to note that Withering's original 1635 London to Bristol road was through Oxford, so probably followed the same route. By this new cross road the charge from Exeter to Bristol was reduced to twopence, and from Exeter to Chester or Oxford threepence; prior to this all such letters passed through London and were charged sixpence.

In 1706 Quash had been appointed Receiver General for Taxes for parts of Devon, with a responsibility for transmitting large sums of money to London. This transmission was normally by drafts on private bankers, to save physical transport of the money with its dangers of robbery or accident, and implied access to and acceptance in a world far removed from that of the normal postmaster. Possibly from about 1708 and the settling of the Oxford cross road, it seems that the size of his business began to outgrow his capabilities, and serious trouble started to build up for Quash. He seems to have been consistently in arrears for quite large sums, and doubtless this was aggravated by the increase in 1711 of one penny on most postage rates.

From 1 June 1711, the date of the increase, most contract farms ceased and the farmers became managers of their area, taking 10% of the net produce of their letters after excluding bad and overtaxed letters, and salaries as deputies. The report makes clear that this was by agreement owing to the difficulty of assessing fair rents in view of the new rates: Quash was debited with his existing rent of £700 for 1711/12 and most of it for the year ending 25 March 1713. It seems, therefore, that he continued as the only farmer, but failed to charge the penny increase on his letters, for the entry reads 'due from Mr Joseph Quash of Exeter for the Adiconall duty of one penny per letter in the Cross Road from June 1, 1711 to Feb 14 1713, £1640.4.9'. This appears to have been paid, but a further claim for £2,000 on 13 February 1712/13 caused Quash to abscond, and he was declared bankrupt. A later claim by Francis Manaton, Receiver General of Taxes for Co. Cornwall, was lodged in April 1714 declaring that he had paid Quash £3,500, who drew three bills on Oswald Hoskins in London who accepted them; before they became payable both Quash and Hoskins were bankrupt. In 1718 is recorded a Treasury reference to a petition by Joseph Quash, praying allowance for considerable losses in having to transmit £254,391 in specie to the Exchequer over six years as bills were not obtainable.

One feels great sympathy for this pioneer of the cross post, who only now is being recognized — statues still standing commemorate men of lesser calibre. Yet it will be as the man who introduced provincial town stamps, and who recognized the ability of Ralph Allen, trained him, and gave him his chance that Quash will be well known in Postal History; two unimportant accidents compared with his life's work. It seems that he was an outstanding employee as postmaster or manager of hundreds of miles of post road, but not successful as a farmer in his own right. In 1708/9 his farm was 'for letters between London and towns in Somerset, Gloucester, Worcester, Oxford, Hereford, Devon, Shropshire and South Wales', yet the rent paid was the same as 1706 — £600 a year, and he was never liable for more than £700. Earlier farmers with districts a fraction of his area and importance paid twice this sum, but it is notable that in the period 1706-10 when Quash was a farmer their rents did not increase much either — was he too late to catch the increase in correspondence? Bigg was farming parts of Middlesex, Hertfordshire, and Bucks with Banbury and Warwick at £1,100 in 1706, compared with £300 in 1693 but only £1,180 in 1710. The roads farmed by Quash should have been much more valuable. It is certain that his lack of financial control betrayed his postal acumen, and this seems to have been accelerated by national conditions making difficult the transmission of money, and folly in selection of his financial associates.

It has been said above that on 1 June 1711 most of the farmers became managers of their areas at salaries plus 10% of the net revenue, from which various expenses had to be met, and that this was by mutual agreement because of uncertainties in the effect of increased postal rates. A discrepancy is that whilst it is stated clearly that this takes effect from the date of the new postage rates (1st June 1711), the farmers' accounts are debited with rents for one half year ended 29 September 1711. Quash is the only one charged a full year. Comparative figures taken from the General Accounts Books 1711-20 in GPO Records are:

Comparative figures taken from the General Accounts Books 1711-20 in GPO Records are:

| Farmer and location | Rental 1710-11 | Salary 1712-13 |
| --- | --- | --- |
| Edward Hall, of Rye | £150 | £235 |
| William Rawson & Sarah Wainwright, Ferrybridge | £1470 | £422.14. 0 |
| John Smith & Matthew Staughton, Wellingborough | £1570 | £590 |
| John George, Thetford | £400 | £268 |
| Thos. Attwood, St. Neots | £240 | £235 |
| Samuel Johnson, Walden | £400 | £367. 4. 6 |
| John Brett, Tonbridge | £330 | £167.10. 0 |
| John Barnes, Chichester | £1550 | £755. 1. 0 |
| Richard Bigg, Buckingham | £1180 | £821 |

In the 1712/13 salary list, Wainwright had been replaced by Skipton and George by Thos. Lee.

Accurate details of the farms are sparse, but the *Calendar of Treasury Books Vol. XXI, 1706-07* describes them in this year as:—

Edward Hall of Hastings: Farmer of all letters London to and from Hastings, Battle, Cranbrooke, Biddendon, Tenterden, Appledore, Hurst Green, Lyd, New Romney, Hythe and Folkestone £145

Mathew Staughton and John Smith of Wellingborough: London to and from Sheffield, Chesterfield, Mansfield, Melton Mowbray, Oakham, Uppingham, Woodburn, Ampthill, Bedford, Kettering, Rockingham. £1,500

Wiliam Rawson and Sarah Wainwright: London and Ferrybridge, Tadcaster, and the towns formerly belonging to those stages, Settle, Kirby Lonsdale with places adjacent not exceeding the half-way to any other post town in the Northern or Chester Roads. £1,400

Thomas Atwood of St. Neots: London to St. Neots, Biggleswade, Stevenage, Welling, Hatfield etc. £240

John Howlett of Thetford: Walsingham and other places in Co. Norfolk £350

Henry Warren of Whitechapel: Havering at Bower, Lambourne, Haybridge and other places in Cos. Herts, Essex, Sussex and Cambridge. £400
(Sussex in this farm would seem to be an error).

John Brett of Tonbridge: Several towns in Cos. Kent and Sussex £330

John Barnes of Chichester: Arundel, Petworth Hazelmore, Godolmin, Guildford, Kingston, and other places in Cos. Surrey, Sussex and Southampton £1,550

Richard Begg of Winslow, Co. Bucks: Edgework (Edgeware), Stanmore, Watford, Kings Henley, Hempstead, Barkhamstead, Buckingham, Chesham, Agmondisham, Gt. Marlow, Wendover, Banbury, Warwick. £1,100

Rentals above are taken from the Post Office Accounts 1706/7.

The Salary List for 1713/14 (year ending 25 March 1714) is fascinating, for some postmasters have a second entry — e.g. 'John Miles of Bridgewater, X road salary from February the 13th 1912 to December the 25th 1713 at 20£ p. Ann — £17.10', all these being for a little less than a year's salary. This shows that the accounts were based on the old calendar, so February 1712 is now February 1713. If these entries are rearranged by the roads, it is seen that all offices on the Exeter-Chester and Bristol-Oxford roads are listed, so it must be the first time the Post Office took over the cross post salaries formerly paid by Quash, and this gives the routes. His rent of £700 was debited up to this same day — £622. 4. 5.

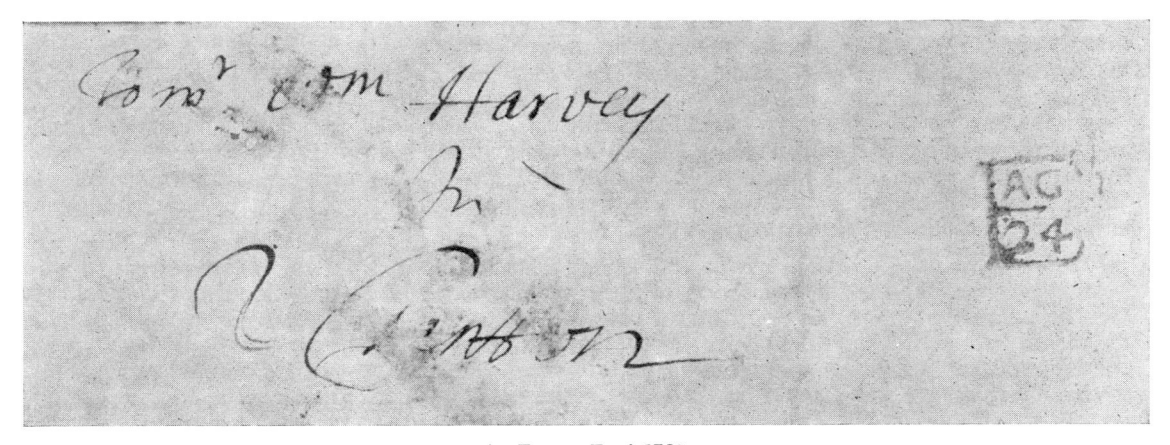

*An Exeter E of 1700.*

Full details tabulate as follows (some offices have only a cross post entry, not being on a General Post road). Extracts are from G.P.O. Salary books 1713/14, ending 25 March 1714.

| Stage | Postmaster | Salary | Cross Postmaster | Cross salary |
|---|---|---|---|---|
| Exeter | Nath Gist | £130 | William Kitto | £100 |
| Tiverton | John Pengelly | 20 | same | 30 |
| Wellington | William Bowring | 10 | same | 40 |
| Taunton | Thomas Butler, later Francis Stanley | 40 | same | 44 |
| Bridgewater | John Miles | 20 | same | 20 |
| Wells | — | — | Edward Wood | 70 |
| Bristol | Henry Pine | 114 | same | 102.10. 0. |
| Wotton under Edge | — | — | Thomas Knee | 45 |
| Gloucester | William Nichols | 50 | same | 70 |
| Tewkesbury | Edward Pearce | 12 | same | 25 |
| Worcester | George Glyn | 40 | same | 42 |
| Kidderminster | William Hill | 11 | same | 35 |
| Bridgenorth | — | — | John Edons | 35 |
| Shrewsbury | Martha Burgis | 45 | same | 40 |
| Whitchurch | — | — | Joan Roycroft | 35 |
| Chester | Thomas Reynell then Edward Palister | 55 | same | 35 |
| Bath | Ralph Allen | 25 | same | 110 |
| Devizes | Ben Streat | 25 | same | 25 |
| Marlborough | Thos. Hunt | 40 | same | 12 |
| Wantage | Francis Stanley | 100 | same | 60 |
| Abingdon | John Lumly | 40 | Eliza Carter, then John Lumly | 12 |
| Oxford | John Ween | 90 | John Pottle | 60 |

Spelling of one or two names may be wrong, as the writing is difficult. As it is known that other postal historians have examined this salary list, it is difficult to see why the importance was not realised.

Salaries are graded according to the work, some stages having no ordinary salary as they were not on a direct or branch road. Francis Stanley managed the Hungerford branch, as well as being postmaster of various stages as far away as Taunton. His two salaries for Wantage are high, and his postmasterships seem to include Taunton, Hungerford Branch (£200) Wantage, Wantage X Post, and Highworth (£110, being 'one ½ of all lrs down and one third of lres up'). Similarly it is not clear why John Powell should combine Lancaster (£6 a year) with Cirencester (£50 and 'one 3rd part of all lettrs more than they did amount to in the year 1793 for carring and fetching the lettrs from Wooton Unredge £103.12.—' total £153.12.—), 1793 must be a surprising slip for 1693. It must be remembered, however, that the amount of 'riding work'— provision of horses and riders, had a big influence on the salary.

In response to questioning by the auditors on the accounts 1710/11, it was stated that some postmasters were allowed a proportion of the revenue instead of a salary because villages and Gentlemen's seats were so far apart that if paid by a salary they would probably not collect and deliver the letters. It is worth remembering that an important country house might well have more correspondence than a large market town, so this was not favoured treatment but realism. Later in the questioning it was stated that the large Wantage salary included taking the bag back and forward to Abingdon three times a week, maintaining deputies at several towns and villages (including Lambourn and Ilsley) and conveying their mail.

It is not yet certain what happened on the Exeter-Chester cross road on 13 February 1712/13 but Thomas Heywood, postmaster of Warrington, was paid £31 in November 1722 for spending 62 days travelling the Chester road between 25 March 1713 and 1 August 1714 to settle the accounts of By-letters (the account was then lost for eight years). It is probable this was to settle differences and difficulties, and the Warrington postmaster may have been chosen as far removed and impartial. Similarly Francis Stanley was allowed £59.10.— for riding 84 days in the quarter ended Lady Day 1713 for inspecting stages on the Bristol Road — both of these could have been the London roads, but considering the upheaval it is much more probable they were smoothing difficulties on the cross road caused by the change from Quash to Post Office employment. Stanley undoubtedly had the stature with postmasters to do the job, and it is notable that the Bristol road to Exeter was not his road. Probably another entry not yet found was for another postmaster to settle his Oxford road.

Looking down the list of cross post salaries the point is inescapable that Allen of Bath received the highest salary, £110. Part of this was for a greater amount of riding work. Much as one may want to glamourize him, is it likely that elderly men who had been in the service before Allen was born would accept a manager of nineteen or twenty? If they did, and it seems probable that he managed or supervised at least part of the cross roads, it speaks volumes for his personality and efficiency and shows that he must have been respected and well known to them — he may have managed these roads for Quash for three or four years.

The large contract farmers, now managing their previous farms on a 10% net basis, carried on until 1716 when they became normal salaried employees with the exception of the Chichester and Ferrybridge farms, which continued on 10% net for some years. The report to the Treasury of 2 March 1716/17 is typical of the worst bureaucracy, claiming that it would save £1,878 when the other two farmers were deprived of their 10% but saying nothing of how these areas would be run without top quality staff. It completely ignored the fact that the saving and the 90% profit taken by the Post Office were only there because these men made the system work at their own risk (when the Post Office had failed consistently) and ended by asking for five more supervising staff in the Chief Office! A sordid story, but not unusual, then or today. Richard Bigg appears to have become a Clerk of the Road very quickly, for newspapers he franked down the road are known in 1715; other farmers may have been promoted too. There is little doubt they were the backbone of the postal service at this time.

Mention has been made of Ralph Allen, but no definite facts have been found about his activities between 1713 and 1720. To bring the story of the cross posts to its climax it is necessary to go back a few years and study this interesting personality. His early years have always been wrapped in mystery and lack of proof remains, but by combining the numerous writings* on him with new research and deduction, a clear probability emerges. The only early date proven is that Allen was baptized on 24 July 1693 at St. Columb, but his memorial at Claverton, near Bath, states that he died on 29 June 1764 'in the 71st year of his age' so he must have been born during the first three weeks of July 1693 if this is correct. No records were kept at this time, of course, but in view of the widespread superstition that a child dying unbaptized was condemned to float between Heaven and Hell for eternity, it would normally take place within a week or so of his birth. What is very doubtful though, is that he was taken from St Blazey Gate (where traditionally his father kept the 'Duke William' Inn) to St Columb, on horseback over pretty bad roads, for baptism. Much more likely was that his mother went to the grandparents at St Columb for his birth, and he was christened there before returning. So circumstantial evidence indicates his birth at St Columb during the first two weeks of July 1693, and traditional St Blazey is wrong.

Although authorized in December 1703, an extension post road south west from Exeter to Truro via Bodmin and Launceston was opened only in December 1704. This was run by the Post Office to serve the midland towns of Cornwall, following a petition 'by Treasurer Godolphin and the Gentry of Cornwall'. Run by the postmasters of Exeter, Plymouth and Launceston in consultation, expenses of £260 were allowed and a full report was required after one year's working. Before this, the only post in Cornwall was along the south coast from Plymouth to

---

*The only two books of importance are Prof. Boyce and *Ralph Allen's own Narrative* by Hopkins and Bond (op. cit.), but earlier writings are quoted.

Market Jew (Marazion) mentioned in Gardiner's Survey of 1677, which dates from 1660 (1635 to Penryn only) and which ran through Looe, Fowey, St Austell, Truro, Penryn and Helston. This road was managed by the postmaster of Plymouth, John Stuckley, and doubtless the new road and the old were made to work well together, being controlled by the same men. Miss Philbrick tells me that she has traced all of this south coast road, and walked parts that are no more than grassy rides or farm lanes five or six feet wide; a useful lesson not to assume that main roads today are the main roads of earlier days.

On visits to St Columb, young Ralph's interest must have been aroused, for the first postmaster, Reskemer Allen, was his uncle (not his grandfather, as is usually stated). Confusion has always resulted from the entry 'Robert Allen' in the salary books for the first year, but this is now proved to be an error, probably a misreading of his very bad signature by a clerk; the debit list of moneys owing shows Reskemer Allen clearly for the first year. Some months before his early death on 8 August 1707 his mother took over, evidently as a temporary measure until Blithe Haycroft (a man) became postmaster in December 1707. At this point Allen was fourteen years old, and the next provable fact is that he became postmaster of Bath on 25 March 1712 aged eighteen. How could this happen? Though not yet at its peak, Bath was one of the most fashionable cities in the country; every activity was ruled by a few despotic families, and it might well have had a greater proportion of literate inhabitants with the need to write letters than any other city in the country. In an office where the postmaster dare not put a foot wrong, the Post Office installed a youth of eighteen who had never (as far as is shown by Bath or postal records) held any official Post Office position before.

It can be assumed that for three years at St Columb he had helped his uncle on occasions, and may well have run the office for his grandmother, but from 1708 the only possible explanation is that he was taken into the Joseph Quash cross post organization and there he blossomed. The accounting centre for the Truro road was Exeter, not London, so Quash would have known about him, and probably took this bright boy to Exeter when Gertrude Allen gave up St Columb in December 1707. The rise he must have had in two years speaks of powerful local sponsorship, for at this time ability counted for a lot, but not enough to shoot to the top. This may well have come from Sir John Trevelyan, M.P. and High Sheriff for Somerset, as was reported after Allen's death. Outstanding ability, integrity, and the constant interest of a large local landowner could just have done it.

In the early writings on Allen are many contradictory recollections and statements: Allen himself says he was Deputy of Bath from 1710 which is patently impossible (all postmasters legally were Deputy Postmasters to the Postmaster General but to simplify terms in this book this has been ignored), but taken together these writings are valuable. Allen was writing in 1761, so it is much more probable that the date of his big chance was firmly in his mind, 1710, but he came to Bath not as Postmaster, but in Quash's employ to manage the Bristol-Oxford cross post. On this type of reasonable assumption, the story may well be as follows: taken to Exeter in 1708, he did so well that in 1710 he was sent to manage the Bristol to Oxford cross post, with headquarters at Bath, in which job he would have been riding frequently and meeting the other postmasters, in particular such influential figures as Henry Pine and Francis Stanley, and must have impressed them enormously. The failure of Quash cannot have been a sudden thing, and Allen must have known by 1710 or 1711 that all was not well. Above all, he obviously had enormous ambitions and ideas, so must have realized that his opportunities lay in stirring up the lethargic but safe Post Office monopoly. As happens frequently in history, the ideal chance occurred quite soon, for with his great capacity for making friends he must have heard rumours of a scandal involving the Bath City Council and the postmistress, Mrs Collins.

It is not necessary to go deeply into this local scandal, but it would seem that when Mrs Collins was appointed in 1690 the Post Office was moved to her house, as was normal at that time. Unfortunately her house was actually a Church, not used as such since Elizabethan times but never deconsecrated, and with the living bracketed with Mastership of St Johns Hospital adjoining. The incumbent died in December 1711, the matter was laid before the Attorney General in February and on 25 March 1712 Allen replaced Mrs Collins. One can quite see that this would not do in Bath, but instinctively there is now a strong feeling that some pieces are missing — it is too

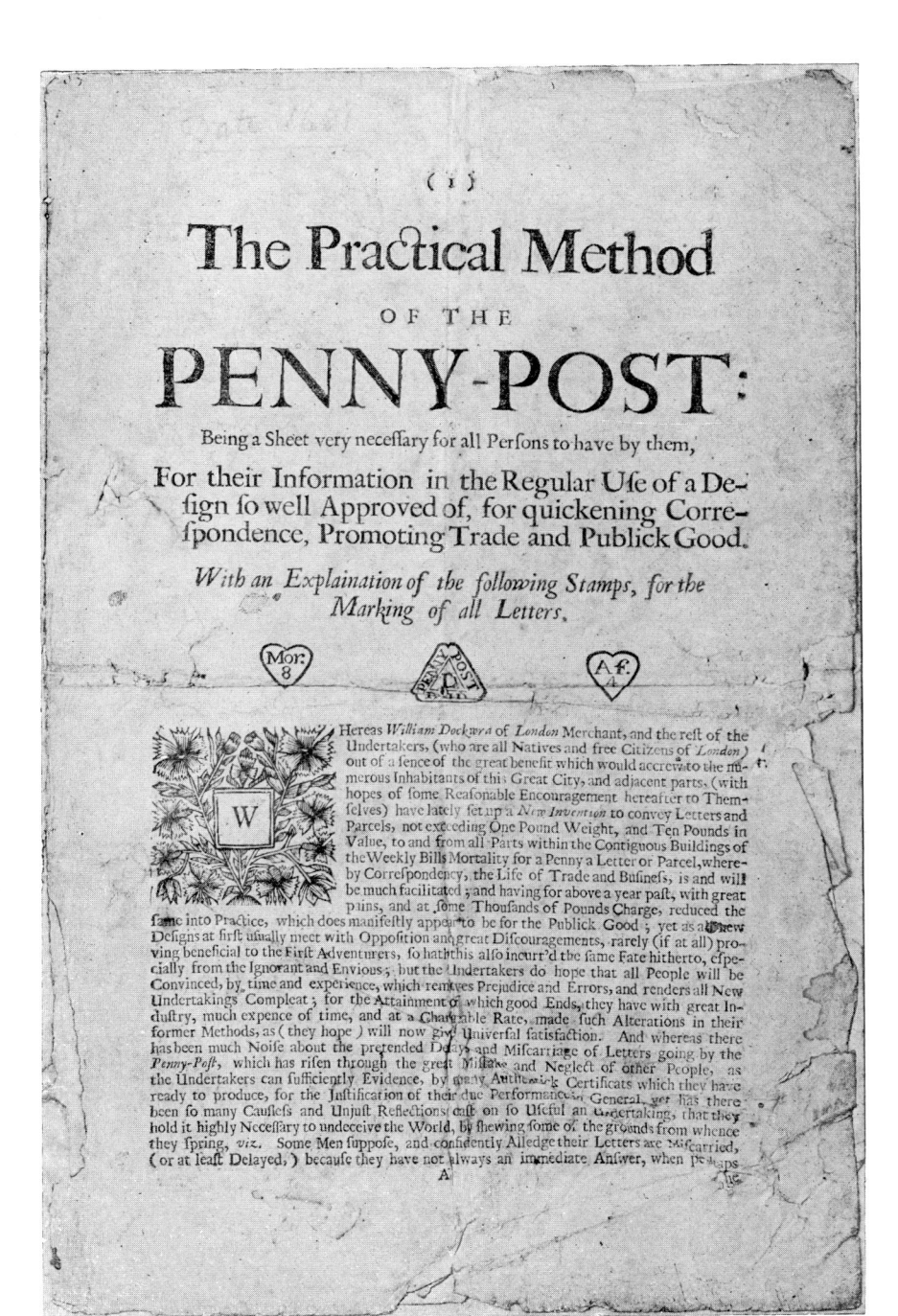

*An advertising leaflet for the Dockwra Penny Post in London (page 27).*

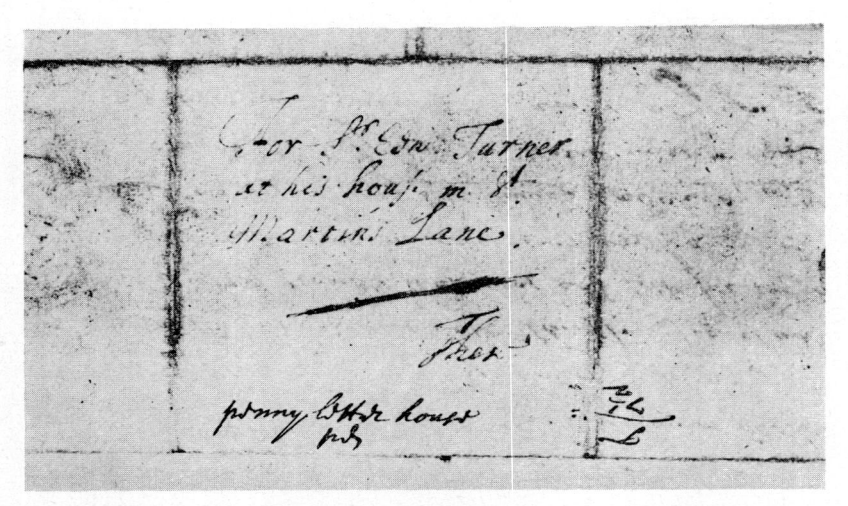

*The earliest known letter carried in the Dockwra Post, 18 May 1680, endorsed 'penny letter house pd.' and T 7½ (probably Temple 7.30 p.m.) (reproduced by courtesy of the County Archivist, West Sussex Records Office).*

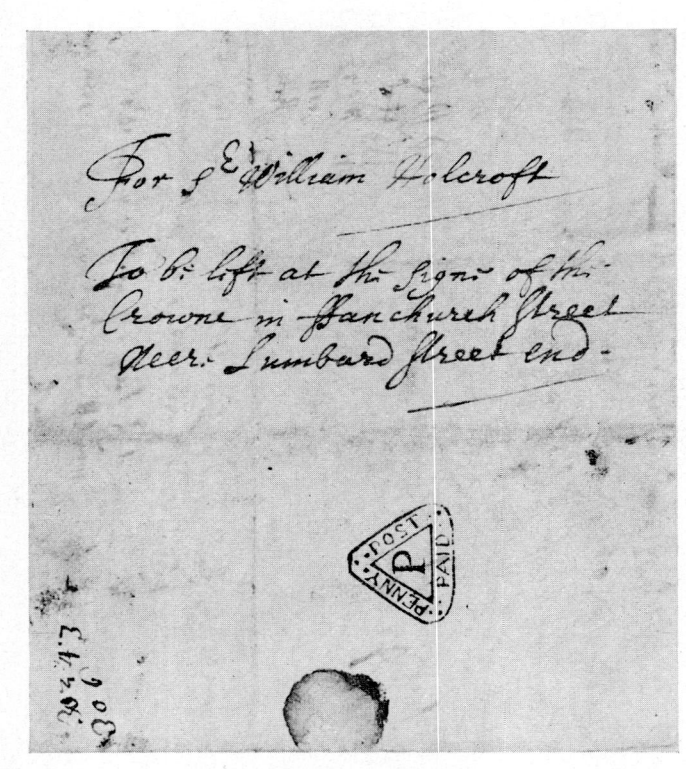

*A 'Dockwra' stamp (possibly used in Murray's post) of 25 January 1680/81 (reproduced by courtesy of the National Postal Museum).*

Plate 10

*Shooters Hill: the execution of George Webb and Richard Russell for Highway Robbery, 19 August 1805. In background is the Admiralty Telegraph shutter (to Dover) and Severndroog Castle (reproduced by courtesy of the Greenwich and Lewisham Antiquarian Society) (page 77).*

*London Twopenny Post; the inner dotted line shows the Town area before, the inner continuous circle after April 1831. The outer dotted line is the Country area before, the continuous circle after November 1833 (although Hampton continued inside) (page 74).*

**Plate 11**

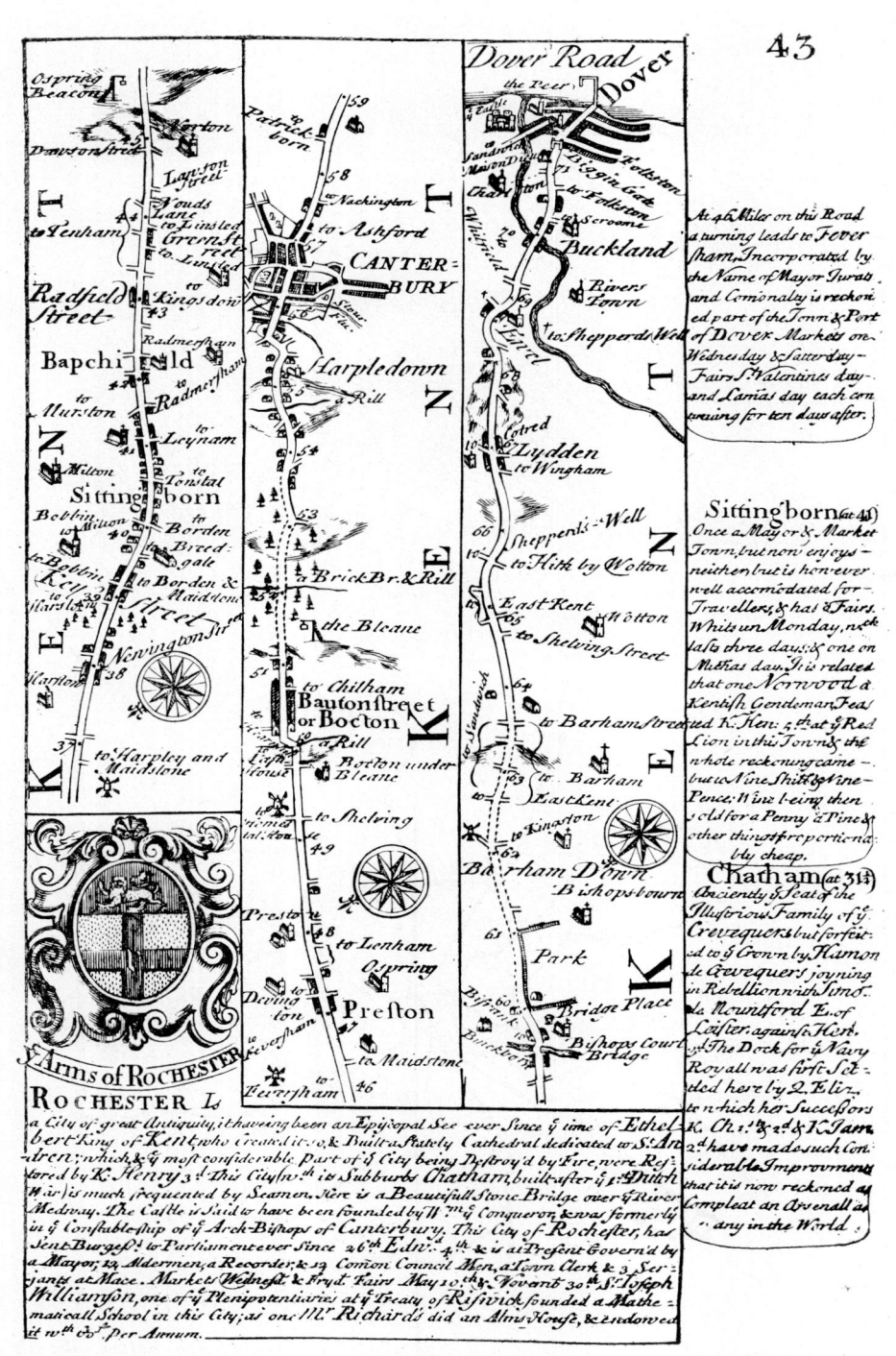

*An example of the 'strip map' begun by John Ogilby. This is from 'Britannia Depicta' by Emanuel Bowen, 1720.*

**Plate 12**

glib. London authority was further removed than South America is today, and this very remoteness forced the Post Office only three years later to appoint a Surveyor for each road. The Surveyors were very capable top men from London, whose job was each to travel his road continually, with full power to take decisions on the spot and (just as important) to keep London in touch with what happened in the provinces. Superficially the Bath action smells of unnecessary panic, for although the Council came out badly, it was not more than a local affair and if serious, new premises could soon have been found for Mrs Collins. If she was really involved (and there is no evidence of this) an experienced postmaster should have been brought in from another town.

Rather than either of these normal courses, it seems to have been decided to do what can only be described as borrow Ralph Allen from Quash on a part-time basis, so they must have wanted him very badly indeed. He became Bath postmaster employed by the Post Office, whilst still cross postmaster employed by Quash. Even with four years work for Quash, possibly two of them administrative, he would have been nearly unknown in London, and it was in London that decisions were made. It seems fantastic, and speaks of more weighty backing than is known — one wonders if Trevelyan was a personal friend of either Postmaster General. Allen is known to have had later associations (by 1715) with Field Marshal Wade, and it is this calibre of support that must have secured the position. Strongly in his favour would have been that whilst well known in Bath, he was free of ties with any of the local people involved. Another contributory factor would be that if the postal system in the South West was soon to suffer a complete upheaval, they wanted to cause as little dislocation as possible in other offices before this, and to make sure that Allen (the youth who really knew the cross posts and Quash's system) came into Post Office employment. On his side, there is little doubt that Allen could see himself shortly without an employer, and was doing his best to get into the Post Office. Some training or probationary period would be expected, as Quash's methods must have been different from the Post Office, but as there is no evidence it must be assumed that this coaching was unpaid. If a London inspector had been watching Quash, it is possible that he reported very favourably on Allen.

In the 1713/14 accounts, with Allen's salary of £25 and cross road salary of £110 are two items back-dated to 15 April 1712. One is additional salary of £15 a year, making £40 in all, the other an additional £20 a year for two letter carriers. The first could be rent for his post office, as unlike Mrs Collins he would not have suitable accommodation, but the entry 'two letter carriers' is more interesting. In the accounts for 1714/15, the next year, the three entries are consolidated into a single salary entry of £60 to conform with standard practice that all office expenses are included in the salary; no other town has a similar entry for letter carriers, and Bath would have less need for them than many cities, being compact. Bearing in mind that the writer feels he was the only postmaster maintaining offices for two masters, it seems probable that the salaries were for a clerk in each office, and they were entered as letter carriers because they had a lower rate of pay than clerks (this we know from Gardiner, who gives the rate for London letter carriers as 8/- a week, window men and sorters £30 a year).

Confirmation that he was still working for Quash comes from the earliest known letter from Allen, now lying in Bath City Library. Addressed 'to Mr Oswald Hoskyns at the Black Moors Head In Kings Street nere the Guild Hall In London' on 29 October 1712 it is endorsed 'Free R Allen' and a charge is erased so his postmaster's right of franking was accepted. It encloses two drafts and begins 'By my masters orders enclosed'— knowing that it was Hoskyns who was bankrupt at the same time as Quash, these orders can only have been money for Quash's account. If a letter from Allen could be found before 25 March we should know whether postmasters on farmed roads had a franking privilege, but this is doubtful.

On 13 February 1712/13 came the upheaval. The summons was served on Joseph Quash for £2,200 and 'being bankrupt, he fled'. There is much more here than is known at present, and research could be very rewarding. Is Prof. Boyce correct in saying that Quash paid the £1,640.4.9 for one penny a letter on the cross post and £165 for the by-letters (total £1,804. 4. 9) and if so why the £2,200? Study of the figures below makes one think it was this £1,805 plus a small working debit (it was normal practice in all Government service at this time to use the Government money you collected for as long as possible). His debit balances were: 1701 £152, 1702 £171, 1703 £409, 1704 £92, 1705 £492, 1706 credit £131, 1707 not in the list, 1708 £6, 1709 £180, 1710 £344, 1711

£934, 1712 £369, 1713 £2,295. If the £1,805 was paid, it reinforces the feeling that he was a loyal servant caught in happenings beyond his control, and that the Post Office wanted to be rid of him so piled on everything. Were they unable for some reason to terminate his farm in 1711 with the others, and used this as an excuse? The prosecution was on 13 February for trial in the Trinity Term (June-July), so investigation of his position must have gone on for at least a year before February to prepare the case: why then was he left in control of his network and charged the full rental up to this day, and in particular why did Francis Manaton pay him £3,500 for transmission to London a day or two before the prosecution? This makes it clear that there can have been little question of dishonesty, for if the Post Office had doubts considerable enough to investigate him for a year or more, and their case was complete, why on earth was not the Receiver of Taxes for Cornwall warned not to use Quash for transmitting funds? Or was he asked to use him? Was the bankruptcy of Hoskins the effect or a contributory cause? Quash's petition of 1718 that he had been unable to obtain bills on London, and that much of £254,391 paid to the Exchequer had to be conveyed in specie causing very great expense, is relevant here. Equally relevant could be another entry in the Calender of Treasury Books, 16 August 1715 —'re Manaton — that houses and lands seized from Quash are of little value, for want of necessary repairs . . . that he may become a purchaser at a reasonable valuation'. So Manaton bought all the houses and property owned by Quash from the Treasury very reasonably!

It is not yet known why all the cross post salaries entered separately for the first time in the 1713/14 accounts (year ending 25 March 1714) are only from 13 February to 25 December. Possibly the last three months was a period of reassessment to see how the system worked as run by the Post Office, but one would certainly expect the postmasters to be paid. Salaries included expenses of the office, and seem to have been dependent as much on the amount of riding work done from the office as its importance, but it is difficult to avoid the conclusion that Allen with £110 was in a supervisory capacity over at least a part of the road, possibly the Bristol to Oxford branch. Throughout his life he showed a remarkable capacity for making friends, and his training with Quash probably fitted him much more for this than the normal work of a postmaster.

In 1715 Surveyors were appointed for the first time; they were in effect travelling representatives of the Postmasters General and as such were of considerable importance. Over the years the system depended on them more and more, both to keep the Chief Office in touch with the provinces and offer recommendations for improvements, and to keep the provincial postmaster in touch with London — they were the oil which lubricated the works. Doubtless, Allen would soon appreciate their importance to him, and there can be little doubt that his natural honesty, scrupulous accuracy and enthusiasm must have impressed his surveyor. It would be primarily on his recommendation that the Postmasters General considered an application from Allen to farm all the cross and by-post letters throughout the country in 1719. In his 1761 narrative, he had little opinion of the early surveyors, but this could be retrospective colouring.

On 8 February 1719/20 the Postmasters General wrote to the Treasury mentioning no names but saying that they considered the only way to improve the revenue from the by and cross posts, which had been near £4,000 a year for some years, was to farm it. They had received an offer of £5,000 a year for a contract for ten years, but proposed to accept an improved offer to £6,000 a year for seven years with prospects of a great improvement at the end of this term. Several additional officers at the expense of the Farmer would be nominated by the Post Office. In a supplement appended is an account of the Country letters for 1719, totalling £7,911. The draft contract being passed by the Attorney General, it was signed by Allen on 12 April 1720, with a declaration added on the 17 June that Country letters, or those which had always passed through London, should still pass through London and not be included in the farm.

The Agreement specified equal quarterly payments of £1,500, and excluded the postage on Irish letters and the Scotch and Packet letter postage and Franked letters. It gave the Postmasters General power to nominate Surveyors and Postmasters, with their salaries, bound them to observe any instructions of the Postmasters General and Allen to observe the official postage rates. Allen was bound to provide a post at least three days a week, have horses ready to convey expresses or persons riding post, and maintain five miles per hour average for the conveyance of the mail. A later clause, requiring him to set up other posts and stages as needed if sanctioned by the

Postmasters General, would in effect give him power to enlarge the cross post system throughout the country, providing he did not divert any letters which had always passed through London. This afterthought of June may appear the completely dead hand on improvements, for it would seem impossible to increase or speed the mail if it had to travel unnecessarily to London and out again, but in practice it appears not to have been enforced providing the total value of these Country letters did not fall. The Post Office was evidently concerned to preserve the profitable letters which paid double postage, and in fact Allen managed to increase these despite his widespread cross posts.

Although the contract included all by-posts and way letters in England, it specified clearly cross post letters on the Exeter-Bristol-Chester and Oxford roads only, and to ensure there was no doubt gave the full route. This has misled Professor Boyce in stating that he was given the cross posts of Western England only; the fact is that this was the only one in existence. The preliminary letter to the Treasury and the clause requiring him to set up more posts and stages as necessary leaves no doubt that in both posts Allen covered all England, and the notice in the London Gazette of 15 April 1720 says 'a farm of all the Bye-Way and Cross Road letters throughout England and Wales. After 24 June next the postage of no bye-way or Cross Road letters is anywhere to be demanded but at the place they are sent from'. This would seem to imply prepayment, but as far as is known the opposite was the case at Allen's insistence, though possibly it applied later.

In an older man of great experience this contract would have been considered foolhardy, but for one of twenty six who had only been a postmaster for seven years, it must have seemed madness. The Post Office rarely succeeded in breaking even on these letters, with a large organization behind it; it could only have been these losses, together with the influence of Allen's friends and the excellent impression he had always made on the Surveyors and Headquarters, that won the day and a seven year contract. He paid a rental of £6,000 when the total income was established at £4,000 a year (he discovered later it was only £3,700) and all expenses, salaries of his postmasters and inspectors, and agreed to adhere to charges authorized by Parliament and approval of the Postmasters General in all appointments and salaries. In the early years of his farm he lost heavily, and detailed accounts of money received and spent had to be submitted, but he said later that this had been waived after 1734, when confidence in his ability had grown. In later years nobody had any idea of his expenses or profits, but in 1763 his gross revenue is known to have been £33,243, expenses £15,550 and rent still £6,000, giving a theoretical profit of £11,692. At the same time Allen estimated the saving to the revenue and increase in Post Office receipts through his labours during the same period (1720-61) at £1,516,870, an average for forty years of about £40,000 a year when his last and highest profit might possibly have been £11,700. It would be fair to say that throughout his farms, he made for the Post Office in clear profit ten times the profit he made for himself, and that nobody in the Post Office could have done it.

Every succeeding seventh year he received a new contract, each at the same rental of £6,000 a year but each imposing stiffer terms and an enlargement of his cross posts at no expense to the revenue. He relates that at the 1741 renewal it was desired to raise his rent, which he agreed was fair, but said that either the Postmasters General could have this increased rent or a large extension of his service. They preferred the latter, and this was the pattern for future contracts. Posts three days a week he made six-day, and he started a number of important new posts across country to save the time-wasting and expensive London journeys. At his death in 1764 a reasonably efficient service was running, vastly different from 1720 and probably 1740. He gave fair details in *Ralph Allen's Own Narrative* (op. cit.) but much verification and elaboration needs to be done before accurate details can be published.

Two extracts should be quoted, the first to show how he was able to make such improvements that the existing services became profitable before attempting to extend. Talking of the method of carriage he says:

> 'To give a slight idea of the nature of this conveyance; The Bye & way Letters were thrown promiscuously, together into one large bagg, which was to be opened at every stage by the Deputy, or any inferior servant of the house, to pick out of the whole heap, what might belong to his own delivery and the rest put back again into this large Bagg, with such

Bye Letters as he shou'd have to send to distant places, from his own Stage. But what was still worse than all this. It was the constant practice to demand and receive the Postage of all such Letters before they were put into any of the Country Post Offices, Hence (from the general temptation of destroying these Letters for the sake of the Postage) the joynt mischiefs of Embezling the Revenue and interrupting and obstructing the Commerce fell naturely in, to support and inflame one another. Indeed they were then risen to such a height, and, consequently the discredit & disrepute of this conveyance grown so notorious that many Traders & others in divers parts of the Kingdom, had recourse to various contrivances of private and clandestine conveyance for their speedier and safer Correspondence; whereby it became unavoidable but that other Branches of the Post Office revenue shou'd be greatly impair'd, as well as this.'

Talking of his methods he says:

'These Checks Mr. Allen first conceived and rendered practicable: And as they were the means and sole means of securing that revenue to the Public, which his other regulations had enabled him to raise & increase, it may not be improper just to mention how they were form'd. He so contrived, that every Postmaster on the same Road, and in all the Branches in the same Road, shou'd check and be checked, by every other: Nay further, this Security against frauds was extended even to operate reciprocally between the Postmasters on different Roads and on the different Branches of different Roads, by means of certain regulations which he kept in places where these different Roads are intersected by Crofs road Branches; and which, for this reason, he chose to call Key Towns.'

This method of checking was doubtless the root of his success, and the Post Office did their best to discover the details. It seems probable that Allen remembered how the contract farmers were treated in 1711-16, and Dockwra before them, and knew that once the Post Office was capable of running by-posts and cross posts at a profit, he would lose his contract. Whatever the reason, it remained a close secret, but he agreed at the 1734 renewal that a clause should be inserted that on his death all books and papers became the property of the Post Office. They had to wait another thirty years to learn how it had been done. From the 1741 contract many improvements were made at Allen's expense, with the increase in the revenue to go to the Crown; this the Post Office preferred to an increased rental.

Surprisingly he found time to direct other enterprises, including the Avon canal and development of the Bath Stone quarries, from which came part of his later fortune. Much of Professor Boyce's book studies and records the man from all angles, his friends and his influence on them, both local, political, and especially artistic. Those interested are recommended to read it, for Allen made a considerable mark on his times by his friendships in the literary field, his benefactions, and his example. Primarily though, he dragged the postal system out of its seventeenth century torpor, set new standards of honesty and efficiency, and won loyalty by insistence on just perquisites and rewards for honest and efficient staff. A remarkable epitaph, but his personality must have been outstanding in any age, more so in the eighteenth century.

By 1735 he was living at Widcombe but he kept his house in Bath, and in 1741 the splendid mansion of Prior Park, designed by the famous Bath architect John Wood in a magnificent setting just below his stone quarries on Combe Down, was completed. Designed in three massive buildings joined by a colonnade, the west wing housed the offices of his cross post organization, and the east the stables and postboys. In 1748 he passed the postmastership of Bath to his brother Philip, and concerned himself with his national organization until his death on 29 June 1764 aged seventy. On his death, the whole system reverted to the Post Office and moved to Lombard Street, with his nephew (also Philip) as Resident Surveyor and Comptroller.

The influence of these farmers of the cross and by-posts cannot be overestimated. The Post Office was happy to run its six main road services and have a guaranteed and increasing payment from men who were forced to develop their areas to make a profit: they took the risks, and without them the postal service would have borne little resemblance to the widespread system that was Allen's legacy. The use of distinguishing stamps for the towns of posting is one example. Although they are known from 1697 on the cross post and 1698 in Ireland, town stamps only came into general use in 1705 and dropped out of favour again from 1710 to 1719. There can now be no doubt that their introduction was due to Quash and their consistent use from 1720 was the result of insistence by Ralph Allen, for these farmers had to ensure that they received the correct postage for cross and by-post letters; in default the revenue would go to the Post Office.

---

Two years after this cross post section was written comes a new discovery which shows that postal history is a living subject about which we still know very little. For many years to come we can all make discoveries — this is the fun of it. Much has been said about Joseph Quash, and it is hoped that the reader shares the author's feeling that here was an outstanding man who was forced into bankruptcy in 1713 by circumstances beyond his control, and by petty backbiting. Allen went from strength to strength, but nothing was known of Quash after the oblivion and dishonour of bankruptcy. Often we wondered what happened to him.

Now Mrs Aubrey Emonet has found in the Cornish Records Office, Truro, some documents indicating strongly a happy ending, and which may throw light on Allen's earliest years. In the Carlyon papers she has found:

A bond for administration of her husband's estate signed by Elizabeth Allen, dated 8 July 1731 (Ralph's mother on his father's death).

Two bonds for administration of his parents' estates signed by Ralph Allen, dated 23 March 1731/2. It appears that Elizabeth died before Philip's estate was settled, so Ralph had to take over both.

An inventory of the goods left by Philip Allen, 3 July 1731, totalling £78. 7. 6. (one Nagg at £4, two cowes and one young calfe £5, nine sheep and five lambs £2.17. 6., personal and inn furniture, etc.).

A lease of a parcel of land to build a dwelling, known as Archers Upper Moore, part of a tenement called Tregrean at St Blazey. This is dated 21 December 1702, and describes Philip Allen as Vintner.

A lease of one-third of the cellar and the two keys adjacent, at a fishing cove called Hallean in the parish of St Austell, dated 27 February 1715/16. This describes Philip as Innkeeper, of St Blazey.

The two last are of considerable interest, but not of importance until more can be discovered. Innkeeper and Vintner would be interchangeable terms, and if Philip built a house at Archers Upper Moore to get away from the inn (or some other purpose) in 1703, Ralph was nine years old at this time. The first deed of administration tells us his mother's name was Elizabeth, not Ann, and fixes his father's death, but the other two are most important because beneath Ralph's signatures are those of Philip Allen (his younger brother) and Joseph Quash. They are guaranteeing Ralph's honest administration of the wills for a sum twice the value of the estates, so the first point is that Quash must have paid his debts or been discharged — a bankrupt cannot be a guarantor. More important, these are purely family documents, and when Ralph Allen could have asked anyone of a hundred people to sign them with his brother he asked Quash, eighteen years after he had dropped into oblivion. At this early stage it is only safe to say that it proves he was a very close family friend, but the probabilities are much greater.

Ralph would seem to have been too young to shoulder the enormous responsibility he did shoulder in 1720, and Philip was younger with no apparent experience. Again, the enormous amount of administration, checking, and supervision was well beyond the capacity of one man however brilliant and energetic. The Post Office had failed with cross posts because they could not supervise and check the peculation of their postmasters: Allen could do so, and he succeeded, but the work would have been heavy. Here is the perfect answer, for Quash knew much more about cross posts than Allen, he had trained Allen, and would seem to have been his right-hand man throughout. He may have gone to Bath to help, but certainly from 1720 things such as the revival of the use of town stamps bear his hallmark. Possibly he lived with the family after his bankruptcy, but it shows Allen's gratitude and acknowledgement of the debt he owed.

**Chapter 6**

# PROVINCIAL TOWN STAMPS

IT IS possible that the earliest provincial stamps to show the origin of a letter are from the Chichester road farmed by Robert Tayer. As has been said under Cross Posts, Tayer was the Postmaster of Chichester by 1673, then managed the entire Branch road to London. He seems to have resisted Col Whitley's persuasion to farm the road for some years, but by 1682 he did so. Also from 1673 Whitley was writing to Tayer 'provide a stamp to distinguish yours from other letters, let your stamp be some figure, & larger than the stamp at the office' (this information is from Brigadier G. A. Viner and J. J. Greenwood). It is not known why Whitley wanted the Chichester Branch letters distinguished, but he had considerable trouble with Tayer. At this period, of course, 'the stamp at the office' would be the Bishop Mark type of London date stamp.

As with the offer of the farm, Tayer appears to have resisted a stamp successfully until 1681, when some letters from the Worplesdon, Farnham, and Chichester area are struck with a peculiar 'hot cross bun' type of stamp, unlike anything else in British postal history (Fig. 26). Although it is not possible to prove it at present, the coincidences are of such strength that it is very probable that this stamp was to distinguish letters coming from the Chichester road, and that Whitley insisted it was used when Tayer took over the farm of this road. It occurs in various sizes but even the smallest is larger than the Bishop Mark of that time, and the pattern is exactly the same as an early map of the city of Chichester. It is known from 1681 to 1686, and is very rare.

Two letters of 1683 in the O. W. Newport collection of Channel Islands bear different stamps 'D'JARSEY' of a similar rudimentary type, but the author is not quite happy about them. It would be more satisfactory if some confirming examples turned up from an indisputable correspondence, but the amount of mail from Jersey at this time was small. These may have been struck in France.

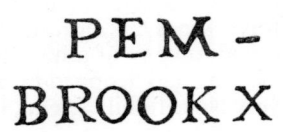

Fig 26    Fig 27    Fig 28    Fig 29    † Fig 30

The first true town stamps are from Exeter and Bristol, the termini of the original 1696 cross post. Both are known from 1697 with 'Bishop Mark' type stamps (Figs 27-28), the earliest movable date stamps by ninety years in England, London's first being 1787. It is not certain, but probable that the dates were changed. The stamps consist of a large E or B with the month and date in the two segments; an albino S is known, but more details are required of this stamp. The other terminus, Chester, had a large C with HES/TER inside (Fig 29) but as all known examples of this are addressed to London it is doubtful if it is a cross post stamp. By all the rules it should be one, though.

Other cross post stamps have been found recently with X incorporated, Wells and Bridgewater being towns on the Exeter-Bristol road and Oxford the terminus of the only branch. These

46

are WELLS with X below (1709), OXON X framed or unframed in one line (1719-20), BRIDG/WATER X (1709), and PEM-/BROOK X (1713) as two line stamps (Fig 30). How many more were issued is not known, but probably to most towns on these roads. Pembroke seems a different case, for although Quash's influence spread to West Wales, no Cross Post could have run from there. The letter is addressed to London, but it is thought that its use on this letter was a mistake. The Pembroke-London branch crossed the Bristol-Chester cross road at Gloucester, so it must have been an instruction to the Gloucester postmaster to turn it North or South West, and not send it to London. As the letter was eight days from Pembroke to London (3-11 May, 1713) it may well have been turned to Bristol and corrected there. Others from the same correspondence in 1713 have a normal PEM/BROOK without the X, and were five or six days only to London.

Surprisingly, Ireland began using townstamps at about the same time, for Strabane is known in 1698, followed by Waterford and Mullingar in 1699. No theories have been produced to explain this, or why the three towns should be selected for this honour — one feels it would need a genius to produce one. If you look at a map, Strabane is a little south-west of Londonderry, near the north coast, Mullingar is right in the centre and Waterford on the south coast. Put a ruler on them, and all three are in a straight line north to south, and are exactly the same distance apart on the map. Can this be a coincidence, when Londonderry should be the obvious choice at the northern end of the line? Derry had a population (in 1871) of 25,200 compared with 4,600 people in Strabane, but had no stamp for another twenty years or so. Derry is slightly out of the line, and a few miles further away, but why should it matter that the three towns were in a straight line and equidistant? The post from Strabane and Mullingar must have been very small indeed in 1698, when only two cities had name stamps in the whole British Isles. It cannot have been connected with cross posts, as there were none, and all Irish posts at this time were the responsibility of one group of farmers.

The first year for normal English town stamps is 1701, with Stone, Bolton, Coventry (Fig 31) and probably others; Wigan is known in this year in manuscript. Numerous towns stamped their names in the 1705-9 period, but few are known from 1710-19. Even towns using them in the first period do not seem to have used them much until 1719-20 when it is evident that a standard type was issued all over the country. Smaller in size of lettering than the 1701-09 stamps, many are spaced in two lines and some are hyphenated (Fig 32). Whereas many had been abbreviated in an apparently senseless fashion (the odd letters dropped being replaced by stops — AB.N.DON, HUNT.N.TON, CHIP.NHAM, etc.) the 1720 types are in full. From this date (with the same small lettering) some are framed in an attractive manner, and only the rarity of material from the provinces in this period prevents proper study.

BOLTON
† Fig 31

WINCHES
TER
† Fig 32

WARE
HAM
Fig 33

BIRMINGHAM
Fig 34

CAMBRIDGE
Fig 35

KINGSTON
Fig 36

TORRINGTON
Fig 37

BRISTOL
FEB 27 99
Fig 38

DARTFORD
† Fig 39

† these are actual size, all others are reduced 20%

By the 1740s town stamps are easier to find, though still pretty rare, and must have been in fairly general use by post towns; the 1760s bring them in quantity. Standard patterns and types make it clear that nearly all were issued officially from London, but locally made exceptions occur to add interest. Lettering became larger in the 1760-70s then smaller again, and when dates are collected for the whole country it should be evident that from the 1720 issue no further attempt was made to standardize stamps until 1799. New stamps were probably issued as requested, and the size and shape sent would be that currently in vogue — after straight lines, two lines were popular (even names as short as EXE/TER or DEVI/ZES), then arc, serpentine, and horseshoe (Figs 33-37). These are normally struck in black ink though some were blue, all shades from red to purple and, in the 1830s, yellow. Single lines were more popular from the 1780s, but many old stamps continued for many years.

The first dated stamps of Bristol and Exeter had no successor among Post-towns until 1798, when Manchester and a few ports received a stamp with the date underneath in two straight lines (Fig 38). Most stamps of this type were sent to islands in the Caribbean, and L. E. Britnor discovered a revealing letter from Lloyds Coffee House which explains their origin well.* Apparently uninsured vessels which sank shortly after sailing from West Indian islands were being covered by letters sent as duplicates on the next available ship, and as no dated stamps were in use the fraud was impossible to prove. The Postmasters General agreed with the Secretary, Sir Francis Freeling, that dated stamps were necessary, and two line types as Fig 38 were sent out shortly afterwards.

Also in late 1798 there appears to have begun the second attempt to standardize town stamps, for most important towns are known from 1799 to 1801 using a new recognizable type with small lettering in a single line (Fig 39). These are scarce to very rare, for in 1801 came the second general issue of mileage stamps (see next section), and many would have been used only a year or so.

The joy of studying town stamps lies in the exceptions, and though some were made locally, many doubtless were issued from London. It has proved impossible to lay down rules on design or issue of town stamps, and possibly designs could be ordered at the discretion of the Surveyor.

Bristol again sets the pace, for a whole series of town stamps follows the 'Bishop Mark B', all incorporating RIS and TOL within the segments of a large B. These are used for general post and cross post letters, and there may be fifteen or twenty different stamps. Whitchurch (Hants) pioneered the arc and horseshoe types with a hybrid in the 1760s, thirty years before they came into general use.

Stockport is outstanding by reason of the unique shapes, brilliant magenta ink and consistent large scale use which makes some of them fairly readily available today. Evidently Peter Board-

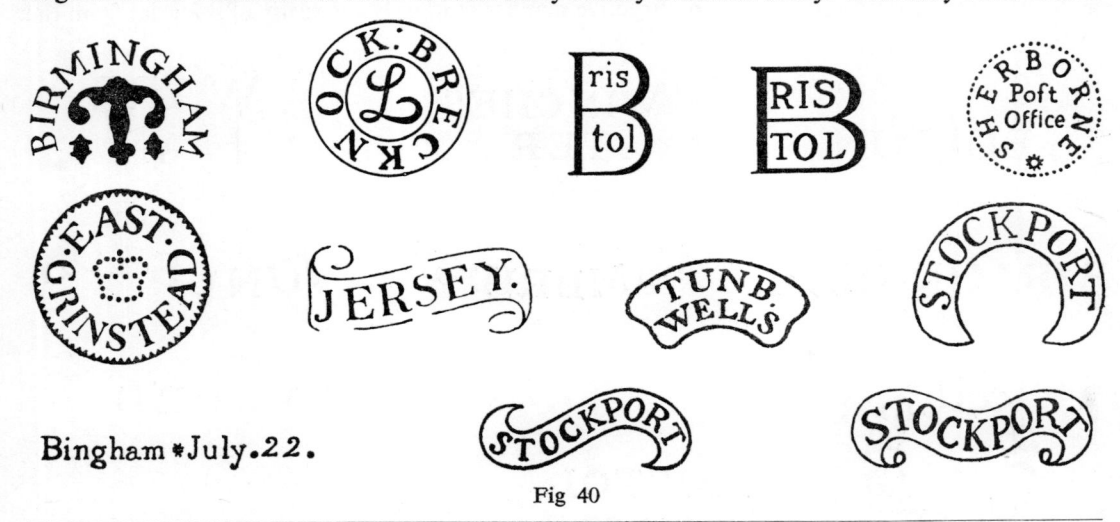

Fig 40

* Reported in *Stamp Collecting* of 11 January 1963, now published by Harris Publications, 42 Maiden Lane, London W.C.2.

man, Stockport Postmaster from 1774, was an individualist who disliked the dull stamps he was sent and the carbon black ink he should have used, so he embarked on the long series of scrolls, crescents, ovals, horseshoes and large circles which enliven many collections today; we are truly thankful for them. He seems to have obeyed orders, for he started in the period when the mileage from London had to be shown in the stamp; this he did, but fitted it into his own design.

A number of other post towns used distinctive stamps for short periods, amongst which might be mentioned Chester, influenced by its connection with Bristol (a large C enclosing HES/TER, Fig 29), Birmingham's beautiful 'chandelier', Jersey and Guernsey scrolls, circular stamps for Bristol and Reading (both early), Sherborne surrounding 'Post/office' and East Grinstead surrounding a crown (East Grinstead is found in other distinctive types, but all are rare). The framed straight line types in 1720-40 were widespread, and must have had a special meaning, but all are rare so study is difficult. Late abbreviations are few but FALM:o, ASHBY/Z and TUN-WELLS are examples; it is possible the former was used by the Packet agents, Fox and Co. Three line stamps were rarely used. If two towns had the same name, a letter was sometimes used for the county — Bury S and Bury L, Bradford W and Bradford Y.

Inks were normally black before 1800, though Stockport and Norwich used Magenta widely and a few towns used shades of red or blue. A surprising number of villages which were not post towns had a stamp issued, and it seems to have been at the discretion of the Surveyor. A good example of this is Melton, Suffolk, which used an arc MELTON.S from 1788 until at least 1840 (by which time it looked pretty battered), for sixty years later Melton still was not a post town. Two letters extant from John Palmer to the Vicar give the answer. Palmer at this time was riding high, having introduced the Mail Coaches, and was Comptroller General. His cousin had married the Vicar of Melton, and in one letter, 2 June 1788, Palmer says: 'I have ordered a stamp to be sent to Melton, and hope your Postmaster will under you care of him, do very well again — I beg you will write to me at all times when you think I can be of use to you or your friends'. Others were also probably ordered by favour.

The Postmaster of Hatherleigh, a sub-office of Okehampton, appears to have seen the Bristol B. and gone further, for in the 1760s a plain H was used (Fig 42). Another sub-office to leave its mark was Coggeshall: Bristol and Exeter had movable date stamps from 1698-1720, but no provincial city had one from 1720-98, when the packet type (Fig 38) was sent to a few major ports. London had its first in 1787, yet in 1790, eight years before any provincial city, Coggeshall,

† Fig 41

† Fig 42

a small Essex village under Kelvedon, used a large double circle stamp with a movable date in the centre (Fig 41). This must have been made for the receiver by a blacksmith friend for the first dated sub-office stamps are about sixty years later. These are freaks of local initiative at which one can but stare in awe. Forty years later, Hatherleigh had 219 houses and 12,200 inhabitants yet they assumed that the postmasters of Carlisle or Norwich or Aberdeen, seeing H on a letter as Fig 42, would realize it stood for Hatherleigh. Coggeshall with 593 houses and 2,469 inhabitants, had no official post at all at this time (see Local Delivery).

**Mileage Stamps**

Mileage stamps came into use from 1784 as shown in Fig 43, but were found to be so inaccurate that after four or five years the GPO reverted to the issue of town stamps. Probably owing to this short life, the 1784 type seems to be the only class of handstamp issued solely to post towns. All are pretty scarce, many are very rare, and doubtless some are still unknown. From 1750 pressure had been brought on the Turnpike Trusts to erect milestones along their roads, but these mileages were estimated and showed considerable discrepancies in themselves, or when compared with Paterson's travellers' guide to the roads which appeared soon afterwards. Charges for letters were so inaccurate that inspectors were kept busy in London and large sums must have been lost each year (it is notable that corrections are always upwards). The introduction of the mileage from London in the town stamps of 1784 enabled the receiving clerk to add his distance from London (which he would know) to that of the sending town, and check the charge endorsed by the latter. Most letters still passed through London, despite the growth of cross posts.

As stated above, issue of the mileage stamps ceased in 1788 or 1789, though use of these handstamps continued and is found very occasionally after 1800, Warwick being known in 1811. Apparently the idea was considered good, for the Postmaster General instructed John Cary, an engraver, mapmaker and printseller, to prepare a survey of all the principal roads in the country under the supervision of Thomas Hasker, Superintendent of Mail Coaches. Measurements were obtained by a machine consisting of a wheel about four feet in diameter, connected to a clock to record the number of rotations and pushed along the road by a long handle. It is said that measurements were checked by travelling in each direction, but one cannot but feel that it would be a miracle if a wheel was pushed from London to Edinburgh and clocked exactly the figure recorded from Edinburgh to London; it must have been averaged, if it was done each way.

STOCKPORT 176    STOCKPORT 176    LEEDS 193    78 SOUTH AMPTON

**Fig 43**

It is interesting to see that this has returned in a similar but smaller machine now being used to measure the width of busy roads, and proving much easier than a tape.

Although Cary made his measurements from various points in London, his figures were adjusted to read from the General Post Office, which in the case of Hyde Park Corner meant adding three or four miles. This is one of the reasons that figures in contemporary road books rarely agree with mileages in the handstamps. His termini were probably:

North Road to Berwick and Edinburgh from SHOREDITCH CHURCH via Tottenham, Waltham Cross, Stamford and Doncaster.

Norwich Road via Newmarket and Bury, as above as far as Royston.

Essex Road to Yarmouth from WHITECHAPEL CHURCH via Ilford, Colchester and Ipswich.
Kent Road to Dover and Deal from LONDON BRIDGE (South side) via Rochester and Canterbury.

Brighton Road from WESTMINSTER BRIDGE (South side) via Croydon, Ryegate and Crawley.

Portsmouth Road from the STONES END, BOROUGH, via Battersea, Kingston, Guildford and Petersfield.

West Road to Plymouth from HYDE PARK CORNER via Hounslow, Salisbury, Crewkerne and Exeter.

Bristol Road from HYDE PARK CORNER via Reading, Chippenham and Bath.

Milford Road to Ireland as above to Maidenhead, Oxford, Gloucester and Brecon.

Holyhead Road to Ireland from HICKS HALL, SMITHFIELD, via Highgate, Barnet, Stafford and Chester (at times this was from TYBURN TREE to Barnet).

North West Road as above to St. Albans, Leicester, Manchester, Lancaster and Carlisle.

Articles on mileage stamps by J. K. Sidebottom in the Postal History Society Bulletins Nos. 24 and 28 (1943) must be treated with caution, for they contain a number of errors. Study of the routes and numbers of the mail coaches is badly needed, for students have little idea of the complete pattern of coaches at various periods.

Cary produced his first official *Delineation of the Great Roads, both direct and cross roads throughout England and Wales* in 1798, and began a struggle with the established Col. Daniel Paterson, whose road book was then in its 11th edition. These books must have been invaluable to the Georgian traveller, and are indispensable to the postal historian of today. His results must have gone first to the Post Office, and when the rates were increased in 1801 (all steps were miles, thus eliminating any charge by stages) a completely new series of stamps with corrected mileages was issued as Fig 44, based on Cary's distances.

Both the 1784 and 1801 types of stamp are normally straight line, and were standard issue all over the country. The former are usually large and heavy, frequently in two lines and with the mileage before, after, or beneath the name, but the 1801 stamps are much lighter and smaller, in one line with the mileage below in a rectangular box. The earliest variation from the standard 1801 type came in the next year, when Fig 38 was re-issued as a three line stamp with mileage above. This type is rare, Manchester being the commonest, followed by Liverpool, Bristol and Hull. From 1803, circular stamps began to be used as Fig 45 with the mileage at the bottom dated and later undated. At about the same time the box surrounding the figures became a line above and below (Fig. 46) and it is thought that (possibly with the odd exception) no boxed mileages were issued after 1803.

As with town stamps, the interesting local varieties of mileage stamps add interest to the study. In the 1784 type, Stockport again stressed its individuality, Sheffield and Nottingham also had horseshoes; Berwick, whose stamps throughout seem to have been both English and Scottish in type, placed a line on each side of the mileage below the name which could be said to be the forerunner of later Scottish mileages. In later types LEEK/150 and LEEK/154 both were enclosed in a box, Caistor L (Lincs), Tunbridge Wells and Portsmouth in a circle, whilst Bristol had a dotted circle. In 1803 Manchester used the first circular mileage stamp, having 185 at the top and the name below reading outwards (Fig 45). It seems to have been unsatisfactory, as

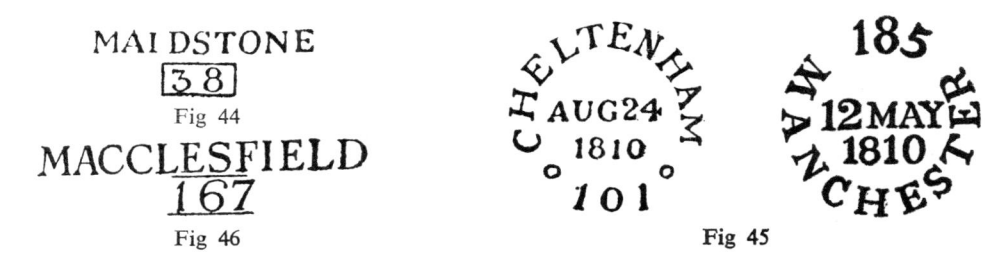

MAIDSTONE
[3 8]
Fig 44

MACCLESFIELD
167
Fig 46

CHELTENHAM
AUG 24
1810
101
Fig 45

185
MANCHESTER
12 MAY
1810

all others have the mileage below, and may have been experimental. It was used, however, for many years. Some towns had arcs to join the name and mileage, and rare varieties include Bristol and Coventry with fleurons, and Hull with double arcs. A selection is shown in Fig 47. Others had a circle at each side, and a unique Bath stamp used for a long time had three stars; this is quite easy to obtain. The major types of widespread use seem to be:

    1784: the first issue as Fig 43, large letters in one or two lines.

    1801: standard, a straight line with boxed mileage beneath (Fig 44).

after 1803: (1)   similar, but Fig 46 with lines above and below the mileage, or

            (2)   circular in numerous variations, the earlier ones having some ornament each side of the mileage, as Fig 47.

Fig. 46 comes occasionally with no lines to the mileage, but it is very doubtful if more than a dozen or so were issued in this way. Nearly all examples of English frameless straight line mileages can be ascribed to bad cutting or wear. It was, however, normal for Irish towns to have a plain mileage without a box or lines. Another source of variety is that many towns have two different figures for the distance from London. In some cases this was from a reassessment, but more often a change in the route.

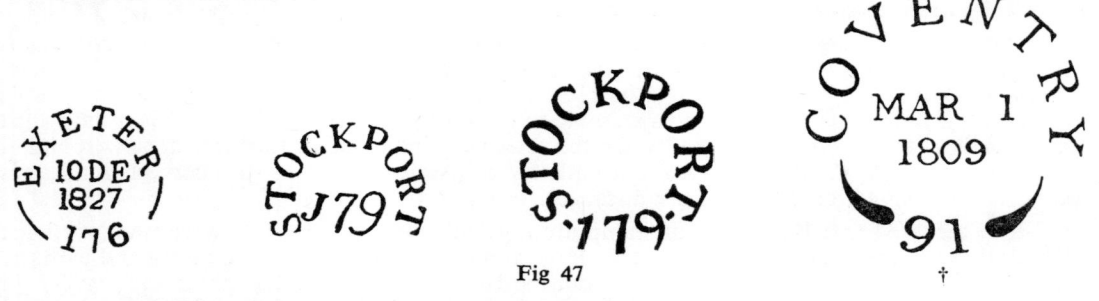

**Fig 47**

After the issue of 1801 no attempt seems to have been made to enforce their use, for this boxed type was used for only a few months in Bath before reverting to straight line town stamps. Bath even used new sizes of town stamp before adopting circular designs of mileage in 1808, and as one of the cultural and social centres of the country it would be under a degree of scrutiny. Generally they had uninterrupted use, however, until 1829 when the first of a number of orders was sent to all postmasters to check the mileage figure, and cut it out if found to be incorrect.

Mileages erased can be found in all types of stamp, and were probably caused most often by reassessment of the distance from London. Cary had done a wonderful job, but it had been hurried and the slightest warping or damage to his wheels could soon lose or gain a mile or two in a hundred. Other causes were a change of route (the charge was levied on the miles travelled, not the shortest route) and errors in ordering or manufacture. Another source of error is that some sub-offices had stamps showing the mileage of their post town: in the case of Blackpool, the rate was a penny more than the Preston figure it carried and (probably with others) it seems to have been withdrawn for this reason. Anyway, it is not clear why it was issued: most sub-offices did not have a stamp, although much later a clutch of four Midland villages appear using mileages of Leicester (Mountsorrell/97) and Loughborough (Kegworth, Cavendish Bridge and Shardelow, all 109). Some in other areas are known, so it seems that the Surveyor was entitled to order where he thought fit. Much more research is needed here.

**Later Town Stamps**

Books were issued to postmasters listing every post town, and against each they were instructed to enter the route and charge from their office, so probably familiarity with these books made mileage figures redundant. Anyway, from about 1829 two arcs began to replace the mileage in dated or undated circular stamps, the latter being stated to have been sent to offices with the annual revenue of less than £1,000. Some smaller offices still used their mileage stamps after 1840 and most of these show a fair amount of wear. In the 1830s a few small straight line stamps came back to minor offices which do not look like mileage erased, and quite a number of sub-offices all over the country were issued with a distinctive type with upper and lower case italic lettering (Fig 48). These and the fleuron types (Fig 48a) were penny post sub-offices.

Town sub-offices began to use stamps for the first time in 1837 and the final change to be recorded came in 1843, when the serif lettering standard for 150 years changed to sans-serif.

† Fig 47      Fig 48      Fig 48a      Fig 49

With the increasing volume of mail began a sensible precaution which continues to this day — provision of blank handstamps with a box of loose type to be made up for any subordinate office which needed it. The time was coming when certain classes of Post Office business had to bear a dated stamp, and this made these travelling or skeleton kits a vital part of the equipment of every Head Office to cover damage to permanent stamps or rushes of mail for various reasons — Christmas and Valentine cards, local events, etc. From about 1836 or 1837 they are recognizable in various shapes, Fig 49, and form an interesting subject for study, for by their very nature they were usually used for short periods (often a few days) though they may recur at intervals made in a similar way. Most early examples can be recognized by their 'inverted pear' shape, having the name in an arc with a two-line date and a number or a cross below, and normally spacing of the letters varies slightly. Later examples vary in type, many being enclosed in a large circle.

Although just outside the period of this book, town stamps come into prominence as cancellations of adhesive stamps. A number occur on the 1840 1d black, and are of interest but not of importance as being local variations. Two must be mentioned, however, as they are above this level. Firstly the Wessex group: in 1842-3 an area comprising Dorset, South Somerset and South East Devon cancelled 1d reds with their dated town stamps. No research appears to have been done, but this bears the hallmark of a controlled GPO experiment, for large and small offices within an area took part for a limited period, and papers may well be lying in GPO records. Secondly, the rectangular framed Exeter which occurs occasionally in the mid 1850s. Exeter was always a major office, controlling the South Western area and not at all the sort of office from which one expects fancy variations. How did Exeter get a serif stamp in a rectangular frame in the 1850s, anyway, apart from the problem of why they used it to cancel stamps? It looks like a stamp issued for internal P.O. use on documents etc., but the mystery is only heightened by the fact that every example seen by the author on cover has a perfectly normal san-serif Exeter dated stamp on the reverse. Why should they change stamps for every letter, increasing the labour five-fold? If by chance Exeter broke its numeral and had no usable travelling (or skeleton) stamp, the obvious thing to do was cancel with the normal circular date stamp which it used as a backstamp.

## Chapter 7

# THE FRANKING SYSTEM

ALTHOUGH it is very probable that letters from members of both Houses of Parliament were always carried free of charge in the post, there is no specific written authority until 1652. This was because it was unnecessary — until 1635 nobody paid for the postal carriage of letters; either you could get your letters into the Royal Mail, or you made private arrangements. From 1635 to 1642 it could have arisen, but letters charged in this period are of such rarity it is impossible to judge. Members would have letters carried free if they could, and the situation was so difficult between King and Parliament that it is very doubtful if Charles would object, adding fuel to the fire unnecessarily. From 1642 any post that ran was closed, maintained by Parliament or the King, so again the matter of payment did not arise. Ten years later, however, it became important. The Royalists were defeated, Parliament's confidence was restored and it was thought safe to open the post for any private letters. The decision was reached to farm it for a fixed sum, but the farmer had to know the conditions of the contract, and on which classes of mail he could rely for his revenue. An efficient running service was worth much more than a skeleton which had to be built up, so for a year or two before the farm was granted efforts were made by Prideaux to popularise the post, and make it efficient and successful. In 1652 an order by the Council of State laid down that all letters of Members should be free if endorsed 'for the Service of the Commonwealth'. They should be signed by the senders or their clerks. The Ordinance of 1654, confirming John Manley as farmer, repeats this franking for Members and various Officers of State, with no restriction of its use to the session of Parliament. Members of both Houses may have enjoyed the privilege of free letters at all times of the year.

The Franking System was not mentioned in the first postage act of 1656 which was to regulate the post as it affected the public, and free carriage of Parliament's own mail was authorized by special resolution, if at all. The attitude of Cromwellian Parliaments was overbearing, arrogant, and intolerant, and it is typical that whilst they legislated for the people, their own rules were not even mentioned. The 1654 regulations for Manley's farm seem clearly applicable whether the House was in session or not, and if this privilege had been removed in 1656 one would have expected to find speech after speech about the iniquities of the new regulations. Most authors state that a Commons order of 29 September 1656 which directed 'that the Post Letters directed to the severall members of this House be brought to the doors of this House, and they be free from postage as formerly' shows that franking was allowed only during sessions of Parliament; this is open to considerable doubt. The Parliament buildings were small at this time, but presumably out of session their letters could be collected. 1656 was a time of revulsion, when the new elections were so unpalatable to the Puritans that over 100 elected members were excluded by a heavy army guard, and another sixty refused their seats in protest. A year before had been Col. John Penruddock's rising of Royalists in Wiltshire, which had been put down mercilessly and the insurgents transported to Barbados. The country was divided into eleven districts, each commanded by a major-general selected for his ruthless puritan ideals, so it stretches belief too far to say that the members who were elected, and were accepted by the army for their implacable views, voluntarily restricted their right to free postage. Why should they — they were still the victors? It had always been an accepted fact that they had free postage. The Commons sat very little in this period — three weeks in 1655, fourteen in 1656, six months in 1657, and only two weeks in 1658, so it would have been a serious loss. It is much more probable that this is a continuance of the

Carolean policy of opening letters to know what was happening in the country, but collecting them together in a more open form than ever Charles had dared. It is probable, therefore, that letters to or from members were free at all times until the Restoration.

The 1660 Bill before the Restoration Parliament made no mention of franking, but an amending clause was written in before being sent to the Lords authorizing free carriage of all letters to or from Members. It was passed by a narrow majority despite heavy opposition, but was promptly thrown out again when it reached the House of Lords. Despite this, the terms of his farm compelled Bishop to carry single letters free during the sessions of Parliament, and a compensatory reduction of £500 in his payment was voted because so many members refused to pay charges on letters overweight and out of time. The situation was difficult, for the King had only recently returned and the last thing he wanted was further trouble with the Commons, so he authorized free carriage by Royal Warrant. The words used (14 May 1661 quoted by Howard Robinson) are revealing, and may have been chosen to underline the disagreement: 'The King being informed by the principal Secretaries of State that the Members of Parliament seem unwilling to pay for the postage of their letters during the sitting of Parliament, his Majesty was thereupon graciously pleased to give direction to the farmers of his Post Office that all single letters, but not packets, sent by the Post Office to or from any member of either House of Parliament, go free, without payment of anything for the post thereof'.

Thus began franking by Royal Warrant, and it is assumed that it was owing to this technicality that no Free handstamps were used in England, Wales, or Scotland until 1764, when the Post Office revenues passed from the Crown to the State. Why Ireland should have used FREE stamps sixty years before this is not clear, but theories could be advanced. Fig 50 shows a type known from 1706-10, in 1707 is a 'Free', and from 1721 FREE was used. Letters were carried solely on the authority of the address, or the signature of the Member in the lower left corner; officials empowered to frank letters put their office after their name. Succeeding contracts to farm the post had a clause for reductions to be allowed for extra franking grants, but on the appointment as Postmasters General of Sir Robert Cotton and Sir Thomas Frankland in 1693 came the first of a long series of attempts to curb within reasonable limits the abuses of a series of greedy legislatures.

The abuses of the franking system are illustrated by innumerable examples in most books on the Post Office, and remarkable reading they make. Secretaries of State had always had more freedom, but some warrants exhorted even them to frank no letters other than those on official business. Members of Parliament showered on their friends signed blank sheets, and the recognized method of thanking one's host of the weekend was to leave him a parcel of franks. Many M.P.s were taken on the boards of large businesses purely to frank the mail and have their names used in the address to free incoming letters, and an examination of surviving free letters shows that a good proportion did not qualify legally. A detailed listing is given by Hyde*, but it is doubtful if all the articles listed as carried in Post Office Packet Boats were free. His list is taken from a fascinating letter from Frank Ives Scudamore†, and whilst the remainder may have been paid for, the first item: 'Fifteen couples of hounds, sent to the King of the Romans with a free pass' definitely was not. Apparently each hound had a 'Free' label round its neck. A letter is recorded of 1715, signed by both Postmasters General to a Member which began: 'Having observed a letter . . . that arrived in an Irish mail frank't with your name in Ireland, and knowing you are in England. . . .'. In 1718 the Irish Parliament sat for three months, the gross revenue (including theoretical postage on Frees) of the Irish office for 1718 was £14,592 and the net revenue (postage actually paid) was £3,066. In 1719, when it sat for nine months the gross revenue rose to £19,522 but the net revenue fell to £753 (Joyce, page 142). One feels that anyone paying postage in Ireland was a fool. Servants were tipped with franks, and forgery grew rife. When an inspector was sent to Irish towns for a week each, he found at Waterford 234 forgeries in 588 franked letters, Kilkenny had 425 forged and 510 genuine, and all the other towns had more forged than genuine

---

* The Royal Mail by J. Wilson Hyde: Blackwood 1885.

† Reprinted as Appendix A to the First Report of the Postmaster General, 1855. Scudamore was asked by Frederick Hill to provide notes on the early Post Office from surviving records, and his racy story is well worth reading. The first section of this report is a useful historical summary of the Post Office.

signatures. Apart from forgery, the volume is staggering — Gowran (whose literate population must have been very small) had 407 franks (212 forged) in about a week (Joyce pages 190-191). No wonder Ireland was the only country to have a special 'COUNTERFEIT' stamp.

Newspapers had always been franked to postmasters by the six Clerks of the Roads, either for their subscribing customers or to be hired out on loan. Soon after the Act of 1711 raised postage rates, booksellers began to write the names of Members with impunity, and the cooperation of the newly-appointed Surveyors shortly afterwards accelerated the growing business of franking newspapers. This was recognized unofficially as part of the salary of the Surveyors and the Clerks of the Roads, so when postage was included in the 1d newspaper stamp of 1836 they received increases in salary and allowances to compensate for the loss.

Little could be done to check the abuses sanctioned by law, and the legislature was notably tardy to impose effective restraints on its own privileges. Doubtless the postal officials did their best and Robinson (page 115) quotes Edward Cave, a supervisor of franks, as saying to a Parliamentary Commission in 1735 that he always disallowed if in doubt or if the entire superscription was not in the hand of the Member; if it was legal, restitution could be obtained. However, try as they would, the inspectors had no power to stop the floods through various loop holes, and Ralph Allen stated that whereas the chargeable value of franked letters was £25,000 in 1715, it had risen to more than £50,000 by 1741: on his death in 1764 the value was £170,000, and the weight was estimated to equal that of all charged letters. Franks were said to be five-sixths of the total Irish mail.

Authorities appear to differ on the dates of some of the restrictions on franks, but the major ones for Members of both Houses of Parliament seem to be:

1693 Only allowable during a session, and for forty days before and after: by the letter of the law this was a relaxation, for Bishop's farm and the Royal Warrants both granted franking during sessions of Parliament only. It seems, however, that whilst this was the law, in practice Members refused to pay at any time, and this had been condoned. The 1693 wording, therefore, may have been an acceptable and enforceable compromise, and became the standard duration of franks.

1715 or 1764* The entire address to be in his own hand and a two ounce limit imposed. No letter to a member was free unless sent to his principal residence, or any newspaper to be franked unless entirely in print. The latter was to prevent Members enclosing heavier letters in newspapers, and the entire address in his own hand would make forgery more difficult. It also increased the time taken considerably.

1764 Franking authorized by Act of Parliament, a consequence of the handing over of Crown revenue to the State in exchange for a Civil List. Forgery of franks was judged to be a felony, punishable by transportation for seven years. Printed proceedings and votes of Parliament and newspapers must now be sent with open ends.

1784 In addition to his signature and the address, the Member must write the town of posting and the date in full. This seems to have been the most effective measure of all, cutting drastically those given or sent to friends. Blank sheets could still be dated a week ahead and addressed, but the letter would have to be sent to that person on the day endorsed.

1795 The limit of weight was reduced to one ounce, and each Member was allowed to send only ten letters and receive fifteen each day. The Member must be within twenty miles of the place at which letters bearing his frank were posted, on that day or the day before. This gave rise to special handstamps 'Above Number', 'Above Weight', etc. and from this date franks are seen which were charged because of an error in the date or town of posting. It was the last important restrictive act and again had a considerable but temporary success, until methods of evasion were found.

---

* 1715 taken from G. Brumell, The Franking System, published privately 1936, a very good booklet for its date. His view is reinforced by the evidence of Edward Cave quoted above. The 1st Report of the Postmaster General (1855) gives the date as 1764, and in view of the fact that most Free letters before 1764 examined have the address in a hand different from the signature, it must be accepted that this came in probably in 1764. Brumell could well have been misled, but it is far from clear how the Inspector of Franks could be so wrong. The evidence of most surviving letters plus a historical summary by the Postmaster General must be accepted.

*Unusual East Grinstead handstamps, the framed example being 1746, the circular seal type 1792, and both the others 1799 (page 48).*

**Plate 13**

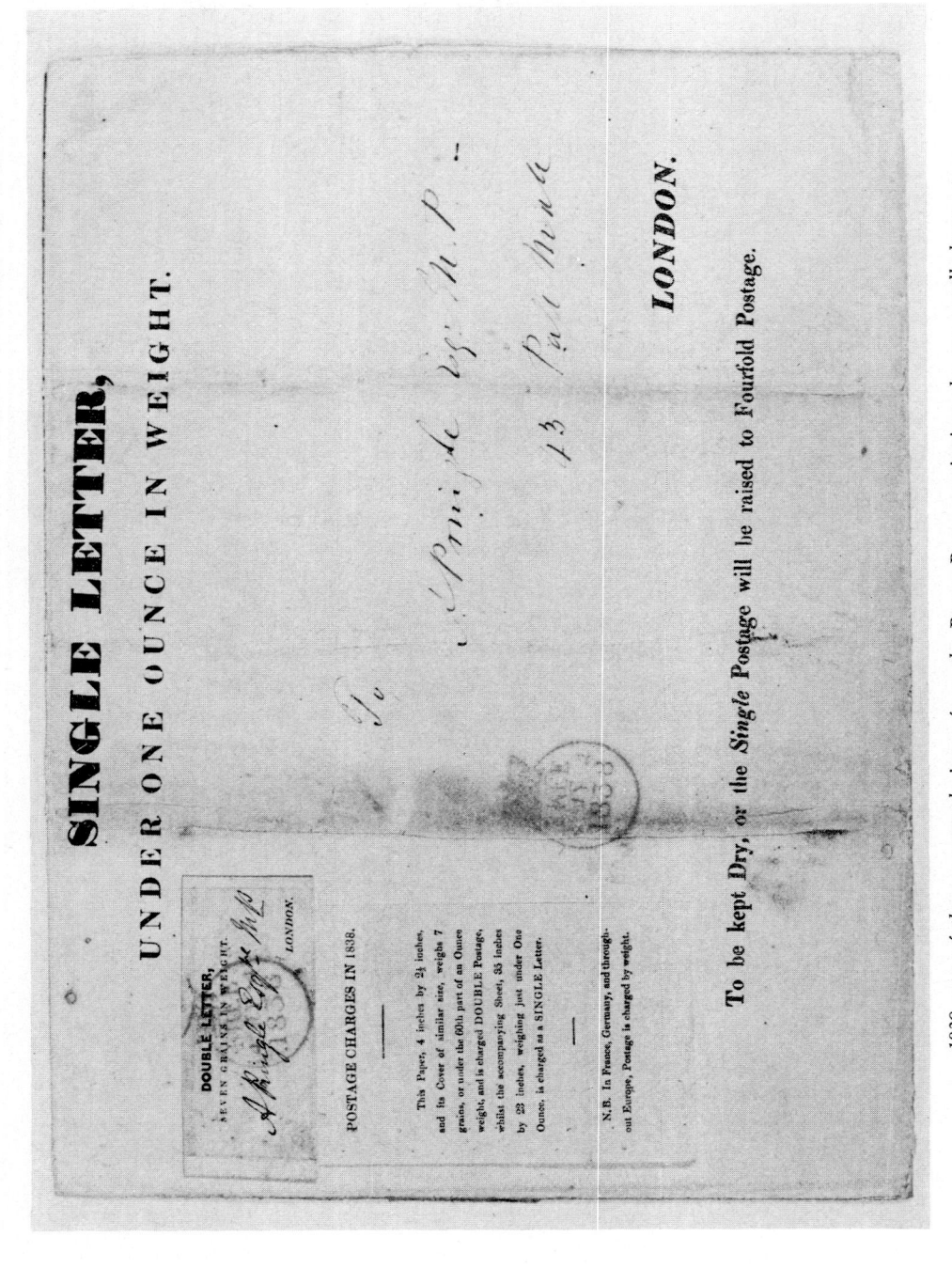

1839, one of the propaganda items from the Penny Postage agitation: the two small sheets at left would be charged twice the postage of the very large sheet which is sixty times their weight. These and others made MPs realise the idiocy of the postal rates, especially as these were sent Free (page 125).

Plate 14

# POST OFFICE REGULATIONS.

ON AND AFTER THE **10th January,** a Letter not exceeding HALF AN OUNCE IN WEIGHT, may be sent from any part of the United Kingdom, to any other part, for ONE PENNY, if paid when posted, or for TWO PENCE if paid when delivered.

## THE SCALE OF RATES,

If paid when posted, is as follows, for all Letters, whether sent by the General or by any Local Post,

Not exceeding ½ Ounce .................... **One Penny.**
Exceeding ½ Ounce, but not exceeding 1 Ounce **Twopence.**
Ditto 1 Ounce ............. 2 Ounces **Fourpence.**
Ditto 2 Ounces ............. 3 Ounces **Sixpence.**

and so on; an additional Two-pence for every additional Ounce. With but few exceptions, the WEIGHT is limited to Sixteen Ounces.

*If not paid when posted, double the above Rates are charged on Inland Letters.*

## COLONIAL LETTERS.

If sent by Packet Twelve Times, if by Private Ship Eight Times, the above Rates.

## FOREIGN LETTERS.

The Packet Rates which vary, will be seen at the Post Office. The Ship Rates are the same as the Ship Rates for Colonial Letters.

As regards Foreign and Colonial Letters, there is no limitation as to weight. All sent outwards, with a few exceptions, which may be learnt at the Post Office, must be paid when posted as heretofore.

Letters intended to go by Private Ship must be marked "*Ship Letter.*"

Some arrangements of minor importance, which are omitted in this Notice, may be seen in that placarded at the Post Office.

No Articles should be transmitted by Post which are liable to *injury by being stamped,* or by being crushed in the Bags.

It is particularly requested that all Letters may be *fully* and *legibly addressed,* and *posted as early* as convenient.

*January 7th,* 1840.

By Authority:—J. Hartnell, London.

*1840. The notice announcing Penny Postage. It would be interesting to know what were the 'arrangements of minor importance' (page 131) (reproduced by courtesy of the Post Office).*

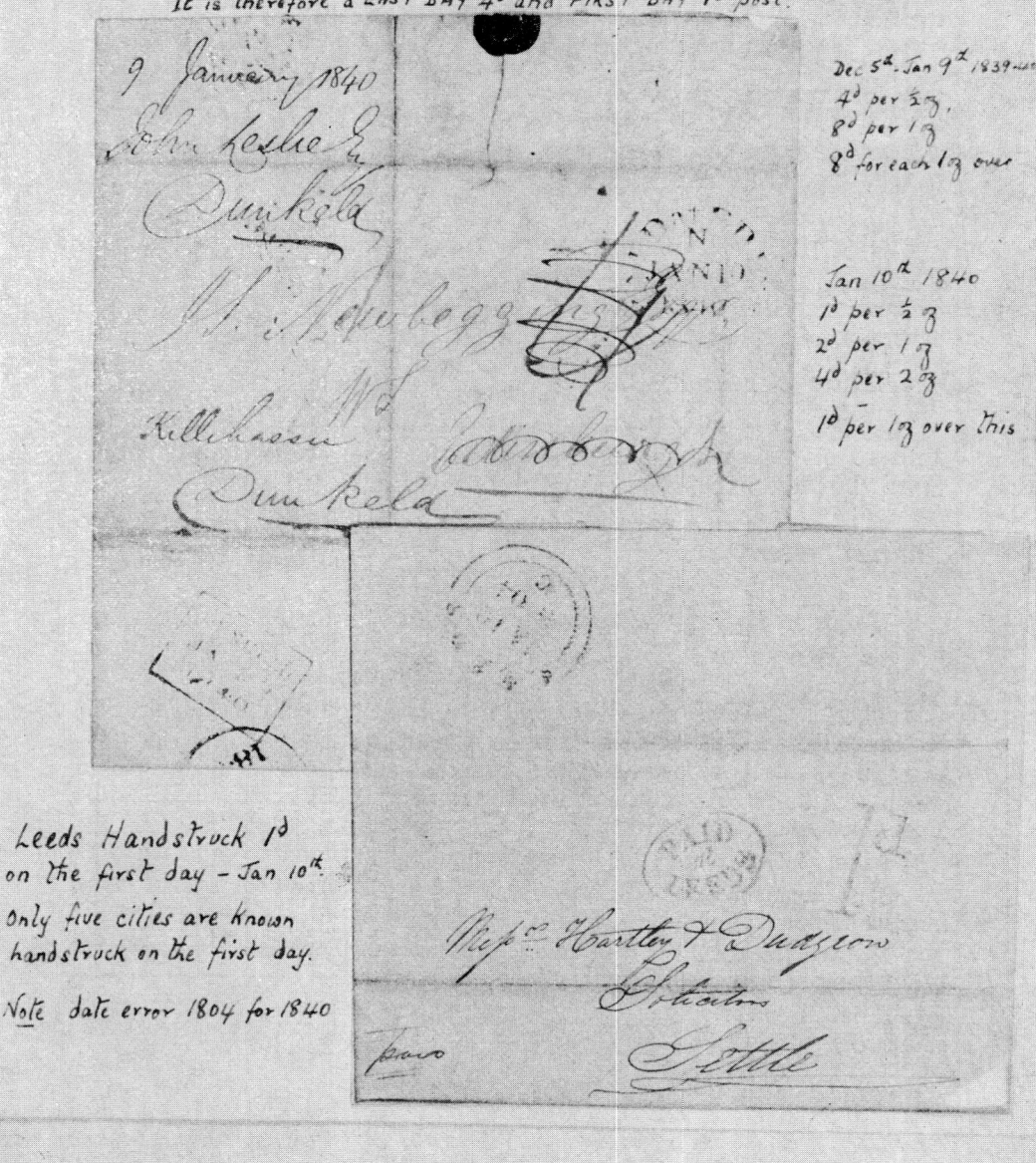

*10 January 1840. The top letter was posted on 9 January, the last day of the 4d. post, and was forwarded the next day at 1d. Few towns had a new handstamp ready for the 10th, as shown at Leeds on the lower cover.*

**Plate 16**

Although a degree of success was won in controlling abuses by Members, an increasing bureaucracy had multiplied enormously the officials given free franking. This problem was just as serious, but here the Post Office was powerless to control it. You could not tell an Under Secretary of State that he could send only ten letters, and there is little doubt that many officials were just as shameless in using the system for their private purposes. Figures are revealing, for those given here (from various sources) are all estimated postage lost by franking:

1670, £4,000: 1677, £7,200: 1715, £25,740 (excluding Post Office clerks, and divided into Parliamentary £17,470, State £8,270): 1741 over £50,000: 1764, £170,000. It would be interesting to find further figures divided between Parliament and Government.

The pattern from 1764 (the first serious attempt to reduce the abuse) was a reduction after each restriction, followed by a steady increase. Before 1764, with revenue going to the Crown it is notable that little attempt at control had been made, and the feeling is inescapable that, being someone else's money, postal charges were fair game for all to avoid. From 1764, however, some attempt had to be made to balance the accounts when the bill was paid by those who elected the legislators, but these attacks of conscience lasted only a matter of months. Generally speaking, the problem was beyond control.

A notice to all Postmasters from the G.P.O. of 11 June 1790 makes clear the method of application of the regulations. Parliament was dissolved that day, so all letters posted from the 12th should be charged normally: those from Public Officers exempt by law were still free. The new Parliament would meet on 10 August, so letters arriving from 1 July (or as soon as the election of a Member was announced after that date) should pass free. Postmasters were told to watch newspapers for announcements of elections, and to inform the Secretary by the very first post of election of all Members in their area. Thus it is clear that whilst forty days franking was allowed after a session, it stopped immediately on a dissolution as there were no Members elected.

Although the franking privilege extended anywhere in the British Isles (excluding the outlying islands), only the three capital cities used stamps, but Edinburgh used only one stamp occasionally between 1772 and 1788 (Fig 51). The reason for the latter oddity is at present beyond explanation, for a lot of free letters were sent to and from Scotland. Letters posted in the provinces were still made out in the same way, but were struck with no distinctive stamp. Apart from official letters and those from and to the Lords and Commons, various other categories of mail were free. Some special cases arose, and these letters were authorized by printing (or sometimes endorsing) on the letter wrapper. Typical is a free cover of 1837 printed at the top 'Office of Poor Law Commissioners, pursuant of Act of Parliament passed in the Fifth year of the Reign of His Majesty King William the Fourth' and below 'Sent in pursuance of the 18th Section of the 4th and 5th Wm. IV c 76'. Each had to be signed by the Secretary, though later many used stamps (especially L.T.R. or Land Tax Registry, which sent by the thousand). An interesting case to illustrate the difficulty of drawing a line is Chelsea Hospital, which normally had no privilege but received hundreds of letters from out-pensioners, many living in Ireland. Chelsea forwarded their charged letters to the Adjutant General, whose mail was free, and the charge was erased. Thus, these charged letters were delivered to Chelsea who endorsed 'on official business' and signed it, readdressed singly each one and returned them to the Post Office for delivery in Whitehall, from whence they must be carried again to Chelsea. Can you wonder the Post Office developed a creeping paralysis? Later, Chelsea and Greenwich Hospitals had the franking privilege.

In addition, very large quantities of Parliamentary Proceedings were carried free, probably from the beginning of the publication of Hansard in 1803. Earlier examples of franked private parliamentary news letters are very rare. Early examples are endorsed 'Par Pro', but from 1837 a wide variety of printed wrappers was used; these continue to the present day and are an important part of a study of the franking system. On 10 January 1840 all free letters ceased, so official letters were struck with a PAID stamp similar to the FREE of Fig 61 which had been used from 1807 with many minor varieties.

Charity letters and those for educational purposes are another aspect of franking, and in England, Wales, and Scotland the latter appear to have been left to the judgement of the Secretary. Numerous letters to Sir Francis Freeling endorsed with his reply make it evident that he was under constant pressure to frank letters, and particularly books, and that if these served an educational purpose he did so on occasions. The majority, even from personal friends, he turned down as not being for the national benefit, and reading them one is aware of scrupulous fairness in his judgement. It is probable that charities required sanction of the Postmaster General rather than the Secretary, for if accepted they could involve large numbers of letters.

Fig 50   Fig 51   Fig 52   Fig 53   Fig 54

Fig 55   Fig 56   Fig 57   Fig 58

Often Freeling had to sign each one, sometimes countersigning above the charity secretary. A good example of this is the Waterloo Subscription, the only one in England known using a hand stamp. In other cases F. Freeling was printed on the wrapper, but even the early Land Tax Registry forms are signed individually by him. It would be difficult to devise a more cumbersome system, and one can only admire the enormous amount of work he got through. Scotland appears to have had the same system, but those signed by D. Wedderburn or Augustus Godby normally are stamped with a three line TO BE/DELIVERED/FREE (Edinburgh having no normal Free stamp).

Ireland in 1819 authorized Charity letters to pass at a penny per dozen after the first twelve, which paid one penny each within Ireland, but does not seem to have made reductions on letters addressed to the charities. Special stamps were used on rare occasions, and some printed inside that replies could be sent free addressed to Sir Edward Lees, Secretary to the Irish Post Office. From 1832 a standard rate of 2d a letter came in for transmission to or from Irish charities, the printed heading being sufficient.

It is remarkable that whilst Dublin used FREE stamps extensively from 1707, Edinburgh used one stamp from 1772-88 only, the very rare FREE/E in a circle (Fig 51). Could it be that the Scots were more honest than English or Irish? No towns other than the three capital cities had a Free stamp, letters posted elsewhere received normal town stamps but have no charge endorsed. From 1784 the only free letters just signed (with no manuscript town and date of posting above the address, or Government office sending it) are from Post Office officials and some members of the Royal Household.

Handstamps began in 1764 in London, the first being 'FREE' enclosed in a circle (Fig 52) (frequently the F is taller 1764-66). This was standard until 1787, when began a series of more elaborate stamps, with a movable date from 1791. This new series (Figs 53-55 etc.), incorporated the initial of the Inspector of Franks on duty, and Brumell says that C was Charles Colston, Inspector from 1777 to 1797, S was James Stafford, Inspector for By-Days (days on which little mail left London), who was replaced in November 1789 by A, a man at present unknown, and P was J. Palmer, an Inspector from 1789-95. The initial of the Inspector was omitted from the stamp from 1797, presumably as it was unnecessary. For two years, mid 1797 to 1799, evening duty was distinguished by a stamp with the outer ring double (Fig 56), but this was then dropped until June 1806. Figs 57-60 show other types, of which only Fig 59 is comparatively easy to find.

58

In July 1807 a completely new style came in, FREE and a date in two lines enclosed in a circle and surmounted by a crown, similar to Fig. 61. The earliest morning stamp is a smaller circle (25 mm.) with the crown completely outside the circle, and is very difficult to find. The corresponding double ringed stamp has a crown well into the circle, and there is no doubt that single and double ring stamps with the crown across the circle were used for morning and evening duties respectively from 1808. Each January and July two new stamps were issued with single and double ring, the crowns varying considerably in detail and position; being delicately engraved, the crown must have been liable to wear or damage and there is evidence that some were replaced. The only exception is July 1839 when it seems the Post Office awaited publication of the reform recommendations, and the new type did not appear until October. From 1814 a cross is sometimes found below the date in both stamps (Fig 61) to distinguish a second (or additional) stamp for use if required. Early copies of the cross are scarce in the morning stamp, but grow more common from 1825-30.

In 1837 more changes began to appear. Hitherto the figure 3 had a round top, both in the day and the year, but in January 1837 the new stamp came out with a flat-topped 3 in the year figures. In January 1838 this was extended to include the day too, and all figures 3 had a flat top from then until the very late issue of the second series of stamps in 1839. At this point, while the day figures remained the same size and style, the year in the new (and last) series of stamps was very small, and invariably the 3 had a round top. Also in 1837 (July) a new stamp was introduced, larger at $28\frac{1}{2}$ mm. diameter, an unusually lavish crown set deeply across the single ring, smaller year figures with a flat-topped 3 set high in the frame, and beneath them a large E. This was in addition to the normal morning stamp, which was renewed as usual in July. Although this first E stamp is rare, examples are known from June 1837 to March 1838.

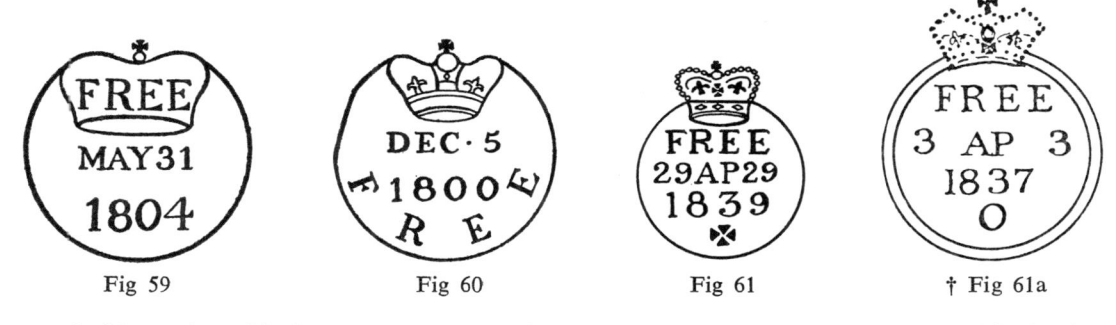

Fig 59  Fig 60  Fig 61  † Fig 61a

In November 1837 began a new series of special stamps which can be recognised by having the crown sitting on top of the circle (not entering it), no line to complete the elipse at the base of the crown, and being still in the larger size of $28\frac{1}{2}$ mm. Originally there was a croix-patée below very similar to the usual additional morning duty stamp, and it may have been confusion over this that brought a change. From February 1838 it was used with N below, May 1838 no letter at all, and June 1838 E below. Frequently it is said that the N stamp was used on mail into London by the Grand Northern Railway (in some copies the N is omitted or very unclear) but this cannot be accepted for in the early part of its use no mail came south of Birmingham by rail, and it does not explain the code E. It is partly true, though, for there is no doubt that Chief office duties were reorganized for carriage by rail. From 1784 the post had all come into London in the early morning, and been sent from London at night, so single and double ring free stamps were enough to distinguish them, but railway mail began to arrive or leave at other times. It is very tempting to say that E stands for evening and N for night, the double ring being afternoon, but this does not quite fit the facts.

The only major variation from the basic design was the Free stamp used in the Foreign Branch, a crown on a rectangle, not a circle (Fig 62). Two stamps were made, the other having the upper corners chamfered. Both are very rare, as the franking privilege to or from overseas addresses was allowed to very few officials, the letters must be on business only, and they must have been carefully inspected. Most examples are addressed to Naval vessels.

59

The last type of 'Free' stamp is one of the enigmas of Postal History, a historical mystery better than most fiction. Despite the help of archivists and historical experts on the problem, an explanation of its use still defies us, and one can only hope it may be solved in time. When Brumell wrote his booklet he described the two known copies, but was unable to explain them: thirty-five years later a few more have turned up and we are still unable to explain them. We have, however, disproved his guess that it had special clerical uses. Considerable help from J. W. Lovegrove, and from many others, is acknowledged gratefully. The stamp itself was similar to the new day mail stamp described above, but double-rimmed, and, apart from one example mentioned later, used only a round-topped 3 in the year figures. However, beneath the year was inserted an O (Fig 61a). Since every example known is a 'front' (the address leaf cut down to the address panel only) a word on their origin may fill in the background.

From the late 1780s a hobby grew amongst well-bred young ladies of collecting all the autographs possible, and by 1800 large quantities of free letters were cut down to the address rectangle, for they were signed in the corner. These fronts were mounted in albums, some beautifully bound, which can still be bought. One album just found had eleven O fronts, of which six had the O sideways — all to Viscount Anson. One could be pardoned for concluding from this that it is common, yet specialists have examined albums in their hundreds, many containing a thousand or more franks, and have not seen one single O of either type. This gives the first clue — the use of this stamp was very definitely restricted to some certain type of mail; it does not turn up in the normal way, but the few who had them probably received quite a number. It must be remembered that the contents of an album reflect only the friends of the collector (unless they were bought from the dealers who had thriving businesses in these fronts), and nothing else. Unfortunately the Anson fronts were loose, so may not have been in the original collection.

All the known genuine examples of the O are from one stamp, probably spanning thirty-seven years. As all before the 1837 reorganisation are outward letters from London, they would have the evening stamp anyway, so it is possible that a single-ringed morning stamp awaits discovery.

Numerous pages were written originally on this fascinating stamp, but these were too technical so the facts must be summarized. The O is important because:

    a. On the evidence of one dated 1 March 1803 (struck over an identical stamp of 26 February) it is the forerunner by four years and the pattern of the normal free stamps (similar to Fig 61) in their millions from mid-1807.

    b. It is the only pre-adhesive stamp to be faked contemporarily (or nearly so) and it was also struck by favour.

    c. It has been found outside the permitted period for franking of forty days before and after the session of Parliament. Its importance was such that it over-rode the normal regulations, in date or in area, for one is known that passed Free in the London Twopenny Post, where franking was not allowed.

    d. Copies found bear no relation to the average incidence: it seems to occur in a small circle of people, and have a much higher proportion than normal of women and the Church. Nearly all have a strong naval connection.

Regarding b. above, an album purchased by Leslie Ray twenty years ago contained a good number of perfectly genuine fronts to which a free O hand stamp, faked from a genuine strike, had been added: as no date plugs were made the date was omitted, but sometimes it had 18 of the year (this may be a second faked stamp made by the forger). The accepted explanation is that autograph collectors preferred those with attractive red stamps, so somebody embellished a number. This must have been done before the 1850's, and was probably 1840-50 (it is doubtful if anyone would dare to reproduce a special free frank whilst it was in use, and the collecting of autograph fronts died in the 1850's). The Anson fronts are all from the autograph collection formed by his mother, the Countess of Lichfield, and current opinion is that whilst both the fronts and the stamp are perfectly genuine, the use of the stamp with O turned sideways is not genuine. No others have been found, and it must be remembered that her husband was Postmaster General at the time, so many things could have happened. The explanation favoured at present is fundamentally similar to the above; Lady Lichfield preferred her autograph fronts with attractive red stamps, so (possibly at breakfast one morning) she asked her husband to take some with him to the Post Office and have them 'improved'. As free franking had ceased and the stamps had lost all meaning, probably he would not object but the postal official to whom they were given was conscientious and not too happy. He could not argue with the Postmaster General, but to ensure that they were recognizable he turned the O sideways before using the stamp.

The fascinating question arising from these hypotheses is why both of these people selected the O stamp to make their improvements? The first man just wanted a free stamp, and if it was chance the odds were at least ten thousand to one against selecting one with an O as pattern. If there were two fakes, how could they both be O's accidentally? The postal clerk presumably could have used any of the free stamps, and the fact that in all cases this stamp was used would imply that both men were aware of a special use which made it safer or more interesting to use. It should be remembered that these two are the only contemporary fakes of any pre-adhesive stamps known to the author, yet many hundreds must have been lying around unguarded in post offices all over the country.

There is a line of thought that none of the O's is genuine, but this ignores too many important points. Firstly, these fronts must have had a different free stamp if they did not have the O: the fakes are nearly all on fronts which should not have had a London stamp at all, but the genuine ones do require a free stamp. Secondly, details are known of two examples of the sideways O which are still in the family papers, and presumably have never been out of Lady Lichfield's collection. If the doubtful sideways ones could not have been faked then the normals must be right. Thirdly, it is most improbable that two people independently would make an imaginary stamp of the same variety, and make it exactly the same, with the same broken frame. It must have existed to be reproduced. Fourthly, it is only in recent years that these have been worth money. Yet the O stamps were known in 1936, written about and some were described by George Brumell, although little interest was taken in them.

There is little doubt that O stands for Official — in a stamp of this nature what else could it have stood for? One front sent from Plymouth by Thomas Bewes to Lewis Hertslet, the Foreign Office librarian, had been charged double rate 1/10d, but this was crossed out, 'Official J.B.' endorsed and the heading Plymouth underlined three times, then the Free O stamp was struck. This implies that it was struck as the letter was official by virtue of its Plymouth origin. What type of Official? Government correspondence received the normal Free stamp until 10 January 1840, when it received a similar stamp worded PAID. Charity letters had special facilities, either signed by Freeling or with the heading of the Act if specially authorised on a temporary basis. Nearly all Post Office stamps refer to the service given to the letter, but this one seems to refer to

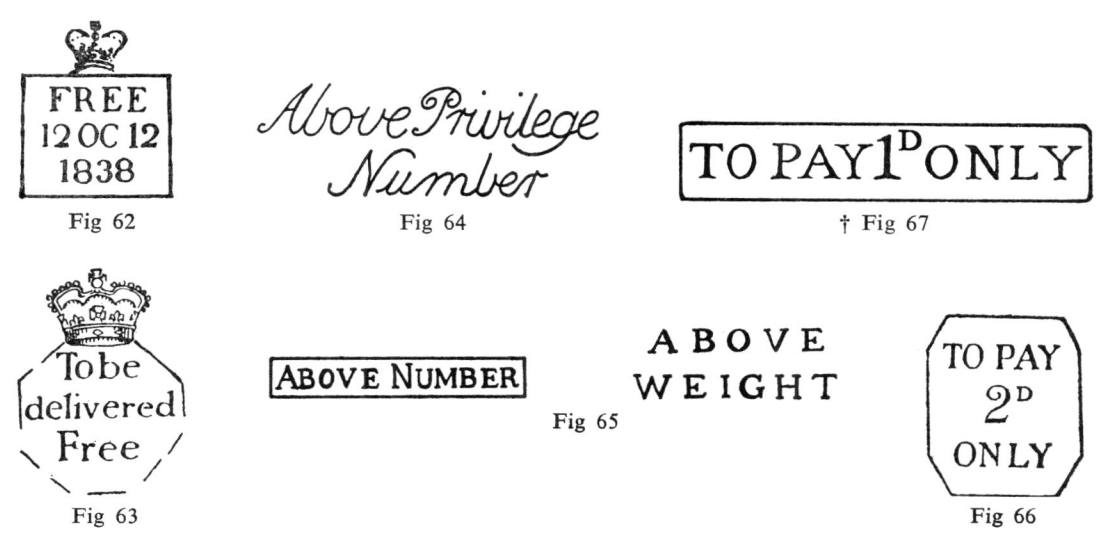

Fig 62

Fig 64

† Fig 67

Fig 63

Fig 65

Fig 66

the letter itself.  From analysis of the senders' addressees and everything to do with them, the address and the town of origin of all known examples, two possibilities emerge.  It is just possible that these were letters opened by order of the Secretary of State, for security purposes.  It is much more probable that the senders worked for intelligence, and the addressees were ordinary, innocuous people used as posting boxes for security letters.

It is a most interesting problem, but it is by no means certain that the answer will ever be found.  The naval connection runs through every one, an example of this being an O front addressed to Twining's Tea Warehouse.  If this had contained an order for tea, all theories would have been disproved, but by chance a normal letter to the same man at Twinings Tea Warehouse was recognised.  This letter was completely naval, and amongst the usual chat gives information where ships were going, and asks for an appointment to a specified ship for a friend.  It is a peculiar tea broker who has a power of appointment in the Admiralty, and coincidences like this must be considered nearly conclusive.

Associated stamps are interesting —'To be delivered Free' enclosed in an oval, octagon, or circle surmounted by a crown (Fig 63), was used for odd administrative purposes (letters from Freeling or the Postmaster General, Soldiers Letters and occasional letters which were overcharged).  A variety of 'Above Weight', 'Above Privilege Number', etc. as Figs 64-65 was used from about 1800 in cases where an abuse was detected.  Finally, as franked letters were not exempt from local Penny Post or Twopenny Post charges, various 'To Pay 1d Only' or 'To Pay 2d Only' (Figs 66-67) stamps were used to emphasize these charges.  A circular 'Put in after date' is in the Post Office record books as issued in 1832, but no example is known.

## Chapter 8

# JOHN PALMER AND THE MAIL COACHES

IT IS usual to think of the coach as a fairly recent introduction, but this is far from the truth. Coaches of a sort go back to the Romans, Athenians, and the original Olympic Games where horses were always harnessed for chariot races, never ridden; it is fair to say that at most times the leaders of a country have shown a preference for a vehicle, rather than horseback. Cicero remarked in a letter from Britain that the only things worth taking back from these islands were the chariots, of which he wished to have one for a pattern. The marks made by the wheels of these same chariots scraping the stone pillars at the entrance to the amphitheatre at Caerleon can still be seen, and little reminder should be needed of Boadicea and the devastating handling of chariots by the Iceni of East Anglia. Early coaches were little more than wheels put on a litter, and written references go back only to the early Middle Ages.

By the last years of Elizabeth the traffic congestion in London was so bad that it was proposed (the Bill was thrown out by the House of Lords) that nobody below a certain rank should keep a coach in London unless they had paid £50 subsidy. A similar measure taxing the coach £40 a year was apparently made law in 1619, and Charles I in 1635-6 issued a proclamation 'for restraint of the multitude and promiscuous use of coaches about London and Westminster'. Writings and early prints of junctions such as Seven Dials (Upper St Martins Lane) show they were just as dangerous as today, for a car is easier to control than a horse.

This, of course, was in a few major cities, and travel in the country was very different. John Taylor's 'Carriers Cosmography' of 1637 lists coaches from as far as Cambridge, and with each succeeding reference the list grows. They had to be of the heaviest possible construction to stand up to the roads, were suspended on chains, and a long journey must have been agony. Stage coaches were generally used by 1700 for long journeys, and ran on schedules during the summer as far as London to York, Exeter, and Chester. Mud, snow and floods still made journeys of this length impossible to a timetable during the winter and a horse was still more comfortable. As the popularity grew, great opposition arose throughout the country for the most remarkable reasons, and a long battle resulted in victory for the stage coaches. It must be remembered that these were normally called Post coaches, and at this time a letter sent by the Post was not sent by the Royal Mail, but probably by private coach. An interesting example of this was sold recently: a letter of 1824 from Berwick to London endorsed 'by the Mail' had a note by the receiver 'Mr Barnes ought to be made to pay the Carriage of this Packet, it having been sent by the Mail instead of the Post and 7/6 charged for it'. Carriage by a Post coach might well have been 1/6 or 2/-.

It is not intended to go into coaches and John Palmer's reforms at great length for most books give a detailed and balanced account. Although important, they are not of the same calibre as, or show the remarkable vision of Witherings or Allen, or the reforms of 1837-40. These men would have been great in any age, whilst Palmer saw two existing organisations and combined them with beneficial results. There is little doubt he was fired with the example of his fellow Bathonian, Allen, and saw himself dictating Post Office policy and making a large fortune in the same way. There was no element of luck about Quash and Allen, but despite Palmer's good fortune in planning this improvement just when the Turnpike Acts had taken effect, and the main roads were becoming passable in reasonable comfort, his administrative ability and personality let him down.

John Palmer was born about 1742, son of a considerable Bath citizen who was a brewer and maltster with other activities. Educated for the Army or the Church, his father gave him the task of promoting a Bill through Parliament to obtain the Royal Charter for a theatre he had recently taken over. He succeeded in 1768 and became manager of the Theatre Royal, Bath, the only theatre with a Royal Charter outside London. In his varied travels he realized that the mail was about the slowest means of conveyance, and made plans to improve it. The traditional postboy ambling on a mule through the countryside at a slow walk was the easiest of victims for a highwayman, and on occasion was in league with him. Frequently he diverged considerably to deliver letters which did not go in the post at all, for it tended to be only the poorest type who would take the job of postboy, and the commerce of the country was reined back to this speed. Ralph Allen based his plans on a rate of six miles an hour for the cross posts during the daylight hours, and might have secured it, but after his death it is probable that speeds were about half that figure. The ten hours for nineteen miles from Exeter to Ashburton cannot have been typical.

Palmer proposed that light coaches be built to carry the mail and a limited number of passengers, with an armed guard and keeping to a strict schedule by night and day. An important side was the emphasis that the mail came first — if passengers were not ready after a meal they must be left behind. With increased security and speed, he was sure the merchants would accept two bitter pills — increased rates of postage, and closing of the mails at the Chief Office at seven or eight, instead of midnight or later, to get the coaches away. He also insisted that they should be free from the tolls which delayed and raised the cost of normal coaches, and pointed out the saving of thousands of pounds the Post Office was paying in large rewards and prosecution costs for mail robberies. Above all, his argument was that if given a really safe, regular, and speedy service the country would pay, and that this was the only answer to the enormous quantities of mail which evaded the Post Office. Originally he proposed the use of soldiers as guards, distributed over the country, but this did not prove practicable. He also proposed further restrictions on franking.

As the coaches would run to a schedule all postmasters would know the time of arrival, and must have the bags sealed and ready. Similarly any tollkeeper, warned by a blast of the horn 250 yards before the gate, who delayed the mail was to be fined forty shillings. Palmer's proposals for increases in the rates of postage were fantastic, for he suggested charging by stages of about twenty miles to replace 1d for one stage, 2d for two stages, 3d below 80 miles and 4d beyond in England. This appears to have been to secure the support of William Pitt at the Treasury, to whom he was introduced by J. J. Pratt the M.P. for Bath.

Pitt's budgetary problems were serious, for the American and French wars had raised the National Debt to a very high level, the civil list was in arrears and his proposed tax on coal was so unpopular it could overturn the shaky Shelburne administration. He therefore gave orders for the earliest trial of Palmer's proposals, but the fall of the government in February 1783 gave the Post Office time to organize. This they did in three large volumes of opposition in language which would have been funny if it had not been pathetic. Howard Robinson quotes much evidence from the Surveyors, including one, Hodgson, who ends a reference to the post and Post Office: 'the constant eye that has been long kept towards their improvement, in all situations and under all circumstances, has made them now almost as perfect as can be'. This was said in opposing a reform which transformed the carriage of mail, and was spoken by the very people who should have initiated Palmer's plan for themselves, years before this. In December 1783 the unhappy coalition of Fox and North fell, and Pitt was Prime Minister at the age of twenty four, combining with it Chancellorship of the Exchequer.

Palmer's star was now strongly in the ascendent, and Pitt gave orders for the trial to start on 1 August; being a Sunday, the first coach left Bristol next day 2 August 1784 at 4 p.m. with a load of mail and four inside passengers, Bath at 5.20 p.m. and reached the GPO Lombard Street at 8 o'clock next morning. The increased postage rates of 1d below 150 miles and 2d beyond this, and the ruling that all free letters must have the place and date of posting endorsed at the top by the person who franked it, came into force on the same day.

The original advertisement of the Swan with Two Necks for the first mailcoach is quoted by Bryant Lillywhite* as follows.

> *MAIL DILIGENCE. To commence Monday August 2nd. The Proprietors of the above carriage having agreed to convey the mail to and from London and Bristol in sixteen hours with a Guard for its protection respectfully inform the Public that it is constructed so as to accommodate Four Inside Passengers in the most convenient manner, that it will set off every Night at Eight O'clock from the Swan with Two Necks Lad's Lane London, and arrive at the Three Tuns Inn Bath before Ten the next Morning and at the Rummer Tavern Bristol at Twelve. Will set off at the said Tavern at Bristol at four O'clock every Afternoon, and arrive at London at Eight o'clock. The price to and from Bristol, Bath and London twenty shillings for each Passenger. No Outsides allowed. Both the Guard and the Coachmen, who will be likewise armed, have given ample security to the Proprietors for their conduct, so that those ladies and Gentlemen, who may be pleased to honour them with their Encouragement, may depend upon every Respect and Attention.*

Despite the obvious success of the experiment, and direct instructions from the Prime Minister that Palmer should be afforded full co-operation and assistance, rearguard opposition from the Post Office (though Joyce says it was trouble with the contractors, not the Post Office) delayed conversion so much that the London-Norwich service (for which contracts had been signed to commence in October) did not begin until 28 March 1785. The first cross post coach was Bristol to Portsmouth in May 1785.

Charles Clear† goes into Palmer's battle to carry out his plan to subdue the Post Office opposition, his trouble with Coach Contractors, his attempts to fill the top positions with his supporters, and to make a fortune on the Allen pattern, in considerable detail. He achieved a very great deal, and succeeded in converting the services to Leeds, Manchester, and Liverpool in July, and Portsmouth, Poole, Gloucester and Swansea, Hereford, Carmarthen and Milford, Worcester and Ludlow, Birmingham and Shrewsbury, Oxford and Cirencester, Chester and Holyhead, Carlisle, Dover, Exeter via Salisbury, and via Wells and Taunton by November 1785. York, Newcastle on Tyne and Scotland followed in 1786 and 1787. Much of the early experimental work appears to have been done at Palmer's own expense, yet not until 5 August 1786 was his appointment as Surveyor and Comptroller General signed.

Palmer's aim was to be in complete control of the running of the Post Office and its expenditure, independent of the Postmasters General, and to secure for himself $2\frac{1}{2}\%$ of the net increase in Post Office revenue. The first was declared impossible in law, and Palmer was made responsible directly to the Postmasters General, a continual source of irritation. Pitt secured for him the financial terms he requested, but insisted that this should be after allowance for the increased postage rates: when the starting figure for his percentage was fixed at £240,000 (revenue £150,000 plus £90,000 allowance for increased rates of postage), Palmer again complained bitterly. It was agreed eventually that he should have an additional salary of £1,500 a year. Worse was to follow, for in July 1787 Lord Walsingham was appointed a joint Postmaster General with Lord Carteret.

All government appointments at this period included a certain amount of payment by perquisite to increase a low salary, but in some departments this had become such an abuse it could no longer be accepted. A Royal Commission had already been set up to investigate; when an unsavoury case involving Carteret came to light Pitt took no direct action, but arranged that the Post Office should come next before the commission. This reflects very badly on Pitt, for Carteret was notorious for signing anything put before him and there are grounds for thinking that he did know the contents of some of them. When Lord Tankerville could stand this no longer and refused to work with him, Carteret went to Pitt and it was Tankerville who was sacked, although he had obtained Pitt's agreement throughout to the reasons for his opposition. Carteret was Postmaster General from January 1771 to September 1789, nearly nineteen years, with seven

---

\* Those interested in coaches, inns, and coffee houses are strongly advised to study his 'London Coffee Houses', George Allen and Unwin 1963, a study extending to 850 pages.   Now his 'London Signs' is published (Allen and Unwin 1972) with 17,500 entries of inns.  It could be no more than an index to his notes, nineteen volumes available for study in the Guildhall Library, London.

† John Palmer, Mail Coach Pioneer, by Charles R. Clear, Blandford Press and the Postal History Society 1955.

partnerships and two periods totalling eight months of sole control; one wonders why. The report could not fail to reveal large numbers of very doubtful situations, so Pitt appointed Walsingham with Carteret to restore some appearance of regularity and order. A man of the highest possible standards, his capacity for work was enormous and he investigated everything, signing nothing that was not proved to be correct, necessary, and fairly charged.

Thus receded Palmer's hopes. In the first years both men seem to have avoided trouble. Walsingham appears to have genuinely supported Palmer's reforms and done his best to accommodate him, but insisted on regarding him as completely under his control, like all other employees. Palmer, doubtless, was much bothered and delayed by Walsingham's flow of minutes and requests, and had little wish to have emphasized his subordinate position. Charles Clear sums up the situation in talking of the revelations made in a 1790 letter from Palmer to his deputy Charles Bonnor:

"This is clearly the true Palmer — his inner soul — speaking, a determined, forceful and energetic personality, generous to his friends but highly distrustful and jealous, and indeed aggressive to those who opposed or, as he thought, opposed his ambitions. Even his ambitions, although guiltless enough, were scarcely of the highest and most altruistic order. He certainly had in view the advancement and improvement of commerce and industry; but this was clearly secondary to his main, but not unnatural objective, to make a considerable fortune as surely and as quickly as possible.'

With the coaches running, Palmer may have tried to reorganize the entire Post Office to fit his coach schedules, undoubtedly he still met strong opposition from the Chief Office and provincial postmasters — he put up everyone's backs. In 1787-8 he brought all possible influence to obtain the farm of the London Penny Post, a foolish attempt with little chance of success, of which more details are given in Chapter 9. He concentrated on placing friends in important positions, the best posts going to two Bristol men Charles Bonnor and Francis Freeling. The two could not have been more dissimilar. Freeling, of whom there will be more later, was chosen by Palmer to settle the first cross mail coach from Bristol through Salisbury to Portsmouth in 1785. He was then promoted to the Resident Surveyor, on whom fell most of the organizing work, and proved a most capable and loyal supporter. Bonnor, whom Palmer made his deputy and intimate, was the worst possible choice and highlights Palmer's inability to judge character. A reasonably successful actor, his unfinished apprenticeship as coach-builder explains some of his value to Palmer, but he was not the type to be in charge of the Inland office during Palmer's long absences, or to be the recipient of letters pouring out his jealousy and frustration. He was always in financial trouble, and even a suspicious burglary, then in desperation a fire (both affecting only his papers) could not conceal Bonnor's doubtful dealings.

In 1791 Palmer reimbursed to the Post Office a large part of Bonnor's latest deficiencies, and probably this began the general distrust which in 1792 extended Walsingham's battle with Palmer into open warfare. Following a series of doubtful intrigues, Palmer told Bonnor to supply information unofficially to the organizers of a meeting to protest against delayed delivery, and lay all the blame on Walsingham. Bonnor decided to change horses, as might have been expected, and published a pamphlet on 18 February 1792 (three days after the protest meeting) disclosing the whole sordid intrigue. On the same day Palmer suspended his deputy, and, on refusing to reinstate him, was himself suspended by the Postmaster General on 7 March. Doubtless Palmer was confident that Pitt would override Walsingham, and it is possible he might have done so had Bonnor not delivered up letters from Palmer written in the days of their close friendship, sworn affidavits, and certificates from other senior officers (and anything which would harm him). These documents finished Palmer, showing that he had worked consistently to undermine authority, and he was dismissed with an annual pension of £3,000 in consideration of the advantages derived by the public from his plan. He continued the fight for his percentage, but only in 1813 were he and his son successful in getting a bill (their fourth) through Parliament. This granted him £50,000 in settlement of his claim, and he lived a further five years to enjoy it. It was a large sum in 1813, considering that the Post Office should have seen the need for this without his help.

Palmer was greatly honoured during his lifetime, and was always supported in his battles by much of the Press and many leading men. They saw only the very good result, but not how it had been achieved and how much was lost in obtaining it. He was the first to see the possibilities of combining the coach and the postboy, and carried on the conversion with considerable energy and skill, but it is certain that it would have come anyway within a few years. There is doubt about the efficacy of his other reforms, and certainly his intolerance, jealousy, and lack of sound judgement were fatal flaws in a high position. Probably the country should have been more grateful for his selection and promotion of Francis Freeling, but proof of Freeling's value lay in the future. Bonnor had the reward for betrayal of his friend for two years, but was never granted more than a fraction of the power and less than half the salary of Palmer. Freeling and many others never forgave him, and he was retired compulsorily in 1795. Freeling was appointed in 1797 joint Secretary with the elderly Anthony Todd, and became Secretary on Todd's death in 1798: Freeling, too, died in harness in 1836 having been virtually a dictator of Post Office affairs for forty years.

The mailcoach became identified to a remarkable extent with its period, and had a profound social effect. It was responsible for a great burst of road improvement under Metcalf, McAdam, and Telford, and brought a degree of glamour to drab lives. The departure of the coaches from the General Post Office every evening became one of the sights of London, and in times of trouble so great was its power to spread news that printed handbills were prepared for the guard to distribute to postmasters (and doubtless to ensure that his shouted tidings were correct). The coach and the mails were completely in charge of the guard, and in case of delay or accident his orders were to unharness horses and ride on with the bags. It is no small thing that Charles Clear can state that probably no mail coach was ever robbed by highwaymen, and certainly not during Palmer's lifetime, but this claim has not been verified. Only three passengers were allowed outside (four in Scotland): this was increased later to seven but nobody ever sat with the guard. He must have a clear view and be ready.

Joyce states that about 220 mail coaches ran regular schedules in Great Britain in 1811, but due to attempts and threats to reimpose tolls on them the numbers dropped sharply and in 1836 he puts the number at 104, all four-horsed. Probably twenty eight of these were from London. He quotes many post roads that were decoached. The damage the mailcoaches did to the roads was considerable, and the arguments of the Turnpike Trusts must be received with sympathy when they found difficulty in showing a reasonable return to encourage investment, were bound by law to maintain the state of the road, and could levy nothing on the most frequent vehicles using it.

Mailcoaches were never owned by the Post Office, who gave contracts to supply a coach for stretches of each road to various contractors; horses were changed much more frequently. The first Bristol to London coach was contracted by Wilson & Co of London and Williams & Co of Bath, but existing coach construction was too light to stand up to the roads. Besant designed a patent coach, and when he secured the exclusive right to supply the contractors he went into partnership with Vidler, a large coachbuilder on Millbank. On Besant's death Vidler held the monopoly until 1836, and for a charge of $2\frac{1}{2}$d the double mile of the coach journey he supplied the coaches, his men drove them from the General Post Office to Millbank, cleaned, serviced, and returned them to the inn in time for the next run. The London to Exeter coach was changed at Salisbury only, whilst to Edinburgh it changed at Huntingdon, Grantham, Doncaster, York, Newcastle, and Berwick (there were more than forty changes of horses on this run).

### Inns and Coffee Houses

Although the hundred years of stage coaches before 1784 had produced a number of very important inns tied to their schedules, the mail coaches increased their numbers and importance. They operated as parcel depots, poste restante addresses for letters, and to an extent replaced the coffee houses as centres of activity. Leigh's Guide to London 1841 estimates there were 200 inns, 400 taverns and 500 coffee houses in London, though this last figure seems very high. Cary lists the following London inns in his 1812 guide to the roads (the number of coaches leaving from each inn is in brackets):—

Angel, St. Clements, Strand (19)
Angel, Angel St., St Martins le Grand (5)
Bell and Crown, Holborn (15)

Old Bell, Holborn (13)
Belle Sauvage, Ludgate Hill (10) (see White Horse)
Black Lion, Water Lane, Fleet St. (8)
Blossoms, Lawrence Lane, Cheapside (10)
Blue Boar, Whitechapel (14)
Bolt in Tun, Fleet Street (18)
Bull, Bishopsgate Street (6)
Bull, Holborn (10)
Bull, Whitechapel (10)
Bull and Mouth, Bull and Mouth Street (35)
Cross Keys, Gracechurch Street (10)
Cross Keys, St John Street (1)
Four Swans, Bishopsgate St (7)
George, Borough (5)
George and Blue Boar, Holborn (20)
Gerrards Hall, Basing Lane, Bread Street, and Black Bear, Piccadilly (5)
Golden Cross, Charing Cross (48)
Golden Lion, St John Street (4)
Green Dragon, Bishopsgate St (3)
King's Arms, Snow Hill (3)
New Inn, Old Bailey (3)
Ram, Smithfield (1)
Saracens Head, Snow Hill (22)
Saracens Head, Aldgate (11)
Saracens Head, Friday Street, Cheapside (2)
Spread Eagle, Gracechurch Street (26)
Spur Inn, Borough (1)
Swan with Two Necks, Lad Lane (26)
Three Cups, Aldersgate Street (3)
Three Nuns, Whitechapel (7)
White Horse, Fetter Lane; Cross Keys, Wood Street; and Belle Sauvage (28)
White Horse, Friday Street (1)
Waldegrave's General Coach Office, Bishopsgate Within (6)
Windmill, St Johns Street (2)

    Numbers are not an accurate guide, giving no idea of the importance of the coaches. One of the most famous inns was the Swan with Two Necks, which horsed fourteen mail coaches including the original Bristol, the Liverpool, Manchester, Portsmouth, Holyhead, and Devonport. The Devonport was proud to be always a fraction faster than any other coach, and was the only named mail coach — Quicksilver. The innkeepers were normally proprietors, or at least partners, in their ordinary coaches, and under William Waterhouse and later Robert Chaplin the Swan must have been a wonderful sight. Chaplin also owned the Spread Eagle, Gracechurch Street, and Robinson states that at his peak he owned seventy coaches and 1,800 horses, having to change on average a third of his horses every year. A bill for the Swan of 1820, when still owned by Waterhouse, lists the Royal Mails starting there as Bristol via Chippenham, Bath via Devizes, Plymouth via Taunton, Exeter via Salisbury, Falmouth, Birmingham, Liverpool via Litchfield, Manchester via Leicester, Carlisle via Preston, Norwich via Ipswich, Norwich via Bury, and Weymouth. A remarkable array — the Exeter coach was the one that had the famous attack by a lioness in 1816, near the Pheasant Inn between Salisbury and Stockbridge*.

    The Bull and Mouth, opposite the GPO, was always a close rival, and in 1836 horsed eleven of the twenty eight mail coaches. Edward Sherman owned nearly as many coaches as Chaplin, and must have had well over a thousand horses. Robert Nelson of the Beau Sauvage, Ibberson of the George and Blue Boar, William Horne of the Golden Cross (later he owned the George and Blue Boar as well) and Mrs Mountain of the Saracens Head were equally famous, and all must

---

    * For details, and much else of interest, see the Post Office Historical Summary No. 8 — The Mail Coach service.

papers in the Post Office show that no hamlet was too small for his benevolent attention. His reign was the period of development of local posts, and he was always ready to bend regulations and accept a loss if the inhabitants gained and it showed a prospect of long-term benefit to the Post Office in the wider sense. His grasp of postal minutiae, attention to detail, and energy were tremendous, despite which he had time to become in no small way a confidant and patron of the Arts, as had Allen. It is evident, however, that he stayed too long. Whilst his complete dedication and incorruptibility had been invaluable, his genuine belief that the Post Office was perfect (and hence his opposition to any major change) and that higher postage rates were the natural solution to all evils laid it open to devastating attack. His last years were saddened by an utter inability to see why so many people were dissatisfied.

Chapter 9

# LONDON — THE 1794 REFORMS AND LATER

FROM 1680, when William Dockwra saw his opportunity and started a private post, the London Penny Post continued practically unchanged. One has the feeling it had been a cosy backwater for a hundred years — why spoil it? This peace was threatened in 1787/8 when John Palmer pressed for the farm of the London Penny Post, and offered to pay as annual rent the equal of the highest net revenue recorded. If granted, he offered to relinquish his agreed percentage of the increased profit of the Post Office due to the mail coaches. Palmer must have known the parlous condition of London's post, and may well have seen his chance of profits to equal those of Ralph Allen. Possibly he expected to be given the farm from gratitude, but really should have known better. In earlier days the Post Office had been keen to farm out risky and unprofitable minor roads (probably after burning their fingers on the 1674 cross post) but there was never any suggestion of farming the post on the six major roads. The London post would certainly be considered of major importance, the equal of the Dover, Chester, or North roads.

At the same time, Palmer sent Edward Johnson to survey the post in and around London, and the days of the Penny Post providing a sinecure for senior staff were over. Johnson was another protégé of Palmer (like Francis Freeling and Bonnor), a former letter carrier, and seems to have given him no more loyalty than they gave. The dates are important, and do not appear to have been studied in relation to each other: the list starts from the appointment of Walsingham, for it was probably a combination of mutual antagonism and Palmer's looking for new worlds to conquer that began the trouble.

| | |
|---|---|
| July, 1787 | — Lord Walsingham appointed Postmaster General. |
| Winter, 1787/8 | — Palmer offered to farm the London Post. |
| Spring, 1788 | — Palmer sent Johnson to survey the London Penny Post. |
| March, 1792 | — Palmer was suspended as Comptroller General. |
| May, 1792 | — Postmasters General tell the Treasury they have Johnson's report. |
| July, 1792 | — Johnson's report is submitted to the Postmasters General. |
| September, 1792 | — They send Johnson's report to the Treasury. |
| April, 1793 | — John Palmer is finally dismissed. |
| April, 1793 | — Manchester provincial penny post is started. |
| March, 1794 | — London General Post experimental stamps begin. |
| May, 1794 | — London Penny Post experimental stamps begin. |

It is clear that Palmer had lost the sympathy of his nominees. Less than two months after Palmer's suspension the Postmasters General, in applying for an allowance for Johnson, wrote to the Treasury:

'Mr Edward Johnson of this office was sent four years ago by Mr Palmer to survey the districts round London for the purpose of establishing a new Penny Post Office; Mr Palmer much approved his plan, and Mr Johnson has now laid it before us.' This is dated 14 May, 1792, but Johnson's report is dated 14th July, 1792, so it may have been returned to him for alteration. Another peculiarity is the delay of two years in trying the reforms, during which time Johnson was adviser for the introduction of the first provincial penny posts in Manchester, Birmingham

# TO ALL POSTMASTERS
## AND
## SUB-POSTMASTERS.

GENERAL POST OFFICE,
25th April, 1840.

IT has been decided that Postage Stamps are to be brought into use forthwith, and as it will be necessary that every such Stamp should be cancelled at the Post Office or Sub-Post Office where the Letter bearing the same may be posted, I herewith forward, for your use, an *Obliterating Stamp*, with which you will efface the Postage Stamp upon every Letter despatched from your Office. *Red Composition* must be used for this purpose, and I annex directions for making it, with an Impression of the Stamp.

As the Stamps will come into operation by the *6th of May*, I must desire you will not fail to provide yourself with the necessary supply of Red Composition by that time.

---

*Directions for Preparing the Red Stamping Composition.*

1 lb. Printer's Red Ink.
1 Pint Linseed Oil.
Half-pint of the Droppings of Sweet Oil.
*To be well mixed.*

By Command,

**W. L. MABERLY,**
SECRETARY.

*The notice sending the Maltese Cross cancellation ready for May 6th (page 136) (reproduced by courtesy of the Post Office).*

Plate 17

*The courtyard of a coaching inn, probably the Bull and Mouth, published in 1874 by Fores from a painting by C. C. Henderson (not contemporary, and it is uncertain whether a London-Glasgow mail coach passed through Manchester) (reproduced by courtesy of the Post Office).*

**Plate 18**

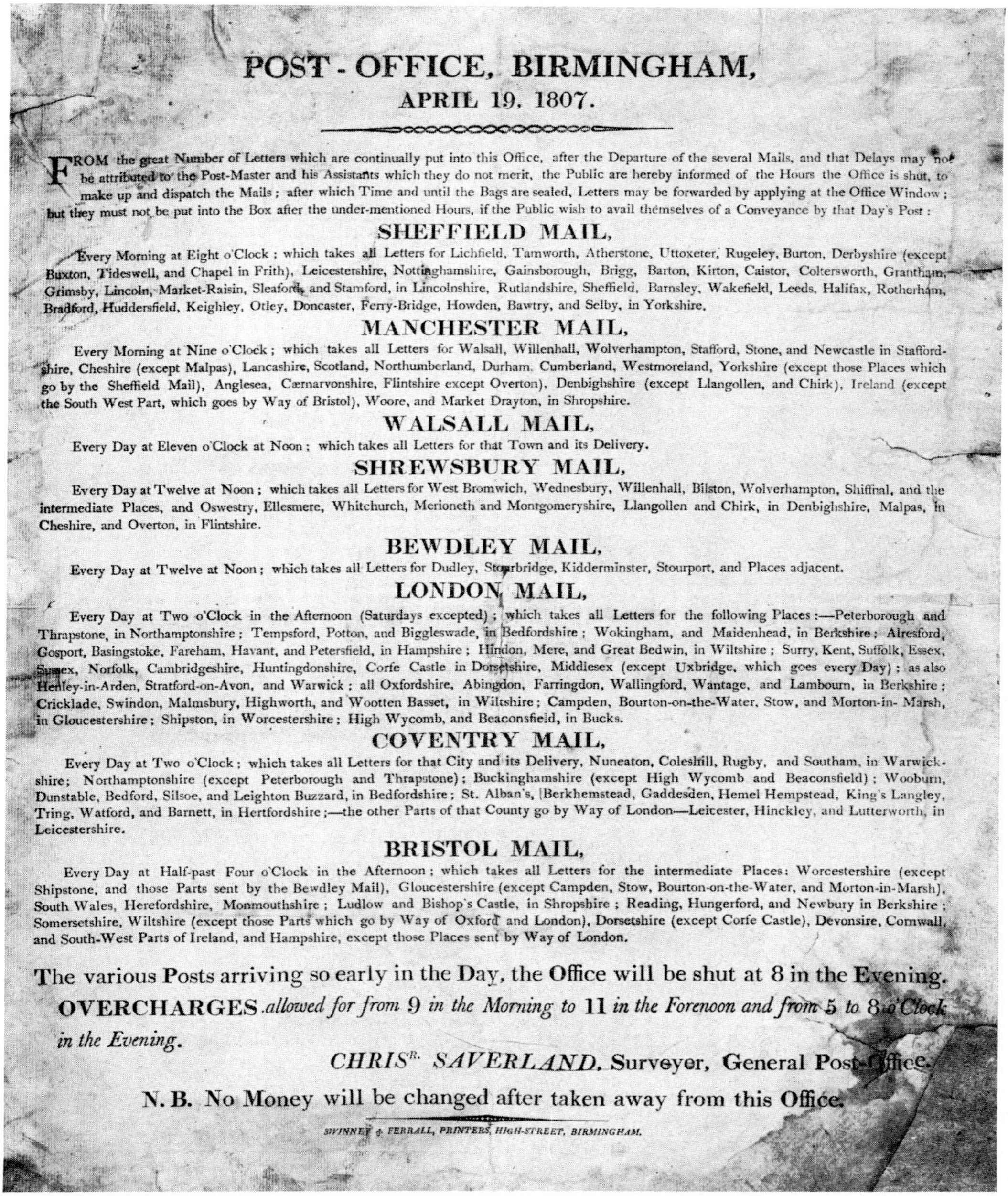

# POST-OFFICE, BIRMINGHAM,
## APRIL 19, 1807.

FROM the great Number of Letters which are continually put into this Office, after the Departure of the several Mails, and that Delays may not be attributed to the Post-Master and his Assistants which they do not merit, the Public are hereby informed of the Hours the Office is shut, to make up and dispatch the Mails; after which Time and until the Bags are sealed, Letters may be forwarded by applying at the Office Window; but they must not be put into the Box after the under-mentioned Hours, if the Public wish to avail themselves of a Conveyance by that Day's Post:

## SHEFFIELD MAIL,

Every Morning at Eight o'Clock; which takes all Letters for Lichfield, Tamworth, Atherstone, Uttoxeter, Rugeley, Burton, Derbyshire (except Buxton, Tideswell, and Chapel in Frith), Leicestershire, Nottinghamshire, Gainsborough, Brigg, Barton, Kirton, Caistor, Coltersworth, Grantham, Grimsby, Lincoln, Market-Raisin, Sleaford, and Stamford, in Lincolnshire, Rutlandshire, Sheffield, Barnsley, Wakefield, Leeds, Halifax, Rotherham, Bradford, Huddersfield, Keighley, Otley, Doncaster, Ferry-Bridge, Howden, Bawtry, and Selby, in Yorkshire.

## MANCHESTER MAIL,

Every Morning at Nine o'Clock; which takes all Letters for Walsall, Willenhall, Wolverhampton, Stafford, Stone, and Newcastle in Staffordshire, Cheshire (except Malpas), Lancashire, Scotland, Northumberland, Durham, Cumberland, Westmoreland, Yorkshire (except those Places which go by the Sheffield Mail), Anglesea, Cærnarvonshire, Flintshire except Overton), Denbighshire (except Llangollen, and Chirk), Ireland (except the South West Part, which goes by Way of Bristol), Woore, and Market Drayton, in Shropshire.

## WALSALL MAIL,

Every Day at Eleven o'Clock at Noon; which takes all Letters for that Town and its Delivery.

## SHREWSBURY MAIL,

Every Day at Twelve at Noon; which takes all Letters for West Bromwich, Wednesbury, Willenhall, Bilston, Wolverhampton, Shiffnal, and the intermediate Places, and Oswestry, Ellesmere, Whitchurch, Merioneth and Montgomeryshire, Llangollen and Chirk, in Denbighshire, Malpas, in Cheshire, and Overton, in Flintshire.

## BEWDLEY MAIL,

Every Day at Twelve at Noon; which takes all Letters for Dudley, Stourbridge, Kidderminster, Stourport, and Places adjacent.

## LONDON MAIL,

Every Day at Two o'Clock in the Afternoon (Saturdays excepted); which takes all Letters for the following Places:—Peterborough and Thrapstone, in Northamptonshire; Tempsford, Potton, and Biggleswade, in Bedfordshire; Wokingham, and Maidenhead, in Berkshire; Alresford, Gosport, Basingstoke, Fareham, Havant, and Petersfield, in Hampshire; Hindon, Mere, and Great Bedwin, in Wiltshire; Surry, Kent, Suffolk, Essex, Sussex, Norfolk, Cambridgeshire, Huntingdonshire, Corfe Castle in Dorsetshire, Middlesex (except Uxbridge, which goes every Day); as also Henley-in-Arden, Stratford-upon-Avon, and Warwick; all Oxfordshire, Abingdon, Farringdon, Wallingford, Wantage, and Lambourn, in Berkshire; Cricklade, Swindon, Malmsbury, Highworth, and Wootten Basset, in Wiltshire; Campden, Bourton-on-the-Water, Stow, and Morton-in-Marsh, in Gloucestershire; Shipston, in Worcestershire; High Wycomb, and Beaconsfield, in Bucks.

## COVENTRY MAIL,

Every Day at Two o'Clock; which takes all Letters for that City and its Delivery, Nuneaton, Coleshill, Rugby, and Southam, in Warwickshire; Northamptonshire (except Peterborough and Thrapstone); Buckinghamshire (except High Wycomb and Beaconsfield); Wooburn, Dunstable, Bedford, Silsoe, and Leighton Buzzard, in Bedfordshire; St. Alban's, Berkhemstead, Gaddesden, Hemel Hempstead, King's Langley, Tring, Watford, and Barnett, in Hertfordshire;—the other Parts of that County go by Way of London—Leicester, Hinckley, and Lutterworth, in Leicestershire.

## BRISTOL MAIL,

Every Day at Half-past Four o'Clock in the Afternoon; which takes all Letters for the intermediate Places: Worcestershire (except Shipstone, and those Parts sent by the Bewdley Mail), Gloucestershire (except Campden, Stow, Bourton-on-the-Water, and Morton-in-Marsh), South Wales, Herefordshire, Monmouthshire; Ludlow and Bishop's Castle, in Shropshire; Reading, Hungerford, and Newbury in Berkshire; Somersetshire, Wiltshire (except those Parts which go by Way of Oxford and London), Dorsetshire (except Corfe Castle), Devonsire, Cornwall, and South-West Parts of Ireland, and Hampshire, except those Places sent by Way of London.

The various Posts arriving so early in the Day, the Office will be shut at 8 in the Evening.

OVERCHARGES allowed for from 9 in the Morning to 11 in the Forenoon and from 5 to 8 o'Clock in the Evening.

CHRIS.R SAVERLAND, Surveyor, General Post Office.

N. B. No Money will be changed after taken away from this Office.

SWINNEY & FERRALL, PRINTERS, HIGH-STREET, BIRMINGHAM.

*Times of closing of the mails at Birmingham. Note the first paragraph, which may explain why the TOO LATE of Birmingham is the commonest in England at this time (reproduced by courtesy of the Post Office).*

Plate 19

*The daily statement of the Birmingham Post Office, 1837 (reproduced by permission of the Post Office).*

and Bristol, and probably the reorganized General Post. Nothing appears to be known of the reorganization of the General Post, but it must have been done, and the experimental stamps were in use before those of the Penny Post.

In submitting the plan to the Treasury Commissioners, the Postmasters General began, 'Of all the improvements that have at any time been wanting in the Post Office, a description of the inconveniences of the present Penny Post, would lead to an immense detail and is unnecessary, they are pointed out in Mr Palmer's letter to the Commissioners dated May 2nd 1783.' So Palmer had his eyes on the London Post, and put up a strong case for its reform, fifteen months before his first mail coach ran and five years before he sent Edward Johnson to survey it. This would be during the delay caused by a change of Government. The letter then goes into the detail of the plan, and returns to Palmer near the end, 'Although the Commissioners are stated by Mr Palmer to have been in possession of the general outlines of his plan, which We never saw but which We understand to be the same with that which Mr. Johnson has now communicated to Us and originally communicated to Mr Palmer. . . . The opinion which Mr Palmer entertained of this Plan, being not only beneficial to the Public, but advantageous to the Revenue, as proved by having offered, in his letter to the Commissioners, to give up his salary and percentage if he was allowed to farm it for his life'.

This seems to say that when Johnson submitted his plan to Palmer, his superior who had ordered the investigation, Palmer went straight to the Treasury Commissioners and ignored the Postmaster General completely: this is quite in character, but why was it not sent to them for comment? It would seem that the Commissioners just ignored it.

The main changes proposed in Johnson's plan were:—

(1)  The five offices were reduced to two, the Chief Office in Abchurch Lane, Lombard Street, and the Westminster Office in Gerrard Street, Soho.

(2)  The Town area to have six collections (at 8 a.m., 10 a.m., 12 noon, 2 p.m., 5 p.m., 8 p.m.) and deliveries each day, and the Country area three deliveries but only two collections. Whereas letter carriers had always collected each delivery from their main office (this could be five miles or more), two country deliveries were now to be sent out by horse messengers to the Receiving Houses and the third by mail coach if possible. These messengers would bring back the letters collected.

(3)  An extra penny was imposed on country letters into the town area. The second penny which had always been charged on town letters into the country (and which had been kept by letter carriers as part of their salary)* was now taken into the revenue.

(4)  Each town walk would have two letter carriers working alternately, as would some country walks where necessary. The receiving offices and walks were to be reorganized so they were of equal importance and amount of work. Letter carriers would increase from 130 to 181, of which one hundred were town area.

(5)  London letters could be sent unpaid in the penny post: for a hundred years prepayment had been compulsory. Letters destined for the General Post still had to be prepaid. It was hoped that this would raise the revenue considerably, for it would prevent receivers destroying the letters and pocketing the pennies. This gives an idea of the state of the penny post between 1780 and 1794 — evidence from all sides indicates that people preferred to send a messenger, or even give a letter to an unknown loiterer. Despite the enormous increase in trade and correspondence through the Industrial Revolution the gross revenue had little more than doubled in eighty years, and the net revenue showed a much smaller increase than that: in the last twenty boom years the net revenue had increased by only £1,300.

---

* Dockwra's post of 1680-82 and the very early Government post covered only the Cities of London and Westminster, and the Borough of Southwark. However, there is no doubt that Dockwra's organization stretched very much further, and towns and villages paid an inhabitant to bring their letters to the nearest receiving house and collect the mail for delivery in the town. This continued after 1683, and the extra 1d for the letter carrier's wages became hallowed by time although still not sanctioned by law (except for the suburbs adjoining). It was fifty years later, in 1731, that the extra penny for country delivery was legalized, but it went to the letter carrier as part of his wages until the 1794 Act.

(6)   The London post was allowed to extend beyond the ten mile radius, and the seven rides are listed as to Mortlake, Woolwich, Woodford, Edmonton, Finchley, Brentford and Mitcham. Although H. C. Westley* states that Wandsworth and Turnham Green were additional rides once a day only, no confirmation has been found and they are not mentioned in Johnson's plan, the contemporary newspapers, or the Report to the Treasury.   Every mention seen is of seven rides.

The 4 oz limit of weight was retained, and allowing for savings and the increased receipts, the cost was considered to be £1,497.  The 1 lb limit of weight imposed by Dockwra had been reduced to 4 ozs. in 1765.  Some points were not accepted — Johnson proposed that country to country letters travelling more than ten miles be charged 3d, but this was thought to be too high.

Although letter carriers of the General Post in London had been given smart uniforms in 1792 (being scarlet coats with blue lapels and lining, a blue waistcoat and a tall hat with golden band), those of the Penny Post were still not allowed them. The Act was passed on 28 March 1794, with effect from 1st June, and Johnson was made Deputy-Controller to be made Controller when Mr Walcot 'is promoted, resigns, or dies'.

These reforms went a long way to restore confidence in the Post Office inside London, and resulted in dramatic increases in mail despite the extra charges: the postal receipts doubled in the next year.  Howard Robinson quotes the following figures for gross and net revenue:—

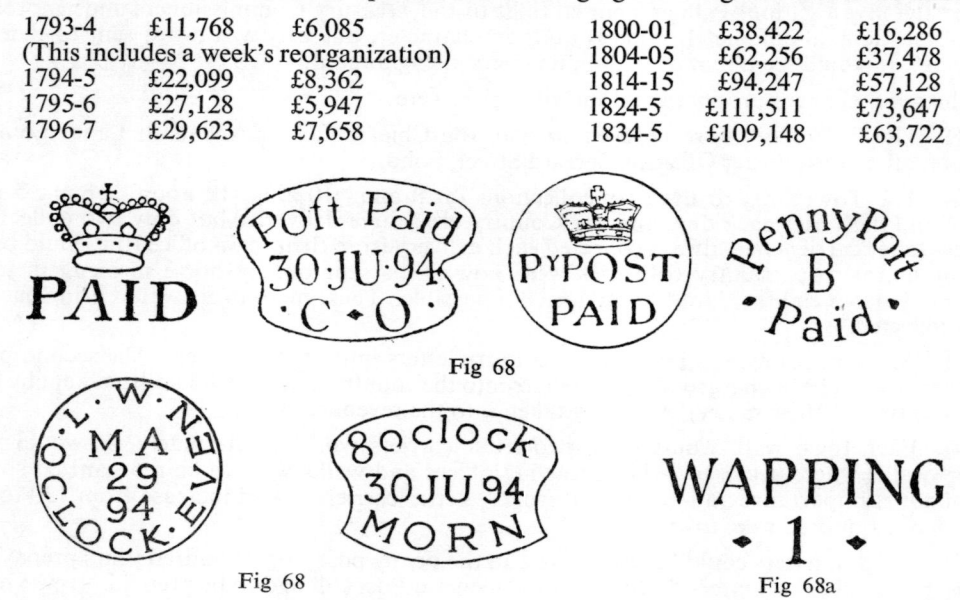

| | | | | | |
|---|---|---|---|---|---|
| 1793-4 | £11,768 | £6,085 | 1800-01 | £38,422 | £16,286 |
| (This includes a week's reorganization) | | | 1804-05 | £62,256 | £37,478 |
| 1794-5 | £22,099 | £8,362 | 1814-15 | £94,247 | £57,128 |
| 1795-6 | £27,128 | £5,947 | 1824-5 | £111,511 | £73,647 |
| 1796-7 | £29,623 | £7,658 | 1834-5 | £109,148 | £63,722 |

Fig 68

Fig 68   Fig 68a

In 1801 the last surviving part of the Penny Post went when letters within the Town area were raised to 2d, and in 1805 a differential was restored when those between Town and Country areas became 3d.  In July 1834 the Westminster office was abolished as a Chief Office, probably because the fine new building at St Martins-le-Grand (opened in 1829) was adequate to house the whole administration.  Before 1834, date stamps can be distinguished easily because those of the Chief Office had the month before the day, whilst Westminster office had the day first.

Some of the experimental stamps of the London Penny Post are shown in Fig 68, and the standard types which followed them in Figs 69-71. The former were used from May to December, 1794. It is apparent from a study of these and the previous triangular stamps that everything was changed. Five offices merged into two, the 'Dockwra type' stamps finished their hundred-year

---

* A very detailed article on the 1794 reforms, quoting the documents in full, in *The Postal History Society Bulletin*, Nos. 88-91, 1957.

run, as did the time stamps, unpaid stamps, and receivers names — nothing survived the Johnson blitz. For the first time proper date stamps were used which included the time of posting (never thought necessary in the general post date stamps), and the receiving houses used their location.

There are problems that have defied solution, are interesting, and quite important. In the first period 1794-1801 a large range of stamps occurs with the office in a straight line, and 1, 2, or 3 below (Fig. 68a). One or two offices are known with all three numbers, but most are not, and the stamps are very popular and pretty rare. It has been said that the numbers represented the delivery, and that they were letters collected by the letter carriers ringing their bells whilst returning to their office. The latter part may be true — they could be "Bellman" letters,* and the extra penny charged for them would account for their scarcity. If the numbers were the delivery, however, Town offices should be from 1 to 6, and later numbers very much more common than the early ones, so they are not deliveries.

The numbers could represent walks, for many areas did not have three walks and 1 would be the business area. An attractive stamp is DEW/BLACKMOOR ST. 3 — Dew was a wax-chandler in Blackmoor Street, so must have been a receiver, although why he should have his name in his stamp is not known. Although there is a large overlap in the dates of these numbered stamps and the new receiving house stamps, there is no overlap known at present in the stamps of any one office. If they are the "Bellman" letters, all offices should have used a different stamp on letters brought there normally, and the two should run concurrently. As they do not, it is an indication

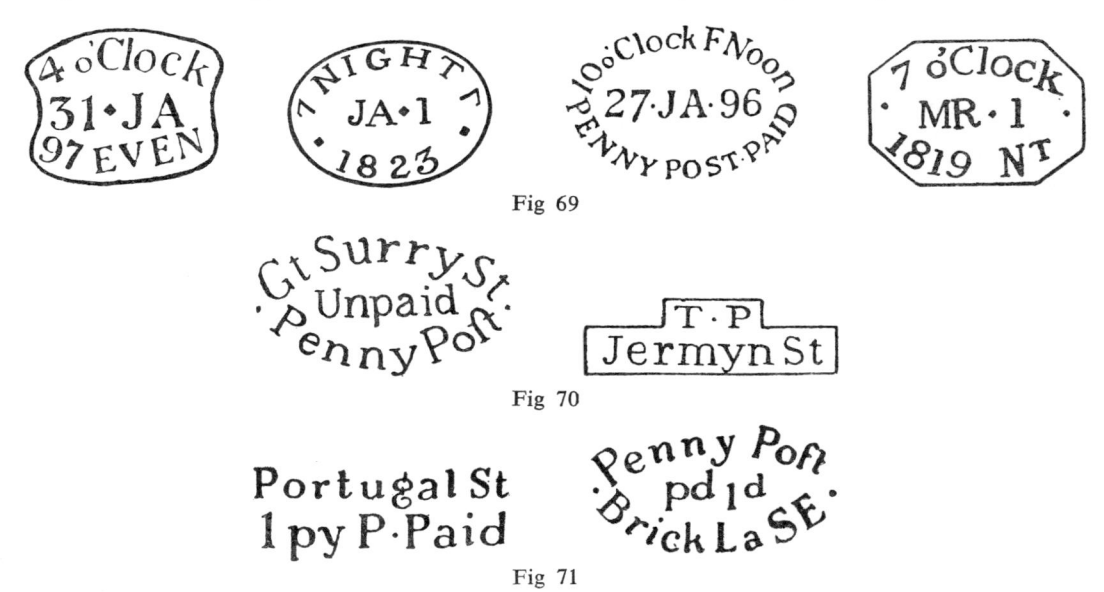

Fig 69

Fig 70

Fig 71

---

*Letter carriers carried large handbells in London, which they rang whilst walking back from a delivery. The letters collected by them were charged a penny extra, but might catch a mail after the offices had closed for it, so it acted as a late fee system. They carried a locked pouch with a slit for insertion of the letters, and remained part of the London scene until 1846. It is not known how these letters were marked.

The beginning of the Bellman is unknown, but Charles Povey's Halfpenny Post in 1709 is definitely too late: this is often quoted. Frank Staff in *The Penny Post* makes early mention, and gives their London end as 1846: a letter of 1701 from Lady Mary Coke which ends 'The Bell rings for my letter, and makes me lose the happiness of fancying I am talking with my dear', and another in the same year from Thomas Jennens 'The Bell rings for my letter'. Todd illustrates a handbill of Dockwra (plate 13) containing the phrase 'yet some persons by neglect of this useful contrivance, have preferred the Bell-man, and other obscure persons, rather than the use of the Penny Post, on whom they might more confidently reply. . . .' So Bellmen were collecting letters in opposition to Dockwra. This cannot have been the Post Office, it must have been the porters and private carriers who attacked his receiving houses in 1680. As these were made illegal with Dockwra in 1683, the Post Office may have adopted bells then, or before 1701.

that this may have been the usual receiving house stamp. Study is made more difficult by the scarcity of penny post letters of any kind in 1794, which may show how the public had lost faith in the London post. In the same period, PAID is known used with this type of stamp for Mortlake and UNPAID for Holborn Hill, but no Unpaid for Mortlake, Paid for Holborn Hill, or either for any other office, has been seen.

Another mystery surrounds the paid stamp of the Chief Offices a little later. In 1794 these were issued for both offices with PENNY POST PAID in an arc below, as Fig 69, in 1796 they were enclosed in an oval frame, and in 1801 new stamps read TWO PENNY P. PAID for the new charges. In 1805 the Country area was raised to 3d, and an 1807 example with the month, before day (Chief Office) is known with THREE PENNY P. PAID. No other copy has turned up though it should not be rare, and numerous letters to the country area have 3 on the front but the two penny stamp on the reverse. Possibly it was broken, and not replaced.

In 1823 occurred an example of the personal vagaries that make postal history so interesting. A new series of stamps was cut for both offices, and as the time was repeated each side to balance, the cutter reversed (in mirror image) the time on one side. This is noticeable in 12, 2, 4 and 7, but 8 defeated him as irreversible. In February a correct set came in, but both were used until nearly the end of 1823.

George Brumell* published a most useful list of charges within the London Post which simplifies them considerably:

|  | Dockwra 1680 | Govt. 1683 | 1794 | 1801 | 1805 | 1831 | 4d Post 5.12.1839 |  |
|---|---|---|---|---|---|---|---|---|
| Within the Town Area | 1d | 1d | 1d | 2d | 2d | 2d | 2d Unpaid | † |
| Town to Country, or within Country | 1d + 1d | 1d + 1d | 2d | 2d | 3d | 3d | 3d Unpaid | † |
| Country to Town area | 1d | 1d | 2d | 2d | 3d | 3d | 3d Unpaid | † |
| Town to General Post | 1d | 1d | 1d | 2d | 2d | free | — |  |
| Country area to General Post | 1d | 1d | 1d | 2d | 2d | 2d | — |  |
| General Post delivered by P.P. in Town | — | free | free | free | free | free | — |  |
| General Post delivered in Country | — | 1d | 1d | 2d* | 2d | 2d | — |  |

\* No charge was laid down, but 2d was usually charged for General Post letters from 1801.

† Fourpenny post letters from 5 December 1839 to 9 January 1840 were 1d prepaid anywhere in London.

Fig 72

Nothing is known definitely about the reorganization of the General Post, although Col G. R. Crouch lists a number of jobs abolished as unnecessary in *The Postal History Society Bulletin* No. 11, 1939. It may have been planned by Edward Johnson during the two year delay in implementing his reform of the London Penny Post, for he seems to have been the organization expert at this time: he was adviser for the Bristol, Birmingham, and Manchester Penny Post

---

\* The Local Posts of London 1680-1840 by George Brumell: Philatelic Adviser Handbook No. 2, 1938, now republished by R. C. Alcock Ltd.

have been great characters and superb organizers. F. E. Baines* states that in Exeter, coaching was responsible for the employment of over 3,000 people in one parish alone (St Sidwells).

As only the Inns are listed above, the Gloucester Coffee House is omitted, but this could rival most of them for coaching activities. In a collection of Time Bills (the official Post Office schedules) for mail coaches, no Inn is mentioned by name, but the Gloucester Coffee House is listed thus as the first stop for the Western Road coaches. Coaches loaded passengers at the Inns before proceeding to the General Post Office, Lombard Street, to collect the guard and his mail bags, but within a year or two of these Time Bills (probably by 1795) the guards for Western Road coaches were taken in carts with their mail bags to the Gloucester Coffee House, where their coaches were waiting. This may have been to ease the heavy congestion at Lombard Street (until 1829 when the GPO was moved to St Martin le Grand).

Taverns and Inns go back to the guest houses and lodgings attached to the Monasteries, the only places open to travellers in the Dark Ages. Theirs is a continuous history for a thousand years, but it was much later that Coffee Houses rose to become national institutions, and lasted as such for about two hundred years. They were the meeting places for the business of cities, and decisions taken there affected the life of the whole community. Starting in London just before the Restoration, they multiplied rapidly and with a severe shortage of accommodation after the Great Fire of 1666 coffee houses soon provided rooms for meetings of every description, auctions, etc. These meetings and the competition led gradually to a specialization, either by the occupation of their patrons or the area of their interests.

Many trades and businesses developed close links with one or more, and it is not surprising to find that the famous association of Edward Lloyd and the growing insurance market induced him to move his coffee house just a door or two from the General Post Office, the main centre of news and intelligence. A West Indies merchant sailing to London who had no address here might well collect his letters from the Jamaica Coffee House, whilst a merchant from India would probably use the Jerusalem. Others had a clientele chiefly political, literary, artistic, sporting, or with some other common interest. Many appear to have charged a subscription for use of their facilities, which would include use of the poste restante address (and presumably their payment of charges on letters taken in), and provision of the home and overseas newsletters and news sheets of interest to their patrons, shipping intelligence, and facilities for posting letters. On a recent visit to Vienna, it was interesting to see coffee houses with the same atmosphere and function as those of London two hundred years ago. To sit and talk for an hour was normal, and all the newspapers and journals are provided clipped to old boards.

Newspapers and the post are dealt with elsewhere, but one of the reasons for attempts to suppress or license coffee houses was the seditious and illegal newsletters available. The internal and external intelligence services seem to have been efficient, however, and found it easier to maintain surveillance of dubious activities if they were concentrated. Bags were hung in the major coffee houses for letters, and throughout most of the eighteenth century the Post Office strove unsuccessfully to control their private handling of letters, and collect the due postage. There must have hung a large board of notices of general interest, for a number have survived advertising lost and stolen property. They were issued by the Beadle of the Goldsmiths Company, who still have a book recording the man who walked round to pin them up. It was a big system, as numbers are 11,000 to 12,000, and many offer a reward 'and no questions asked.' Many newspaper advertisements asked for replies to coffee houses, and doubtless they acted as forwarding agents if required.

By 1799 the Post Office Packets were so slow, expensive to run, and overseas packet rates so high, that it was cheaper to send three letters by different ships to ensure arrival, than to send one by the Packet. Still the Packets lost money, partly because so many officials had their perquisites, so the Post Office tried to enrol the leading coffee house proprietors as agents of the Post Office. This failed, as might have been expected, and it was not until 1814 that the Post Office took resolute action. The Ship Letter Act of this year made it illegal to give letters to ships' crew privately, but such uproar arose that it was agreed that on payment of one third the packet rate the letter would be stamped 'Post Paid Withdrawn Ship Letter' and handed back to the sender,

---

* Forty Years at the Post Office, Macmillan 1895, pages 38-41.

who could then give it to the ship of his choice. Again this failed, and the 1815 act solved the problem of cost by requiring all ships to carry letters for the Post Office on payment of a reasonable sum, and twopence a letter to the captain. It did not stop the coffee houses making their own arrangements for sending letters, but at least it reduced considerably the cost of the Post Office Packet Boats. Changing conditions reduced the need for, and importance of coffee houses, and gradually they declined.

A link with inns and coffee houses is provided by tradesmen's tokens, which date back to Edward I but reached their peak in three periods: the last of these about 1790-1810, was the largest. Small coins were disliked by the Mint, which felt that manufacture of halfpennies or pennies was really beneath it, so in times of shortage tradesmen provided their own. Perhaps it is typical that Queen Elizabeth refused to have her image on coins of a base metal, as being beneath her dignity as a monarch, so no copper coins were struck by the Mint with her head. Such a craze did tokens become in the early nineteenth century that many were fraudulent (having no place to exchange for a coin of the realm, or very light weight), others were faked, and some even were imaginary: useless tokens were produced in large numbers, in the same way that stamps were produced for imaginary countries or in fictitious issues in the 1890s. Five in the last period (about 1790-1810) have a general postal interest, of which three have a mailcoach and an inscription to John Palmer, and the others were issued by the Swan with Two Necks and the George and Blue Boar. Two John Palmer tokens and the Swan with Two Necks should be available at reasonable prices, but the other two are pretty rare. The rare Palmer has 1797 replacing a cypher on the reverse. All these were halfpennies, and are well worth a place in a postal history collection. There are variations in them, but one cannot go far wrong with these five, but as with other collections it is wise to known more about it if you wish to go deeper.

## Decline: Coaches and Sir Francis Freeling

The decline of the coach was due solely to development of the railways: as they expanded and increased their speed, coaches just could not compete. Although the Stockton to Darlington railway opened to carry the public and goods on 27 September 1825, it was with the opening of the Manchester to Liverpool line on 15 September 1830 that they really hit the headlines with the first fatality. When the Home Secretary, William Huskisson, was struck by the train and killed during the opening ceremonial journey in view of thousands of visitors in stands, all development and running of railways was very nearly stopped as too dangerous. They survived, however, and there may have been the first experimental carriage of mail on this line on 11 November 1830. There does not seem to have been any regular contract for carrying mail, however, until 1837-8 and London was linked to Birmingham and the North West in September 1838. From then, mailcoaches suffered a gradual rundown, and the last from London (to Norwich via Newmarket) was withdrawn on 3 April 1846, the last from Manchester in 1858, and probably the last of all in Scotland in 1874. A revival occurred in the Parcels coaches run by the Post Office from 1887, which were introduced to Brighton to break the railway monopoly of long distance carriage and reduce the unacceptably high charges they demanded. Soon parcels coaches were running to Manchester and other long hauls, but they only improved on the old coaches by one m.p.h. With the introduction of motor-coaches for these parcel runs in 1898, the horsedrawn mail coach had really met its Waterloo.

A remarkable coincidence is that the reign of Sir Francis Freeling is closely bound up with the supremacy of the mail coach. A protégé of Palmer, he played a considerable part in the running of the first mail coach of August 1784, and rode in the first cross mail coach in 1785. He reigned supreme in a way unbelievable to modern thought throughout its career, and in his decline authorized its death warrant by the first carriage of mail by railway. Freeling died still in harness in June 1836, a year before the railways began to compete seriously with the mail coaches.

Despite the personal sniping fashionable during his later years from politicians, Freeling can now be seen to be a great man; probably the only one produced inside the Post Office during the two hundred years to 1840. Damning as this statement must be, it is even more so when it is realized that his greatness was solely as an administrator. As Resident Surveyor, Assistant Secretary, Joint Secretary, and Secretary from 1798, his word was law for fifty years, during which time he strove to do his best for everybody within the framework he developed. His establishments, but this would not have been a full-time job. Changes in the General Post cannot have been fundamental if once again the stamps are a guide. The circular date stamp of the General Post continued unchanged for another five years, as did the current Free stamps, so the only sign of experiment was in the Paids, where three trial designs as Fig 72 were used between March and December. After nine months they returned to the type that had been used from 1787-94, and these continued for another seven years. Initials used by the Receivers had already ended in 1790, and the receiving house addresses continued unchanged in stamps for many years. It would seem that in the General Post it was mainly an adjustment of staff to the new mail coach era.

**The London Bye and Cross Post**

The Penny Post was completely separate from the General Post, although its headquarters were round the corner in Abchurch Lane. They each had their own letter carriers and receiving houses, and the only point of contact and exchange was the Chief Office. Thus, although a letter addressed to Reading was handed in only half a mile from the first coach stop at Hounslow, it still had to go into the Chief Office of the Twopenny Post, be handed over to the General Post, and sent out again along the same road. Although some receivers appear to have acted for both posts, it is probable they kept different rooms or counters for the two posts, and certainly the letters were kept separately.

The first improvement started on 5 July 1809, when began a system for sorting and exchange so that letters from one place to another on the same ride need not go through the Chief Office. A number of Country Sorting Offices were established, and these used a large stamp with the name around a circle and MG or EV above the date (Morning or Evening) (Fig 73). In 1832 a light cart from the Chief Office linked with the Westminster Office and sorting offices on the Hounslow Ride, which saved a half-hour, but still there was no connection with other rides, or with the General Post letters which formed probably half the London delivery. This came in December 1834 when coaches to the west picked up at Hounslow (their first stop) suburban mail for towns on the Western, Bristol, and South Wales roads. Incoming coaches dropped bags there from these towns with the letters for Chelsea, Brompton, Kensington etc. It was a big saving in time and money, for whereas General Post letters had to pay twopence extra for local postage into the Chief Office and out again, these new bye letters paid only a penny to or from Hounslow and saved at least three hours. So successful did it prove, that all the major coach roads were given the same system at the old boundary of the London post — the point where they stopped anyway for their first change of horses.

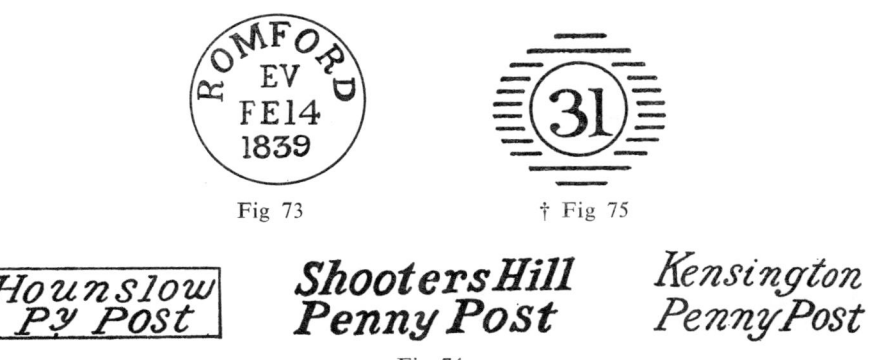

Fig 73

† Fig 75

Fig 74

In March 1835 a sub-office was opened on Shooters Hill for the Dover Road coach to exchange bags, and arrangements similar to Hounslow began at Barnet in July 1835 for the Chester and Holyhead road to Ireland, Waltham Cross in March 1836 for the Great North Road, and Croydon in May 1836 for the Brighton Road. Kingston came into the scheme for the Portsmouth Road at a date between July 1836 and January 1837. These later additions changed the whole system, for the bye-posts of 1809 which were established to sort local mail only, grew from 1834 to process general post letters (Hounslow had letters from seven coaches) and now were added the letters from other roads as well. It became in 1836 a fully-fledged cross post inside London and in a quiet way this was revolutionary. Until Quash's Bristol to Exeter post of 1696, it is fair to say that 95% of all post passed through the Chief Office, the oddment being some letters addressed on the same road (many of these were given to carriers or friends, and one's servants delivered local letters). In forty years from 1720, Allen reduced this percentage considerably, a fall that continued after his death; now we see the same progression in London's post a century later, first the local letters and then cross posts. This centralization had been for one purpose only — financial control and checking, any short cuts laying the Post Office open to the pocketing of a proportion of the revenue by postmasters.

Hounslow was selected by Freeling to try the scheme, for he said that with seven coaches on that road it was the most difficult area. Hounslow, Barnet, Waltham Cross, Kingston and Croydon were similar in that all were both General Post towns and London Threepenny Post towns, and had existing penny posts in the provincial system to villages outside the London area, so it was possible to extend these to other places inside the area. All used the same Penny Post handstamps on both types of letters (Fig 74) which is unfair to postal historians but is a good exercise in that 'it separates the men from the boys'. To make identification easier, the following rules will help;

(1) Letters must be to or from an address within the London twelve mile area, and from or to a provincial address.

(2) Under no circumstances can they have been in to the Chief Office; a few letters are known which should be cross post but have a Chief Office backstamp — these are interesting but of small value and are probably missorted.

(3) To remove the penny post element, the provincial half of (1) above must be, say, more than ten miles beyond the London boundary.

(4) It is probable that before 5 December 1839 they must have a penny post handstamp of the provincial type, but this is not certain yet. This shows that the penny was paid in addition to the General Post charge. The author would be interested to hear details of more covers in the London Cross Post before 10 January 1840 to be sure.

Shooters Hill was the exception, being little more than a steep hill, with a large inn (the Bull) a beacon and a gibbet (usually furnished with one or more corpses) at the top. Throughout history it had been the worst place on the only road worthy of the name in the country, and it is probable that from Roman days the road went over the crest only because any other route was vulnerable to attack from the crest or the river.* From 1739 a new, wider road was built at the lowest point of the hill just south of the old road, and in 1817 with convict labour from the hulks at Woolwich the crest was lowered considerable, and the gradient made easier at each side. Even then, passengers had to get out of the coach and walk up quite frequently. Mrs Farley quotes 'The Memoirs of William Hickey' published in 1761 as saying of the Bull, and Logon the proprietor, 'out and out the most expensive tavern in all England, where however you will be served in a princely style and find every article of the very best', but adds that invitations to dinners and entertainments usually had printed on them 'Armed men in attendance'. The main building was demolished in 1854, but when the last part was pulled down in 1881 a sealed cellar was found, containing a table on which lay a finely chased horse-pistol.

When Freeling wanted to establish a drop on the Dover Road there was no office suitable, for Dartford was too far away on the Kent side of the Bull, Blackheath and Deptford too near London with the consequent increase in the cost of riding work, and the coach did not pass through Bexley, Woolwich or Eltham. He therefore established an office at Shooters Hill (possibly in the Bull) to make up bye bags for all towns on the Dover Road, and others branching from it (e.g. Maidstone), and this was the only dropping point which was not also a General

---

\* For those wishing to read further, a most interesting article by Mrs D. Farley appeared in the Transactions of the Greenwich and Lewisham Antiquarian Society, Vol VIII, Number 1, 1973 (it is not postal, but is very interesting). Available from Greenwich Local History Library, Woodlands, Mycenae Road, Blackheath S.E.3

Post town. Stitt Dibden states that a messenger rode from Shooters Hill each morning with the letters to Blackheath, Greenwich, Deptford and New Cross, and returned with outgoing letters in the evening. One walked from Blackheath to Lewisham, and another from Shooters Hill to Woolwich. It seems doubtful if he continued to Greenwich, for its letters were always sent from Blackheath, the London ride continuing to Charlton and Woolwich.

Hounslow, Shooters Hill, and Barnet were all bye-posts originally, (i.e. along or feeding into one post road) but with the establishment of a drop at Waltham Cross in March 1836 Barnet became a cross post as well, exchanging letters between the Holyhead and Great North Roads. The same happened later with Hounslow when Kingston was included, and villages such as Kensington sent their letters to both according to which road they needed. However, letters with penny post stamps from the offices under Kingston (Chessington, Long Ditton, East or West Moulsey, Thames Ditton, Tolworth, or Weston Green) are not cross post as they were never inside the London area.

Although a letter from Freeling to the Postmaster General on 4 October 1834 says 'Your Lordship is aware that I have long had a favourite scheme in contemplation, and that at various times I consulted your predecessor upon it, and that he greatly encouraged it' this was written three months after the change of government, and it seems likely that he was taking a degree of credit due to Lords Richmond and Althorp. This is based on a reading of the characters involved. Although Freeling was very conscious of the need for improvements of this type, he was strongly against sources of loss to the revenue, and letters paid a penny less under this system whilst expenses increased. On the other hand, it is absolutely typical of the reforms introduced by Chancellor Althorp (see Chapter 13) and he is felt to be more probable as the originator of the scheme, but unable to carry it out through the fall of the government.

On 10 January 1840 the extra charge is presumed to have ceased, but some offices continued using the penny post handstamps. All the suburban sorting offices must have been issued with the Maltese Cross cancellations to use on the adhesive stamps, and in 1844 they were issued with Fig 75, the new numeral cancellations in a barred oval. The numbers run along the rides;

| | |
|---|---|
| 1- 3 Highgate to Whetstone | 22-23 Eltham and Bexley |
| 4- 6 Hampstead to Edgeware | 24-26 Dulwich to Beckenham |
| 7-11 Stoke Newington to Enfield | 27-30 Clapham to Carshalton |
| 12-17 Bow to Chigwell and Ilford | 31-36 Wandsworth to Hampton |
| 18-21 Deptford to Woolwich | 37-41 Brompton to Brentford |

Note that the same numbers in a diamond have no connection, and were all used in the Chief Office. It is not known when the system ended.

Examples of letters to illustrate the system are:

Brentford via Kingston to Andover. Marlborough via Hounslow to Hampton Court. Tiverton via Hounslow to Kensington. Brighton via Croydon to Clapham. Whetstone via Barnet to Market Harborough.

Examples which are not London Cross Post, but look similar are Reigate via Croydon Penny Post to Shirley, and Fareham via Kingston Penny Post to Thames Ditton. This is because neither Shirley nor Thames Ditton were in the London Post.

**Chapter 10**

# PROVINCIAL LOCAL DELIVERY

THERE is little doubt that from earliest times arrangements were made to collect their mail from the nearest post road by towns and villages. The possibility of Bishops Stortford running a penny post in 1690 has already been mentioned. Little research has been done on private posts of any kind, but it is most probable that a consistent pattern will be found: if the need was there, the service came from one direction or another. The limiting factor to be remembered in rural posts is not that people could not write, but that there was no need for them to write. There is evidence of municipal posts to London well before 1600 — these were cases where a town council hired a messenger as occasion demanded (or in certain cases had a salaried messenger) to carry its letters. Most of these letters would be for fairly local delivery to large landowners, and the few London letters would be carried to the nearest main road and handed to the messenger of a major city, who would have enough mail to make a scheduled run. Occasionally a solicitor or tradesman would have a London letter, and the messenger would carry this too for an agreed fee, but the entire life of the people was focussed locally and most had no need for a letter for years at a time. It is doubtful if the 1635 opening of the post had time to affect greatly these private arrangements before the complete disruption of 1641-2.

From 1660 correspondence grew considerably in volume, but still towns and even cities away from the six post roads collected their mail from the nearest of these roads by a private letter carrier who received payment per letter. If there was a postmaster, he was primarily a supplier of post horses and would run the post as a sideline to this and his innkeeping. As has been said earlier, the monopoly of hiring horses for travellers riding post, and the power to requisition horses from travellers at other inns were the most valuable parts of a postmaster's appointment, and this monopoly continued until 1780. There is a strong probability that postal historians always have overestimated the degree of organization of the post, and popular maps showing post roads to all points of the compass should be treated with suspicion. A case has just turned up in the 1670s of the Postmaster of Launceston, officially appointed, who received no salary, and had no post.* He had to collect the Launceston post at his own expense from Exeter, for which he was allowed to charge three pence a letter over the normal postage. Doubtless these cases were widespread. Again, many town name stamps 1705-15 are of very small towns which were road junctions, whilst stamps for large towns nearby are unknown, so it is evident that the appointment of a Postmaster was as much for horses and communication as for letters.

The Post Office encouraged local initiative in providing extra services, for they had no desire to spread much beyond the six post roads and a few major byposts that could support themselves, and had no objection to their postmasters running local services. Only when the Post Office decided to run the service itself did it take action, and even in 1844 Rowland Hill wrote of vast areas the size of a smaller county in which there was no government post at all. At the present state of knowledge, therefore, the picture up to the early 1700s must be a dozen or so roads, with postmasters off these roads collecting the mail and sometimes delivering it as a private enterprise. Not till the 1740s did Ralph Allen really make an impression, and this must have been small compared with the size of the problem.

---

*\* Devon and Cornwall, a postal survey 1500-1791* by David B. Cornelius. The Postal History Society 1973.

The 1765 Act (5 George 3 Cap 25) is concerned largely with mail going overseas, but allowed the setting up of 'a Penny Post Office' in any city or town in Great Britain, Ireland, or America, as thought convenient. Charges were to be the same as the London Penny Post. The next paragraph is important, stating that when such penny posts are established, no person may collect or deliver letters without a license from the Postmaster. The clear implication is that until a penny post was established, any person could run a private post for towns and villages, and there is no doubt that these private posts were the backbone of the postal system for many more years. A year before, on Ralph Allen's death, the Post Office had succeeded to his cross post system and his secrets; Allen had brought the post to a great number of places most efficiently but it is doubtful if the Post Office improved it much for many years after 1764.

Delivery of letters came into great prominence in 1772-4 when the inhabitants of Sandwich in Kent decided to contest in law the right of their postmaster to charge a fee for delivery of letters. At some former time, crosspost and bypost letters had been delivered free, although London letters had always had a delivery charge added as the postmaster's perquisite. Joyce* gives most interesting details of this and other cases, but here they must be summarized. The Kings Bench found in favour of the inhabitants, holding that where usage was free delivery, it must be adhered to. Ipswich then put in a slightly different case — whether the postmaster could demand any sum above the legal postage, and if not whether he could make the inhabitants collect their letters. Again the verdict was against the Post Office, and many towns where there had never been a free delivery claimed one. The Postmasters General were in a panic, for they could see that they would have to deliver to 'every hole and corner of the land'. Joyce says that of 440 post towns, seventy six were in the position of Sandwich, and had had free delivery at some time. The remainder, like Ipswich, had no traditional right but could now claim a delivery. The Attorney General favoured the Post Office in believing it unfair to expect them to deliver to houses, and held that delivery at the post office was enough, so the Post Office brought a case against Hungerford; here it could be proved that no free delivery had ever been given. In a long summing-up, the Lord Chief Justice (Lord Mansfield) held that the Post Office in some cases had demanded the delivery charge as a duty, and this it was not, for duties could be imposed only by Parliament. It would be a 'monstrous inconvenience' if everyone had to go to the post office every day to see if by chance there was a letter for him, and he mentioned the Bath and Gloucester cases before finding against the Post Office: he added that the Post Office should have gone to Parliament for clarification of the law. The other Judges concurred with equal emphasis that it was the duty of the Post Office to deliver within the limits of every post town, without extra charge. The Attorney General accepted this verdict, and refused to sanction an appeal, so there the matter rested.

These and other cases are well worth detailed study, for they show both litigants and the law at their best. If the Post Office had taken on staff to deliver as ordered, postal rates would probably have doubled (and imagine the howl that would have erupted then). Joyce considers it doubtful if one single letter carrier was employed by the Post Office outside London when Sandwich brought its case!! Yet one understands the feelings of a householder living next door to his post office when charged a penny in addition to the very high general post rates. The end of the story seems to be a masterpiece of inactivity by the Post Office, and surprisingly they were allowed to get away with it. Other towns were left with the postmaster continuing to charge for his private delivery service, and only those making themselves thoroughly unpleasant had a free delivery. With this historical background, one understands Freeling's snub to the Surveyor who thought the Minehead postmistress did too well from her private post.

It could be coincidence that during these cases the Post Office introduced the second penny post, in Dublin: equally it could have been to show that they were doing their best. Starting on 11 October 1773, with eighteen receiving houses in the town but only two deliveries a day, the Dublin penny post cannot have had much success and this may account for the rarity of early material. The Penny Post Office was situated in the General Post Office Yard, and sent out deliveries at 9 a.m. and 4 p.m. every day except Sundays. As in London, prepayment of 1d was

---

* The History of the Post Office by Herbert Joyce, 1893, pps 197-201, probably the most reliable of the early writers.

DUBLIN PENNY POST

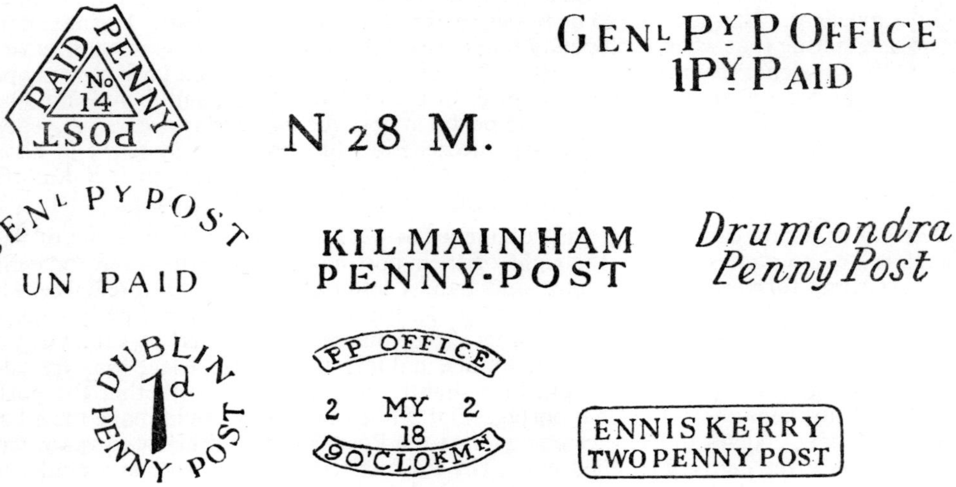

Fig 76

compulsory, and an outer area was established at a twopenny charge. From 1782 'Dockwra type' triangular stamps are known with a receiving house number in the centre (Fig 76), but none is known after 1784, the year in which the Irish Post Office was separated from England. It seems that they hastened to discard all signs of English control, and Howard Robinson gives details of the typical overstaffing and chaos that caused it to run consistently at a loss. It is the sorry story of free franking in Ireland over again. The only other stamp used regularly in early days was a date stamp in one straight line, abbreviated — N 28M being November 28, Morning. Recently F. E. Dixon discovered 'PENNY POST NOT PAID' enclosed in a circle and a handstruck 1d, on a letter dated 1788, but he adds that whilst dozens in this correspondence were delivered by hand, only three had been posted. In 1810 the Dublin Penny Post was completely reorganized by Lord Clancarty, a strong Irish Postmaster General, and a wider range of stamps was introduced; but despite these and later improvements 1823 was the first year to show a profit, after fifty years of accumulated losses. In 1831 the Irish Post Office came under London again, and in the next year the first provincial penny posts were running: with the shaky Dublin system, it is understandable that extension to the provinces was too risky before this.

PROVINCIAL PENNY POST

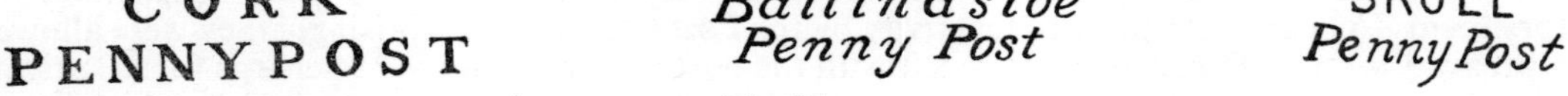

Fig 76

Three months after Dublin's local post began, a remarkably colourful character appeared on the postal scene in Edinburgh. Peter Williamson, or 'Indian Pete', has caught the eye of every author so a detailed biography is unnecessary. Most of these Edinburgh details are taken from an admirable book recently published by A. Bruce Auckland and J. J. Bonar.* Born about 1730, he was kidnapped as a young boy in Aberdeen, sent to America, and was fortunate to be purchased by a Scotsman who had himself been kidnapped as a youth. Evidently with fellow feeling he treated Peter very well, educated him, and gave him his freedom and a substantial legacy on his death. Marrying and settling as a farmer, his farm was sacked by Indians and he was carried off

---

* *Penny Posts of Edinburgh and District* by Auckland and Bonar, Scottish Postmark Group, 1972.

but escaped. He later joined the British Army fighting the French and Indians, was wounded and captured by the French but was exchanged and discharged as unfit in 1757. Publishing the story to raise money, Peter's accusations caused Aberdeen magistrates and merchants to treat him as a vagabond and expel him, but from Edinburgh he sued the Corporation of Aberdeen and received substantial damages.

The numerous inventions to his credit included a portable printing press, and he published the first Edinburgh Directories and other books. Probably the knowledge of Edinburgh he gained in this, the influential friends he made at his coffee stall in the Hall of Parliament House, and the starting of the Dublin Penny Post combined as the spur for him to begin a penny post in Edinburgh. His first advertisement was in the Caledonian Mercury for 17 January 1774, and as this was thrice-weekly it could mark the beginning of the properly organised post. In December 1773 a few letters are known bearing an irregular stamp made from loose type, and these may be letters handed to his coffee stall for delivery; it seems probable that his post grew from this beginning.

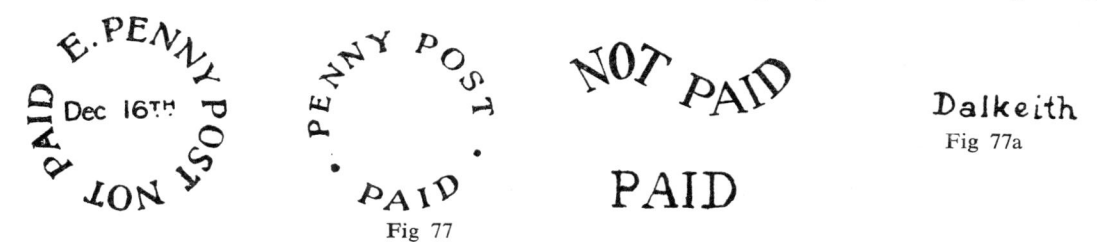

Fig 77

Dalkeith
Fig 77a

His first advertisement read,

"PENNY POST — LETTERS and SMALL PARCELS will be delivered to whom directed, every hour throughout the day, from nine o clock in the morning till nine at night, for one penny each letter or bundle, within an English mile of the cross of Edinburgh, to the west and south, and as far as north and south Leith — The following places are appointed for taking in letters etc for the PENNY POST — P. Williamson printer in Dunbar's close, Lawn Market; by Mr John Wilson, bookseller, front of the Exchange; by Mr James Grant, grocer, head of Halkerston's wynd; by Mr Patrick Lees, grocer, back of the City guard: by Mr James Anderson, grocer, head of Chambers close; by Mr Patrick Thomson, grocer, head of Dunbar's close; by Mr John Andrew, grocer, head of James's court; by Mr William Lockhart, shoemaker, Cowgatehead; by Mr William Ramage, grocer, Bristo street; by Mr John Rae, merchant, Grassmarket; by Mr Archibald Campbell, grocer, opposite St. Johns St, Canongate; by Mr. Alexander Lamond, merchant, east end of Crosscausey; by Mr John Gilbert, taylor, head of Leith Walk; by Mr. William Ronald, merchant, Tolbooth wynd, Leith, and by Mr Robert Williamson, vintner, on the shore of Leith."

From the beginning of 1774 two series of stamps begin for paid and unpaid letters, as Fig 77. It is probable that his stamps were made up from the type in his printing works, for all show signs of a homemade amateurism, and are usually irregular. Some have the date struck separately across the centre, and these are scarcer. It is not certain if more than one stamp each for paid and unpaid letters was used, and gaps between types makes it difficult to see what happened. Although the circular unpaid stamp is known until 1790 late examples are so worn as to be hardly readable. Few letters were paid, yet the circular paid stamp is unknown after 1777 which indicates that a number of unpaid stamps may have been used. In 1781 and 1790 two sizes of 'PAID' stamps are known and the circular unpaid was replaced by a serpentine stamp from 1790-93. All stamps of the Peter Williamson post are pretty rare, and very popular. In 1793 he was granted a pension of £25 a year, and Edinburgh's local post became a Government service. He had faced a certain amount of competition from the Clerk of the English Road (who ran his own penny post in Musselburgh, Dalkeith and Preston Pans with stamps as Fig 77a in lower case lettering) and another private post in Leith, but undoubtedly his post was very successful, and a benefit to the citizens. The Post Office from 1793 used a most attractive range of stamps for both the Chief Office and sub-offices, and they form an interesting group to collect (Fig 78).

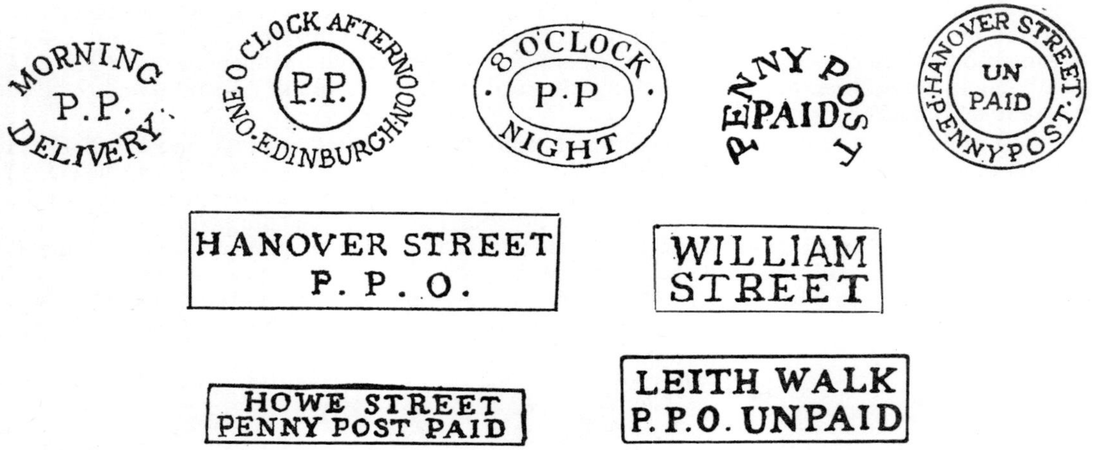

Fig 78

Whilst plans were being prepared to take over in Edinburgh, the first provincial penny posts began in Manchester, Bristol and Birmingham, all in 1793. Other places considered were Liverpool, Bath, Newcastle, York, Coventry, Leeds, Norwich, Exeter and Sheffield, but these were held over, as was Glasgow in Scotland. Some writers on this service have expressed surprise that the Post Office was so slow to extend the service in the 1790s, and suggest the 'local authorities' were possibly to blame: a study of postal documents available disproves this, as does the consideration of the background. London, whose service had run for a hundred years and more, had been allowed to run down badly, probably made little profit overall, and was in the throes of complete reorganization at a considerably increased cost. Dublin, the only other working example, had lost money in every year since it was founded twenty years before, and must have been very deeply in the red. Freeling was young, keen, very able and a strong believer in a local delivery system, but was newly appointed as Resident Surveyor in London. Despite his enthusiasm for local delivery he had to tread warily. Anthony Todd had been Secretary to the Post Office since 1762, thirty years, and was firmly entrenched. If Freeling was careful he was next in line, but Todd was against innovations or disturbances, and there were limits to the risk he would stand — why should he at his age, with a comfortable position.

Joyce goes into the salary position thoroughly, and says that the Secretary's was nominally unchanged since 1703 at £200 a year. Although this was an age when every salary and wage had perquisites officially recognized to assist it, Todd had each year a commission of $2\frac{1}{2}\%$ on the entire Packet ship expenditure (£2,136), a bye-salary the origin of which is unknown (£75), coach hire allowance (£100), Lloyds coffee house paid £100, fees on commissions and deputations (£154), twenty chaldrons of coal, twelve dozen wax and sixty four dozen tallow candles (valued by him at £103), an unfurnished residence and stables at the Post Office, eight pounds of tea and two dozen arrack from the East India Co. He still retained his former post as Clerk to the Foreign Branch, for which he received a salary of £50, an allowance of £100, £15 for coach hire, ten chaldrons of coal and thirty two dozen candles. The total was well over £3,000, so it is understandable that he would never resign and wanted only a quiet life. It is therefore greatly to Freeling's credit that despite the losses being made on the Dublin service, he got agreement to take over the Williamson post at Edinburgh and launched Birmingham, Bristol, and Manchester. Probably he was willing to try a penny post in the ten other cities, but the reports from the Surveyors on the spot were strongly against them. Liverpool, for example, was held over because although the revenue from general post letters was large (at £25,000 gross in 1799), it was separated from Cheshire by the Mersey, and had little beyond the town area. It had been found already that revenue in town areas was small, people preferring to save the penny by delivering the letters themselves. A further point to deter Freeling was that most postmasters were against the introduction of penny posts, whose revenue went to the Post Office — they had their private delivery service whose profits they kept, and they did not see why the Post Office should deprive them of it. Later, most of them were compensated.

Freeling had thirteen provincial cities on his short list from the reports sent in by the surveyors, and these were reduced to the three most likely to show profit: it is probable that if these had shown losses from the operation after two or three years, the whole proposal would have been scrapped, for a good start was essential. It may have been the coincidence that a change was necessary in Manchester that made this the first, but as part of the operation Sarah Willatt was pensioned at £120 a year, a sum that was well deserved. She became Postmistress on the death of her husband in 1772, and appears to have borne the entire work of the office with the assistance of a daughter and one letter carrier; two other daughters having contracted an illness from their postal work that resulted in their deaths. The surviving daughter was granted a personal pension of £40 p.a. after her mother's death.

It is probable that Stitt Dibden is correct in saying that Manchester began on 15 April 1793, although Calvert* makes it clear that it was intended to start on 5 April and a printed handbill dated 8 April says that four offices were open at Deansgate, Salford, High St, and Bank top near Piccadilly, with the Principal Office in Back Square and deliveries three times a day. The handbill continues that one penny would be charged for letters within the town, twopence for those in the country district. Letters might be put into the receiving houses for the General Post on prepayment of one penny. Letters were dispatched for delivery in Middleton, Ashton-under-line, Staley-bridge, Oldham, Saddleworth, and other places. An announcement in 'The Mercury' of 15 April changes the positions slightly, and places the principal office in Queen St, St Annes. Reports by the Surveyor, George Western, make clear that only three country offices could be set up (for good pay in London was considered nothing in Manchester) — Ashton to include Staleybridge, Oldham to cover Saddleworth, and Middleton. Eight letter carriers were authorized if six were insufficient and it was hoped to show a clear profit of £300 p.a.

In fact it got off to a flying start, quickly made £119 after paying letter carriers and receivers, and brought a clear gain to the revenue of £586 in the first year. Freeling must have been well satisfied with the results of his careful preparations. Within a month the Ashton carrier had so much business that he could not return until midnight, whilst at Oldham they had the advantage of an innkeeper who had been well established for many years with a private post — this was always a busy office. However, local agitation called it 'a common pot house' and the post was moved. In 1794 the penny post was extended towards Radcliffe, and three new receiving houses were opened at Dobcross, Staleybridge and Saddleworth: these used oval stamps as Fig 79, numbered 4, 5 and 6 from their opening until 1802. Meantime from 1800 Ashton, Oldham and Middleton used 1, 2 and 3 in a rectangle as Fig 80: all numbers except 7 and 11 are known in this type. From 1812 offices 1, 3, 4, 5 and 8 may be found in a square frame (Fig 81).

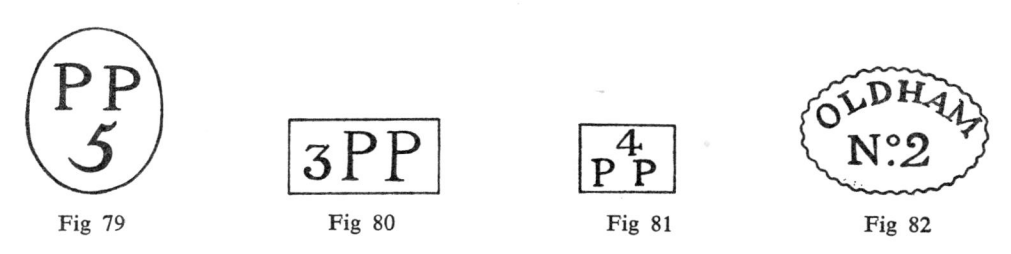

Fig 79

Fig 80

Fig 81

Fig 82

---

* Charles Calvert in 'A History of the Manchester Post Office, 1625-1900', published by J. E. Lea, Manchester 1970, appears to have confused the intention with the fact. Many authors quote the handbill of the 8th which says that the offices are open, but this could have been printed some weeks before the 5th. Dibden (in private notes) transcribes letters from the GPO Records which may not have been seen by Calvert. On 11 April Freeling sent the handbill to their Lordships, saying that Mr Western (the northern Surveyor) would circulate it on the day the Penny Post commenced, and later 'As Mr Western states that the Penny Post will begin next Monday'. On 16 April he confirms it should have begun on the previous day, and on the 23rd he encloses a report on it. It seems conclusive that 15 April 1793 marks the start of the first provincial penny post.

As the penny post system grew, more offices were added, and those known with numbered stamps are:

| | | | |
|---|---|---|---|
| 1 | Ashton-under-line | 7 | Didsbury |
| 2 | Oldham | 8 | Cheadle |
| 3 | Middleton | 9 | Wilmslow |
| 4 | Dobcross | 10 | Flixton |
| 5 | Staleybridge | 11 | ? Eccles |
| 6 | Saddleworth | 12 | Ratcliffe |

From 1814 Oldham used an attractive series incorporating its No 2 office number, some in serrated oval frames as Fig 82, which may have been to the design of the postmaster. A change in policy occurred in 1824, from which date new stamps as Fig 83 showed village names in types similar (but not identical) to the rest of the country. Some have P.P. below, others are framed. Manchester was also the only English town to have PENNY P. UNPAID, similar to Edinburgh but unframed and still with no town name. Why 1, 2 and 3 had no stamps until 1800 when 4, 5 and 6 had them in 1794 is not known. The first used by the town offices were oval as Fig 84 from 1809, for Ardwick, Ancoats, Salford, and Knott Mill.

Three months later a Penny Post began in a city of a very different nature, Bristol. The capital of the West Country for hundreds of years and enormously wealthy from shipping and trade with the colonies in America and the West Indies, Bristol was a close second to London in every way. However, whereas Manchester was young, thrusting, and growing very fast from the Industrial Revolution, Bristol's staid solidity placed it in a decline. It had suffered a very severe blow in the loss of the American plantations ten years before, and was engaged in a battle to preserve its very life blood, the slave trade. Why Bristol refused to adapt itself and accept the inevitable is a fascinating question, but by 1793 it had already lost part of its power, and by 1840 was just another city. Bristol used Fig 85, a circular design numbered 1 to 11, but no example of 4 to 6 has been found. 7 and 11 occur from 1794, 9 from 1796, 10 from 1799, 8 from 1803, 1 from 1810, 2 from 1812 and 3 from 1813. One or two letters are known with P P U (Penny Post Unpaid) about 1808.

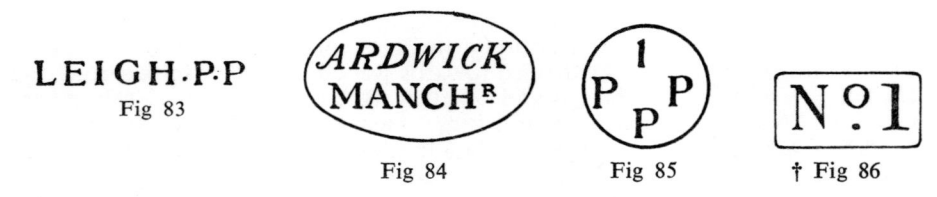

LEIGH·P·P
Fig 83

ARDWICK
MANCHᴿ
Fig 84

P 1 P
 P
Fig 85

Nº 1
† Fig 86

Ian M. Warn reports that the 1794 Bristol Directory lists five town receiving house addresses plus Hotwells and Clifton, and it adds that there are letter carriers to thirteen named villages. Directories from 1797 to 1814 give addresses of only Hotwells and Clifton receiving houses, but retain the details of country villages served, so there is little doubt that the town receiving houses were closed within a year or two for lack of business. On this basis it is fairly safe to guess that the Chief Office was numbered 1, town receiving houses 2 to 6. Hotwells and Clifton are known to be 7 and 8 at this period, but later the numbers were reallocated, Clifton being 1. 9 to 11 open up the possibility of stamps to 20 for the villages, but Geoffrey Oxley thinks it much more probable these numbers are for the rides and not offices. Presumably 1 was retained by the Chief Office to stamp letters that had been missed, but it seems that 2 must have been reallocated later. The farthest town office was ten minutes walk from the post office, so it is understandable that they were closed. It is likely that the numbers went to 12 in this early type.

Bristol Penny Post grew to cover a wide area, and differed from Manchester in using 'Bristol Penny Post' stamps, whilst the village struck the number in a rectangular frame as Fig 86. This was standard practice throughout the country until 1837, but Bristol continued with numbers to the end, and with numbers over 70 is by far the highest recorded for any penny post system. This does not mean that there were seventy offices at one time, as some may have been vacant.

Although out of context by date, a problem which worries many students can be mentioned here as it concerns Bristol. Although delivery did not start to every house on 10 January 1840, all evidence points to the last extra charges (including penny posts) having ended abruptly on this day. This will be gone into in detail later, but confirmation comes from a definite statement by Rowland Hill to this effect. It was made in a pamphlet of 1844 which surveys the working of Uniform Penny Postage*, and he should have known. Why, then, should the Post Office issue a large group of thirty five new penny post stamps to villages under Exeter on 30 October 1840, as well as other small groups in 1840 and 1841? Above all, why should Bristol have been issued with new types of three line penny post stamps with a movable date (which were more expensive) in January 1842, January 1844 and April 1847? These were used until 1852, twelve years after the penny charge had ended. In the front of one of the Proof Impression books in Post Office Records is a manuscript record of the prices of new stamps contracted for three years from 1 October 1842; most are not identifiable with certainty and no names are mentioned. Below a double line are entries which are named, Scottish, and much too cheap. These are:—

| Missent to Edinbro | brass stamp | 3/9 |
| 2 | brass do | 1/6 |
| 1 | do do | 1/6 |
| Aberbrothwick Penny Post | do do | 3/9 |

Arguments have continued since this entry was discovered: why the double rule which makes clear that those above it are not the same as those below, why should these be named stamps, why Scottish when the Scottish stamps were made in Edinburgh in 1842, and had separate contracts? Above all, why should prices be about a third of the prices above the line, agreed in London? There are suggestions that by some mistake in the contract, penny post stamps at 3/9d were so much cheaper than circular undated town stamps at 8/2d that the Post Office took advantage of it, and continued issuing them as name stamps when they were pointless. The author cannot agree with this because it ignores:

(1) the double line, which infers that this was the end of the contract agreed, (2) those above the line are prices of general types, those below are for individual named stamps, (3) those below the line, being Scottish, have no connection with the contract specified, (4) it is not likely a mistake of this kind would occur, or that the Post Office would take unfair advantage of it; if they did, they would issue all penny post stamps, and not a few isolated groups between the more expensive circular stamps, (5) it can have no connection with the group of Exeter stamps in 1840 and certainly not with those of Bristol in 1847, as the contract was 1842-45 only.

It seems most probable that entries below the line are notes on the comparable Scottish contract for reference, although possibly out of date, and that this has no connection. It is difficult to suppress a feeling that a penny delivery charge may have survived in certain cases, and Rowland Hill overlooked it. Another way in which Bristol covers can be unusual is that sometimes they have two different numbers on one letter. These are from receiving houses off the main routes, and the second number is the office at the junction with this route.

In late August 1793 started the third provincial post at Birmingham, on similar lines. In the London Gazette five town receiving houses have the addresses given (all of whom were grocers) and various villages are named in the country area. Here again, prepayment of 1d or 2d was optional, but for letters to be forwarded by the London or Cross mails it was compulsory. At this period, all penny posts were regarded as a local arrangement, and the charge could not be collected outside the area. Its introduction was shortly after the Postmaster of Birmingham, Mr Gottwaltz, was declared insolvent with debts of £4,000, but Mr Woodcock, one of his sureties, carried on the office until the Surveyor arrived to establish the Penny Post. Surprisingly it does not seem to have delayed it, and the first six weeks brought in produce of £47.17.0, but troubles were soon to come. Parts of these are well documented in the Post Office Records, and authors who mention the fight of Bilston and Halesowen normally say that they stayed out of the Penny Post — this is incorrect. It is clear that their private letter carriers were stopped, and both were in the scheme for about three months, after which they were removed and their own letter carriers resumed.

---

* *The State and Prospects of Penny Postage* by Rowland Hill, published by Charles Knight 1844.

The trouble was that letters had been delivered for a halfpenny (or less in some cases), and evidently the whole Birmingham scheme nearly foundered. The London Gazette notice listed, in addition to the five town offices, letter carriers to be dispatched 'every day except Monday to Solihull, Knowle, Sutton Coldfield, Hales Owen, Dudley, West Bromwich, Tipston, Wednesbury, Darlaston, Willenhall, Bilstone, and to the intermediate and adjacent places'. Disagreement exists here, for there is no evidence to show that Dudley, Willenhall, and Darlaston ever co-operated, and they may have been released in the same way as Bilston and Halesowen. Tipton came in very much later, so that was six failures out of eleven. Original allocations of numbers and the later issues reallocated are:

| *Original allocations* | | *Later issues* | |
|---|---|---|---|
| 6 | Solihull | 1 | Brierley Hill |
| 7 | Knowle | 4 | Oldbury |
| 10 | West Bromwich | 8 | Tipton |
| 11 | Wednesbury | 14 | Castle Bromwich |
| 12 | Sutton Coldfield | 15 | Handsworth |

No letters bearing 2, 3, 5, 9 or 13 have yet been seen. Is this like Bristol, with the five town offices occupying 1 to 5? It is very probable that the 1793 allocations were from 1 to 12 only. We do not know enough to be certain, but the psychological angle is important. These three penny posts were vital to Freeling's success and advancement, and he received regular reports. Town offices were excluded from the numbering in Manchester, but were included in Bristol, and this seems a typical summing-up of the two places. Money meant much more in Manchester than Bristol at this time, and it seemed likely that people would prefer to walk with a letter to the chief office in Manchester, but use the town receiving offices in Bristol. On this analysis, Birmingham had a closer affinity with Manchester, and the town receiving houses would be of smaller importance, unnumbered. As it happens, the Manchester ones just survived, and the Bristol ones were closed. At present it is uncertain if Birmingham's original allocation included the town offices.

Birmingham continued throughout with the same design of paid and unpaid numbered stamps for the country area (Fig 87), some being used after 1840, but new villages coming into the scheme had their name in the stamp. From 1825 the town offices had a different series, the normal village 'No 1' (Fig 86) in a rectangle, and these letters were struck with 'Birmingham Py. Post' in two lines at the Chief Office.

Fig 87

Fig 88

The only other penny posts set up in the early period were Glasgow in 1800 and Liverpool (which had developed considerably since the unfavourable report of 1792) in 1801. By this time, Manchester, Bristol and Birmingham were well established and showing a fair return, particularly in letters put in for the General Post. The gross produce of letters at Liverpool had been over £25,000 in 1799, the highest in the Kingdom, and only its geographical division by the Mersey had delayed it. The first quarter's produce of £71.9.9 must have been satisfactory when compared with well established Birmingham £268, Bristol £257, and Manchester £174 in 1801, but the figures for the same quarter in 1806 and 1807 are surprising — Birmingham £208. 9. 8d and £222.12.10, Bristol £238. 1. 4 and £267. 9. 8, Manchester £227. 3. 3 and £257. 1. 6, Liverpool £76. 1. 4 and £103. 8. 9. Another fact that may have delayed Liverpool is that its postmaster's private delivery at a halfpenny a letter brought a clear profit of over £100 after expenses, and Thomas Statham only retired in 1798 after forty-five years as Postmaster. It would have been expensive to buy him out earlier. The area covered was still only the small town area until 1825, when it was much enlarged and six receiving houses opened: in the first year their revenue was £170 with expenses only £36. An area of about six miles radius from the centre was now in the penny post

The Bath to London mailcoach in the very early morning. The guard is exchanging bags with the postmaster at his bedroom window without stopping the coach (reproduced by permission of the Post Office).

Plate 21

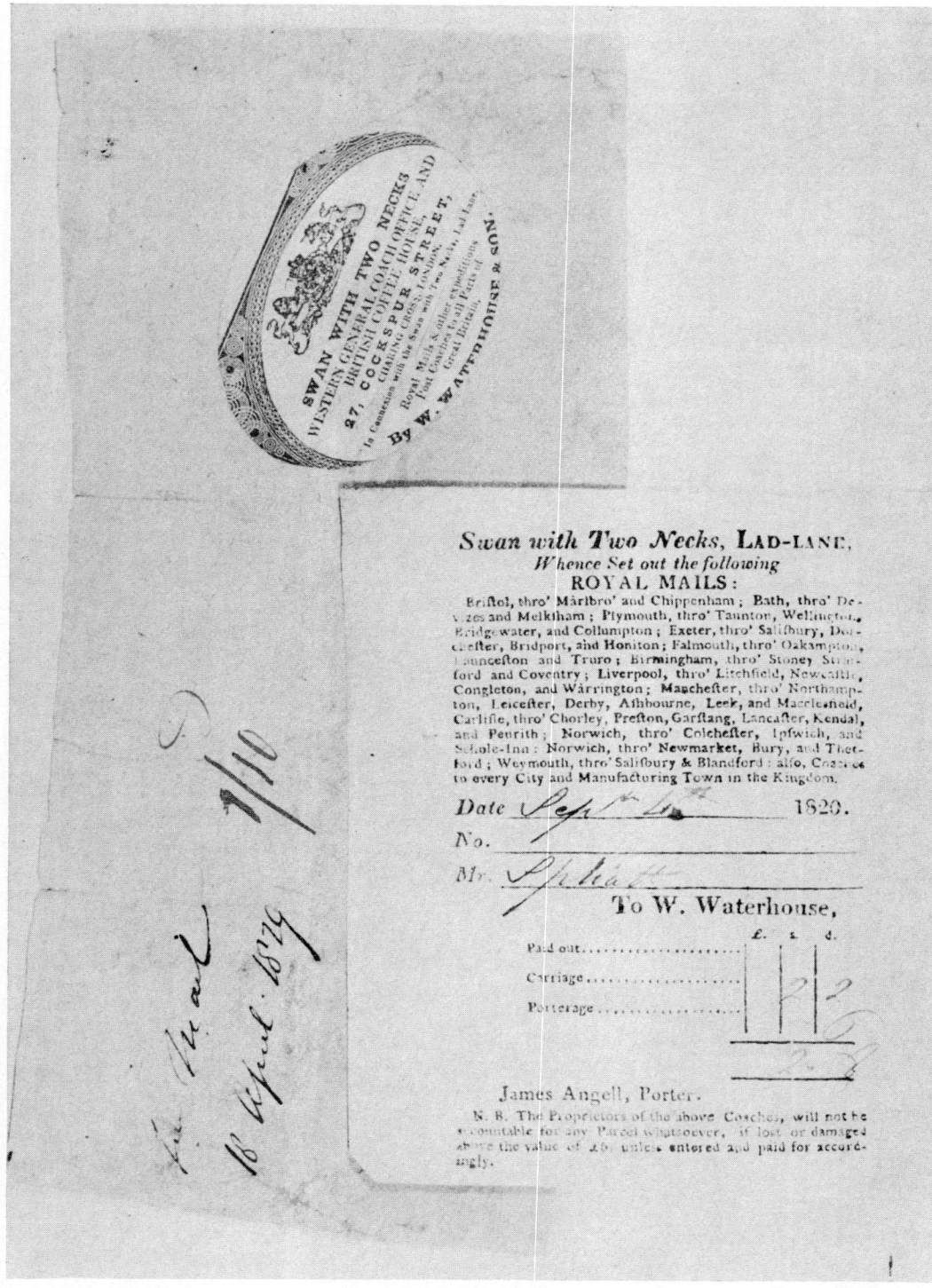

*Swan with Two Necks; part of the wrapper of a parcel sent from the Swan with its label stuck on, and a bill which lists the mailcoaches from the inn in 1820.*

**Plate 22**

# GENERAL POST-OFFICE,

### August 6, 1814.

WHEREAS CEPHUS BATES, the Rider conveying a Foreign Mail in a Cart from Dover towards Canterbury, was stopped about Nine o'Clock on the Evening of the First Instant, upon the Highway opposite the Guide Post to Barfrestone and Eythorne, by two Men on Foot, one of whom violently beat and bruised the Rider, and threatened to blow his Brains out; they robbed him of Thirteen Shillings and Six Pence in Silver, but did not attempt to take the Mail.

The Villain who so violently beat the Rider, had very large Whiskers, and was dressed in long dark Trowsers and a short Jacket.—The other Man was dressed also in dark Trowsers and a long Jacket.

Whoever shall apprehend and convict, or cause to be apprehended and convicted, both or either of the Persons who committed this Robbery, will be entitled to a Reward of

## FIFTY POUNDS,

over and above the Reward given by Act of Parliament for apprehending Highwaymen.

*By Command of the Postmaster-General,*

**FRANCIS FREELING,**

*Secretary.*

*An official notice regarding the robbery of a mail, with a very high reward for 1814. Note that the Foreign Mail came from Dover in a cart at this period (reproduced by courtesy of the Post Office).*

**Plate 23**

*The PANDORA, employed in the Packet Service from 1833 to 1842 (reproduced by courtesy of Alan W. Robertson).*

area, including Aintree, Garston, Walton, Wavertree and West Derby. The only stamp used had been 'Paid 1' Fig 88, but now fleurons came for Bootle, Crosby, Seacombe, Upton and Woodside as Fig 48a. No example of Upton is known.

**The Fifth Clause Post of 1801**

Analysis of the penny post details above gives an overall picture which is very favourable to Francis Freeling, and explains the curious timing of events. Although young and very new in his position, he showed traits characteristic of him to the end — undoubted genius as an administrator but lack of the spark that marks the innovator. Responsible to a Secretary who lived very well and had no desire for change, but fired with ambition to supply the need for local services away from the post roads, he adopted his surveyors' recommendations in 1793 and took no chances. Five were enough for the moment, for he would have to build them up, consolidate, and analyse their results. By 1800 he had realized the drawbacks of penny posts as well as their advantages: that they suited some places but not all. There are numerous examples of the persuasion he had to use on their Lordships — writing of the Shaftesbury post in 1806 he said:

'I beg to remark that where these Village Posts do no more than barely cover the expenses incurred separately for them, they are to be considered as highly satisfactory, for the complete accomodation they give to places, for the most part very ill served before their establishment, cannot fail to produce an increased number of Letters, the General Rates on which are felt in the total Revenue of the Post Towns to which the Villages are attached, though the separate amount cannot be stated. In some instances, we have perceived the Revenue of such Post Towns largely increased a year or two after such a Post has been established.'

It was a long time since one had heard of a leading postal official who saw beyond the immediate profit or loss.

His experiences persuaded him that apart from the cities of Liverpool and Glasgow, it was wiser to leave postmasters running their own town posts, and to concentrate on connecting villages with their post town in a more flexible manner. In writing of Liverpool whilst waiting for reports in January 1800, he could not resist saying: 'I beg to add that all these Country Posts originated with me, and have ever been a favourite scheme, and I have much regretted that hitherto no new circumstances could justify their extension.' The strong opposition in Birmingham undoubtedly influenced him to caution.

The 1801 postage act, 41 George 3 Cap 7, increased all postage rates, but the fifth clause was most important. It empowered the Postmaster General to collect or deliver to places that were not post towns, letters at such charges as were agreed with the inhabitants. The sixth clause emphasized that this power was not exclusive, and did not hinder the inhabitants from making their own arrangements for their letters. One cannot recollect any other example of the Post Office providing a service which they agreed should be in competition with existing arrangements. This gave Freeling the opportunity to run a variety of posts, each gauged to the needs of the particular area; a large number of 5th clause posts were set up, but there were no more penny posts for some years. The eighth clause allowed guarantees to be given to the Post Office by individuals or villages to cover losses incurred in the running of posts established under the fifth clause, and this was used in some cases (see later section). An interesting point which does not appear to have been noticed by writers is that the preamble of the 1801 Act repealed the 1765 Act, and every mention in later clauses of penny posts applied to London only. It would appear therefore that from 1801 all provincial penny posts were illegal: the date when they were legalized again has not yet been discovered, but the Post Office must have had a nasty shock when this was noticed.

The act came into effect on 5 April 1801, but it is uncertain if any 5th Clause posts ran successfully in that year. Kelvedon had two private posts, and because the one run by the Postmaster was losing ground to the post run by the Coggeshall villagers the former was to be made 5th Clause, but in October Coggeshall refused to agree. Nearby, Colchester to Dedham and Stratford in December 1801 may have been the only one. In January 1802 Watlington's private post from Tetsworth was unsatisfactory, so the receiver was subsidized £10 a year under the act. In February Epsom began to Ewell, Cheam, Sutton, and Banstead at one penny, whilst in May came Lamberhurst to Goudhurst and Flimwell to Ticehurst, Wadhurst, and Burwash. Esher,

Watford, Newcastle Staffs., and Newport Pagnell must have been about the same time. Maidstone, Dartford, Tunbridge, and Foots Cray all started in September 1802, and Leeds was in October.

A later report gives the second year's expenses and quarterly revenue of the earliest 5th Clause Posts as:

| Town | Expenses | Revenue to 5.7.02 | to 10.10.02 | to 5.1.03 | to 5.4.03 |
|---|---|---|---|---|---|
| Dartford | £ 49.19. 0 | — | £ 4. 3.10 | £ 18. 2. 1 | £ 16.18. 7 |
| Esher | £ 69.18. 0 | £ 18. 4. 1 | £ 21. 1. 8 | £ 18. 2. 7 | £ 20 est |
| Maidstone | £ 62 | — | £ 3. 2. 7 | £ 20. 1.10 | £ 20 est |
| Watford | £ 59. 8. 0 | £ 16.19.10 | £ 18. 1. 2 | £ 15. 9. 8 | £ 15.12. 4 |
| Tetsworth | £ 23. | £ 6. 6. 4 | £ 6. 0. 5 | £ 6. 5. 3 | £ 5.11. 9 |
| Newcastle, Staffs | £ 374. 2. 0 | £101.13. 3 | £106.13. 0 | £ 99. 0. 4 | £104.12. 4 |
| Leeds | £ 16. | — | £ 9.11. 1 | £ 9.12. 1 | £ 14.15.11 |
| Newport Pagnall | £ 49.17. 0 | £ 12. 9. 4 | £ 14.16. 4 | £ 15.14. 3 | £ 16. 0. 3 |
| Epsom | £ 66.16. 0 | £ 25.16. 3 | £ 29. 0. 8 | £ 26. 7. 3 | £ 26. 6. 4 |
| Footscray | £ 55. 4. 0 | — | £ 3.18. 4 | £ 15. 0. 4 | £ 14. 7.11 |
| Lamberhurst | £ 135.10. 0 | £ 18. 3. 9 | £ 31.14. 8 | £ 28. 5. 6 | £ 26.18. 5 |
| Tunbridge | £ 70. | — | £ 2.13. 8 | £ 16 est | £ 14. 7.11 |
| Colchester | ? | £ 20.19. 2 | £ 23.11. 5 | £ 22.19. 8 | £ 21. 8. 5 |
| Total | £1031.14. 0 | £220.12. 0 | £274. 8.10 | £311. 0.10 | £317. 2. 0 |

Although the profit is little over £100, it would be thought very satisfactory considering that many included some expenses for setting up the new post, and for new towns the revenue was only part of the first quarter. Probably it was equivalent to £250 in a normal year's running.

Fifth clause posts have been misunderstood consistently by all writers, and although this will do little more than whet the appetite, at least the fundamentals are believed sound. The thing to be borne in mind is that there were two distinct types of post. In the first period it was really a penny post under another name, tailored to the individual area and without its complications. Freeling was always willing to learn, and experience of the troubles with the penny posts in Dublin, Manchester, Bristol, and Birmingham convinced him that a more flexible system (to allow for differences in each of the areas) was necessary. Thus came the replacement of the exclusive right to run a post, but at a fixed penny a letter, by the non-exclusive 1801 system. Under this he could arrange anything suitable to both the Post Office and the inhabitants. In the second period (after 1809) it was anything but a penny post, and was used where a penny post was unsuitable. No handstamps have been found for the first period, but a number were used in the second and more may be found.

The table above gives the position in April 1803, and from this date there was a regular increase in posts opened. To mention a few recorded in the Post Office Records 1807-8:

Chipnam to Corsham and Pickwick was opened 15 February 1806 at a penny a letter either way: Expenses £31.4.0, Income £45.

Shaftesbury to Hindon opened 15 July 1805, a penny either way.

Bridgewater to Stowey at a penny a letter.

Axminster to Seaton, Beer, and Colyton at a penny a letter opened 3 February 1806.

Peterborough to Thorney and Crowland service was disturbed by the Boston coach (introduced 5 July 1807) but the ride was continued to Thorney at 21/- a week, the same as Spalding. A daily horse post was proposed on 20 August 1807 from Peterborough to Thorney and Crowland. Thorney inhabitants to pay threepence a letter on delivery, one penny a letter sent, which should bring £75.15.0 against expenses of £86, but as £9. 2. 6 had been paid to the Thorney post for many years, there would be no loss. It adds that the post for Crowland had been wholly private, and partly so for Thorney, so evidently a penny a letter was paid by Thorney people, and the Post

Office subsidized it at £9. 2. 6 a year. There are quite a few references to the Post Office assisting a private post in this way. Bampton to Dulverton had been a private 3-day post, was made a 5th clause post on 31 July 1807 at 1d a letter.

Southampton to Beaulieu was started 18 January 1806 but was opposed by the inhabitants; later agreed at 1d a letter, ½d a newspaper. Botley came in on 28 March 1807 also at a penny a letter. Chertsey had been a private delivery from Staines, paying a penny each way, but became a 5th clause from 12 April 1806, including Egham, Thorpe, and St Annes Hill, paying a penny on deliveries only, collections free. Blandford to Sturminster 5th clause began 30 March 1807 at a penny a letter, Guildford 5th clause ended in March 1808. Details of many more of these posts can be found in Freeling's minutes in Post Office Records.

Discussing Bridport to Beaminster with the Postmasters General, Freeling says that the only 5th clause posts that will be agreed in the future are dependent towns such as Beaminster; all villages or scattered houses will be made penny posts (see Olney later). This change of policy was forced on the Post Office by two serious defects in the 1801 act — the lack of exclusive rights to carry the mail, and the ruling some years before that although franked letters and newspapers were charged in the penny post, they must not be charged in the 5th clause post. This was not a sharp change, but during 1808-11 most of these posts were made penny posts. When things settled down, there emerged a pattern which was haphazard in the extreme, but seems to have worked. It is probable that Newcastle under Lyme, which was by far the largest 5th clause office in the 1803 list with receipts of £412 p.a., continued right through from 1801 to 1840 but even here, as in some other places, a penny post system was combined with it. Probably Newcastle had ten 5th clause post villages in the later handstamped period, and three in the penny post, but Bristol with seventy-odd in the penny post had only one 5th clause office whose letters were stamped — Thornbury. Bristol had other 5th clause villages over to Weston at an earlier date.

In this later period penny posts were the rule, and 5th clause posts the exception. They were all either 'dependent towns' as stated by Freeling, or odd places where a penny post was not a workable answer.

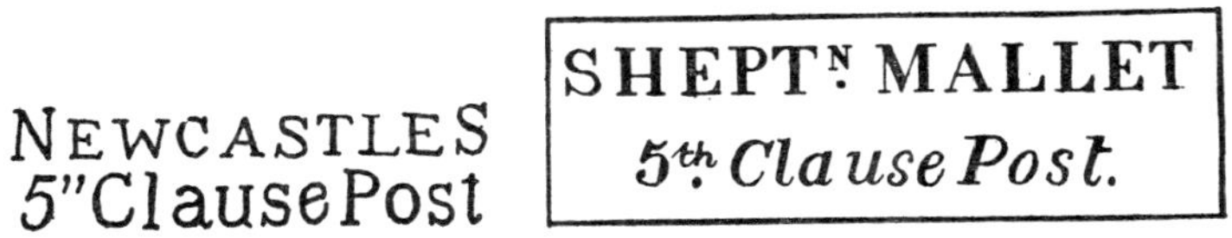

NEWCASTLES
5"ClausePost

SHEPT.ᴺ MALLET
5ᵗʰ. Clause Post.

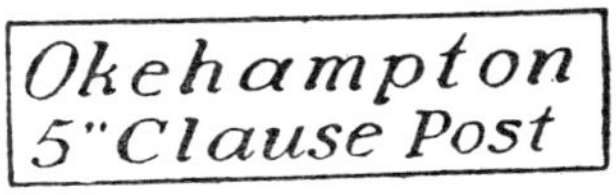

Okehampton
5"Clause Post

Fig 90

Fig 91

Wincanton
5" Cl: Post

SHAFTESBURY
5ᵀᴴ Cᴸ Post

Bristol
5"ClsPost

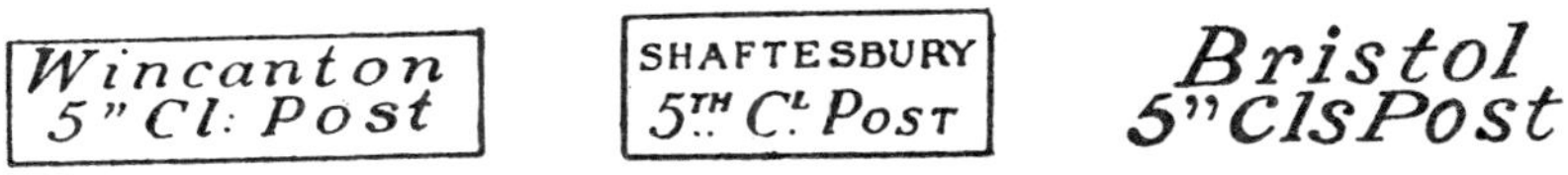

Fig 92

Handstamps of the 5th clause post vary quite a lot, and are unknown before 1816 (i.e. well into the second period of the posts). Broadly speaking, the types are similar to the penny posts, earliest issues having the town in capitals, clause post in lower case lettering (Fig 90). Then the town comes in lower case (Fig 91) and the later types have clause abbreviated (Fig 92). Towns known using handstamps (of which some are of the greatest rarity) are: Adderbury, Bristol, Crewkerne, Holdsworthy, Ilminster, Middlewich, Newcastle (Staffs), Okehampton, Shaftesbury, Shepton Mallet, Taunton and Wincanton, and in Wales Haverfordwest, Llaugharne, Pembroke and St Clairs.

A point which must be remembered is that the 5th clause post was purely a local arrangement, and therefore Freeling makes it clear that whilst penny post charges could be added to the General Post charge, 5th clause charges must be paid by the inhabitants who had agreed to the charge. This means that outward local charges must be prepaid (even when GP charges were unpaid), so they were not included in the manuscript figures on the front of the letter. Complications arose over 'open boxes' for outward mail, and again Freeling was adamant against them.

Open boxes were slits in the walls of receiving houses, through which people could slip unpaid letters into a locked box within. These were used as soon as the idea of penny post charges was accepted throughout the country, and were made compulsory in the early stages of the enlarged penny post system:

PMG Report Vol 30/289                                                                                                 7th August 1811
My Lords

I have the honour to propose to Your Lordships that all the Penny Post Receivers in the Country be ordered to keep open Letter Boxes, into which the Public may if they please, deposit their letters without paying the penny rate. The penny, when not paid, to be added to the General or Bye charge on the Letter.

At Bath and other Towns, where the Letter Boxes are thus open, it has been found most agreeable to the Inhabitants and, on a general scale, is likely to be most productive to the Revenue, for experience does show that the payment of any charge on putting a Letter into an Office operates as a restriction.

I am, therefore, of opinion that as there is no special advantage in taking the penny at the time the Letter is put in, it is very advisable that Your Lordships should order it to be discontinued everywhere.

The modern Acts of Parliament relating to the Twopenny Post in this Metropolis and its vicinity have purposely left the option with the writer.

                                                                                All which etc

Approved Chichester
        Sandwich

It is interesting that although London had insisted that the penny was prepaid from 1680 to the 1794 reorganization, this report called the permission to send local letters unpaid a most profitable part of the new plan. The London reform of 1794 had still insisted that General Post letters have local charges prepaid, and the penny posts of Birmingham, Manchester and Bristol of the year before had the same regulation. London relaxed this in or before 1796, with the introduction of the triangular 'PENNY POST NOT PAID' stamp, and the others may have done the same, but the earliest Provincial unpaid stamps known are 1808. It seems that the local charge was not allowed to be debited to people outside the area until they had become used to it, the service was known universally, and was expanding to other parts of the country. Manchester adopted open boxes in April 1804, and probably Bristol and Birmingham did the same.

Open boxes were still not allowed in 5th clause posts, for each was a private arrangement between the Postmaster General and the inhabitants, and the differing charges could not be enforced outside the area of that agreement. People were used to paying a halfpenny, penny, or even fourpence on handing in an unpaid letter, but unfortunately this means that the 5th clause rate does not show in the charge marked on the letter unless it is a local one. The same applies to inward letters — only the General Post rate is marked on the cover. This rule on open boxes was relaxed later, but probably in selected strong posts only, for the Post Office circulation map of 1823 has a diagram of the Newcastle Potteries offices, saying below: '5th clause post with open boxes, the Penny, when not paid, charged on delivery'. In 1825 Freeling had further doubts when the Western District Surveyor pressed for open boxes in the Bristol to Weston post; he took further legal opinion and again laid down that no open boxes could be allowed under the 5th clause, underlining 'the inhabitants must pay'. It is not clear if those at Newcastle were stopped.

An illustration of the local nature of 5th clause charges is Taunton, where the Halliday correspondence has provided a number of answers. The only letters bearing the Taunton 5th clause stamp are those from the village (in this case Old Cleeve) to Taunton 1818-19, although if any had been addressed to other 5th clause villages they should have had it. During this period letters going beyond Taunton were not stamped (although they may have had the No 3 receiving house stamp of Torr), probably because it was no concern of anybody else. Letters to Cleeve from Taunton do not have it, as it was added to the written charge automatically so was unnecessary, and the pity is that in 1819 the direction of the letters changes to inwards to Cleeve, so there is no clue how long it ran. The 1823 map shows Torr in the penny post, and Dunster as the only 5th clause office. A further surprise was that it appears to have been run at the general post charge of fourpence plus one penny for delivery in Taunton, so the advantage is not obvious. However, these letters were carried by the boy who took the general post letters from Taunton to Minehead (the latter being a post town not on a post road), and without the local receiving houses letters would have to be posted and collected from Taunton or Minehead, although they passed the door. In the local post, they would be posted or collected from Torr. Presumably a penny post would have entailed too great a loss, but it would be interesting to know how much was charged within the post — say Cleeve to Dunster.

Another large correspondence has shed light on the Charing and Maidstone district of Kent. For long an area of private posts, it is fortunate that there appears to be endorsed on the back of each letter the actual sum paid, if different from the figure on the front. Almost invariably the figure on the back is one penny more than the charge on the front: a postmaster's private post, one would say. Yet there is much more to it than that, and there is much here we do not understand.

Study of the papers in Post Office Records raises a number of problems so one can give only an outline here: this is a good example of the problems which make postal history so fascinating. On 25 September 1802 Freeling (Post 42, Book 21, pages 598 on) reported on the request of Sir Wm. Geary for a direct post from Maidstone to Tonbridge. Mr Aust, the Surveyor, proposed to do three things:

(1) guard the mail from Rochester to Maidstone
(2) establish a direct post from Tonbridge to Maidstone
(3) serve the villages upon or near the road by an arrangement under the 5th clause of 41 George 3.

'The direct post is to be tried experimentally under Sir Wm. Geary's indemnity against the expense agreeable to the 8th clause of the same act. Establishment of this direct post, giving to two parallel roads an opportunity of sending expeditiously instead of through London as at present, and opening to them a general and convenient communication with many parts of the County of Kent and into Sussex is certainly a regulation of the first accommodation to persons interested in it.' Mr Aust stated the expense as £151.10. 0 per annum, of which Sir Wm. Geary would guarantee £72. 2. 6, 'the villages will be served part by special messenger from Maidstone and part by a delivery from different receiving houses where the Rides will drop the Bags — the extra pence collected in this latter part of the delivery Mr Aust proposes with great fairness should be reckoned as revenue and go in aid of Sir Wm. Geary's guarantee. The other villages it is proposed to serve by a special messenger at an expense of £54. 2. 0 p.a., which Mr Aust is confident will be repaid.'

In his report, Aust breaks down the expense of the direct post as:

| | |
|---|---|
| For conveying from Maidstone and Rochester, £5 per mile p.a. | £45 |
| Waiting time at Rochester, 6d a day or, p.a. | £ 9. 2. 6 |
| Guards wages, 7s a week or, p.a. | £18. 5. 0 |
| Conveying mail Maidstone and Tonbridge, £5 per mile p.a. | £70 |
| Waiting time at Tonbridge 7s a week or, p.a. | £ 9. 2. 6 |

As this ride was in the middle of the night these costs were considered cheap (the timing was worked in with the London-Dover and London-Hastings mails), the three receiving houses were Hadlow, Mereworth and Wateringbury (to be charged on Tonbridge), and one penny a letter or ½d a newspaper was to be charged. Another post to Tovill, East and West Farleigh, Teston, Yalding, Hunton and Linton was also under the 5th clause, for which the costs were the messenger's wages (for 22 miles a day) of £49.18.0 and a Receiver at Yalding £4. 4. 0. This post would not lose, so was outside the guarantee.

The Kent County Archivist reports that Sir William Geary's residence was Oxenhoath, at West Peckham (adjacent to Mereworth), and that he was an M.P. for the county at this period. He had acceded to the baronetcy and estate in 1796, and came of a services family, his father being an Admiral. As an M.P. with free postage there would be little personal benefit from this post, so why should he be willing to pay up to £72 a year for it? Perhaps one of his constituents controlled a number of votes, and could bring pressure on Sir William Geary to carry this through for him. Certain it is that somebody would save a large sum in postage from the shorter route, and was willing to pay for it.

The postal implications appear strange, to put it mildly, and need much study linked with an analysis of the letters carried on the roads concerned. Firstly, Sir William just wanted a cross post similar to the hundreds already established by Ralph Allen and others: probably he had little knowledge of the 5th clause post. It can be assumed that Freeling refused an ordinary post, so Geary offered to guarantee the loss, but as cross posts were General Post (and no mechanism existed to accept guarantees for the General Post) it was disguised as a 5th clause local post. It was illegal to run these between two post towns, so each town ran one to the same villages, meeting and exchanging the General Post bags. So far this is typical Freeling, bending but not breaking the law if it provided a needed service (if the two 5th clause messengers met there was no reason why they should not carry and exchange General Post bags as well—in Taunton the reverse applied), but look a little deeper. Maidstone is the county town of Kent, and probably had a branch post from Rochester in 1661. Certainly by 1677 this branch continued through Maidstone as far as Ashford, and even in 1641 it had been necessary for the Corporation to issue an order stopping the 'unlimited number of postmen' going from Maidstone to the City of London. Only Richard Baldwyn on Monday, John Saywell on Wednesday and Samuel Skilton on Friday were authorized: if they journeyed on other days they forfeited 5s, and other people not sanctioned by the Mayor were fined 10s.*

The relevant facts and deductions are:

(1) A cross post was needed for general post letters, linking two old established roads, and to avoid loss it could only be done under guarantee. As guarantees had been legalized in the previous year for local posts only, two local posts were established which exchanged letters in the middle.

(2) The cost of these two local posts is given as £70, but there is no charge for salaries at the three receiving houses of Hadlow, Mereworth and Wateringbury (probably £4. 4. 0 each). The guarantee could not be more than the cost (assuming these receivers were unpaid) and the balance of £2. 2. 6 can bear no relation to the cost of three receivers, so £72. 2. 6 cannot have been the full cost of his part of the post.

(3) A guarantee of half the cost was normal, and was considered safe, for if the loss exceeded half the cost the post would be stopped.

(4) It is impossible to make £72. 2. 6 from any combination of expenses, even ignoring the £70.

(5) The phrase that Mr Aust proposes with great fairness that the extra pence collected should go in aid of Sir William's guarantee is revealing, for what other revenue was there to set against it legally? If the penny a letter he mentions was added to General Post letters as well (e.g. those from Rochester to Hastings) and deducted from the guarantee this charge was completely illegal, yet where else could the revenue come from? This seems to be proof of the General Post nature of the guarantee, in fact if not in name. Charges in the General Post were laid down by Act of Parliament, and even local General Post charges such as the Milford to Waterford halfpenny required a special Act.

Accepting, therefore, that the guarantee must have been for all the items listed by Mr Aust, Sir William was charged for the following in addition to the cost of the new post he wanted — charged for them in the sense that he would refund up to £72. 2. 6 of any failure to cover these expenses:

(1) the cost of the Rochester to Maidstone post, which the Post Office had run for at least one hundred and forty years before this without assistance.

---

* *The Postal History of Maidstone*, S. J. Muggeridge, Postal History Society, 1972.

(2) a guard who had not before been thought necessary. Incidentally, how did one guard a horse post without a charge for a second horse — did he ride pillion?

(3) waiting time for the two postboys to link with their respective mails.

The only reasonable expense in this £81.10. 0 is the waiting time at Tonbridge, £9. 2. 6. It seems very much like blackmail, but much more work has to be done before this and the Charing post are understood.

To revert to Charing, which was never in this 5th clause system, it would appear to have maintained its private post until joining the Maidstone penny post system in 1817 as No 8 receiving house. Letters from the 1790s show this with, say, a 4d charge on the front and 5d on the back (well before the act of 1801) and these continue through the years with the extra penny. Confirmation comes from a letter from Freeling of 2 November 1818 (PMG 33/505) saying that the Postmaster of Maidstone had charged an extra penny on all penny post letters delivered by him, applying it as a perquisite to his own use: he thinks it was done through ignorance of the regulations and suggests the offence is pardoned. At this time local letters can be found charged either twopence or threepence, but from 1819 they are a regular penny.

Yet there is much evidence against this, for in 1801-2 Charing was issued with a boxed mileage stamp of a type usually sent to post towns. There are exceptions, of course, but it is an indication and it seems to have been used for about three years only. Secondly, analysis of letters from London to Weller Norwood at Charing shows that until 1816 or later postage was 8d + 1d (rated by London at 50-80 miles) but from 1819 or earlier the charge was 7d + 1d (rated by London at 30-50 miles). No letters are available at the moment between these dates, but it would seem that when Charing came into Maidstone Penny Post in 1817 the order went out that letters were to be charged to Maidstone (below 50 miles) rather than to Charing (above 50 miles). Yet if the Post Office provided no service from Maidstone to Charing (although the post boy rode through there on the way to Ashford) London letters should always have been charged to Maidstone; if they did provide a service, how is it that the Maidstone postmaster could add a penny to each letter when they were already rated to Charing?

Thirdly, in Post Office Records is a map of 1813 which complicates matters still further. A large number of villages are marked 'R.H'— receiving houses: this is to be expected on penny post and 5th clause routes, but many are on main or General Post routes. In particular, Charing and other villages on the Rochester-Maidstone-Ashford road (which incidentally is shown as continuing to Brabourne Barracks) are so marked. These must have been General Post receiving houses, one would assume, and nothing is known of village GP R.H. If they were, there is no possible reason for the postmaster of Maidstone to add his extra penny, but it would explain London charging letters for 51 miles (8d) and not for 38 miles (7d). Fourthly, letters from Sandwich to Charing are addressed either via Ashford or Maidstone, the former being a penny less, yet on this 1813 map and in all records seen there is no connection between the coastal road from Dover to Romney (where it ended, with no road on to Rye) and the Ashford road at Brabourne: evidently there must have been a linkage of some sort. The numerous other discrepancies in the existing letters, when compared with the regulations, make one say that there will be no solution until much more work and study have been done.

Another interesting story is the post from Newport Pagnel to Oulney, Bucks. Oulney had been served by a 5th clause post at a penny, but the inhabitants wanted it at a halfpenny. This was refused, for the produce was only £59. 5. 8 a year with expenses at £57.17. 0. In a minute of 5 January 1808 Freeling stated that he had instructed that no further messengers be sent for the present 'for the people of Oulney absolutely mean to discontinue paying the Penny'. He recommended imposition of a penny post, but late in the month had second thoughts, for Oulney was a market town which had had a small allowance for its post: revenue was probably between £200 and £300 a year* and it was wiser to make it a sub-post town to Newport. This important document deals with the general situation (PMG Reports Vol 27/521) and ends —'I beg further to remark that the Penny Post Act has, with respect to the Country, been almost dormant after excepting the great Towns of Manchester, Birmingham, Liverpool and Bristol. The 5th Clause of

---

* This is an interesting admission — private carriers were taking four times as much mail as the Post Office.

the 41st Geo. 3, Cap. 7 was introduced for the purpose of trying experiments by agreement with the Inhabitants, and all the Posts under it would have answered well if Franks and Newspapers had not been lately declared to be excepted from charge, under the Penny Post they are not and, therefore, that is the preferable mode for the future and experience has shown in the other Posts if there be a sufficient number of Letters at the outset to pay the extra expenses, the Letters are afterwards sure to increase, and that Revenue and Public convenience proceed together. I think it necessary to mention to Your Lordships that some years ago a Post, under the 11 of the King was proposed to this neighbourhood, but at that time the private messengers had influence with too many of the Inhabitants to enable the Postmaster General to do it with any success, and perhaps it may now be the same, which shows the preferable nature of Penny Posts, as they allow no option.

All which etc. F. Freeling.

To be settled at the next Board.
        Sandwich

I think a trial should be made.
        Sandwich
        Chichester'

However, things got so bad that all post to Oulney was withdrawn, and the inhabitants were left to make their own arrangements by private messengers from 5 April 1808. In October 1810 they asked for an official post again, and the Surveyor (Mr Scott) proposed a superb compromise which was endorsed by Freeling—that again under the 5th clause all letters delivered in Oulney should be charged one penny, but no charge to be made for the letters returned from there. This in effect granted the people their request, assuming that a person wrote as many letters as he received, but allowed the Post Office to maintain its penny charge. Finally on 7 November 1810 he reports that the expenses of re-establishing the post were £64. 8. 0 and the extra pence on the letters were nearly the same. The Oulney Receiver, who had continued to act for the locals all the time, had asked for his post office allowance for the two and a half years, but as he was a ringleader in the agitation this was refused. He kept his job, though.

**Later Provincial Penny Posts**

It is impossible to go into this in detail for a book should be written on this subject alone. The ramifications are enormous, and the legal complications considerable. As has been said above, most local posts were run under the 5th clause of the Act of 1801 until it was found that free letters and newspapers could not be charged, although they could in the penny posts. From 1808 there was a move from 5th clause to penny posts to counteract this, and from then the growth of penny posts all over the country was very steady. The Select Committee on Postage report of 1837 lists more than a thousand penny posts, and yet a letter from Col. Maberley (Secretary to the Post Office after the death of Freeling) gives timely warning to those students who grasp odd facts without proper background information. This recollected that a very large number were omitted; the details were needed urgently, so he just asked the Surveyors and they compiled the lists from memory, or with inadequate checking. Even documents of the greatest importance can have mistakes, and can be open to suspicion if they disagree with the known facts. Another danger is that many show only the intention, and may not have been carried out.

Shifnal in Shropshire may possibly have been the first penny post after the major cities of 1793-1800, for its establishment to Wenlock, Broseley, and Madeley was notified on 20 October 1806, with expenses of £176. 1. 3 and estimated produce of £238. 8. 0. This is very early. Most of the 1808-9 posts were conversions, some of which caused trouble with the local people. Coggeshall in Essex is remarkable for having used a large circular town stamp with movable date plugs in 1790 (see Fig 41 under town stamps): this is only three years after London had its first movable date stamps, and thirteen years before any city in the British Isles (unless one includes the Bristol and Exeter Bishop marks of a hundred years before.) There is nothing like it, and it was considered the work of a local blacksmith for a receiver who was proud of his position. Recently a note of Stitt Dibden's has been found that on 2 November 1809 Freeling minuted the Postmaster General that the private messenger employed from Coggeshall to its post-town of Kelvedon was accused of fraud, but the inhabitants wished him to continue. As his employment would be illegal if a penny post was established, it seemed a good opportunity to introduce one, and Freeling added 'coggeshall is a place where measures of Government meet with much opposition. The Penny Post messenger is to be armed with a brace of pistols.' It must be, therefore, that the Coggeshall stamp is the date stamp of a private post, not a Post Office receiver. Kelvedon Penny Post stamp is one of the earliest, being known in 1811, and Coggeshall was its only receiving house.

Many others in addition to Birmingham, Oulney and Kelvedon were enforced against violent local opposition, in some cases so strong that the Post Office had to give in and revert to a 5th clause or private post. In other cases the opposite applies; opposition to the terms of a 5th clause post hastened its conversion — local posts in general seem to have been a headache to poor Francis Freeling. Blandford to Sturminster became a penny post in 1808 because the local people objected to the extra charge of twopence for delivery. Again, sometimes local troubles were used as an excuse for conversion, but in many cases the only reason was the advantage to the Post Office of the penny post system, with its monopoly of letter carrying and the charges allowed on Free letters and newspapers. Legal bickering was extensive and voluminous, residents of Cheltenham even trying to insist that letters put into the penny post 'to be kept until called for' should not be charged any postage at all. This naturally was refused — they could have the letters delivered, but if they preferred to collect them they must pay the penny. Other cases included the man in Bath whose garden backed on to the free delivery area, but his house was clearly in the penny post.

Ottery St Mary is another village with an interesting story, and, like Kelvedon, its letters with Honiton Penny Post are among the earliest stamps, starting in 1811. Could it be that the trouble spots were issued with stamps first, to enable an accurate check to be kept on letters and revenue from them? On 18 April 1811 the Surveyor (our old friend Mr Aust) had reported that the Honiton 5th clause post to Ottery was still losing money, now £12. 8. 0 per annum, and he proposed to convert it to a penny post which should pay its way. Despite this loss Mr Horsey, the receiver, was dissatisfied with his £10 p.a. salary and had gone to the lengths of resigning in protest. He wanted to be reinstated when Mr Baker, a respectable shopkeeper, was found to be happy with the salary of £10, but it was accepted that they could not 'indulge such capricious behaviour' and Mr Baker was appointed. A month later a letter from Ottery has a 'Penny Post Unpaid' stamp*, so they must have moved very rapidly. Logic tells us that this must have been struck at Honiton, and yet there are discrepancies of ink etc., which could indicate that it was applied at Ottery. The normal Honiton Penny Post is known from August 1811, but in 1819 Ottery possessed a town stamp, and was using two different 164 mileage stamps in 1823 and 1824-5. This is most surprising; sometimes stamps were issued by favour to places not post towns, but three different ones is rather excessive for a penny post receiving office. It may have been a post town for a year or two. In June 1826 it returned to the fold with the normal boxed 'No 13' (Fig 86) struck at Ottery and 'Honiton Penny Post' at Honiton, but in November went off the rails again with a home-made '13 OTTERY' stamp. Letters may have either Exeter or Honiton Penny Posts, so it sent letters in both direction (see the illegal twopenny posts later). In August 1827 the normal No 13 receiving house stamp returned, but in 1833 a new local 'OTTERY 13' appeared, and an unclear strike of September 1831 could even be 14 OTTERY. Finally 1839-40 saw the use of a named village stamp — Ottery St Mary Penny Post. These covers are listed by Vernon Rowe, and form quite an array for a small village receiving house.†

Ottery St Mary received its number 13 from the Exeter Penny Post, although it began in the Honiton group, and early letters via Honiton have no number. It may have been made a Post Town in 1819-25, as it is difficult otherwise to explain the use of a town stamp and two mileage stamps 1819-25. Although the principles of the allocation of stamps are not known, some sub-offices given stamps have the mileage of their post-town, not their own distance from London: in this case, however, 164 is Ottery itself (Exeter 176, Honiton 159). It is difficult to see three stamps issued by favour in a few years, and local pride probably inspired the two later stamps 13

---

\* Abergavenny and probably Bath are the only other towns known with unpaid stamps in the normal series.
† 'Postal History International' October 1972, Proud Bailey Ltd., 25 Meeting House Lane, Brighton.

OTTERY and OTTERY 13. Similar examples occur for OLDHAM No 2, SEATON No 2, and Newent No 3. It is unsafe to be dogmatic about receiving house numbers at present, for some systems changed to accommodate new villages, others used the next numbers, depending on the area. Some filled vacant numbers with new offices, others added on. Systems are known where a clockwise allocation was held to strictly, causing a change of other numbers to accommodate a new office. It is just possible that if the 14 OTTERY stamp is proved beyond doubt the numbers were changed about 1828-9, then returned to normal in 1832, but it is more probable 14 was an error. Mr Rowe finds that 13 had been used by Broadclyst before its allocation to Ottery, and Exeter was a big system.

Many other cases of equal interest can be found, and a great deal of work remains to be done. The types of stamp issued seem to be fairly consistent by date — in certain periods certain types were cut. Nearly all the early stamps (from 1811) used Fig 93, with the town name in capital letters and Penny Post beneath in lower case, but two interesting exceptions are Romford (which had the name in lower case) and Exeter (which was entirely capital letters, enclosed in a rectangle, Fig 94). It may be that these were experiments to compare the appearance and both occur for one other town — the former for Ross, the latter Berwick. A few towns then had the first standard type abbreviated to Py P, but in the middle period the majority showed both lines lower case, in a rectangular frame. Again, some stamps abbreviated Penny to Py. In the 1830s most issues were unframed, and Bristol, Bath, Exeter, Taunton, Southampton, Blandford, Devonport and Plymouth used a three line stamp with a movable date in the middle line. These would have been more expensive, and the allocation seems peculiar. The others are lower case stamps and to 1837 are normal lettering, similar to the earlier stamps. In this year a change of policy occurred, for Col. Maberley (who had just become Secretary on the death of Freeling) admits that the Post

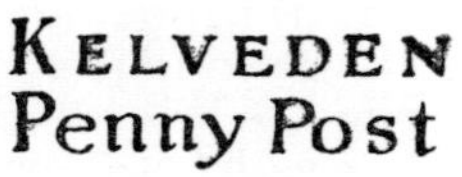

**KELVEDEN**
Penny Post

Fig 93

EXETER
PENNY POST

Fig 94

*London Colney*
*Penny Post*

Fig 95

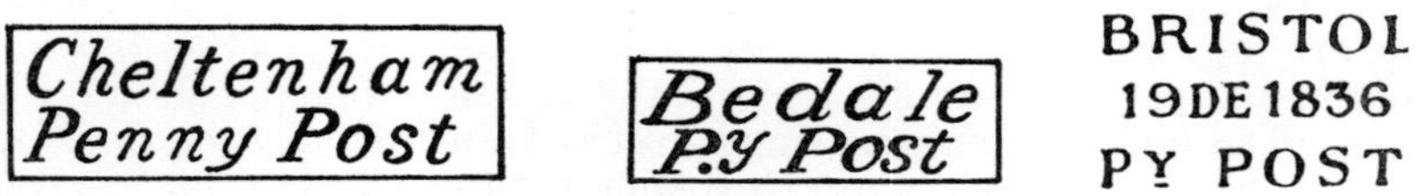

*Cheltenham*
*Penny Post*

*Bedale*
*Py Post*

Fig 96

BRISTOL
19 DE 1836
PY POST

Office in London did not know what was going on, and had no certainty whether local charges were included in the General Post charge or not. It was necessary to reverse the policy observed since the penny post stamps began, and replace the village numbered stamp with the village name. This entailed issuing a very large number of new penny post stamps, and he adds that some cities which had no penny post system would also be issued with stamps for letters collected by the carriers on their rounds, the pence from these letters being frequently pocketed. This 1837 type is called the village type, and though similar to the earlier type it is recognizable by the thin light lettering which is narrower, oval letters which had been more round, and closer spacing. This is Fig 95, and some other standards are Fig 96. It is curious that major cities such as Leicester and Colchester should use the 'village type', but presumably the former was for those collected by the letter carriers, and the latter was to replace a stamp very badly worn. The type depends on the date of issue.

A final point with regard to Col. Maberley's remark mentioned above about charging in the local posts. This was written shortly after the investigation by the Select Committee of 1835 into the penny posts, and in the Ninth Report (pages 66-7) it is made clear that in many places where penny posts existed, delivery of town letters was a perquisite of the postmaster at a halfpenny or one penny; the penny post supplied villages nearby. George Welch said under examination that the total sum paid for private delivery in a town was never large, but had to correct his evidence later, saying then that postmasters such as Newcastle and Brighton received large sums from this source. It would appear that these sums were taken into the revenue shortly after the enquiry, and a penny post stamp might have been issued if none was in use. Suddenly in 1837, more than 250 towns and cities were given penny post stamps, and every one was a post town in its own right. As to charges written on a letter, observation leads one to think that as a general rule unpaid local charges on posting were included in the figure written by the sending post town. This could not include penny posts for delivery, the charge was not altered later to include them, so these were additional. Thus if a penny post stamp is at the sending end of the journey it is included, but if at the delivering end it is not. The same rule applies to London mail (where it could be checked) to or from the provinces. If there is a penny post at each end it is probable that one is additional and one is included.

**Guaranteed Posts**

Until recent years it was said that there was only one guaranteed post — Glencarradle which was probably across to the island of Jura, and used a stamp from 1840. It is now certain that guaranteed posts were widespread in the thinly populated parts of England, Wales and Ireland in addition to Scotland, but no idea of their extent has yet been obtained. No other handstamps were used, as far as is known at present. Briefly they are post office deliveries to villages and houses which were uneconomical, and which would only be undertaken on condition that the loss incurred was guaranteed by the local people. This system began under the 5th clause posts, being authorized by the 8th clause of that Act, but the writer has strong objection to the statements of reputable authors that the 5th clause posts were a guaranteed system, and that the inhabitants agreed to make up the loss. Some go so far as to state that 5th clause were not part of the official Post Office, and the messengers were employed by the Village. This is utter confusion of the facts, and has arisen from the 9th Report mentioned above, page 66. George Welch did say that they were guaranteed, but he was speaking of the posts in 1837, and nowhere does he *imply* that they were unofficial posts run by the inhabitants. The Act of 1801 gave no power to the Post Office to claim back losses on the posts unless guaranteed, and frequent references in Freeling minutes show that some did run at a loss without recompense. Ottery St Mary has already been mentioned, and many others have been seen. Proof that usually the Post Office had no power to enforce repayment of losses by the inhabitants is the number that were stopped after a year or two because they lost too much money.

The explanation lies probably in the uses to which this clause was put. Its value was to give freedom to both sides to make any agreement that suited the local conditions, and whilst in the 1801-10 period it is certain that most local posts were run at an agreed flat price per letter, there was nothing to prevent the Post Office saying that posts which showed consistent losses would have to cease unless the local people would guarantee the loss. There may be a combination of both — in 1808-9 Chester to Northwich was abandoned, and the guarantors were required to make up the deficit (PMG reports Vol 26, page 639). Another means of balancing the books was that in some cases it was agreed that franks and newspapers should be charged a penny, although this was specifically disallowed by decision of the Law Officers. Thus on 27 August 1810 Freeling asks permission to run posts from Norwich to Loddon and to an area to the east of Coltishall, in both cases at twopence every letter and one penny for newspapers (the former would include free letters). The letter carriers were to be paid fifteen shillings a week, the receivers £8 per annum, and although these payments were secured out of the revenue, the post was dependent on guarantees against loss being forthcoming. Similarly in 1807 a post from Knaresborough to Ripley in Yorkshire had been established at one penny halfpenny per letter on delivery, but the letter box to be free (i.e. no local charge on outward letters). Sir John Ingleby and Mr Trappes guaranteed this post, but regularly it lost money and in March 1812 a minute was approved to try it as a penny post for a year, and to wind it up if still unsuccessful.

This period may well have been forgotten by George Welch in 1837, or possibly he was not in the Post Office thirty years before he spoke. It seems that if unpromising 5th clause posts were run by the Post Office at the request of local people, these were guaranteed, but the large majority the Post Office wanted run, and on these there was no guarantee. Things had changed in the 1830s for most were converted to penny posts, and those left were unlikely to lose, but there had been a considerable growth in what might be called requested services. Large estates and villages wanted their post delivering, and the best way was guaranteed posts, for they knew they were receiving it at the bare cost to the Post Office. After the 1840 reforms it is likely that they increased, or certainly large sums came in annually from guarantees. They may have continued where needed until nearly 1900, when free delivery of some sort became a reality all over the British Isles. This period will be dealt with in more detail under Uniform Penny Postage.

**The Illegal Twopenny Post**

This is a subject about which one has to be careful in the present state of knowledge, for it is difficult to state facts. To recapitulate for a moment, from 1635 'to post a letter' meant that it was sent by the General Post from one post town to another post town, and had to be collected. From 1682-3 when Dockwra was suppressed, the phrase was enlarged to include a post inside London, and we had the General Post Office and the Penny Post Office. That was all for nearly a hundred years, until Dublin had its Penny Post, and from 1793 Edinburgh and the three major cities. Nowhere else in the British Isles did the Post Office provide any local service at all before 1801, although many private posts existed. Thus the General Post rates are most important, and especially the minimum rate (being the lowest charge to use the post). Before 1711 the minimum was twopence below eighty miles, and until 1765 this was threepence. In that year it was realized that threepence for a mile or two kept large quantities of letters in the hands of the private carriers, so new rates were introduced below this of a penny for one post stage (varying from eight to fifteen miles) and twopence for two stages. In 1784 this became twopence and threepence, eighty miles being fourpence, and 1796 saw the variable stages eliminated (again with a heavy increase) and the minimum threepence for fifteen miles. In 1805 the lowest General Post charge was made fourpence, an appalling imposition because the 5th clause posts could not apply to letters between two post towns. This meant that whilst letters to a village from the post town twenty miles distant could be one penny, those between two post towns five miles apart must cost fourpence, twenty miles fivepence.

It is not known how the movement started, for the story is confused by 5th clause posts, private postmaster's posts, and carriers' letters, but letters rated twopence can be found right through the period when there was no such charge. Some of them were postmasters' private posts, but all have mileage, circular date stamps etc. and this could not apply where a penny post was in operation in that direction. There is evidence that an unofficial movement developed among some postmasters who realized that this minimum of fourpence was exorbitant. Two probable reasons for this are:

1. Postmasters running a 5th clause post in opposition to private carriers could not compete against the carrier's penny or halfpenny.
2. In areas where a penny post operated (excluding all private carriage of mail by law) some postmasters realized the iniquity of sending letters fifteen to twenty miles for a penny in one direction, and fourpence for four or five miles in another, purely because the latter was to another post-town. They had to live with the inhabitants who must have been very rude about it.

It is impossible to pinpoint the beginning or the details, but a realization grew that if they could run a 5th clause or penny post to an intermediate village, house, or even a tree, and the neighbouring town ran their penny post to the same house or tree, letters could be exchanged for twopence (actually 1d + 1d). This was half the authorized rate allowed between two post towns, however near, and may be the reason some villages were offices in two posts. Two cases have been described already in which this bending of the law was done officially — Maidstone to Tunbridge and Exeter to Honiton, using Mereworth and Ottery St Mary as joint receiving houses for two 5th clause posts. Others from about 1800 may have been official or private, but it would be difficult for Freeling to stop it in some towns when he suggested it for others. Even more surprising is that Ottery continued to do it under the penny post, for the twenty mile journey should have been fivepence and regulations for the penny posts were rigid. As there was no increase for heavier letters, the loss was greater than it would appear.

This spread to other penny posts, and came into the open in 1818 in the case of Plymouth to

Plymouth Dock (renamed Devonport 1 January 1824). Only two miles apart, officially the fourpence charge had been enforced although twopenny letters are believed to have been seen before this date. On 6 November 1818 a letter from Freeling (PMG Reports 407/1818) stated that Plymouth Chamber of Commerce was pressing for the Penny Post Acts to be applied between Plymouth, Stonehouse and Dock. On the analogy of Croydon being threepence in the London post, although a Post Town, the Solicitor considered it would be legal to charge a twopenny rate; it was hoped this would stop the fall in revenue (which was down from £170 to £120 in three years) and it was accepted. Letters in the General Post for Stonehouse were charged one penny extra, as were those for delivery in the town of posting, but those posted in one town for another were charged twopence. The reduction caused another sharp fall in revenue to £45!

It must be understood that this applies only to mail between two post towns less than fifteen miles apart; letters in some penny posts had been subject to a twopenny charge for the outer (country) area since 1793, and as more were established larger cities adopted it where necessary. Some Scottish offices used a stamped 2, but in England Leeds seems the only office. Sheffield and Harrogate used stamps as Fig 97 with twopenny post in words, but both are very rare.

*TwoPennyPost*

† Fig 97

In 1833 this charge was authorized from Edinburgh to Leith, and then Greenock to Port Glasgow, Paisley to Johnstone, Falkirk to Grangemouth, Linlithgow to Boness, and Anstruther to Pittenweem, all being under three miles apart. In December 1835 came Harrogate to Knaresborough, and although only Ramsgate to Margate and Portsmouth to Gosport are mentioned, the words 'and several other places similarly situated' show that more had been recognized officially since 1833 in England. The number of towns known from letters well before 1833, however, is evidence that this was a movement started by the postmasters themselves quite without authority, which became so strong that Freeling was forced to give in: he makes clear that before 1833 the only one authorized was Plymouth to Devonport.

Late in 1836 a blow fell when the legal advisers to the Post Office reversed their decision, and ruled that there were no grounds in law for a twopenny charge anywhere outside London. This ruling applied to both the outer areas of the provincial penny posts and to General Post towns, and the logic is obscure. On two previous occasions the solicitors to the Post Office had confirmed its legality without doubt, and the 1765 Act clearly stated that they should be at the same rates as the Penny Post settled within the Cities of London and Westminster, and Borough of Southwark and parts adjacent: the twopenny and threepenny rates in London were never doubted. The ruling was accepted, and with effect from about 1 January 1837 all twopenny rates were made either one penny or reverted to fourpence. The circular sent to Surveyors was dated 24 December. Freeling was not willing to let this pass however, and got agreement to have the law changed to allow half the rate for half the distance. Fifteen miles being uneven when halved, the amendment was proposed as seven miles for twopence, but here Robert Wallace, MP for Greenock 1831-46, (of whom we shall hear much more later) made himself difficult. Paisley to Glasgow was a half mile over the seven, and eventually he secured agreement to a limit of eight miles. Authorization for the new twopenny rate up to eight miles was sent to Lord Lichfield, the Postmaster General, on 25 November 1837. The earliest date for the legal charge would be about 1 December 1837, and it remained until 1840. It applied to all towns below eight miles, not only to those which had had the rate before, so new towns can be found from 1838: Aldborough and Yoxford paid fourpence to Saxmundham in 1836, twopence in 1838. This story appears to be one of some postmasters finding a legal loophole which the Post Office was unwilling to block, and which later they recognized as just. Plymouth to Devonport became a penny post in this later period, which continued to 1840. Margate seems to have used its oval ship letter stamp, with the words 'Ship Letter' removed, on these twopenny letters only.

## Chapter 11

# INSTRUCTIONAL STAMPS

THESE are a vast and popular field, but as most are self-explanatory there is not a lot to be said. There are no really fundamental issues to be discussed — if a letter is struck with TOO LATE, it can be accepted that it was posted after the time for closing that particular mail, a late fee was not paid, and so the letter was held over until the next post. The most one can do, therefore, is to chronicle facts, for types vary considerably.

**More to Pay**

These stamps were used in London from 1800, but do not appear to have been used in the provinces until after 1840. Letters earlier than 1840 on which an extra charge was payable have it endorsed in manuscript. London began with a rare and very attractive MORE TO/PAY in a crescent, surmounted by a crown (Fig 98) but from 1813 these words come in one line in a rectangle, then three lines enclosed in a double circle. Variants of the latter stamp run through until 1845. Closely associated were 'In all' stamps, which began in 1760 for use in London on letters in the General Post only. Before this date 'in all' can be found written (usually against a second charge) in cases of redirection or where the original computation was to London only. From the 1780s it is not found handstruck, and no explanation can be given, but in 1810 a similar In All, again in script letters but with capital A, occurs sometimes on letters in the Twopenny Post.

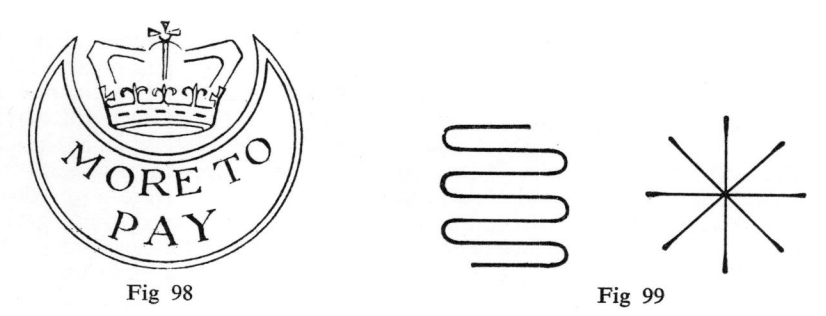

Fig 98

Fig 99

**Charge Marks**

A series of numeral stamps from 2 to 6 occurs for the various London charges, 2 and 3 being normal in the twopenny and threepenny posts and adding nothing to the value of a letter. 1 has not been seen in London before 1840, and the first 2, a very large (40 mm and above) figure, is very scarce. 3 was round-topped, but country offices of London used a flat-top 3 for cross and by-post letters only and these are difficult to find. Paddington and other offices used blue for their stamps for a time. 4 to 6 occur only as combination rates, and are also scarce. Associated with these are squiggles or crosses (Fig 99) used as erasure marks for the old charge. On inland letters red figures (manuscript or stamped) are always used for paid letters, black for unpaid charges to be settled by the recipient. Most cases of the former in black are due to oxidation of the ink, but the instruction was not observed scrupulously if a paid handstamp was struck alongside, or on overseas letters. In the Indian zone unpaid letters were called 'Bearing', in other parts occasionally 'Forward'. Both mean the same — the postal charge is borne forward with the letter.

In the provinces stamped figures were used very occasionally for the rate to London, for this was needed most frequently. Reading used a large 4, and 5 is known when the postage increased in 1796. Woburn, at 42 miles from London exactly the same as Reading, had to have a 7 when it used a stamp in 1814-19, so much had postal charges increased. The only other one seen is 5 from Broxbourne, and this is interesting because its parent post town of Waltham Cross did not use a 4 stamp. So much mail went to London from one banking family that Broxbourne, the No 2 receiving house, added the penny post to 4d of the General Post and used 5. In both of these last two examples the volume of mail from one house was probably larger than many post towns, so it was not favouritism, but reality. Godalming and Northwich have been recorded, but have not been seen by the writer. Scotland can boast a remarkable case with the small 2 used by Montrose in 1742-3, fifty years before England's earliest figures. This charge stamp to Edinburgh can be assumed to be privately made by the postmaster.

In the penny post, Edinburgh and Glasgow used 1 and 2 stamps in the inner and outer areas, whilst Liverpool's and East Anglia's use of handstruck 1 on some penny post letters, and Leeds use of a 2, have already been mentioned in the later penny post section.

**Crowns**

Crowns were struck usually by London, Edinburgh, and Dublin over an old charge as authority to cancel it. It was incorporated also in a number of other stamps (e.g. Frees and always at the top), but its presence can always be traced to the need to authorize something — the seal of Government. Crowns alone became larger as time progressed, and more elaborately decorated. At the turn of the century a simple smaller type comes in, and very occasionally this is enclosed in a circle with a small table letter outside at the top. An earlier small ornate crown in a circle, about 1765-7 is also rare. Early crowns are black, the middle period can be black, red or purple, and later ones red. Examples are shown as Fig 100. Edinburgh used a plain one, more square than London, until a smaller crown was associated with G.R. in 1814. These are Fig 101. On the accession of Queen Victoria this did not change, but Glasgow began using V Crown R in red then black, the latter for an unexplained purpose, not a change in rate. This is a very scarce stamp, and in black can be found with 1840-41 adhesive 'penny blacks' or 'penny reds'.

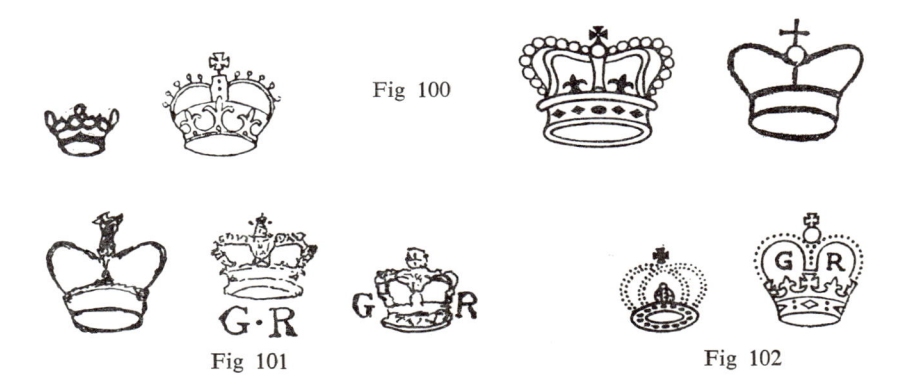

Fig 100

Fig 101          Fig 102

Dublin used a wide variety of ornate crowns, as Fig 102, sometimes associated with other stamps (particularly on Free letters for 'Wrong Date', 'Above Number Privileged', 'Date Altered', 'Member Not in Ireland' etc). These are all rare to very rare, and most attractive, particularly the last which is enclosed in a scroll. The example recorded similar to this but reading 'Member in Ireland' must have been struck in London, for there was no point in striking it when the letter had arrived there. It is hard to understand this degree of rarity, considering how much mail was sent to MPs, many of whom must have gone to Ireland. Evidently neither stamp was used regularly. The only provincial crown seen is a scarce wide one of Brighton, 16 × 12 mm, which seems to have been used on letters they were unable to deliver, or redirected.

## Too Late

Too Late was the most widely issued of all provincial instructional stamps, and quite small post towns can be found using them. They are in a wide variety of shape and sizes, but most are fairly small and in a straight line framed or unframed. Occasionally it was written on a cover, or two stamps of consecutive days were struck on the reverse by the sending town to show it had been held over, if they had no stamp. One or two towns had named stamps —'Ft. George/Too Late' or 'Too Late/by Carlisle' and in others the wording varies —'Too Late for 1st Delivery' at Liverpool, 'Put in after 2 o'clock' at Portsmouth, and 'Too Late N.P.' of Manchester. N.P. probably stands for Night Post, for there were two mails from Manchester to London and (a little earlier) the Carlisle coach for the main mail was timed to arrive at 10.30 pm, a break being allowed until departure at 2.0 am. The earliest seen by the author are Liverpool and Birmingham, 1804, but earlier ones probably exist. Scarcity has little relation to the size of the town, probably it depends more on the convenience or inconvenience of box closing times (it must be remembered there would be various closing times for the different mails throughout the day). Two Bishop marks of consecutive days on a letter probably imply Too Late in London at an earlier period; London did not use plain 'Too Late' until 1840, but 'Put in after 7 o'clock at night' (later 6 o'clock) was used for a long time, and a scarcer 'Too Late for Morning Post' (Fig 103) comes in two sizes 1814-18. The Branch Offices used 'Posted after 7 pm'. Scotland used widely an attractive framed type as Fig 104, frequently called the Mae West from its curves. Apparently each town used different squiggles above and below so they can be identified. With some wording it is not easy to be certain if a stamp is Too Late or Late Fee — that is, whether it was held over or was sent after extra payment, but it is most probable that all were Too Late.

## Late Fee

Late Fee stamps are stated to have been used first in 1797, and Stitt Dibden in 'Late Fee and Too Late Stamps' quotes from the President's Order Book (which he discovered in the GPO) under 4 May 1797 'Mr Stow has this day ordered a stamp to be made for the use of the messengers after 7 o'clock, upon duty at the window in order to distinguish these letters as there arises great difficulty in accounting sometimes for letters which have been delayed, not knowing whether they came in due course or put in with a fee. The stamp is to be used on every letter taken in at the window after 7 pm'. The window was closed at 7.45 to allow for the mail to be bagged by 8.0 pm. This applied to the Chief Office only, and the fee appears to have been sixpence which had to be prepaid, so is not included in the charge marked on the letter. The stamps used are Figs 105 and 106.

Although this was the first handstamp used it was not the start of the Late Fee system. Letters given to the Bellmen in 1700 would go in after the mails were closed, so really this penny can be considered a late fee. The letter quoted above proves that an official system at the window of the Chief Office was running before stamps came in 1797, and London receiving houses probably had a late fee of their own. In the provinces most cities had one, especially because the money was a perquisite of the postmaster. It was left to the individual postmaster whether he accepted letters after the mail closing time or not, but if he did it must be at charges and times officially laid down. As he had to work harder to prepare the bag in time for despatch, the revenue went to him, but it must be remembered that salaries were low in expectation of a number of extras.

Another similar perquisite, incidentally, was private boxes at sums ranging from five shillings to two guineas a year — as a mail was sorted letters were put straight into these boxes, so they could be available an hour or more before delivery. The advantage of the more expensive boxes is not known — Bicester had six different charges for ten boxes, whilst Birmingham let 192, all at a guinea each, but Bristol let 306 at sums from £1. 6. 0 to £7.17. 6 (an income of £487. 3. 9). It was mainly the industrial towns that used boxes freely — Barnsley had 46, Blackburn 35, Bradford Yorks 111 but Bradford Wilts had none. Surprisingly, Bath had 58 and Brighton nil.*

---

\* All these details are from a Return to the House of Commons, 1837, giving details of every post town. It is a most useful document and is probably for the year 1836.

A few towns give the advantages enjoyed by box holders; in Blackburn and Northwich subscribers could post late without fee, whilst Liverpool and Leeds provided a waiting room for them. It is notable that of the towns giving any advantages nearly all English ones put earlier delivery, but Scottish towns state specifically that box holders are not served earlier. In Ireland, Arklow, Ballymena, Belfast, Cork, Clonmell, Drogheda, Dundalk, Galway, Limerick, Navan, Newry all gave credit of from one to three months for postage to their box subscribers — a useful concession. When private boxes started is not known.

To return to Late Fee, it must be remembered that the time of box closing varied with the mail it was desired to send by, and the position of the town geographically. Coaches called at all hours of the day and night, and though details are not available a letter is remembered to Freeling from the Postmaster of Carlisle: he really must have an extra clerk, for it was only possible to close the office for three or four hours of the twenty-four, and if he had five hours sleep he was very fortunate (or words to this effect). Thus in a busy office at a junction there could be six mail times for closing, and each might have a late fee for the last hour. Late Fee pence were taken into the revenue at varying dates, but most between 1840 and 1842. By 1846 a statement could be made in the Guide to Postmasters 'All Late Fee pence go to the revenue'.

Fig 103

Fig 104

Fig 105

Fig 106

† Fig 107

Fig 108

After the early Figs 105 and 106, both of which are very rare, came Figs 107 in 1801 and 108 with the day at the right only from 1807 to 1809, **all having no code letter at the top.** They are in dull purple or black until 1816, when they were struck in the normal red. From 1840 adhesive stamps prepaying a late fee are often put at the left of the envelope, and many later London late fee cancellations have the date in a hexagon.

### Examiners Marks

Examiners Marks is a phrase used to cover a good number of initials, letters, and signs. Many were struck doubtless by an Inspector who verified the rate, route, or weight, but others have meanings difficult to discover. From about 1840 a series of office abbreviations turns up for letters that were undeliverable or out of course — CX for Charing Cross, NR for North Row, PB for Pimlico Branch, PN for Paddington, SY for Stepney etc. In the provinces Brighton sub-offices used E, N and W, Southampton used A, and Plymouth A, B and C. To a certain extent, any letter or design which cannot be explained in any other way is called an Examiners mark. Many show no clue on the letter as to why they were struck, and must be left to conjecture. It is probable that WR and RL stand for West Road and Ride Letter, both being letters collected by the letter carriers, but it is not certain.

### Houses of Parliament

Houses of Parliament mail is a worrying problem, for a number of stamps have been used but all are very scarce to very rare. Before 1840 most of this mail was franked, so no other identifying stamp was needed, and it has always been assumed that all of this was sent straight to the

Chief Office for handling. It is noticeable, however, that a very much larger proportion than would be expected has the Charing Cross Branch backstamp (from its formation in 1829) and this raises the query whether some of the Houses of Parliament mail was handled here. It seems impossible that Charing Cross had a Free handstamp, as the CX backstamp occurs with all four types, but a possible explanation is that these are late letters. There must be a reason, for when a miscellaneous sample of Free entires was sorted, and all were eliminated which could not have originated in Parliament (letters from the country, Sunday postings, those written in other parts of London etc.) half of the remainder between 1830 and 1840 had no backstamp and half had a Charing Cross stamp. There was one Vere St backstamp, but no Lombard St or Borough, so this cannot be coincidence.

The theory that these could be late letters stems from an article on the House of Commons Post Office by Barbara Whittingham-Jones in the Philatelist (Robson Lowe Ltd.), Vol 20 Nos 3-6. She states that in 1820 John Bellamy was directed by the Speaker to make up and forward the last bag to Lombard St as late as possible after 6 o'clock. In 1821 he was ordered to send the first bag at 5 pm to the Receiving House at Bridge St, the second and last bags at 5.30 pm and 6.30 pm 'to meet the cart at Charing Cross'. What cart was this? It seems likely to have been one from the Westminster Chief Office in Gerrard Street, Soho, and this may have been run since its establishment in 1794. As the messenger could hardly wait on the open street with the bag, he probably handed it over in a Receiving House until the Charing Cross Branch Office was opened in 1829, but when Gerrard Street was closed in 1834 some other means of transport must have been arranged. Probably a half hour or more would be allowed after closing the bag for checking, making out the waybill, and carrying to Charing Cross; as Bellamy was a servant of Parliament and not the Post Office it may well have been more to allow for a second checking before the Post Office accepted the bag. Many people delay the writing of letters and miss the mail, so it is very probable that letters that missed the bag by a half-hour could be sent to Charing Cross by private messenger for inclusion; there may have been a messenger every night with these late letters. This would explain the unreasonable number posted at Charing Cross.

This applies only to letters for the General Post, of course, as those in the Twopenny Post were charged normally. These latter were struck with H.P. in large red letters, and although it is known from 1820-42 and there are at least three different stamps, its rarity shows the rooted objection that Members felt to paying for a letter. The rarity of H.P., then, is explainable, but the very great rarity of a circular undated 'House of Commons' (issued on 10 February 1843) and a smaller dated 'Houses of Parliament S.W.' enclosed in a circle, and used with two cancellations HP/1 and HP/2 in horizontal bars in 1859, is inexplicable. The former, being struck on the envelope, would have had a fairly small survival rate, but HP1 and HP2 were stuck on the adhesives. Thanks to the growth of collectors and newspaper competitions, adhesive stamps of this period are extremely common, yet in tens of thousands examined by the writer not one has been found. It is not clear why these handstamps were issued to the Houses of Parliament Post Office if they were used so very rarely, and mail was cancelled with normal Inland Branch diamond obliterations. Why were they used at all? In 1882 a duplex cancellation with 40 in an oval of heavy bars was issued, and this is more common than the earlier types, but in 1889 a series of postage due stamps from $\frac{1}{2}$d with H.C.S.W. are all very rare indeed.

A series of backstamps that is well known, but has not previously been connected with Parliamentary mail, is recognizable by having only a crown above the date (Fig 109). Similar stamps but with a letter at each side of the crown appear to have been used on large envelopes or packets, and have no connection with Parliament. From late 1841 to January 1844 the two letters of the month have serifs, but from 1844 until the end in 1858 the month becomes sanserif. From 1847 to 1855 another stamp of the same series has + below the year, and from 1855 to 1858 this was changed to 1. All are known in black or red, and occur on mail *from* the Houses of Parliament and *to* government offices. It is almost certain that this was a special late collection from Parliament and late delivery to government offices. It is worth repeating that if the crown has a letter at each side above the date it is normal, and has no connection with this special late service.

**Sunday Post**

This is another field where the author is unhappy about the state of knowledge at the present time. Little is known about the way letters were handled, for the small amount of research has concentrated on the special stamps. Two subjects seem fairly clear, the London Twopenny Post and Free letters, so these will be dealt with first. In the Twopenny Post letters which were sent to Country offices on Saturday night were delivered there on Sunday morning, but were hand-stamped before leaving the Chief Office with an interesting 'To be Delivered by 10 Sunday Morning'. There were four varieties as Fig 110, the rectangular stamp also occurs in two lines, and they were to prevent people saying that post office work prevented letter carriers going to church. The very rare type is the unframed oval.

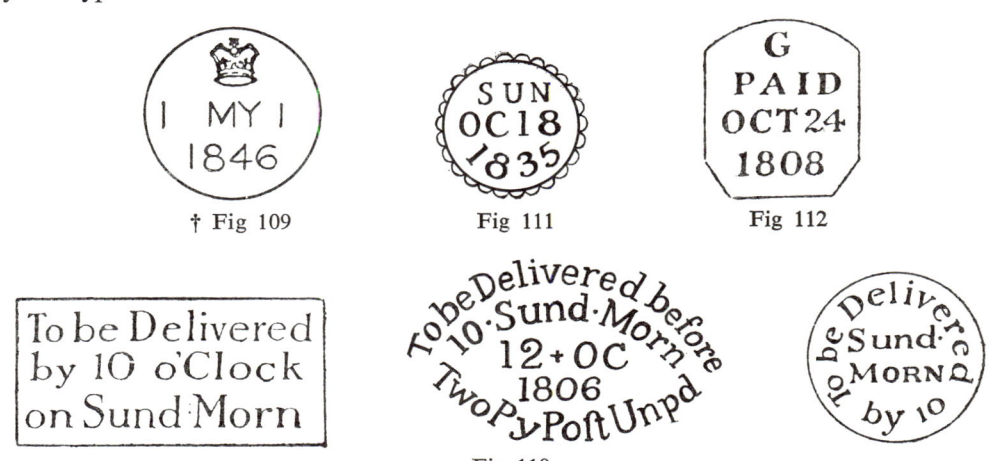

† Fig 109

Fig 111

Fig 112

Fig 110

Letters were accepted on Sunday at the Branch Offices and the Chief Office of the General Post, but were held until the Monday evening coach. Ordinary letters were just held over, but Free letters were more difficult, for stamping and sorting were not done until Monday and yet the date must agree with the posting date in the superscription. To get over this, the normal back-stamp with an S code above the Sunday date was struck on the front of the letter and the Free stamp had Monday's date. There may have been trouble authenticating these free letters, for in 1832 a new stamp of an unusually literal design as Fig 111 was introduced. It is a most attractive stamp, varies considerably in size and number of scollops, and is not rare but is always popular. From 1835 or earlier L, C, or V in a circle was struck in red on the reverse of letters posted at Lombard St, Charing Cross, or Vere St, and it is probable that B was used by the Borough Branch Office in Southwark. Some have no letter, and it is assumed that these were posted at the Chief Office.

The Sunday SUN is found on occasional letters until 1868, being sanserif from 1857 and in later years very small, in red, black, or blue. From 1840 these are for a completely different purpose, at present unknown: they must be different, as the franking privilege had ended and they are prepaid with adhesive stamps. Until the last years they seem to be on normal letters to a variety of addresses, some with the Branch Office L, C, or V on the reverse. The very small latest ones seem to be to or from addresses abroad, sometimes both, and would appear to be a Foreign Branch stamp introduced to explain the delay. An example before the author was from Brazil to Bordeaux, the only London stamps being the red SUN of 1866 and the Anglo-French GB/1F 60c Currency mark. This letter did not go to the Inland Branch at all.

The other Sunday stamps are the General Post date stamps. In 1798-99 Fig. 7a had a table letter outside the ring, and A to H and S are known. Clearly the S is Sunday, and this follows through the types used to 1840. From June to December 1799, on the introduction of Fig 7c., the year was shortened to 99 only, but from 1800 the year was in full. From 1810 to 1840 the day was repeated at each side, and all of these occur with S code. This latter is quite easy to find, but the first three types with Sunday code are all very rare or rare. The latter is normally on the front of Free letters posted in London, and on the back of those into London from the provinces.

With very few exceptions, all the General Post Sunday stamps inwards are from Scotland, Ireland, or the ports of England — Chatham, Dover, Devonport, Plymouth, etc. Why? Another linkage is that for many years from 1777 some letters from Ireland carry a big IRELAND, and this is now known to have been struck in London, and in Scotland for letters carried from Donaghadee to Portpatrick. Proof of this is that between 1798 and 1802 this occurs occasionally with S above for Sunday, and the letters arrived here on Sunday, not posted in Ireland on Sunday. Thus it can be said that from 1798-1802 letters from Scotland or major English ports arriving in London on Sunday received the S code datestamp, Irish letters received the S/IRELAND, but after 1802 both groups received the S datestamp. Finally, the London Paid stamps also used code S on letters from the same restricted areas, in Fig 112. Why are they not found on letters from other English towns? Ireland had a number of Sunday stamps, all have the word in full and all but an octagonal framed date stamp are very rare.

A warning is necessary here: London date stamps code S other than Figs 7a (with S outside the ring) and varieties of 7c (all having the date in straight lines) do not appear to be Sunday stamps. Variations of Fig 7b for example, with one or two rings but the year curved are normal days. It is always wise to check with the calendar.

Two Freeling minutes have been seen (but cannot be quoted) about this period which mention in passing the blank post days in the provinces, arranged so that mail did not arrive in London on a Sunday, and one added "in the case of Liverpool this is Friday". Manchester also is seen to have no post to London on Friday (vide 'A History of the Manchester Post Office' by Calvert, Appendix 6), and it would seem that other provincial towns did the same, yet Liverpool was an important port. If the only coaches arriving on Sunday were the North Road from Scotland, the Chester Road from Ireland, the Dover Road, and West Road from Plymouth, did they bring only one or two bags each, ignoring other towns at which they stopped? We still do not know, but the offices were open. A notice in the Bruce Castle collection says:

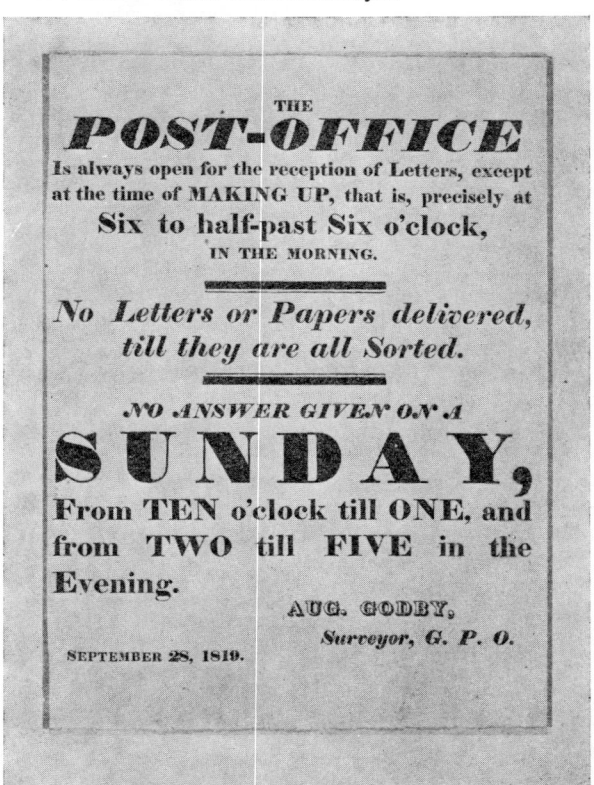

Fig 113

Fig 114

Fig 115

THE
POST-OFFICE
Is always open for the reception of Letters, except at the time of MAKING UP, that is, precisely at
Six to half-past Six o'clock,
IN THE MORNING.

No Letters or Papers delivered, till they are all Sorted.

NO ANSWER GIVEN ON A
SUNDAY,
From TEN o'clock till ONE, and from TWO till FIVE in the Evening.

AUG. GODBY,
Surveyor, G. P. O.

SEPTEMBER 28, 1819.

Unfortunately, we do not know which town it describes, but it must have been about twenty-two hours journey from London. The office cannot have been open all and every night, but it may have meant that the box was open all night, and you could post your letter unpaid through the slit when the office was closed. To quote Manchester again, it seems the office shut from 10 pm until 8 am, so the Preston and Carlisle mail had to be posted before 10 pm to leave on the coach at 2 am; evidently the box was not cleared again.

Finally, references are made occasionally to the coaches being stopped at the outskirts of London on Sunday morning, and apparently an attempt was made to bypass London by some coaches. Also it is said that coaches did go out from London as usual on Sunday night, but they did not take on board any mail until beyond London suburbs. These points have not yet been investigated, but it remains a mystery why London should be treated so differently from the rest of the country.

**Money Letters and Registration**

Although registration was used in the Foreign Branch, and in Ireland from 1827 or earlier, there was none for inland letters in England until 1841: the money letter system was thought to be enough. Introduced in 1792, it had worked quite well but had no compensation for loss. Any letter declared to contain money or valuables had 'money letter" written at the top left corner, was wrapped in a separate waybill and was entered in a register every time it was sorted (this sometimes made the post office staff refer to Money Letters as registered). There was no additional charge, but the enclosure meant that the postage would be doubled or more. The increasing use of money orders reduced the need for money letters, and they ceased on 1st January 1840, but recognition of the need for some safeguard for valuables caused the introduction of registration for inland letters on 6 January 1841. The fee was one shilling in addition to the postage, but still no compensation for loss was allowed although a receipt was given to the sender. The fee was usually prepaid in cash at this period (although most letters have the postage in stamps) so a typical letter has 1/- marked in red ink and a penny or twopence in adhesive stamps. Some are entirely prepaid in cash or stamps. The fee was reduced to sixpence on 1 March 1848, fourpence on 1 August 1862, and finally twopence on 1 January 1878. Until 1856, every registered letter was enclosed in a wrapper, white at first but changed to green after a month or two so that it would be seen immediately the bag was opened. From 1856 they were tied with green silk, later changed to blue and then to the blue lines which are still used today. Special registration had been introduced for bankers' parcels of notes in 1824, stamped with a tall or a broad crown enclosing PAID and the date, but examples are of the greatest rarity, as are the original green wrappers.

The Foreign Branch introduced registration handstamps about 1820, but Alcock and Holland state that a system had run since the 1780s. As a fee of £1.1.0 was charged for letters sent abroad, and 5/- on inward letters additional to the postage prepaid abroad, it was used very little and examples of Fig 113 (in two or three types) are rare. In 1836 the fee was reduced to 2/6d. in either direction, and new stamps as Fig 114 were used. These were used for thirty five years, later ones having sanserif lettering. A stamp that occurs on registered letters from overseas in the absence of Figs 113-114 is F.O. in a circle of dots (Fig 115) but the reason is not clear. At this time (1827-32) various dotted stamps were used in the Foreign Branch, and it is assumed that F.O. stood for Foreign Office.

† Fig 116                                                                                           Fig 117

'Registered' was usually written in manuscript when the system extended in 1841, but London Inland Branch adopted the second type of Foreign Branch stamp (Fig 114). Later a type enclosed in an oval frame became standard. Many provincial towns had attractive local stamps which vary considerably and form a nice group to collect if one can find them. Foreign Branch in the 1850's used the first of three standard types — a crown with the country above and Registered below, joined by arcs. Later the crown was dropped, the wording being first in a framed oval, finally enclosed in a circle, and both were dated. In all three types Prussia is by far the commonest, Hamburg next and the rest are rare. They are shown in Fig 116, and probably each type was issued for Prussia, Hamburg, Holland, Belgium, Belgium via France, Gottenburg, France, Bremen, Spain, Denmark, Sardinia, Malta, Constantinople, Italy and Switzerland.

Ireland had a system of registration in the 1827-31 period or earlier, using Fig 117, but one is not happy to read that all double letters or larger not going to England were given free registration automatically. It can only be interpreted reasonably to mean letters inside Ireland and elsewhere, and why should the Post Office register to Scotland but not England? Did they register freeall letters of two sheets to France or Germany, America or Hong Kong? These were the last years of the independent administration from Dublin, and the office was losing money without adding unnecessary burdens, so if correct how else can it be explained but sheer spite?

## Soldiers and Sailors Letters

Letters written from campaigns go back to the earliest times (mention has been made of the papyrus letter in the British Museum asking for reinforcements in Nubia), and a number exist from Elizabethan times, but not many from this period are available to collectors. There are a few of the Civil War, 1642-48, and of the Wars of Spanish and Austrian Succession, 1702-13 and 1740-48, but not many. The last two are from the Low Countries. Those from America in the Seven Years War 1756-63 and War of Independence 1775-83 are rare, expensive, and very popular, but some from British soldiers and sailors in other areas can be found at this period more cheaply. A point to remember is that letters from those involved in campaigns are of much more interest and value than those from garrison troops, and the value varies greatly according to the contents. A letter describing a well known battle sells for many times the price of the normal soldier's 'hoping this finds you as it leaves me', and the best are fascinating human documents.

On two major points the writer is forced to disagree with standard reference books, the first regarding the original Act of 1795 which authorized a special rate for the forces, the other the special treatment of the East India Company zone.

Nearly all early campaign letters are from officers, for few other ranks could write, and those who could would not impose the very high rates of overseas postage on their families. To take advantage of Ship Letter rates they must be near a busy port, and usually they were inland. It was not until the French Revolutionary War began in 1793 that the problem was important, for before this our armies had been pretty small. In this war we had large numbers of men abroad, and education meant that many more could write, but postage rates were worse than before. Recognizing this problem, an Act was passed on 5 May 1795, to take effect immediately (35 George 3, Cap 53), which reduced the postage on letters to or from soldiers and sailors to one penny, irrespective of where they were posted. This was an important concession, for the press-gangs were at their height, were taking all types of men, and for the first time many soldiers wanted to write home. The Act must have been hurriedly drafted, for the wording was loose and caused confusion in its operation. Every book on postal history says that the penny postal charge must be prepaid by the sender, in either direction, and on any reasonable interpretation there seems little doubt that this was intended. However, it is not what the Act said, and it can now be proved it was not how the Act was interpreted. The first six clauses deal with Parliamentary free letters, and clause seven brings in the penny rate on letters from soldiers, providing the penny is prepaid. Clause eight, however, for letters to soldiers and sailors, clearly says 'which Sum of One Penny shall be paid at the Time of the Delivery thereof', so they were sent unpaid, and the soldier paid both ways. How this has not been seen before cannot be explained, but it is confirmed by an amending Act (46 George 3 Cap 92) of July 1806, eleven years later, which corrects this to the penny paid at the time of posting in either direction. Also, the 1806 Act adds the words 'within any part of His Majesty's Dominions' which limit was not imposed in 1795.

The restrictions placed on these letters in both Acts were:

(a) The letter must be on his private affairs.

(b) It applied only up to the rank of Sergeant; all Warrant and Commissioned Officers were excluded and still paid normal postage.

(c) All letters from him must be signed by the Commanding Officer, with the name, rank, and unit of the sender, or addressed with the rank and unit if to him (in which case the letters could be collected only by the addressee, or another person authorized by the C.O., from the nearest Post Office).

(d) He must be engaged on His Majesty's Service at the time.

(e) All letters from him must have the penny prepaid, and, from 1806, those to him must also be prepaid.

(f) After 1806 he must be within some part of His Majesty's Dominions. This was interpreted later to apply to all letters on which the Post Office did not pay fees for carriage to other countries (thus letters from the Crimea were threepence unless brought on a naval vessel, for twopence was paid to the French for carriage via Marseilles). It must have applied also to theatres of battle, for Spain and Portugal had the penny rate from late 1808. Most letters from the Peninsula are from Officers, though, at normal rates.

This surprising discovery was quickly confirmed by unearthing a naval correspondence (tucked away many years ago) between Hugh McKibben, a young American pressed into the British navy in 1795, and his Uncle James in Belfast. The first three letters to Hugh at Portsmouth or elsewhere are all penny unpaid from Belfast, then in July 1796 he became a midshipman and paid up to 2/-. Those from him are not made out as sailors letters until June, so four cost his Uncle 10/9d instead of the 4d they should have been: why this should be one cannot say. A final mystery are two to Hugh in 1799-1800, addressed as sailing master of the Aurora, which travelled at one penny each unpaid from Cockermouth to Portsmouth. These five unpaid penny letters confirm the rate, yet why has everybody overlooked it? They also confirm the difficulties for the Post Office in interpreting the Act. Stitt Dibden quotes various orders* clarifying it, including free carriage in the London Penny Post and exclusion if the letter contained a money order (the latter being rescinded six days later). He also quotes an order of 21 July 1798 which included Sergeant Majors in the privilege, and an order of 1813 and the Consolidation Act of 1837 which again excluded them.

Although it is widely stated that there was an Officer's rate of sixpence a letter, no example of this has been seen by the writer earlier than 1857 which cannot be explained as a normal rate, and he doubts if it was introduced. Before 1854 their letters seem to have incurred normal overseas postage, in the Crimea 1854-7 they were given the same 3d rate as other ranks (1d plus 2d transit through France) and the uniform 6d rate to all parts came in on 1 June 1857.

Examples of correct addressing are in the 1813 notice, and these styles were normally observed. Across the top he wrote his name, rank, and unit, all underlined, and then the address, whilst the signature of the Commanding Officer is usually in the lower left corner. Some letters seen recently show that on occasion these inscriptions were not read, the letter being accepted on its layout. A missionary in Ceylon, when writing to the secretary of the Methodist Missionary Society, seems regularly to have written across the top. One example reads 'From Matura, July 31 1830 Single sheet Post Paid to Ship' which is underlined: at the bottom left, again cut off by rules at the right angle, is 'Per John Craig'. A number of these letters got through, being stamped with the large 'India Soldiers, London, 3', and were accepted as soldiers letters. He wrote very clearly, so presumably felt that if the Post Office was misled by them it was their own fault, but it looks so much like a soldiers letter that it is not what one expects from missionaries.

In 1799 an attempt was made to drive the French army out of Holland, and the mixed British and Russian force captured the Dutch fleet and had some success. Bad organization and training placed it in an impossible position for the winter, and the army signed a convention and withdrew after two months, but kept the Dutch fleet. This minor diversion is of considerable interest to postal historians, however, as it saw the first Army Post Office. Before this expedition, the only postmark occurring on army letters is a monogram type AB in circle from the army in Belgium

---

* *Postage Rates of H.M. Forces 1795-1899*, published by the Postal History Society 1963.

1743-5, and it is now considered that this is a Belgian stamp for 'Armee Britannique'. It occurs only on letters from the British army, however, and is a very interesting and scarce mark, but was not an Army Post Office. It is a source of wonder that if this first A.P.O., run for only two months between 14 September and 10 November 1799 with an army of only 15,000 men, could be made a success, the experiment should not be repeated for exactly a hundred years. The Peninsular War involved ten times this number of men and lasted six years, yet there is no evidence that an Army Post Office was formed again for any campaign until the Boer War.

The post office set up by Henry Darlot in Holland is described in full detail by Stitt Dibden (op. cit.) and makes an interesting story. Darlot seems to have been a man with ideas, and had put up a scheme two years before to reduce frauds by the twenty letter carriers of the Foreign Branch. He seems to have needed ideas, for he was given five days to procure all personal and official necessities, plus 'a servant, a strong one-horse chaise, a stout draft horse, a saddle horse, tent, bedstead, furniture, a sword and pistol, and a distinctive uniform, a blue coat with red collar and cuffs, cockaded hat and a cockade.' For all this, Darlot was allowed one hundred guineas, but having to pay thirty guineas for the chaise and thirty-six guineas for the first horse, he was allowed a further fifty guineas. His other expenses included 'A Boat Cloak at 2 guineas, a Beaver Driving Coat at £2, one Callico Banyan (or jacket) at 2 guineas, a drab livery Surtout (overcoat) at £2.12.6, a Green Baize Bag at 5/-, a Cabin Trunk at £2.10.0, a Camp-bedstead and Biddy at £9.10.0, 2 pairs of Sheets and 2 Pillow Cases for 3 guineas, a regimental sword with silver and gold fillings at £2.12.0, and a Crimson and Gold Reg. Sword knot at fourteen shillings.'

Poor Darlot found he had a difficult task, for the letters arrived only partly sorted, a great number of people were not attached to any regiment, and everybody was so impatient that when a mail arrived 'I am beset by at least a hundred of them' who would not wait for the Drum-majors to collect the mail. He had to collect and be responsible for the postage, yet was paid in the money of five or six different countries and was presented every day with orders on the money order office which the troops received on embarkation, and which really he had no authority to take. He was receiving and sending mail both direct to London and by naval transport to Yarmouth, and insisted that he must have two trained clerks (who presumably had not time to be sent). He received twenty nine mails from England, which included £94 dead letters, and on his return his balance was:

| | |
|---|---|
| Postage collected on letters from Holland ... ... ... ... ... ... | £451. 3. 6. |
| „ „ „ „ to Holland ... ... ... ... ... ... | £404. 4. 6. |
| Paid Letters ... ... ... ... ... ... ... ... | £224. 1. 0. |
| | £1,079. 9. 0. |
| Less expenses (including Darlot's expenses both in England and Holland) | 306. 2. 6. |
| Advertisements in newspapers informing the public of the arrangements ... | 50. 0. 0. |
| Darlot's remuneration at 20/- a day ... ... ... ... ... ... | 80. 0. 0. |
| | £436. 2. 6. |
| Leaving a Balance of ... ... ... ... ... ... ... ... | £643. 6. 6. |

Two stamps were used by Darlot —'Army Bag' and 'Post Paid Army Bag' shown as Fig 118, both are very rare. It seems that an Officers' rate of sixpence *in addition to inland postage* was used (very different from a sixpence flat rate which is usually talked of) but no letters at the penny flat rate have been seen from other ranks.

Fig 118

Fig 119

The largest amount of Army mail pre-1855 was undoubtedly from the Peninsular War 1808-14, and the background to Wellington's campaigns is well known to all. It was the first time that entire countries were really mobilized for war,* and that large armies in the modern sense were in the pitched battles, and yet little detail is known of the handling of mail. It seems to have been done through the Embassy at Lisbon for both Portugal and Spain, direct to Falmouth, and it would seem probable that two types of bags were made up — those forward to London unopened, and those for sorting at Falmouth. Before this, Falmouth had acted as a port only, and forwarded all the packet mail to London, but half the army mail from Lisbon has not been through London. Some letters have a Lisbon straight line stamp on the front, and were probably handed in to the office there; others have a greenish-blue Lisbon/F stamp struck at Falmouth, and these were handed in to the ships and put in the pouch or 'portmantle' carried for loose letters. A very few were put into the civilian Portuguese Post Office, and bear their stamps, but the large majority have no stamps of origin. The letters can be of considerable interest, and are well worth examining.

In this period, prisoners of war were taken in large numbers for the first time, and letters from them are of interest. They were in the charge of the Transport Office, and this used an oval stamp 'Transport Office/Prisoners of War' as Fig 119. Most prisoners were working on farms in various parts of the country on parole, and their letters frequently have no special stamps. The hard core of trouble-makers were in Dartmoor (newly built for the purpose) or on the old hulks at Plymouth, Portsmouth, and other ports. Some of the Dartmoor letters have a script censor mark 'Exd. JM' (Fig 120) and one stamp known of a hulk is 'VETERAN'.

Finally, the other area of disagreement is the soldiers and sailors letters from India. The Honourable East India Company had always had its own army, of a semi-official nature, and carried all the mail in its own ships to this country. The Post Office found it uneconomical to run packets to India, and yet the 1799 Ship Letter Act attempted to impose a ship letter charge of half the packet rate for a comparable run (1/9d a single letter) in addition to the inland postage. It did no work for this charge, and even worse, proposed to charge the Company's boxes full of their own letters. After a short skirmish the Post Office agreed to leave the Company's letters alone as long as their ships turned over to the Post Office all normal mail they carried. This was the least they could offer, for they could not carry them themselves, and paid nothing for their

Fig 120    Fig 121    Fig 122

---

* The sociological development of warfare would make an interesting series of articles, but this is not the place. Civil War must be excluded, for this has always been tragic in its effect and affected the whole country: the terrible conflict of loyalties in the individual or in brother fighting against brother makes it a thing to be avoided at any cost. However, one feels that the Crusades etc. corresponded to the Saturday afternoon football match — a good way to get away from the wife for a bit. How else could one have a Hundred Years War with France? Three hundred years later war was developing from a gentlemanly pastime into a serious business, with many more professionals and a greater use of the press gangs required. It was only the industrial revolution in Britain and then Napoleon (with all the wrong ideas on war) who spoiled it: not until 1805-6 did the Post Office begin to have trouble sailing packets into French ports. From 1793 mail had been sent freely from England to France and the occupied territory, although we were at war; but Napoleon's unsporting attitude, that war was a serious business to be prosecuted with all possible weapons, complicated things for Freeling. Whilst all our major south and east coast ports received cartel ships under flag of truce, he allowed them into Morlaix only, a fishing village with no facilities. A fine article by S. W. Shelton (*Postal History nos* 186, 188, 190, 1974-5) shows how this change of attitude forced our packets further north to Scandinavia, from whence letters were smuggled into French territory. With this loss of amateur status, war lost its attraction, so gentlemen went on the grand tour after the battle, and collected souvenirs — Waterloo had large numbers of British within a week to see the sights.

carriage. It flared up again in 1814, when the Post Office took new powers to stop Ship Letters outwards which the Company could not possibly accept. They refused to carry Post Office bags of letters, and a new act of 1815 gave in to the extent of treating letters carried by East Indiamen completely differently from those on other ships or the packets.

This is very relevant to soldiers letters from this area (which included Ceylon, Cape of Good Hope, St Helena, etc.), for a series of stamps began in 1823 with 'India Soldier &c' and the port below, having a large 1 or 3 in the centre (Fig. 121). Remember, all soldiers and sailors letters were one penny if prepaid, twopence if unpaid, plus any extra charges incurred, but all of these stamps were clearly unpaid. The charges are explained in the Act as a sea postage of twopence plus one penny Inland postage, unless delivered to this country free of any charge, in which case there was an inland charge of one penny only. But no soldiers letter ever incurred an inland charge from 1795, it was one penny to the door — an example on hand was from Quebec through London and Dublin to Cork, then readdressed from Cork-Dublin-London to Cheltenham, all for one penny prepaid in Canada. It is quite apparent the Post Office was covering up here, and the explanation may be that in India soldiers letters were carried free of charge, so it seems likely the East India Co. refused to collect the pence for prepayment to this country. Having just lost the major battle, the Post Office had no means to enforce it, so agreed that these soldiers letters should be sent with the penny unpaid, but dare not admit it. More research is needed here, but it seems to be the only explanation which fits. No act has been seen which makes the India soldiers' penny optional, and it is most unlikely it was ever passed by Parliament, but details may be found in the Post Office Records.

The commonest port for these stamps by far is London, followed by Liverpool, Portsmouth and Plymouth in that order. Deal and Dover are rarer, and Bristol and Weymouth are very rare. A smaller size stamp, not enclosed in a circle, was used by London and Liverpool from 1838 to 1840, and in 1841 a new rate of fourpence came in, surrounded by 'Soldiers and Seamans Letter by Ship' (Fig 122). The explanation of this new rate has not been found yet, but probably it was connected with the new P. and O contract for the mails to India.

## The Additional Halfpenny Tax

The frequent tolls paid to the turnpike trusts were a considerable expense to stage coaches and travellers, in return for which the trusts were bound to keep those stretches of road in good condition. Invariably it is stated that the mail coaches were exempted from tolls by the act of 15 July 1785 (25 Geo. 3 cap 57), but the author has seen no evidence of what happened before this date. Did mail coaches for the first year of their existence pay toll? Studying "The Papers relative to the Agreement made by Government with Mr Palmer", 1797, it is apparent that exemption of some type was arranged, but the details are not stated anywhere. In Palmer's letter to Mr Pitt, 5 May 1785, he says "The Contracts are made for the greater part of the Kingdom, from London, for the allowance of Guards, and the exemption of Turnpike-Tolls only" (page 43, appendix 4); this could be interpreted as a lump payment to each trust in commutation of tolls. Considerable payments would have to be made until exemption was allowed by parliament. The exemption from tolls by the 1785 act did not apply to Ireland at any time, and this system was adopted here.

Exemption caused considerable opposition from the turnpike trusts, for mail coaches carried passengers too, were regular and frequent users of the road and were said to do more damage than anything else with their high speeds and thinner wheels. After twenty-eight years' opposition, trusts in Scotland succeeded in securing liability for tolls of four-wheeled mail coaches from June 1813. In England they continued free however, and all other mail carriages (providing they carried no passengers) were still exempt in Scotland. Turnpike trusts promptly increased tolls to recover their losses, so that the additional halfpenny postage imposed in June 1813 on all letters carried in Scotland by mail coach fell far short of compensating for this expense. J. K. Sidebottom* states that although the cost of toll charges had been estimated at £6,865 per

---

* The three studies of the Additional ½d are Sidebottom in the Bulletin of The Postal History Society Nos 33 and 71 (June 1945 and November 1953), Kenneth Hodgson in the same journal, on English handstamps only, Nos 176, 177 and 179 (1972-1973) and W. G. Stitt Dibden "The additional halfpenny mail tax 1813-39" published by The Postal History Society, 1963.

annum, the new rates incurred payment of £11,759. Something had to be done, and rather than double the surcharge on letters the Post Office decided to reduce the number of four-wheeled coaches in Scotland, on which toll could be charged. Mail coaches must not be stopped for tolls, but payment was made from the "Revenue of the Post Office in Scotland". Joyce says that the fear that this repeal from exemption would spread to England made the Post Office reduce the number of mail coaches there, but this did not happen.

The "exempt towns" have caused great argument, and are studied in some detail by Stitt Dibden. There is no doubt he is right in saying that it is the entire journey that must be considered, and not just the Scottish end. If a letter was carried in a four-wheeled coach in Scotland for even one mile of a long journey the halfpenny was added; as the notices that have been found are issued from London, the only towns exempt in 1813 were Coldsteam, Earlston, Hawick, Galashiels, Jedburgh, Kelso, Melrose and St Boswells Green. Letters addressed to all other Scottish towns from England went on the Glasgow or Edinburgh coaches, so were subject to the surcharge, but some would not have the halfpenny added if they were local; e.g. London to Paisley had the surcharge, whereas Glasgow to Paisley may not, for it reverted to a horse post. Much more study of this decoaching is needed, with letters showing the presence or absence of the halfpenny. Large areas, particularly in the northwest of Scotland, should not have the charge on internal letters  Probably it was difficult for post towns to administer, and mistakes were frequent. As the charge was General Post, Free letters still passed free, and it is most doubtful if any penny post letters (not going in the General Post) would be carried by a coach. Soldiers penny letters were also exempt.

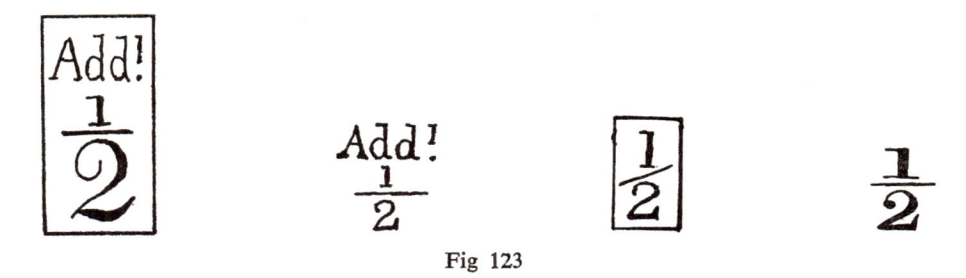

Fig 123

The charge was first imposed on 8 June 1813, and stamps for it are known from 10 June so everything was ready. Four main types are illustrated, of which the first large design was used for all early issues, but the variation is wide and some are completely different. Allocation of covers to a particular town may be a very complicated job, as shown by the uncertainty as to whether some towns and cities ever used a ½ stamp. In 1813 stamps were probably restricted to Edinburgh, Glasgow, London, Berwick and Carlisle, but over the years even the small Scottish towns were issued with them. In England it was the important forward offices (those used to channel mail on to the long-distance routes), and two apparent omissions which are surprising are Birmingham and Chester. Both were major forwarding offices and should have used stamps. A hundred years later Birmingham was such a focal point within easy reach of every large port that it was issued with a ship letter stamp. The first example caused furious arguments as to whether this Birmingham/Ship was used on canal mail, for it could not be further from the sea; the answer came out eventually that it was the ideal centre to rush mail for cancelling from any port that was overloaded, and though much of this importance came with the railways, by 1825-30 (when a number of English towns first had a ½d) it would justify its use as much as Newcastle, Exeter or Bristol.

English Addl ½d stamps that are confirmed are Berwick 1813-39, Carlisle 1813-39, Falmouth in green 1823-39, Newcastle in blue shades to green 1825-28, Liverpool 1826-39, Manchester red 1831-39, occasionally in black 1832-36, Bristol 1835-39, Exeter 1836-37 and London 1813-39. All are black unless specified; Berwick also used green 1823-39 and Carlisle red 1833-38, but there is no importance in the colour. In Ireland, Dublin was the only example, using the second stamp illustrated but with the bar extending the full width, in black 1825-33 and 1836-39, in red 1835-6.

These dates are taken from Kenneth Hodgson's article. Falmouth was used on the packet mail coming in, chiefly from the West Indies, and Exeter (a very small ½ easily overlooked) is by far the rarest. It did not multiply for larger letters, being a flat rate.

Many years ago the author noticed some letters with a halfpenny in the charge which had been nowhere near Scotland and began to ask why it was there. Three years later the answer came in an act of 21 June 1836. As has been said in discussing the Civil War, Milford as a port goes back to Elizabethan days at least, and apparently the last part of the road had scarcely been repaired since her death. The improved road, forking at St Clears and running along the south side of the Haven to Pembroke Naval Dockyard, ran into financial trouble in 1833 and it was proposed to subsidize the turnpike trusts by a levy of a halfpenny a letter carried from Waterford to the new packet station at Hobbs Point, adjoining the Dock. Just why the station was moved from the north to the south bank anyway is not clear at the moment, possibly to keep everything together. Freeling fought nobly against this idea that the cost of maintenance of roads could come from a local surcharge on letters carried along them, but by 1836 the fight had gone out of him and he was overborne. No stamps were used, but letters can be recognized by the charge (which was ½d a sheet, so doubled up for larger letters) and the invariable Waterford backstamp. If there is a Dublin stamp it must be before the Waterford date on letters from Ireland, after it on letters to Ireland. They must not be to or from Scotland. The rarity and interest of these Welsh ½d's are not yet fully appreciated.

Chapter 12

# THE REFORMS OF 1839-40

THE story told so far should have given the general impression that whilst the Post Office had doubtless done its best, it had been pretty uninspired in its ideas. The damning fact is that in two hundred years of public service it had not produced a single person from within the organization with vision, and the courage to rebel against the entrenched permanent staff. Every single important innovation was thrust on an unwilling office from outside. Samuel Jude probably carried the first regular public letters at a charge, but he was a merchant; Witherings organized the Foreign then the Inland post but he was a Court official working for the Earl of Warwick; Dockwra and Ralph Allen may have been two of the greatest pioneers but one was a merchant, the other was apprenticed to a postmaster in the private cross post he ran. Allen's first post office job was 'in at the deep end', as Postmaster of Bath, one of the most important positions in the country at that time. When he secured a farm of the cross post system they had to give him a fairly free hand, and he kept secret his methods so well that although the Post Office knew he made a fortune they dare not refuse renewals of his contract, for they could not have run his system efficiently. There is little doubt that Allen remembered hearing of the fate of Dockwra only thirty years before, and was not going to allow the Post Office to take by force a second time a fully organized service. Palmer again (though not in the same class) was from the theatre.

Against these men, each of whom saw his opportunity in a public need, and had the courage to press on, the Post Office could set only Freeling from their own ranks. As has been said, he was not comparable for his great strength was as an administrator, not an innovator, and like Todd his allowances were so great that he could not afford to retire. He would have received a pension based on a salary of £500 a year, yet he was receiving £4,565. Nearly £3,000 was compensation for profits from the privilege of sending newspapers to the colonies, £700 was salary as Resident Surveyor which was continued when he became joint Secretary in 1797 and the post was abolished, and the remainder was in lieu of a flat in the the Post Office. It must be said clearly that this was normal for the times, that he devoted his life to the Post Office, carried the entire weight himself with humanity, and always did his best for everyone concerned. Yet even Joyce (a most balanced postal official reared in the Freeling tradition) had to say that it was a tragedy both for the country and for Freeling's reputation that he did not retire when St Martins le Grand opened in 1829. This was the peak of his career. He became Secretary at a time when postage rates were rising fast to pay for the war with republican France, they rose even faster with the Napoleonic and Peninsular Wars, and he was quite unable to see why people grumbled at this natural course of events. From 1812, a letter from London to North Scotland if a single sheet would cost 1/5d, or to Bedford, Oxford, or Cambridge 8d: if two small sheets or a letter and envelope it was twice these charges, and if it weighed one ounce Scotland was 5/8d and Bedford 2/8d. One ounce is half the present minimum rate, so who can wonder that so few individuals wrote letters.

This, then, is the background to a gradual revolt amongst those who accounted for a large proportion of the letters in this country — the merchants, solicitors, and traders. More research is needed into the background of this opposition, but again there is the same pattern of an important reform being forced on a reluctant Post Office by outsiders. Although the clamour for reform was loud, and growing louder, there is little doubt that the only thing which forced the postal officials to take notice was their complete inability to combat the smuggling of letters, and enforce on the largest users the charges they had decreed. With their refusal to try new methods and cut their costs, it was the mail in quantity from the business houses on which they relied to support the single letter of an ordinary citizen, and more and more business houses evaded payment of postage. Packet letters could cost £1 very easily, and the carriers conveyed box after box of freight to the ports, each containing hundreds of letters which paid the Post Office not a penny. Letters are not hard to find inwards from South America (14/- per ounce) or elsewhere brought in this way and posted in London for a total charge of twopence to the Post Office. Methods of evasion were as varied as they were widespread, and if a consignment was detected the breach of law was usually settled for an agreed lump sum, the letters were put into the post and the carrier continued sending his next consignment.

In 1836 the financial situation was made worse by reduction of the newspaper tax (which included free postage) from fourpence to one penny, both irrespective of distance. This released a flood of large newspaper packets into the postal system with no compensating saving in methods of handling, and was probably responsible for bringing together a group of people whose ideas were to prove irresistable. Of long standing in postal agitation was Robert Wallace, MP for Greenock; then came a group including Charles Knight, the Hill brothers, and Lord Brougham who were writing and publishing for the education of the working classes; and finally was the committee of merchants whose leaders were George Moffatt, Henry Cole, W. H. Ashurst, and Joshua Bates. Despite the reputation gained later by Rowland Hill, the most important of these people must inevitably be Robert Wallace, as Frank Staff said some years ago. To mention but two factual reasons, (1) it was the three years of his postal agitation that roused the interest of the others, and gave them a common focal point, and (2) he was the Chairman of the Select Committee on Postage of 1838, whose recommendations made inevitable a uniform rate of postage irrespective of distance. Furthermore, three times on vital issues the voting of the Committee was equal, and each time Wallace cast his vote in favour of the reforms: if he had cast it against, the cause would have been lost. Thus it can be said that he started the movement, and it was entirely his voting that brought it from the realms of theory to fact: this should be enough for the reputation of any man. Whilst it is probable that Wallace would have achieved a considerable degree of reform without Hill, it is certain that Hill could have done little (or might never have been interested) without Wallace.

Robert Wallace was elected as their first member by the new Parliamentary division of Greenock at the 'Reform Bill' election of 1832. It is curious that whilst postal historians have thought of him as a young fire-eater with Post Office reform as his platform, in fact he was nearly sixty when first elected. It may be the combination of his slightly rabble-rousing tactics in speeches, which were certainly vicious in their attack on the Post Office, and the feeling that members new in this 'Reform' election were all youngsters intent on setting the world right. Anyway, when Hill made a speech at a meeting in Greenock in March 1850 to launch a testimonial fund for Robert Wallace he was able to describe him as 'my esteemed and venerable friend' (and Hill was then fifty-five years old). Probably his background of a Glasgow mercantile family, and his constituency being a busy manufacturing area at the mouth of the Clyde, gave Wallace the realization that the chief handicap to the country at that time was the Post Office.

The group of merchants and bankers is quite straightforward, for their interests and livelihood depended on quick, secure and cheap communication. This is not to say that they were less admirable or honourable, for their were not. No doubt many of them were activated by the same impulses and frustrations as Wallace or the 'education group', but it so happened that their material interests lay in the same direction. In fairness it should be pointed out that although this group (with the legal profession) provided a large proportion of postal revenue, they had taken most effective steps to avoid the worst of it so their gain was smaller. To this extent their actions were altruistic.

Finally comes the group of men who were working for the extension of cheap but genuine education for the toiling masses, the situations described so fluently by Charles Dickens: in fact, it is surprising that as far as we know Dickens was not involved, although he was a little young. The focal point was the Society for the Diffusion of Useful Knowledge, and its journal, the weekly

'Penny Magazine' which was published by Charles Knight and printed by William Clowes (who in 1840 printed the Mulready envelope). It was obviously helpful to this group in their efforts to spread education as widely as possible that postage rates should come down.

Yet curiously enough the first warning shots came from the one source it would be thought laughable to suggest — the Treasury. Lord Althorp, Chancellor of the Exchequer from 1830 to 1834 was probably the first holder of this office to realize that it was vital to the country to re-organize the Post Office, even if this meant spending large sums, and he must be given full credit for reversing the 'dead hand' policy of his predecessors and department. His first action was to insist that the free delivery boundary of the General Post in London should be made a circle three miles from St Martins (at a cost of £25,000, and taking effect from April 1831) despite Freeling's strongly expressed view that it was too costly. Shortly after this he insisted that the Twopenny Post boundary should be a twelve mile circle, and then, turning to the Packet service, he persuaded the Government that there was no need for the Post Office to run its own vessels (or borrow from the Navy) but to put it to tender, with a preference for steam. The tender accepted was from the General Steam Navigation Company, which ran from London, so this was the deathblow of Harwich as a packet port to the Continent.

The final reform of Lord Althorp cut right to the foundations of the senior staffing at St Martins — the privilege of sending newspapers to postmasters for country subscribers. Their monopoly of early days by franking had been reduced considerably since postage was included in the tax, but numbers sent were increasing steadily: of about thirteen million sent by post in 1830 (11,862,000 in 1829) the clerks of the roads still handled well over one-tenth. Despite the opposition, this was stopped from 5 April 1834, and those who suffered were compensated handsomely. It is interesting to note that the next reforms (according to Joyce and Howard Robinson) were to have been an attack on Freeling's autocratic power, the stopping of perquisites to senior staff instead of proper salaries, and a lowering of the general level of postage rates. If Lord Althorp and the Duke of Richmond had remained longer in their posts there might well have been drastic reductions in the charges for letters in 1835; these would probably have delayed for a long time the introduction of one uniform rate, charges by weight, and the use of adhesive stamps. However, Earl Grey's government resigned and the opportunity was lost, but anyway there is no evidence that they were thinking along the lines that Wallace and Hill developed so the greater good might have been lost. Althorp must have worked well with his Postmaster General,* the Duke of Richmond who, according to Joyce, once opened a Diplomatic Bag for the Colonial Office and found it full of letters to bankers, merchants, and Army Agents representing a postage loss of £60. Richmond refused to accept his salary for a considerable time, and was working in his office or talking with letter carriers and sorters at all hours of the day and night. Nothing like this had happened since the days of Lord Walsingham. He appears to have concentrated on improving the administration and left the reforms to the Chancellor, taking the view that they should come by changing the law, not bending it.

One of Richmond's first tasks was arranging the reunification of the English and Irish offices, which occurred in 1831. This had the curious effect of giving him a second patent, as Postmaster General of the United Kingdom, when the ink was scarcely dry on his first as Postmaster General of Great Britain. It was no easy task, for the state of the Irish office has already been mentioned. The Irish Postmasters General, Lords Rosse and O'Neill, had been in office for more than twenty years but had been seen rarely. The office had been ruled for more than fifty years by the Lees, father and son, John Lees (a Scotsman) having been appointed in 1774 and Edward joining him as joint secretary in 1801. John had been involved in the nasty business of payments to the previous secretary and another unnamed person, of a large part of his salary, and a smell never seemed far away from them. Edward outdid his father in every way. Although papers had to be signed by only one of 'the Earls', if it was inconvenient or a matter too doubtful even for them, he had been known to sign them as having been 'passed by the Board, present The Earls': later he was forced to admit to a committee of the Commons that only once had he seen them present in the same room, and that was a drawing room. The staff was swollen by innumerable practising bankers,

---

* Only one Postmaster General has been appointed since the death in office of the Marquess of Salisbury on 13 June 1823. The Earl of Chichester, the last joint holder of the position, carried on alone from that date.

attorneys, merchants clerks, and Government employees who valued the position for the power it gave to send free all the letters they or their employers required, and have immediate access to the mail of themselves or their rivals. The Receiver General was a private banker and money lender, we are told by Joyce, and two Express clerks ran a remarkable arrangement for newspapers by subscription on behalf of the Clerks of the Road; this involved frequently the holding back till next evening of all papers but their own in addition to enjoying free postage. It was impossible for the Dublin booksellers to compete — if a subscriber received his copy of the Edinburgh Review a day later and was charged 2/6 more postage than his friend (whose copy came through the British Newspaper Office, General Post Office, Dublin), he would lose the subscriber. It is not surprising in these conditions that the Dublin Penny Post had made losses in every one of the fifty years since its foundation.

There were many other differences and troubles between the British and Irish Post Offices, not least regarding the carriage of the mail between the two countries. In 1813 Lees announced that letters from Ireland would be sent to this country in Irish wherries from Howth, and in 1819 he combined with others to form the Dublin Steam Packet Company, both actions being well within his rights and succeeding in extracting better terms from Freeling in London. The former action was aimed primarily at securing the packet postage of twopence a letter, for Ireland had been paid an allowance of £4,000 a year whilst they were carried in English boats but now received the packet postage plus the extra postage for the mileage from Dublin to Howth, which they thought considerably more than £4,000. After six weeks Freeling gave in and doubled their allowance after pressure from London merchants who disliked the increased postage and irregular arrival of letters. The latter aimed at the passengers, for the Post Office chartered packets at low rentals in consideration of the extra passengers the owners would get, and the owners would not charter if the passenger fares fell too much. The Post Office had been very lax in not encouraging steam vessels, and when Dublin did this in 1819 London was forced to follow suit. Taking action in May 1821, they introduced steam on the Waterford to Milford Haven route in April 1824 and on Portpatrick to Donaghadee in May 1825. However, a large part of the trouble on the route was the shocking conditions of roads through Wales. The longer sea crossing to Liverpool was little disadvantage to steamers compared with the better facilities and road connections, and rival services there captured so much traffic that very large sums had to be spent. These were for making new harbour facilities, roads across Anglesey and through Wales, and especially in building the Menai and Conway bridges. £20,000 was voted for Holyhead improvements in 1815 alone. All these improvements were forced on England reluctantly, and one wonders why the Liverpool route was not adopted as the primary Irish artery. Holyhead was never really suitable, and the saving in sea travel was more than lost by the exposed harbour where entrance or exit was often impossible, the Conway ferry, the very difficult crossing of the Menai Straits from Anglesey, and the appalling roads all the way to Chester. A little earlier Parkgate, on the Dee near Chester, had been used extensively. A letter from Dublin to Cheshire of August 1820 says 'We had a dreadful passage of 4 nights and 3 days, arrived here yesterday, the motion of the vessel is not yet out of my head — you must therefore excuse me'. As it is a report on the business interviews for which he travelled, the journey appears to have been only from Cheshire. The surprising thing is that in 1805 a sum of ten thousand pounds had been voted by Parliament to make Howth a suitable port for the packets from Holyhead. The work should have been completed about five years before Lees used Howth for his small wherries, but it was still not deep enough for the English boats. It has not yet been possible to check what happened to this money.

This, then, was the situation which forced the amalgamation of the British and Irish post offices again by the Duke of Richmond in 1831. The gross abuse of franking has been mentioned before, the overstaffing for friends to obtain incidental benefits, the uncertainty whether mails would fit the sailing of the packets, higher rates of postage, the different length of the mile and currency (127 English miles equalled one hundred Irish miles, and thirteen Irish pence to twelve English pence), and lack of control from the top all made it inevitable. The difference in rates caused Belfast to use an attractive but very rare rate stamp between 1804 and 1806 on prepaid letters, and it is surprising it did not continue. Later letters sometimes had it endorsed in pen, a typical example of 1824 to York having in red ink 'Ir.9, Br 1:3, 2/-' in three lines, and the Belfast 'P. Paid' and mileage stamp. Belfast to Dublin, a distance of eighty miles was ninepence, but even allowing twopence packet charge the English rate seems to be twopence overcharged. The cost of the Menai and Conway bridges was so high that an extra penny was added to rates for each bridge, but they were not in use until 30 January 1826. The first vehicle across was the London to Holyhead mail coach, and the twopence charge was imposed in 1827. As this two shillings was paid in Belfast it is presumably Irish, so seems to be 11d English (170-230 miles) plus 2d English packet charge, plus 2d to convert to Irish pence.

In 1832, following the postal reunion, the relevant Irish acts were published in a package act (2 Geo 4 cap 15) which is very important. It authorized extension of penny posts throughout Ireland and curtailed free franking heavily (on paper at least, making forgery of a frank liable to transportation for seven years). Charities had to be nominated individually by the Postmaster General, and would then qualify for a flat rate of twopence irrespective of distance travelled. Clause 9 authorizes the establishment of Guaranteed Posts, and it is known that they were used widely but none to date has been found using a stamp. By far the most interesting are clauses 6 and 7, for these correspond closely with clauses 5 and 6 of the English 1801 act and state that posts can be run to towns and villages in Ireland, not being post towns, at charges to be agreed with the inhabitants. Clause 7, as does clause 6 of the English act, states clearly that this does not give exclusive rights to carry the mail, and their own carriers can continue. It is remarkable that this should be inserted, considering the trouble that had been caused by it in England, and details are needed of towns that used it. It must be very doubtful if any 6th clause stamps were used, but how nice to find one.

When the Duke of Richmond attempted to have the Irish Post Office accounts audited, he found they had not been checked for fourteen years and were in great confusion. The banker who was Receiver General had died a short time before, so it was the ideal time to straighten things out; when the auditors were just leaving London news came that his bond had been returned immediately after his death. It would have been impossible for Lees to be in ignorance of the state of the Irish accounts, deficiencies must have been very large over the past fourteen years, and yet he said the order to surrender it was given at a Board at which were 'present The Earls'. In fact they were nowhere near Dublin, and were never consulted. In view of this, and his previous record, it passes belief how Sir Edward Lees should be sent to Edinburgh as Secretary to the 'Scotch Post Office', unless it was thought the Edinburgh officials would be able to control him. According to Joyce, the Irish establishment was reduced by half (simply by sacking without any compensation those who rarely attended to their duties in person), salaries of those retained were increased, yet a saving of £10,000 a year resulted. He adds that the Irish accounts for those fourteen years have not been audited to this day.

It was most unfortunate that to follow the fine work of Althorp and Richmond came a year of upheaval, resulting in the firm establishment of Lord Melbourne as Prime Minister and the Earl of Lichfield as Postmaster General: in this twelve months there were four changes in the latter office, and four different holders of it (the Marquess of Conyngham in his second spell lasting only twenty two days). This would play havoc in any Department, particularly as Freeling in this period had lost his grip. Lest readers should compare the superficial facts of the careers of Freeling and Lees as stated (for they worked closely together and were good friends) and think that they were two of a kind, it should be stated that every author stresses (and enormous volumes of his minutes prove amply) that Freeling's motives were always to do the best for the service and the country, and no man can do more. Little evidence is forthcoming that Lees used his judgement beyond the advantage of the Lees family and friends.

Shortly after his election, Robert Wallace began frequent attacks on all aspects of the Post Office which became almost daily, and though constant reiteration tended to lose him serious consideration by many members, he was gaining support. He failed to secure the appointment of a select committee, but it was due to his constant attacks that in 1835 the Treasury appointed Commissioners to enquire into the management of the Post Office. He pointed out that the recommendations of the last three commissions of enquiry had been ignored by Government and the Post Office, the last having reported only five years before (the others were 1788 and 1797), and they had been very similar. He continued his attacks during 1835-7, despite the Commission that was sitting, opposing particularly the practice of charging by the number of sheets inside a letter, the refusal to place the administration under a Board, preferential delivery, the holding over of Sunday's mail in London until Monday evening's coach, and the basis and general level of postage rates. He pointed out that most countries in Europe now charged by weight and not by the sheet (which saved a great amount of work) and the four ounce maximum of the London Twopenny Post could well be adopted as a basic weight for General Post letters. In discussing charges, he recommended large reductions with a maximum of ninepence, but did not visualize a low flat rate all over the country at this time. The Commissioners of 1829 had recommended that one corps of letter carriers should deliver letters of all kinds instead of the wonderful London system by which delivery was triplicated — carriers of the General Post, Twopenny Post, and Foreign Branch solemnly walking the same streets, each delivering his own letters: the Post Office had replied that 'it would be productive of the greatest confusion and delay' although Dublin and Edinburgh already had a unified system, and this again Wallace emphasized. Despite the appointment of the 1835 Commission, he continued his attacks.

Wallace was already gaining a broad degree of support when the Hill family came on the scene — it is put this way because every activity seems to have been a family affair. Thomas Wright Hill was a brass worker in Birmingham, but unconventional and unusual — practical with his hands, with an inventive turn of mind, yet an idealistic theorizer with his head in the clouds. Living some years in Birmingham (where he was involved in the riots), he married Sarah Lea and moved to Kidderminster where Rowland was born in 1795, the third son. The other children, in order of age, were Matthew, Edwin, Arthur, Caroline, Frederick, William, and Sarah. With the bad times he soon had to move — to a large haunted farmhouse outside Wolverhampton, and the young Hill's childhood was in times of hunger and unrest which undoubtedly affected them in later life. When Rowland was seven, his mother persuaded her husband to buy the school of a friend in Birmingham, Hilltop, and when eleven he was teaching the youngest boys: the Hill boys' own education was mainly from their father but partly self-acquired through teaching. Mrs Hill must have been a remarkable woman. The school prospered reasonably, and when it had to enlarge, Hazlewood nearby was built. Their advanced ideas began to attract attention, and with the publication of 'Public Education' a number of influential friends were made. Despite a serious fire at Hazlewood progress continued, and in 1827 their ideas of expanding to London bore fruit when they bought Bruce Castle, a large empty mansion at Tottenham. Both schools were run as a joint enterprise, Rowland being at Bruce Castle and Edwin taking over Hazlewood from their father, who retired (Matthew had become a lawyer). This saw the beginning of the 'Family Fund', a pooling of their resources from which any brother could draw, and of the close family assistance in every way which was of great use to Rowland later.

With his London base at Bruce Castle* his interests expanded and in 1833 Hazlewood was sold to allow Arthur to run Bruce Castle, and Rowland to recuperate from a bout of illhealth. His restless mind considered various outlets, and he accepted the post of English Secretary to the South Australia Association, a colonizing project, in 1835. Matthew had been elected MP for Hull, so of course was brought in to help. Within a year the unsatisfied Rowland was looking around again, and (though he does not put it this way in his autobiography) this seems to have been because the difficulties of colonizing Australia precluded a rapid expansion of the Hill importance for which he searched. He was very interested in the development of a more efficient and rapid printing press, and had also contacted Robert Wallace to obtain information on the reform of the Post Office (both closely linked with the work of the Society for the Diffusion of Useful Knowledge, on whose committee Rowland and Matthew served). Wallace sent him a large load of reports and papers, and it was these (the groundwork already done by Wallace and others) which swung the balance, putting the whole Hill family on to a detailed analysis of the postal system. He retained his position in the South Australia Association until his appointment to the Treasury in 1839.

After a considerable amount of research, tabulation, and sifting of the cabload of documents and reports that Wallace had sent, the brothers reached some most interesting conclusions. There are indications that these were discussed with Wallace before anything was done, and in January

---

* It continued as a school until purchased by the Tottenham Borough Council in 1891. It is now a museum with a most interesting postal history display and collection, and is well worth a visit.

1837 the first copies of a pamphlet, 'Post Office Reform; its Importance and Practicability' were sent to friends and influential acquaintances for comment. This edition can be recognized by 'Private and Confidential' printed on the title page above the heading. The first public edition had many alterations, and incorporated a preface dated Feb. 22, 1837 from 2 Burton Crescent (no Burton Crescent is listed in current maps of London) and there could be three later editions*.

This pamphlet caught the imagination of the public, and must have sold well. In brief, it began by showing that the clear profit paid to the Treasury was less in 1835 than in 1815, despite an enormous increase in the need for letters (revenue from stage coaches had more than doubled in this period.) By reasoning which was probably unfair, he decided that the cost of sending a letter from London to Edinburgh was one thirty-sixth of a penny, yet it was charged more than a shilling, and then (correctly this time) he assessed nearly all the cost as being incurred on handing-in or delivery, and in paying for the very large number of free letters and heavy newspapers to be carried.

From this reasoning he drew three conclusions:

1. As the distance carried had little effect on cost compared with other things, one uniform charge should be made irrespective of the mileage.
2. To save costly accounting and delay for collection of the postage, letters should be prepaid on posting with the full charge.
3. To simplify this charging, letters must be taxed by weight only, irrespective of the number of sheets inside.

He elaborated considerably on methods of implementing these three pillars of his proposals, and decided that one penny per half-ounce was adequate (the private edition said one penny per ounce), that letters posted unpaid should be taxed a fine equal to the postage, and many other points. The methods of collection are interesting, and here we have another example of a change from the private edition to the public, rather surprising to the millions who collect adhesive stamps today. In the former Hill suggested two methods — prepaying by money, and by the use of stamped wrappers on which postage was paid when they were purchased. In the first public edition he adds that a difficulty is that people who cannot write could not address the wrapper if given one by the receiver: 'Perhaps this difficulty might be obviated by using a bit of paper just large enough to bear the stamp, and covered at the back with a glutinous wash, which the bringer might, by applying a little moisture, attach to the back of the letter. . . .' This, then, is the origin of the Penny Black and Twopenny Blue, and the millions of adhesive stamps from all over the world which we collect — no more than an afterthought to get over a problem. He had suggested previously that each receiver be issued with a 'tell-tale stamp' which changed its number each time, to strike on letters paid in cash (double letters having two strikes etc) and show how many pence he had to account for; this was the 'stamp' Hill suggested was struck on gummed paper if the sender did not wish to use a prepaid envelope, and he did not intend them

---

* There is a discrepancy in the editions. Birkbeck Hill, writing for Sir Rowland Hill, says "I had already published the pamphlet previously circulated as private and confidential, and it is to this publication that I have already made repeated reference, under the title 'Post office Reform, Second Edition.' However, after a lapse of thirty eight years and near his deathbed, Hill's memory could have played false. Howard Robinson follows Hill, takes the private as the first edition, the first public of 22 February as the second edition, 15 November as the third edition and says there may have been a fourth in early 1838.

It would be most unusual to call a very small private printing of a book, with no preface and sent to selected people for study and criticism, the first edition. It seems probable that *at the time* the February edition was regarded as the first edition, for it bears no imprint of the edition on the title page, has an important preface, and bears for the first time a publisher's name — Charles Knight and Co. It was largely rewritten and, most important, Hill begins the preface 'A small edition of this pamphlet was printed, and privately circulated, early in the month of January . . . it has enabled me to submit my plan to the consideration of many able men. . . . Their examination has led to some important improvements which, while they remove certain difficulties that attached to the plan in its original form, tend still further to simplify the proposed mechanism.' Without imprint and with the publisher's name, this seems to be considered the first edition.

The only other edition known bears the November date, and imprint of the Third Edition, so there is no doubt about this. A fourth edition was intended in February 1838, but it is doubtful if this was ever produced. There one must leave the problem. Were there only three editions, or four, or even five? It would be interesting if other editions can be traced.

to be printed. He realized the cost of rural delivery was considerably higher than urban delivery, so considered his system was applicable only to 'primary distribution' which was between two post towns or delivered locally. Secondary distribution, from a post town to places of inferior importance, he recognized as a source of loss but thought that even this should just pay its way: this should be examined more fully, but he envisaged a system similar to 5th clause posts for the small villages. As has been mentioned, and will be gone into at greater length shortly, the Uniform Penny Postage which came in 1840 only guaranteed delivery within a post town, and it was about 1900 before free delivery covered all the British Isles.

The pamphlet covers more than a hundred pages, but the summary above is enough, and Howard Robinson gives greater detail. One point which is not usually made, and seems most surprising, is that Hill did not visualize the end of Free Franking, and specifically caters for free letters. Probably he dare not do so, for the privilege was a prerogative jealously guarded, and these were the people who had to recommend his plan. He said that he hoped originally that the Government would adopt his plan without a fight, but when this failed the preface to each succeeding edition grows more outspoken and acid. Timing of the pamphlet was excellent, for the 1835 Commissioners had issued eight reports and were now studying the London local post. Hill was called to give evidence on 13 February 1837 (nine days before the date on which the preface was written to the first public edition of his pamphlet) and Wallace and Col. Maberley appeared later. The recommendations issued in July included the use of prepaid stamped covers experimentally in the London District Post, with prepaid letters reduced to one penny over the whole area (unpaid letters to be unchanged), and the amalgamation of the letter carriers.

The final (10th) report of the 1835 Commissioners was issued in January 1838 on Registration. They (Lords Duncannon and Seymour, and Henry Labouchere) had done a very fine job within their terms of reference, but were fortunate that the current mood for postal reform brought them much more attention than had been given to previous enquiries. They managed to get a degree of action, whereas the reports of their predecessors accumulated dust on the parliamentary shelves (but this needs no explanation in the 1970's, to readers who know all about jumping on bandwaggons). Through them the system of mail coach supply was recast completely, and when Vidler refused their terms the contract was thrown open to tender (he being excluded). They stopped also the incompetence and nest-feathering which had grown in the packet service by handing over the running and supply of the ships to the Admiralty.

Equally important, they secured the transfer of the Money Order Office to the Post Office officially, compared with the semi-official private enterprise status it had enjoyed since 1792. The Post Office had tried to start this in 1791 to prevent thefts of currency from letters, but when their legal advisers found their powers very doubtful they supported a private scheme of the Clerks of the Road. The Clerks did not do very well, so in 1798 responsibility was assumed for it by Daniel Stow, President of the Inland Office, and two partners. To send their orders at an economical rate, Stow & Co are said to have enjoyed free franking, but the author has not heard of any survivors endorsed with their name. The sole partner in 1838 was Mr Watts, who was bought out for above £400 a year, but in Ireland the brother of Sir Edward Lees (who had swapped his post of Clerk of the Munster Road for control of the Irish Money Order Office) secured for this a sum of more than £500 a year, although the business was smaller.

In addition, every report included three sample wrappers and envelopes, which the Commissioners recommended should be used experimentally to prepay letters in the London District Post. These were printed on special paper made by John Dickinson (who had given evidence on this subject) containing regular silk threads, and made under conditions of strict security. Two were printed 'One Penny, not to exceed one ounce' and the other twopence for six ounces.

No doubt everyone concerned expected that these reports would be forgotten more quickly than they had been written, as was shown by Wallace moving for a Select Committee to examine the Hill plan. He withdrew his request when study was promised, but later in May 1837 Lord Ashburton presented a petition in the Lords, and made a strong speech recommending the pamphlet. Both would have awaited publication of the report if they had thought attention would be paid to its recommendations. Hill's pamphlet was raised again in the Lords in the following month, and in this debate the Postmaster General, the Earl of Lichfield, placed himself beyond the pale for postal reformers. He declared that Hill's estimate of 88 million should be 170 million letters annually, so his proposals would require 416 million to equal the present revenue, and ended with the immortal words 'With respect to the plan set forth by Mr Hill, of all the wild and visionary schemes which I have ever hear or read of, it is the most extraordinary' (or extravagant)*. This statement, coming from a man speaking by virtue of his office in the Government, showed the lengths to which the Post Office would go to prevent implementation of the Hill plan.

Its extreme bias had a profound effect on moderate opinion, and unified the work of the three groups already mentioned — Parliamentary, headed by Wallace, Warburton, and Lord Lowther; Educational, led by the Hill brothers, Charles Knight, and Lord Brougham; and Mercantile, with George Moffat, W. H. Ashurst, Henry Cole and Joshua Bates. From early 1838 these three groups worked closely together, and conducted a clever campaign to convince both Parliament and the country that a uniform prepaid rate was not only desirable, but was economically possible. Papers published by the Mercantile Committee alone form a large volume, and a most interesting study: as one example, every member of both Houses and person of influence was sent two letters in the post, free franked so that the Post Office paid for the propaganda against itself. One was a very large sheet measuring $35 \times 22$ inches folded to $12 \times 8\frac{1}{2}$ inches, the other a sheet $4 \times 2\frac{1}{2}$ inches folded to $2\frac{3}{4} \times 1\frac{1}{4}$ inches. The latter enclosed a second sheet the same size, saying 'POSTAGE CHARGES IN 1838: This paper, $4 \times 2\frac{1}{2}$ inches, and its cover of similar size, weighs 7 grains, or under the 60th part of an ounce weight, and is charged DOUBLE postage, whilst the accompanying sheet, $35 \times 23$ inches, weighing just under 1 ounce, is charged as a SINGLE LETTER — N.B. In France, Germany and throughout Europe, Postage is charged by weight'. The large sheet is printed with a similar message, but on the front it has the salutary warning 'To be kept Dry, or the Single Postage will be raised to Fourfold Postage'. This pair was sent from Manningtree to A. Pringle, MP, 43 Pall Mall but they are too rare to be certain of the details of posting. As they were addressed to people with the franking privilege they could be posted free from any office. Sir Henry Cole† describes the amusement caused when fifty pairs were posted at Charing Cross. Fortunately at least two contemporary collections of the propaganda put out by the Mercantile Committee have survived, of which the largest is owned by the Postal History Society. A similar set is now in the National Postal Museum, and they make fascinating reading.

The Mercantile Committee had the brilliant idea of printing evidence, facts, notices of meetings, and general propaganda as a newspaper, the Post Circular, and sending it in the post. There were a number of editions, edited by Henry Cole and printed by Whiting, and they also contained telling caricatures, petitions and much material that needed circulating. As a newspaper it was carried free in the post providing it had the penny newspaper tax stamp, but as newspapers were charged in the London post those addressed to London were solemnly conveyed to a provincial post town, and posted there. One very powerful caricature showed the actual load carried by the Edinburgh mail coach on 2 March 1838, all placed on top of the coach for clarity. There were 2,296 newspapers weighing 273 lbs carried free, 484 franks and a large parcel of stamps also carried free, the franks weighing 47 lbs. The only paid freight was 1,565 letters, with a total postage of £93 and weight of 34 lbs. It was telling propaganda, for of a total of 531 lbs carried, only 34 lbs was paid, and a coach was said to be able to carry more than 1,680 lbs of mail without difficulty. The relative weights are instructive, too, for items to a pound were: newspapers 8.4, franks 10.3, and letters 46, so if the franked letters had been paid each would average $7/7\frac{1}{2}$d postage compared with $1/1\frac{1}{2}$d each for the charged letters. Cole had done fine work as Assistant Keeper of the Public Records, and became Secretary of the Mercantile Committee as well as Editor. He was one of the winners of the Treasury Competition (see later), became

---

\* There is a difference in the reporting of the two journals here, for Hansard says extraordinary whilst the Mirror of Parliament says extravagant: this was liable to occur when the reporting was done privately. The latter was quoted in the Nicholas Nickleby advertisement, Howard Robinson gives the former, whilst Frank Staff gives the latter version. It is felt that extraordinary is more probable, he just could not visualize the scheme, but both show the utter lack of vision and imagination in the Post Office at this time.

† For more details of a fine administrator, see his autobiography: 'Fifty Years of Public Life' published in 2 volumes in 1884.

Hill's assistant at the Treasury in 1839, and later was one of the chief organizers of the 1851 Exhibition.

As has been said, it is interesting to see the same names cropping up in various connections. A long pamphlet by W. H. Ashurst 'Facts and Reasons in support of Mr Rowland Hill's plan for a Universal Penny Postage' covered ninety five pages, and included favourable extracts from the evidence to the Select Committee which had not then been published. One of the people giving evidence of the wide use of trade circulars that would be made with a penny postage was J. W. Parker, publisher to the University of Cambridge. An attractively printed circular is bound in the pamphlet, bearing his name at the Cambridge Bible Warehouse, West Strand, and this was stated to have been submitted for the Treasury Competition of the next year, in the wrapper section. From the educational group too, a good number of pamphlets and articles came, together with articles and letters in newspapers.

One of the cleverest was written by Cole, and is found in part XIII of the first edition of Nicholas Nickleby by Dickens (it had first appeared in the Post Circular). The last page of the advertisements is 'Queen Victoria and the Uniform Penny Postage, a scene at Windsor Castle'. Sure enough, the preceding pages advertise the publications of John W. Parker, and pages before that have the imprint of Whiting (who produced the Post Circular and the Beaufort House essays). Charles Knight, Clowes, Parker, Ashworth, Henry Cole, they all crop up frequently. This scenario at Windsor Castle, an imaginary confrontation between Lord Lichfield and Hill controlled by Queen Victoria and in the presence of the Prime Minister, Lord Melbourne, brings out all the damning evidence and ends with the discomfiture and retirement of Lord Lichfield. Beneath is an appeal for petitions.... 'SUPPORT YOUR QUEEN and the Report of the House of Commons with your Petitions for a UNIFORM PENNY POSTAGE....' Queen Victoria had been on the throne only a year, and it would seem doubtful in the extreme if she had expressed her support (in such outspoken or even in much milder terms) or was pleased when she read the two pages of condemnation put into her mouth:

'The Queen (to Lord Melbourne) — It is clear to me that his Lordship had better retire from the Post Office' and again 'It appears to me, my Lord, that the loss of Col. Maberley to the Post Office would be another great gain to the Public.... My Lord Melbourne, you will please to bear in mind that the Queen agrees with Her faithful Commons in recommending an uniform penny post. If your Lordship has any difficulty in finding a Minister among your party able to carry the measure into effect, I shall apply to my Lord Ashburton or my Lord Lowther, as circumstances may require'. This is heady stuff, but one wonders that they were allowed to ascribe such strong but imaginary views to the Sovereign.

William IV had died five days after Lord Lichfield's famous words mentioned above, but the Whigs were returned (though with a smaller majority) and both Lichfield and the Prime Minister continued in office. Lord Melbourne was much occupied at this time in coaching and training the young Queen in the constitutional history and monarchy, and judging by his pupil a fine job he made. What was totally unexpected by all politicians was the firmness and strength of character that she began to show when she had found her feet, and it makes the imaginary scene in Windsor Castle remarkably prophetic. It ascribes phrases to her that she might well have used later in private, particularly in view of the many petitions which began to come in for a reduction in the level of postage rates. At the same time, no evidence has been seen by the author showing that Queen Victoria had any influence on, or took sides in the battle for a standard postage rate.

Meanwhile the Select Committee on Postage under Robert Wallace's chairmanship (always called the Wallace Committee) had been ploughing through the evidence of a large number of witnesses. The second enormous volume of evidence was published in early August, followed immediately by the third containing its report and conclusions, and an abstract of evidence. It is interesting to wonder why Wallace was made chairman, for usually it is an impartial member, and Wallace was strongly in favour of reform. If it was to remove a vote known to be in favour, it rebounded, for three vital decisions were carried by his casting vote and as chairman he wielded a strong influence throughout. Still, his vote for reform throughout the investigation would probably have carried it without the necessity of a casting vote if an opponent had been the chairman. A very important point frequently overlooked is that the terms of reference of this

Committee were so restricted that they were able to ignore most of the contentious points about the general running of the Post Office and the post, side issues which would have fogged the conclusions, and concentrate: 'to inquire into the present Rates and mode of charging Postage, with a view to such a Reduction thereof as may be made without injury to the Revenue; and for this purpose to examine especially into the mode recommended for charging and collecting Postage in a pamphlet published by Mr Rowland Hill.'

The Post Office, from the evidence of Lord Lichfield and Col. Maberley, came out very badly, but fared better with other senior officials who tended to keep to facts. Surprisingly, Sir Edward Lees came out well, saying that the illegal carriage of letters was the main cause of the difficulties, that a small reduction in rates would make things worse, and the only solution was to go to the lowest possible rates. He added that even the publication of this evidence was bound to make evasion still more serious a problem. Lord Lichfield provided his third estimate of the chargeable letters passing through annually at sixty-seven million (compared with one hundred and seventy million previously stated by him as fact) and his estimate of revenue was equally erratic, being found to contain up to 50% error. It was clear that the Post Office had no figures at all to work on, and Hill's amended figure of seventy eight million (from eighty eight million) was accepted by the Committee and proved to be very nearly right.

The most surprising feature of the evidence was how one witness after another got up and explained in great detail how they defrauded the revenue (one assumes they were protected by the laws of privilege). Thus Mr R. Taylor, a printer and publisher, always received proofs by coach, carrier, or private hand, each packet having a large number of letters from the author, his friends and acquaintances for delivery in London. Dr Lardner had come from Ireland, where in view of the weight of his packages he chose to frank them 'Lord Rosse', the Postmaster General who could frank to any weight. Now in England he estimated his correspondence at 6,000 to 7,000 a year, of which only 2,500 went to the post office at a cost of £30 a year — it would be a very large sum indeed if sent through normal channels without his 'ample supply of franks'. And so the evidence went on, from every walk of life but mainly publishers and booksellers: it was apparent that less than a tenth of letters from the business community paid postage, and that correspondence would increase greatly if it could be sent cheaply. Other types of evasion were old newspapers pricked with a pin or 'sympathetic ink', letters (to be refused) whose only message lay in the form of the address, and so on. Richard Cobden said that not one-sixth of all letters from Manchester to London paid postage. Walsall said one-fiftieth and Glasgow one-tenth. No longer could Post Office representatives deny this evasion, and Maberley even forecast that it would grow much worse with improvements in communication by the new railways and steamships. Just as important were the letters and circulars people would have sent if rates had been lower. It passes belief how Col. Maberley, having made these admissions, could describe the Hill plan as 'utterly fallacious; I thought so from the first moment I read it... a most preposterous one, utterly unsupported by facts and resting entirely on assumption'.

There was then evidence taken as to the desirability of various rates of postage, accepting the need for a flat rate irrespective of distance and charged by weight.

The report itself is a very full document of sixty nine pages, and on most points is strongly in favour of the Hill plan. In some things it went further than Hill — as in the abolition of all franked letters (of sixty two or sixty four million general post letters it was estimated about seven million a year were franked, being 4,813,448 Parliamentary, 2,109,010 of Public Offices, and 77,542 copies of statutes). In others it did not go as far, as in the acceptance of a uniform rate but recommendation of twopence, not one penny, as the charge between post towns irrespective of distance. It accepted charging by weight, and the need to simplify accounting procedure (which would be helped by prepayment by means of the stamped paper), but would not make prepayment compulsory.

Publication of the Report in August 1838 gave a tremendous boost to pressure by the reformers, and Henry Cole states that whereas in 1837 Parliament received five petitions, in 1838 it had 320, and in 1839 it received over 2,000 signed by 262,809 people. One presented by the Duke of Richmond (the former Postmaster General) had collected in twelve hours the signatures of the Lord Mayor and 12,500 merchants of the City of London. The troubles that harassed the

Melbourne government at this time made it very chary of action, but whilst it wavered (and would probably have resisted), a Parliamentary deputation of 150 members, chiefly his own supporters, urged acceptance of the plan. The Attorney General declared in its favour and Lord John Russell, Leader of the Commons, told later that the Cabinet was unanimous in recommending acceptance; Mr Moffat, leader of the Mercantile Committee, said that if the Government had doubts about it, he would form a body to farm the Post Office on the terms proposed, and guarantee to the Government the full amount of revenue it now received.

In early July 1839 the Chancellor of the Exchequer, Thomas Spring-Rice, moved that the Report be received and, in view of the pressure in the intervening year, a rate of one penny per half ounce be recommended. Everybody realized there would be a considerable loss in the first year (Wallace forecast up to £600,000), but the Conservative opposition under Peel was not as strong as was feared and the division produced votes two to one in favour. The Penny Postage Bill was introduced on 18 July, and Tory opposition was so divided and disorganized that it was ready for the Lords before August. Although many had considerable reservations and mixed feelings, the Lords remembered the lesson of the Reform Bill debates some years before and passed it without a division. Thus penny postage (whilst not necessarily immediate) became by law the avowed aim in the very near future.

The national newspapers for some time had been strongly in favour, irrespective of party, and the provincial papers were nearly unanimous, but one or two influential journals were much more reserved. A gem of criticism appeared in the *Quarterly Review* of October 1839. Having ignored the Hill pamphlet for nearly three years, it decided to review it when the battle was over, won and lost. Nailing its colours to the mast, it sailed in with no less than sixty-two pages of vicious opposition to the Hill plan and the recommendations and conduct of the Wallace Committee. It is unsigned, but Robinson states that it was written by J. W. Croker. Although cleverly written, it seems pointless in the extreme unless it was an attempt to rally the divided Conservatives. Croker writes as one who first favoured it, but was rapidly disillusioned on studying it and ended strongly against it. As the only severe criticism of the plan that the writer has seen it is important, but it is not convincing — it is too clever. Croker plays with words, spends pages criticizing a slip caused by a hurried production or a change in conditions in the thirty months since the plan was produced, and from these minor details he damns the whole scheme. A good example of this is that when Hill wrote, the Post Office had a large surplus, which Hill notes and says that reductions in postage rates may be expected anyway from this surplus. The 1837 and 1838 accounts had seen the surplus change to a resounding loss, and Croker makes great play with this change, saying that therefore the whole plan is unworkable and the Government has no right to place the remaining revenue at risk. Without the benefit of hindsight this does not apply — in fact the opposite is the case. The whole basis of the plan, which he ignores, was to cut down administration costs by simplifying the entire system of handling letters, compared with which the transport was nothing. If the plan was right with a large surplus it was much more right with the 1837 deficit of £655,760 and vitally necessary with the added deficit in 1838 of £345,227: with 1839 showing an estimated loss of £860,000 when he wrote, it passes belief how any man, brilliant or foolish, could say it was wrong to cut unnecessary overheads. Throughout the mass of scintillating words run two themes — it is wrong to take a chance, and because nobody objects to paying the fantastically high rates they must be right. This latter theme is an ideal example of Croker's argument. Nobody suffers from the charges except a few very wealthy merchants, for no one else writes letters. The merchants do not have to pay them, as they pass the charges on to their customers, so why take the risk? No comment can do justice to that reasoning.

In early September, only a fortnight after the bill received the Royal Assent, Rowland Hill was offered an appointment in the Treasury to supervise the new measures, but for two years only and at a salary of £500 a year (the same as he received from the South Australia Commission). This was not at all his idea, for he had expected to be appointed Secretary to the Post Office, in a new position responsible not to the Postmaster General but the Prime Minister. Immediately he rushed to Leicester to consult his elder brother Matthew, and they composed a severe letter from Matthew to Rowland, which he forwarded to the Chancellor with a covering letter. This device resulted in the salary being raised to £1,500 a year but still for two years only and still in the

Treasury, with power only to make recommendations to the Chancellor of the Exchequer (now Sir Francis Baring) for the Post Office changes. Hill was very annoyed and hurt about this, with reason because he was afraid that Maberley and Lichfield, but especially Col. Maberley, would try to sabotage the entire scheme. This fear proved to be unjustified, and had it been true the Chancellor had power enough to force compliance from the Post Office. With this appointment, he resigned his position in the South Australia Company.

This action of the Government was very wise; in fact it was the only way in which the scheme could be made to work, for Rowland Hill was anathema to all senior Post Office officials to a man, and they would never have worked with him. The Government wanted the reform to succeed, and the only way they could see was to keep apart Rowland Hill and the Post Office. The arrangement expected by Hill whereby he was responsible to the Prime Minister, and could give orders to anyone in the Post Office, was obviously impossible. It appears that there was more here than has been realized: the Government cannot have thought that he would accept these terms, and they may well have decided to offer the same salary to distract his wrath from the two more important points. If they could divert him from the Post Office to the Treasury on a short two year contract, they would be only too pleased to give way graciously and increase his salary up to the point it should have been anyway.

On Monday morning, 16 September 1839 Rowland Hill began work at the Treasury, to plan the introduction of his reforms. This position gave him access to the practical working of the Post Office, and on his first day he accompanied the Chancellor on a visit there which caused him to revise some of his ideas — before this he had been rigidly excluded. In particular he found that the building at St Martins-le-Grand was already overcrowded in its working area (although it had been open only ten years), but foolishly he resisted the idea of any improvement because it might interfere with his plans for District Offices. He was overruled in this, but the enlargement was not satisfactory to either side, and one wonders what would have happened if the increase in letters had been as large as was expected. His own solution, to rent temporarily part of the famous Bull and Mouth Inn opposite, was refused, as was his logical pressure to unite the two independent sets of letter carriers who still walked the same streets (the Foreign Branch letter carriers had ended before this). He was then sent to Paris to study the organization of the French Post Office, where he was impressed but did not learn very much.

On his return Hill began planning the introduction of a uniform postage, and his plan was sent to the Chancellor on 7 November although dated 2 November. Before his appointment, the Treasury had announced on 23 August a competition for ideas for the stamps and prepaid envelopes to be used, closing on 15 October; Hill's report therefore begins by saying that this will delay the full scheme, but interim changes must be made to maintain interest and prepare the Post Office staff — give them a practice run. They should simplify the operations and accounts, test the practicability of prepayment, and introduce charges by weight to give practice to the staff. Any part that is experimental should be tried first in London, where it could be supervised. He then proposed that in the London post all letters under half an ounce should be charged a penny if prepaid, but be unchanged at twopence or threepence if unpaid: the twopence charged on General Post letters delivered by the twopenny post (in Country areas) should be abolished making rates the same whoever delivered the letter. The General Post retained the 2d rate below eight miles, but all greater distances would be 4d for a half ounce, 8d the ounce and each additional ounce. All additional charges, such as the Scotch and Welsh halfpennies and the Menai and Conway bridge pennies, were to be abolished. Ship letters were to pay these inland charges, but other overseas rates were left unchanged, and sea charges within the British islands (Channel Isles, Isle of Man etc) were removed. He suggested 5 December 1839 to begin these new regulations, and again stressed the desirability of establishing District Offices. These proposals were accepted, and the trial began on that day.

The Act (2 & 3 Vict, Cap 52) came into force on 5 October 1839 for one year only, and simply gave the Treasury powers to fix or amend the rates of postage at any time by weight 'without reference to the Distance or Number of Miles the same shall be conveyed', to alter the regulations for carriage, to suspend the powers of Franking, and the regulations for the Twopenny posts and provincial penny posts, providing the changes were published in the London Gazette ten days in advance. It authorized the Treasury to sanction free carriage of letters written on stamped paper, in stamped envelopes, or having a stamp affixed, and to provide the stamps. It was replaced by a more detailed act on 10 August 1840 (3 & 4 Vict, Cap 96).

Hill awaited the results with considerable anxiety, but 5 December showed an increase of fifty per cent in letters from London. The public had understood the changes very well, for paid letters in the London post rose from below 9,000 to 23,000 although unpaid were the same at 32,000. It was a good start, although the revenue fell from £1,600 to £1,100 and Hill's diary records that the Chancellor was well satisfied: most important was that he could record on 13 December that Bokenham and Smith, the two heads of the Circulation Department, were well satisfied with the practical working, and he had begun to win over the senior practical and permanent staff. Three days later he proposed that the penny rate should come in on 10 January. Sir Francis Baring agreed to this date for the final step, but insisted that all free franked letters must cease on the same day, government or private. The increase had settled at about a quarter of the total, which was well below the expectations, but the staff were coping well.

In Hill's proposals was the suggestion that 4d should be included in the new date stamps to save double work, but this was not done. Nearly all letters of the Uniform 4d period have a manuscript 4, black for unpaid and red for paid letters, but a number of towns in Scotland used 4 stamps regularly which were probably issued from Edinburgh as they are a standard type. What cannot be explained is that whilst a fair number of towns in England used a stamped 4, all are extremely rare and most were used on a few days only. Ipswich and Hertford used two different

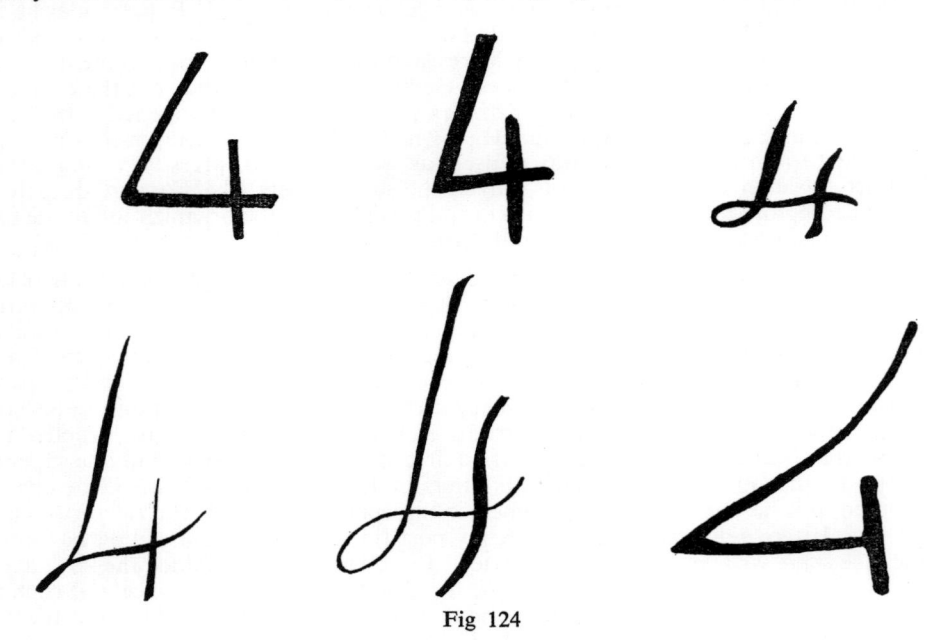

Fig 124

stamps during the month, and most towns are known with written charges as well. Another surprising fact is that London and most major English cities did not use a 4 stamp in this period — Birmingham, Liverpool, Bristol, Manchester could have benefited as much as Dublin, Edinburgh or Glasgow (which seem to have used them consistently). A most useful list by Bryant Lillywhite* of all the letters seen by him in the Uniform Fourpenny period shows the discrepancies quite clearly.

It will be seen that the London Twopenny Post was selected for the trial of prepayment, as

---

* Postal History Society Bulletin 124, March-April 1963.

Hill suggested in his draft. Prepayment had been strongly opposed by senior postal officials, yet it was essential to the success of the plan that handling, and especially delivery, should be speeded up in this way. Until now, for every letter the carrier knocked at the door, waited until it was answered and then until the money was brought, and probably found change, so that in his evidence Robert Smith said that in Central London it was no use giving a carrier more than sixty or seventy letters to deliver in ninety minutes. In residential areas it was difficult to average one and a half minutes a letter*. In the same investigation, Hill pointed out that with prepayment, probably every house would soon be provided with a box so the letter carrier would pass on as fast as he could walk (*page 33). This, then, was the importance of the experiment in London that letters were a penny if prepaid, but twopence or threepence if unpaid, and why Hill must have been so pleased that the forecast resistance to prepayment did not occur. The importance of these London letters is frequently overlooked.

It is a measure of the success of the trial 4d period that after only two weeks, Hill was confident enough of the practicability of his purely theoretical proposals to recommend the introduction of the penny rate three weeks hence, and the Chancellor to accept the date. Thus on 10 January 1840 came the penny postage for which so many had worked. This is the vital date, and 6 May (beloved of stamp collectors) is of very little importance. On and after 10 January a letter sent anywhere in the British Isles cost one penny if under a half ounce and prepaid, or twopence if unpaid: please spare a thought for what this meant. On 9 January the mails were bursting with free letters, but next day nothing was posted free. A letter to northern Scotland weighing an ounce (half the minimum rate today) which was six shillings on 4 December was only fourpence five weeks later, and the single letter came down from $1/5\frac{1}{2}$ to 1d. Letters everywhere without any fuss were one penny. On 6 May (if you were lucky) you had three ways to send your letter where only one had been before, but it made no difference to you sending it, or the charge you paid. In his diary, Hill records that he was up later than the adjacent days (rose at 8h 20m) on the 10th; then the very large letters 'PENNY POSTAGE extended to the whole kingdom this day!!' reveal his exuberance. Later comes a phrase that must have needed hours of control 'I have abstained from going to the P.O. tonight, lest I should embarrass their proceedings'. Is it fair to assume from this that he was not really worried? On the 11th again he only rose at 8.15 am (on 9th it had been 7.45 am) and begins 'The number of letters dispatched last night exceeded all expectations, it was 112,000, of which all but 13,000 or 14,000 were prepaid. Great confusion in the Hall of the P.O. owing to the insufficiency of means for receiving the postage. The number received this morning was nearly 80,000, part of course at the old rate. Mr Baring is in high spirits. It cannot be expected however that this great number will be sustained at present.' Surely this diary displays great confidence in the outcome — the reforms were obviously so right and necessary.

Fig 125

With the new rate of one penny a whole range of new 1d handstamps began, with some towns using a 2 stamp for double letters up to one ounce. One or two towns used 4's for letters up to 2 ozs., Chester and Carlisle continuing the stamp they had used in the uniform 4d period. These makes a very interesting and collectable group, and at present have not received the attention they deserve. Many towns began with manuscript charges and only used a stamp after some years, whilst most London offices used their old penny post stamps; a new handstamp is known on the first day at the Chief Office, but it is doubtful if a dozen towns are known with new handstruck 1d on 10 January. Much checking and research is needed before an accurate listing can be prepared, for errors have crept in. Although some are purely utility, many are most attractive and are very colourful in red.

---

* 9th Report of the 1835 Commissioners, page 17. Robert Smith was the Superintending President of the Twopenny Post.

Fig 125

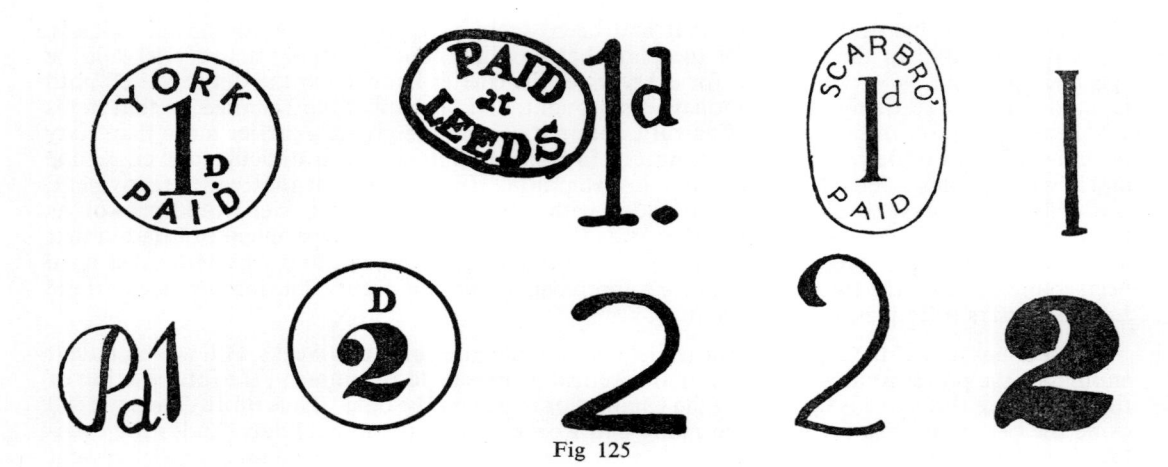

    The projected reforms of 1839-40 brought serious opposition from the stationers, who foresaw that their sales of writing paper would fall seriously if everyone wrote on the stamped sheets. This was not so, of course, as so many more letters were written. A side effect of the reforms was the use of envelopes in this country. Although envelopes had been used in Europe for more than a hundred years before this, use in this period in Britain had been restricted to the London post and free franked letters. In both these posts charges were by weight, but elsewhere the charge was by the sheet and an envelope counted as an extra sheet, so made the letter liable to double rate.* To satisfy the stationers the Mulready envelopes and wrappers (see later) were sold at a farthing each above face value, although this had not been planned. There were reduced rates for purchase in quantity, and these are printed on the flaps of the wrapper.

    As has been said above, Hill introduced into his second pamphlet (the first public edition) a small piece suggesting a third method of prepayment — either payment in cash, use of the stamped wrappers or envelopes, or a small adhesive label gummed on the address side of the letter. His suggestion of a tell-tale stamp struck on the label which kept a record of how many strikes had been made, to be accounted for by the receiver each day, was not accepted by the Treasury, but they were without ideas what to use. There was no guide, for no country had tried it before, so they announced a competition on 23 August 1839, asking for suggestions from the public. It was to be for ideas either for the envelope or the stamp, and had a closing date officially of 15 October. A large number of entries came before the end of the year, and a Treasury minute of 26 December states there had then been more than 2,600 communications. In 'Penny Postage Centenary'† Robson Lowe listed all the known entries, with those sent in subsequently, and this fine article is still the authoritative study of the competition. The entries were very varied, some being finely produced printing whilst others were rough pen sketches. Some did not send an essay at all, but a suggestion for the method, whilst others submitted a large number. In particular Charles Whiting, who had the resources of Beaufort House behind him, submitted about one hundred entries, many being either embossed or two-colour printing. A fair number of the surviving essays have proved impossible to link with the person who entered them, which is a pity.

    Four entries were awarded £100 each, one being shared by James Bogardus and Francis Coffin. The others were Benjamin Cheverton, Henry Cole, and Charles Whiting. None, however, was adopted either for the stamp or the envelope, and Henry Cole states that 'none was deemed sufficient in itself'. As prizes of £200 and £100 had been offered, the money was increased by £100 in view of the entries.

---

    * Frank Staff, in *The Penny Post, 1680-1918* ascribes the first commercial manufacture of envelopes in this country to a stationer named Brewer of Brighton in the early 1820's and thinks this may be because there were so many continental visitors in Brighton and so many franked letters from Brighton at this time. In his own collection he has Venetian envelopes hand made by the sender in a rudimentary fashion going back to the fifteenth century.

    † *Penny Postage Centenary*, published by the Postal History Society, 1940, editor S. Graveson.

Cole states* that he was charged to obtain a design for the envelope, and after consulting the President of the Royal Academy he saw the artists suggested. Sir Francis Baring asked him to see William Mulready in addition, which he did, and Mulready produced his symbolical design two days later (15 December 1839) which was adopted. It was engraved on brass by John Thompson, and not completed until 1 April. This was reproduced, and twelve stereos were bound into a forme to print a sheet. Wrappers (being rectangular) were printed square, but the envelope with flaps open was diamond-shaped, so was sideways in the forme. Each stereo was numbered, the wrappers first, and reconstruction shows that the first five formes were the penny, numbers 1-81 then the twopenny 90-105. Envelopes of the penny (again four formes) ran from 131-189 and the twopenny 195-210. Formes V and VI of the penny wrapper evidently came later, 223-255, and other numbers known were used as replacements. Printing was started by Clowes on 14 April, after different borders around the design had been tried, and the first envelopes were placed on sale at the Chief Office (and probably other selected offices) on 1st May to be read for use on 6 May. Six days later, Hill wrote that ridicule of the envelope had become so strong that some other type of stamp would have to be found for the envelopes. This is sad considering that he had placed all the importance on it, and saw it as the main vehicle for the post of the future. He was very surprised that it was the adhesive label everyone liked and used freely. During the following months the ridicule grew to remarkable proportions, especially by the sale of a large range of caricature envelopes which are so widely collected today, and the Post Office was forced to replace Mulready's design. On 26 January 1841 was issued a new type of envelope, still on the Dickinson silk-thread paper but now plain and inoffensive, with a stamp embossed at the top right corner. This, the first of the 'penny pinks', corresponds to the 'penny red' of the adhesive stamp issue and would probably have been printed in black if it had been a month or two earlier (see later).

Long articles have been written on the production of the world's first adhesive stamps, the 1d black and 2d blue, and this is not the place for a technical treatise. However, some points have still been overlooked, particularly with regard to the timing, and these will be brought out in the course of a general summary of events†. Firstly, there still raged up to 1950 or thereabouts, a remarkable battle between the descendents of the Hill family and those of James Chalmers of Dundee. Many tons of paper were expended in the earlier stages of the battle, firing one broadside of pamphlets after another, and the author well remembers that meetings of the Postal History Society had an uncomfortable atmosphere if both factions attended. Always they would sit on opposite sides of the room, and obviously they had paid no attention to the words of Samuel Graveson, that great pioneer of postal history, in *Penny Postage Centenary* on the subject. Having pointed out that adhesive stamps of the same type had been in use for very many years for deed and document stamps and patent medicines, and that Charles Knight's suggestion of prepaid wrappers had been preceded by some years by Charles Whiting in a submission to the Post Office, Samuel Graveson continues 'May we accept therefore . . . that in a democratic state no invention is the product of one mind only, but the fruit of many minds and of years of trial and experience. How many real inventors have seen others take the credit for something they have passed on to them'.

To the unbiassed observer there is no doubt that the furious argument whether Chalmers suggested stamps before or after Hill, and what they both meant by stamps, is paltry. For more than a hundred years some documents and deeds had had a small line-engraved stamp exactly the size of the postage stamp, adhesive and printed in black, so here from about 1700 is the origin of the penny black. There is no doubt that James Chalmers thought along similar lines to Hill, and produced essays at the same time, but the finished article drew all its inspiration from the little document stamps. 'The Plan' was the important thing, and there has been no suggestion that Chalmers produced a plan for uniform penny postage. Adhesive stamps were only one of the frills added for ease of working and would be useless without the plan, so what was the point of

---

\* *Fifty years of Public Life* by Sir Henry Cole, pages 62-63.

† The standard textbook is *The Line Engraved Postage Stamps of Great Britain, printed by Perkins Bacon & Co* by Sir E. D. Bacon, published by Chas Nissen & Co 1920, and taken from Perkins Bacon's records.

Chalmers making stamps before 1837, as was claimed by Patrick Chalmers, with nowhere to put them?

It is very surprising to see that Hill put out feelers to Perkins Bacon, and inspected their premises on 24 July, nearly two months before he began his work at the Treasury and six weeks before he received any notice that he would be offered a post. It is even more surprising to realize that this visit was whilst the penny postage bill was still in the Commons, and before the Lords had had sight of it — it was in the Lords it was feared it might be blocked. Such was the measure of Hill's confidence that it would be made law, and that when it was law he would be in charge of its application, and this makes doubtful the fears expressed in his book. In the light of this visit, how can the fact that Perkins Bacon did not then enter the Treasury Competition be explained? A letter from Henry Cole shows that he had counted on help from them with his entry, but the plate had not arrived in time, and one from Hill of 12 August warns that he was in no position to remunerate them for expenses they may incur; so it would seem that Perkins Bacon was backing Hill and Cole even before the competition was announced, on a pretty clear understanding that they would receive the order when the time came. It seems a better explanation of why they did not enter, than their official one. At this time they were working on the basis of printing a 'dry stamp' i.e. a stamp which does not require the paper to be dampened before printing. Probably from Perkins Bacon's point of view their actions were just backing a probable winner, but it can be seen why Hill appears to consider the competition a waste of time and barely mentions it in his autobiography. Again, of course, it was not his idea so he would not support it.

This is not implying that there was anything wrong in their actions, but it puts the situation in a most interesting light. Perkins Bacon were a firm of outstanding craftsmanship, and thoroughly worthy of the job. For many years they had held contracts as security printers for bank notes, although they did not secure the contract for the Bank of England notes for which Jacob Perkins had come from America in 1819. Chiefly their reputation was founded on craftsmanship in engraving, and a number of valuable patents of which the 'geometric lathe' (invented by Asa Spencer and purchased by Perkins) was the most important. This made a pattern of lines on the plate which was said to be impossible to reproduce, even by the machine, and was therefore a safeguard against forgery. Perkins formed a partnership first with Gideon Fairman, another American engraver, and then in December 1819 with Charles Heath, at this time engraver to the King. Thus came the firm of Perkins, Fairman, and Heath, and superb advertising sheets are known with this imprint having the Creed, the Lords Prayer, or the Ten Commandments engraved six times, each in a circle the size of a sixpence with superb medallions between. Every letter and word is clearly readable under a glass. Shortly after this, Fairman returned to America and Charles Heath is stated to have been bankrupt by virtue of the amount of money he had put into the firm — surely a peculiar reason for dropping him. More research is needed here to discover what really happened, as will be seen shortly. At about this time J. B. Bacon (who had married Perkins' daughter) became a director, and in 1834 H. P. Petch joined the board which then became Perkins, Bacon & Petch.

As stated above, the standards of Perkins Bacon & Petch for line-engraved printing was probably the equal of anyone, but it was only for recess printing, for which the paper must be moistened. Why then should Hill, Cole, and Bacon have had these discussions in July and August 1839 on dry plate, or surface printing, in which they were not skilled? If evidence of this is needed, it is only necessary to look at the very poor essays they made by surface-printing in 1880 in an attempt to retain the contract for printing the 1d and 2d stamps. Not only was Charles Whiting of Beaufort House a leader in this type of printing, but whereas Perkins Bacon held the important patents in the one field, those in dry printing belonged to Beaufort House: their Congreve principle of multi-colour plates had been widely used for lottery tickets, tickets for the Coronation of King George IV in 1821 etc, as it was most attractive and again was secure against forgery. As Whiting had been a loyal supporter of the penny postage movement from the beginning, did some of their printing, and had more entries in the competition than anyone else, why should Hill discuss with Bacon whether they could print Whiting's essays, instead of Whiting himself. It could be that Beaufort House was not large enough, but one would think with a guaranteed and continuous contract they could expand. This is another unsolved mystery, for it would seem that Perkins Bacon would have to pay heavily to use Beaufort House patents, and it was not their type of work. Whiting himself was only the business head of the firm, and it is possible he did not get on with Hill very well, but this was not unusual. He is mentioned little in Hill's diary, but it starts rather late for this; the odd references are not exactly friendly, and frankly there is a nasty odour hanging around this part of the preparations.

A third point which does not appear to have been remarked upon by most writers is that in a Treasury Minute of 26 December 1839, and in another of 20 February 1840, provision is made for stamping with the Queen's head by Wyon any paper that the public cared to send to Somerset House. This is repeated in *The Times* of 14 April 1840, in an article which could only have been written on official information, or following a visit to the Stamp Office —'The stamp for affixing to letter paper at the Stamp Office, is from a die engraved by Mr Wyon of the Mint. It is an embossed stamp, consisting of a beautifully engraved head of Her Majesty, with a wreathed border to the die. . . .'. Quite obviously the reporter had seen it, yet when adhesive stamps were placed on sale only two weeks later this 'stamping to order' facility had been withdrawn for fear of forgery. It must have been at the last minute (it could have been scrapped through this 'Times' article, which mentions the danger of forgery). The Wyon die was not used until the Mulready envelope was stopped late in 1840, when it began a very long run struck on plain envelopes made from the Dickinson silk-thread paper.

Again, why does nobody point out that the original scheme was to have three colours of stamps, the third being only for use by Government departments? This was given in the Treasury minute of 20 February 1840, but a memo from Hill to Bacon of 26 March adds 'One plate of penny and one of twopenny stamps will be required to supply the Government offices. They are to be distinguished from those used by the public by inserting V.R. in place of the ornaments in the upper corners'. The scheme had thus been changed, the V.R. plate for the penny stamp was made and printed in black, and copies are well known but pretty rare in fine condition. Printing began from it on 14 April 1840 with 174 sheets, and continued on fourteen days until 3 June, when 3,471 sheets had been done, of which 148 sheets were spoiled. The twopenny V.R. plate for government use was not made. Of the penny sheets, Sir E. D. Bacon states that two were registered as 'Imprimatur' sheets'* on 15 April and 9 May, one was sent to Rowland Hill, thirteen ungummed were delivered to Somerset House for circulars to be sent to all Postmasters, and 3,302 sheets were destroyed on 25 January 1843. Five sheets are not accounted for, so this leaves a possible nineteen sheets (or 4,560 stamps) which can exist, and a fine example sells for about £200. So much for the story of the 'V.R.', the abortive stamp for the Government offices.

To return to the important points of background to the preparation of the world's first postage stamps, it would appear that the original intention was for Perkins Bacon to make the plates only, and that the printing should be done at Somerset House (Treasury minute of 20 February 1840) but obviously their premises and presses were not suitable, so the entire job was given to Perkins Bacon. In all the negotiations from July 1839, it seems a foregone conclusion that Perkins Bacon would engrave the plates, and the paper would be provided for them by a separate contract: paper was excluded from all the suggestions for the stamp contract, and was provided by Stacey Wise of Rush Mills, Northampton.

William Wyon who has gone down in history as engraver of the most famous and widely used royal head for adhesive stamps, coinage, and medals, was of the remarkable family of George Wyon of Cologne, a silver chaser. George Wyon came to this country in the train of George I, and no less than seven of his descendants are listed in the *Dictionary of National Biography* as Chief Engravers to the Royal Mint or Chief Engraver of the Seals. William, great-

---

* Perkins Bacon were under compulsion to deliver a sheet (shortly afterwards it became the first five sheets) from every plate as it was made, and this was retained in Somerset House as the Imprimatur sheet for reference. At various times a set of one stamp from every sheet has been given away, until now the sheets in the Post Office lack varying numbers, but on average twenty five to thirty stamps. They are very popular with collectors, are always imperforate and were not gummed; shades of the penny red plates are beautiful, frequently very different from the issued stamps. In some later stamps the other four sheets were perforated and issued in the normal way, so in cases where the plate was not used subsequently (e.g. 2/- plate 3), was used on a different paper (10d on emblem watermarked paper) or printed in a different colour (4d plate 17 in sage-green) these stamps from the four sheets are the only ones issued, and are of the greatest rarity. Rarest of all is 1/- green plate 14, which in good condition could sell for well over £2,000. This was printed in 1876. Imprimaturs of unissued stamps are worth more than normals.

grandson of the original George, was born in Birmingham, and in 1813 (at the age of eighteen) was awarded both their large gold medal and their gold medal by the Society of Arts. With this remarkable achievement he came to London in 1816 and was appointed second engraver to the Mint on the award of Sir Thomas Lawrence after a competition. In 1828 the chief engraver Benedetto Pistrucci was removed to a new post (created specially to make room) of chief medallist, and Wyon was made chief engraver with a special award of £500 for his services from 1823. In 1837 on the accession of Queen Victoria, he engraved her head for a medal struck to commemorate her first visit as Sovereign to the City of London, and she was enchanted by it. This head was used on the majority of service medals and awards for gallantry until the 1880's, and she would not have any other portrait on the adhesive postage stamps of Great Britain to her death in 1901.

Henry Corbould was commissioned to prepare the design of the stamp, and the die adapting the Wyon head and Corbould design was engraved by Charles Heath (mentioned above as an early partner in Perkins, Fairman and Heath). As Charles Heath's eyes were not good in 1839 it is probable the actual work was done by his son Frederick, but anyway the Heaths were paid fifty guineas and Corbould twelve pounds. Proofs were pulled at various stages in the production, but it was decided that it was too lightly engraved for the purpose and was not completed. Work began on a new die which had the head engraved more heavily, on a background of engine-turning very different from the first die. One can only applaud the decisions which resulted in the improved die. Heath's first head has a slightly cross or petulant expression and would never have stood up to the number of plates that were required from it. The legend 'Postage one Penny' was all at the bottom of the stamp giving it an unbalanced look, and the background was diffuse and indefinite. In the new die 'Postage' was at the top, 'One Penny' below, the background was separated into the outer colums of a series of arcs, and the surround which was deep but matt, giving the effect of a framed cameo. The new Heath head, being deeper, gives the impression of strength but not of bad-temper, and being now completely framed is a balanced picture. Above all, the remainder was now a frame for a portrait of magnificent craftsmanship, and the jet black ink of the printing of the penny stamp was absolutely right.

Whilst the shade of black varies little (the intensity and condition of the plate make it appear to vary, but there is very little difference in the colour) the twopenny stamp which accompanied it varies in shade considerably. The blue can be quite pale, but the latest printings in a very deep full blue are magnificent (this colour runs on to the early printings of the new twopenny stamp with white lines added of 1841. The die was engraved in reverse on a flat block of soft steel, then hardened to a remarkable degree. This was transferred to the roller (a thick circular piece of steel taking up to seven impressions around the edge) and the roller was hardened. It was this roller which rocked the impressions into the printing plate, and different impressions on the roller may have been used to lay down consecutive plates. The twopenny stamps were made by removing 'One Penny' from one impression on the roller and engraving 'Two Pence'. The sheet was composed of 240 stamps (twenty rows of twelve impressions), and a letter was punched in each lower corner after the plate was completed, balanced by stars in the upper corners. The corner letters and the stereo numbers of the Mulready envelope were both afterthoughts to make forgery more difficult, it being felt that only one would be made and the Post Office would probably notice a large number passing through with the same number or letters. The top row was lettered AA-AL, the next BA-BL, and so on to TA-TL at the bottom. When the plate was completed it was hardened and was then ready to print. In April 1840 pressure was on Perkins Bacon to print quickly, for the stamps were late, so they used plate 1 in the soft state, possibly plate 2 as well. Plate 1 became so worn that when they had enough plates working it was withdrawn, softened, and every stamp on it was recut, or normally called 'reentered'. This gives two states of the plate and they are called Plate 1a and 1b. Many of plate 1b show signs of the first entry where the roller was not keyed exactly to it, and reentries like this are always popular. Technically, if the repair was made before the plate was used it is a fresh entry, and if made after printing commenced it is a reentry, but in normal terms the reentry is used to cover both.

Both the Mulready and the penny black were sold to the public (if available) on 1 May to be ready for use on 6 May 1840, but the 2d was not ready in time. Printing of the penny labels continued by night as well as by day up to 27 June 1840, for which Perkins Bacon were paid three halfpence a thousand above the contract price. One or two were used postally on the 2nd or 4th, and these would command a very high price today. Through a misprint in a circular, the London receivers were not supplied, and Hill records that this enabled the licensed vendors to charge 1¼d a label, and 15d, 16d or even 18d a dozen for Mulreadies. As sales were so large (a steady half million a day were supplied, recorded on 22 May, and this was not enough) they had no reserve at all, and in his diary on 29 May Hill records that many receiving houses had not received any labels, and vendors were still charging well above face value. They were cancelled with a Maltese Cross stamp struck in red, but there was also trouble with this red ink being cleaned off after the stamp was used.

The 'Directions for preparing the Red Stamping Composition' were:

1 lb Printer's red ink
1 pint Linseed Oil
Half-pint of the droppings of Sweet Oil
To be well mixed

according to a Post Office Circular of 25 April 1840.

The adhesive gum on the back was made from potato starch and supplied by Messrs J. Rawsthorne of Manchester. Here again there was trouble, for Perkins Bacon were craftsmen printers, and had no wish to do the gumming. Although they were allowed an extra halfpenny a thousand stamps for this work (the final contract price being raised from sevenpence a thousand) it was a constant source of annoyance to them, for the public was not used to these labels and licked too hard. In the late 1850's complaints became so numerous that the sheets were gummed twice, and some years later they were said to be gummed three times, drying between each application. Certainly it is very thick indeed, and is responsible for the frightful cracking and disintegration of stamps from most of the later plates of the 1858 series. It is a serious indictment of the collectors of these mint stamps that they will still pay a much higher price for those with gum than those without. It can only be described as utter selfishness (or lunacy) when they know that if the gum is not washed off very soon, every stamp will crack into pieces and be useless. What curious people they are, who prefer to lose all the value for fear that they would lose about a third of it if other people did not wash it off too.

The Speaker of the Commons had approached the Chancellor on 11 January to see if some interim measure could be taken to prevent Members having to waste time waiting to pay cash for their letters. After discussion, special prepaid envelopes were printed for one penny and twopence, bearing the words 'To be posted at the Houses of Parliament only' in black, and these were ready for the opening of the session on 16 January. At the end of the month the two Houses were separated, a penny envelope in black being issued for the Commons and a penny and twopenny for the Lords in red. The latter have 'Temporary' in brackets at the top. It is apparent that so few of the twopenny joint envelopes had been used that they continued in use for the Commons, being in black. All the twopenny envelopes are extremely rare, only one complete example being known (until five turned up recently) of the Houses of Parliament. The author remembers only one being sold of the Lords twopennies. Of the penny envelopes, the House of Lords is rarest, then the Houses of Parliament, and the Commons is easiest to find.

Hill, the Treasury, and the Stamp Office had all been very worried over the prospect of adhesive stamps being used again by chemical removal of the cancellation or other means. They could do little about those that missed the cancellation, but on 21 May his diary records that many ways to clean them had been found, particularly covering the label with isinglass or some other substance to varnish it over. He says these frauds were already numerous enough to cause annoyance, he thinks they will not last but Phillips the chemist with others is working hard on the problem. Between May and the end of 1840 a number of experiments were carried out to remove cancellations with various solutions easily available. These were on small plates of three or twelve stamps specially made, the former being very rare. A crescent at the top right corner of each was blotted out, and from the various colours used they are called "Rainbow Trials". It was decided that there was no ink suitable to cancel a black stamp which was impossible to remove, the only fast ink being black, which was difficult to see anyway if lightly struck. From late September to the end of 1840 four or five large London offices tried using black ink on the black stamp, but it was far from satisfactory and the decision to reverse the inks was made. Thus after a life of about ten months only, the penny stamp in black was replaced by the same in red as stocks were exhausted, beginning in February 1841. The original black plates 1b, 2, 5, 8, 9, and 10 were cleaned and used for red printings, and the new plate 11 was first used in red. After the red printing began it was found that stocks in black would be exhausted before the reds were ready for issue, so once more plates 5, 8, 9, 10 and 11 were cleaned and used for the small 'provisional printing' in black. This was the only black printing from plate 11, and is estimated at 700 sheets. Some plates were repaired before the provisional black printing commenced, and where identifiable these letterings are of great rarity (PB from plate 5 is the outstanding example, as the new entry was badly placed). From February 1841 onwards red brown was the standard colour for the penny.

A final point should be mentioned, for it is not widely remarked. Britain has never had its name on its stamps, and we trust it never will have it incorporated. The reason is that for three years, until Brazil issued the famous 'Bullseyes', all adhesive stamps prepaying postage nationally or internationally were British, for no other country used them. Therefore a name was unnecessary, and it was not used. It is up to every other country to distinguish theirs from ours, and this is still one of the most closely guarded privileges left to us. One hears that at meetings of the Universal Postal Union a 'sour-grapes' motion is tabled about it with monotonous regularity, and in an age when we cannot throw away our few advantages fast enough it is by no means certain it will survive.

Chapter 13

# MARITIME POSTAL HISTORY
## A Short Survey
### By ALAN W. ROBERTSON

MARITIME postal history relates to everything postal connected with letters carried to or from the British Isles by sea. It is usually limited to events and practices within the territorial waters of the British Isles. This facet of our postal history offers particular attractions to the would-be student and collector.

The sea-routes over which the written word travelled between the British Isles, Europe, and the rest of the world, have a history extending over centuries. The period of the expansion of the British Colonial Empire is of exceptional interest as written communications increased in volume, and methods of transmission by sea between the mother country and faraway overseas outposts of the Empire were a remarkable development. Here also was social history in the making, often reflected in the contents of letters from over the seas. *Geographically* the location of the British Isles in relation to the mercantile sea-routes of the world was important, and made a choice of routes possible, the study of which can prove very rewarding. The configuration of our island coastline, together with the location of varying densities of population, considerably influenced the methods and means of transmitting letters to and from the British Isles and also between ports within the kingdom. *Ships and shipping* are of course an integral part of the subject, and the enthusiast in this direction can find ample scope co-relating the names of ships and shipping companies with the letters carried by them, firstly in the days of sail, and later by steamships, famous and otherwise. *The rates and postal charges* on maritime mail varied greatly over different periods of time. The permutations and combinations of postal charges on letters entering and leaving the country by ship offer, to those possessing analytical faculties, a form of mental exercise as entertaining and exacting as anyone could wish. *Sidelines* of the subject are many and varied. To name a few:— the *disinfection* of maritime mail suspected of carrying contagion from overseas; the salvage or rescue of letters from ships which met disaster at sea, usually referred to as '*wreck letters*'; the practices of *forwarding agents* located at many ports in the kingdom; the customary forms of manuscript endorsement on letters by ship, with the sender's prayer in cipher for the safe arrival of the ship and the letter, known as '*talismanic inscriptions*'. These are but a few of the attractions provided by the specific subject of *maritime* postal history, but perhaps the greatest appeal to many is the almost limitless scope the subject offers to the possessor of an enquiring mind. Let us therefore now view some of the foregoing aspects a little more closely, as it were through the eyes of an enquiring layman with inclinations towards the study and collection of maritime postal history material.

---

There are letters showing evidence of having been carried over the seas in the 15th century and earlier. For practical purposes however the period most generally ascribed to the various practices in connection with maritime despatch dates from the mid 1760s to the end of the nineteenth century. There were a few earlier considerations, and some practices are perpetuated in a lesser degree to the present day. In 1766 the first of a series of handstruck identification stamps was issued by the General Post Office for use on maritime mail. From that time until approximately 1900 nearly two thousand types and variations of such maritime handstamps have been recorded. After about 1900 most of the considerations which called for maritime postal identification in the days of sail had become obsolete with the development of steamships.

There are numerous ways of recognizing letters which have been carried by ocean-going vessels. The evidence is usually to be found on the outside of the letter and may appear in one or more forms, the following being the most general:

1. The earliest practice prior to the mid eighteenth century was for the sender to write, adjacent to the address, the name of the ship or the name of the master of the ship by which the letter was despatched.
2. The simple annotation in manuscript 'SHIP' or 'SHIP LETTER' is found on letters mostly prior to the nineteenth century.
3. The use of official maritime postal handstamps, struck on letters by the postal authorities.

(The absence of any of the foregoing exterior evidence on a letter, the contents of which clearly proves its overseas origin, usually indicates that the letter had not been carried by the established legal posts. The illegal avoidance of the postal laws will be discussed later.)

Before proceeding any further it is well to consider the two most frequent and important words connected with our maritime postal history: 'SHIP' and 'PACKET'. These two words are fundamentally so important that if their functional use is not appreciated from the outset, much confusion can result. The technical and practical differences of the two terms will be dealt with under separate headings, but let the would-be enthusiast in his approach to the subject establish firmly in his mind that *Packet Letters* were carried by *Post Office* or Government vessels (Packet Boats) on Post Office mail sea-routes. *Ship Letters* were carried by *private* ships (that is, ships other than Post Office Packets) usually via routes over which no packet services were available to the public.

*Because different postal rates were involved it was necessary to indicate to which of these two categories a letter belonged. The paths of these two run separately, but parallel, throughout the period now to be surveyed.*

## SHIP LETTERS
### (*The transmission of letters by private ship*)

Royal Courier postal services, later including the limited despatch of public "common mayle" between England and the Continent of Europe, date from the fourteenth century and earlier. The 22 mile sea-crossing over the straits of Dover was supplemented later by sea communications across the North Sea. These relatively short sea-passages and the interchange of commerce with Europe resulted in so many opportunities for the written word to pass to and from the Continent, that references to this aspect are omitted.

Not until the end of the seventeenth century did the first *Post Office Packet* service over long sea-routes begin to be established. Prior to that time the only way to send a letter overseas was by private arrangement with the master of a merchant ship sailing towards the destination of the letter. Conversely, residents overseas arranged with masters of ships sailing towards the British Isles to carry their letters to these shores. During this early period, these practices were therefore entirely by private arrangement. The comparative illiteracy of the times, of course, limited correspondence, which in the main was confined to the letters, invoices and bills of the merchant adventurers. By the mid-seventeenth century the seeds of empire were being sown, and with the movement of the early pioneers from the mother country, so the links of correspondence began to be forged particularly with India, the plantation colonies in America, and the West Indies. Merchant ships engaged in the early colonial trade provided the only means of despatching and receiving letters to and from those parts. Letters given to passengers on these ships were usually carried 'by favour' and endorsed in manuscript accordingly.

It was the custom for the owner of a trading ship to advertise that letters handed to him or his agents would be carried to the place of destination of a particular voyage. The masters of such ships also undertook the performance of like services and hung bags at coffee-houses, and other places of congregation, into which the public put their letters. A penny or two was paid by the sender to the master for each letter as his perquisite, but that fee entailed no legal responsibility on his part for their safety en route. This was the customary method of sending letters outwards from the British Isles. Similar arrangements appertained to incoming letters by private sailing ships. On arrival at an English port, the master made what private arrangements he could to send the letters onwards by hand to the addressee, before the establishment of organized posts within the country.

When the Post Office was established, the foregoing practices became subject to entirely new postal regulations in respect of letters brought to these shores by private ships. Inland posts within the country having been established, revenue to sustain the foot and horse posts was raised by charges on letters according to the distances they were carried. It was therefore essential for the Post Office to 'capture' all letters hitherto carried by private arrangement to augment the revenue, and this of course included incoming SHIP letters. Clauses in the Post Office Act of 1660 specifically ordered all masters of incoming private ships to put any letters they carried into the post at their first port of call. Despite the penalties for evading those regulations masters, practiced in the private despatch of letters, often continued their longstanding customs. As a persuasive measure to induce 'bringers' (masters and passengers alike) to put their letters into the post, a 'gratuity' of one penny, later increased to twopence, was paid by the Post Office to the bringer for each letter he handed over. In those days the recipient of a letter paid the amount of postage due, before he could take delivery, and the said 'gratuity' was recovered by the Post Office adding it to the inland amount due from the addressee. At this point let us consider the Post Office procedures which began to apply to an *incoming ship letter* in 1660. Firstly there was the recovery of the 'gratuity' (not always paid out as it appears that many bringers were unaware of their entitlement) if it had been claimed. Secondly, the determination of how many miles the letter would be carried from the port of entry to the addressee, for on this depended the inland postal charge. These charges were calculated by officials at the General Post Office in London, whence all letters were sent at that time. It was therefore necessary for the clerks at the London G.P.O. to know the port of entry from which to calculate the inland charge and whether the gratuity had been paid out. From 1705 the postmaster at the port of entry would strike his town stamp, if he had been issued with one, which justified the charge on the front of the letter (including the captain's penny gratuity). The few letters between 1712 and 1760 with a SHIP handstamp all came into Irish ports more than 40 miles from Dublin; from 1760, Greenock also used a SHIP stamp.

By the mid-eighteenth century, British maritime commerce had vastly increased, and with it the quantity of letters brought in by incoming private ships. To meet this increasing postal traffic to an ever increasing number of ports in the United Kingdom (Act of Union 1710), the Post Office began to issue a series of handstamps which, by incorporating the name of the port and the words 'SHIP LRE' in one handstamp, served the dual purpose of identifying incoming SHIP letters and their port of entry. These began in 1765.

The form of this first two-line unframed type of handstamp is here illustrated (Fig 130) standard in form only, the lettering varied greatly in size, and in one or two cases the handstamp was kept compact by dividing a long town name to make three lines of wording. The distribution of these handstamps was at first limited but within a decade they were in use at a considerable num-

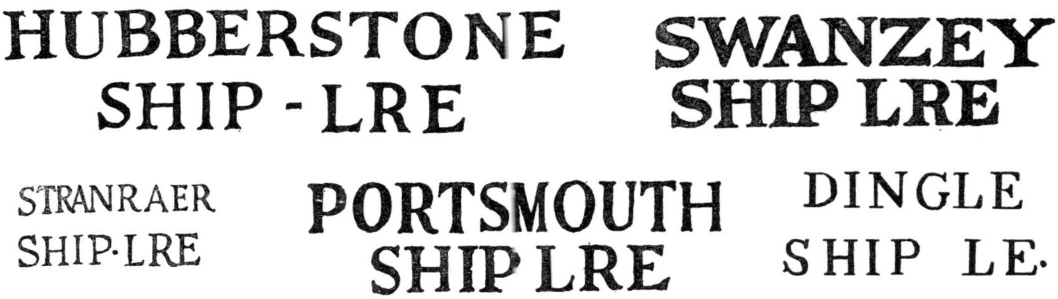

HUBBERSTONE
SHIP - LRE

SWANZEY
SHIP LRE

STRANRAER
SHIP·LRE

PORTSMOUTH
SHIP LRE

DINGLE
SHIP LE.

Fig. 130

ber of ports. Letters struck with this first type of handstamp are regarded as the early 'classics' of Great Britain postal history. The rarity of fine impressions from some of the ports compares with some early classic adhesive postage stamps issued a century later.

From 1766 over the next thirty years, there was a considerable increase in the number of letters carried by incoming private ships. The Post Office Packet mail services were also developing parallel courses but the costs of maintainenance and replacement of war losses were very heavy. These losses had to be met by revenue from the packet postal charges, and the resulting rates were high enough to deter many from sending letters by the packets. As a means of increasing Post Office revenue therefore, a new Ship Letter rate of fourpence was introduced in 1799 on every incoming letter by private ship. As all that the Post Office did was to receive the letter into the inland post and charge the concurrent inland rates, this levy on letters carried by private ships increased the temptation to by-pass the Post Office. So the master's or bringer's gratuity was raised to twopence a letter as a more attractive incentive to put incoming ship letters into the post. It became increasingly obvious that economically it was impossible to provide mail packet services over all sea-routes, and in 1799 the Post Office undertook the *outward* despatch of letters by *private* ships to places not served by the packets, at one half of the estimated packet rate if such a packet service had been in operation. The Post Office in turn paid the master the fee of twopence which he would have received from a member of the public under the old custom of 'private arrangement'. The public were notified in advance of the departure of accredited private ships by means of Post Office and press notices. All of these innovations called for particular administration and so to deal with all matters appertaining to incoming and outgoing letters by *private* ships, the accounting of outward sea-postage, incoming 'levy', gratuities, liaison with ship owners, an entirely separate ship letter office was established at the General Post Office in Lombard Street, London, on the 10th September, 1799.

With the establishment of that new Office, the old original two-line type of ship letter handstamps were withdrawn from the ports and an entirely new type was introduced. Examples of the second series of ship letter handstamps are given in Fig 131.

Fig 131

Once more the general form was standardized with sundry variations of the crown motif, and in some cases, the wording 'Ship Lre' expanded to 'Ship Letter' (for the first time). This type of maritime handstamp continued in use throughout the period of the Napoleonic Wars until near to their conclusion. In 1814 radical Post Office reforms were introduced. The rate on *incoming* ship letters was increased to sixpence, the gratuity at twopence was unaltered, but was now included to make a 'standard' total of eightpence, plus inland postage, due from the addressee on delivery. New rates and procedures on letters to and from India, the East Indies, Mauritius, and the Cape of Good Hope by private ships were established, and the preceding oval type of handstamp was withdrawn and replaced by the third series of Post Office ship letter handstamps. The wording was within a rectangular frame, now generally known as the 'step' type handstamp.

This 'step' type (Fig 132) continued in use from 1814 to 1839 and on surviving ship letters it is the handstamp of most frequent occurrence. The distribution to ports in the United Kingdom was very comprehensive, but whereas larger ports such as Liverpool made very frequent use of the handstamp, its use at other smaller and less frequented ports was sometimes very occasional and letters stamped at some of the smaller offices are, today, of extreme rarity.

```
QUEENBOROUGH
 SHIP LETTER
```

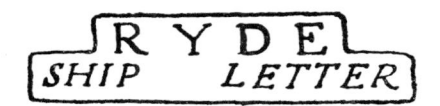

```
   R Y D E
SHIP    LETTER
```

```
SHIP LETTER
  HELSTON
```

Fig 132

The development of the steamship from the time of the mid-1820s was rapid. By the end of the 1830s, the first of the new paddle steamers were crossing the Atlantic. Ocean-going Post Office steam packets, were an even more uneconomical proposition than the sailing packet boats, but the public expected the speed, regularity and efficiency of the steamship to be utilized in the carriage of mail. Beginning with a contract in 1840 with the Cunard company for the carriage of mail between Liverpool, Halifax and Boston, the Post Office contracted with steamship companies for the carriage of the Royal Mail under subsidy. The era of the sailing ship was far from ended, but as the steamer mail contracts were rapidly extended, the public were provided with services much superior to anything the sailing ship could offer. The number of letters sent by private sailing ships declined to an insignificant proportion. Now, however, there were *private steamships*, and if the sender considered it more expedient between the times of the contract mail departures to despatch by private steamer, he could still do so, and such letters continued to be classified as SHIP LETTERS. And so, until the time of the outbreak of World War II, a very small proportion of incoming mail was brought on occasion by incoming private ships. For the purpose of identifying such letters, a limited number of ship letter handstamps were in use until relatively modern times. Examples of the last types of ship letter handstamps in use in the United Kingdom and Ireland are shown in Fig 133.

```
LEITH SHIP LETTER
    JU 5
     03
```

```
 HARWICH
SHIP-LETTER
```

SHIP LETTER
TYNE DOCK
SOUTH SHIELDS

```
SWANSEA
  9 JY
   01
SHIP LETTER
```

Fig 133

## THE POST OFFICE PACKET MAIL SERVICES

The history of the *Post Office Packets* is a vast subject but, because of its official services to the public, records and documentation are abundant. The whole story can be correlated much more tidily than the "ship letter" story, which contained a medley of practices, at times more in the hands of the public than under the control of the Post Office. *Interpretation clause*: Act 1 Victoria 1837. "The terms *Packet Boats* and *Post Office Packets* shall include Vessels employed by or under the Post Office or the Admiralty for the Transmission of Post Letters, and also Ships or Vessels (Though not regularly employed as Packet Boats) for the conveyance of Post Letters under Contract, and also a Ship of War or other Vessel in the Service of Her Majesty in respect of Letters conveyed by it."

In approaching the subject it is well to appreciate geographical and topographical considerations by envisaging a map of the British Isles. We are here concerned with the ways and means, adopted by the postal authorities over the centuries, of transmitting mails beyond the coastline of the kingdom before the advent of the aeroplane. The main *seaborne* mail services fall into three categories, each governed by geographical considerations, thus:—

*The so-called "Domestic" Packet Services* covered specific sea-routes of communication within the perimeter of the British Isles and obviously the oldest and most important were those connecting the land-masses of England, Scotland and Wales with Ireland. *Port Patrick* (S. Scotland) to *Doneghadee* (N. Ireland), *Holyhead* (and Liverpool) to *Kingstown* (Dublin), and *Milford Haven* (S. Wales) to *Waterford* (S. Ireland), were the shortest sea-passages, and the traditional routes of travel. It was natural for the written word to travel over the same courses. *Weymouth* (later Southampton) and the Channel Islands of *Guernsey* and *Jersey* presented peculiar problems. A service from *Whitehaven* (Cumberland) to the *Isle of Man* was established in 1767 and was transferred to *Liverpool* to the *Isle of Man* in August 1822.

The geographical advantages of the shortest sea-route for *Packet Services to and from the Continent of Europe* were frequently rendered impractical because of the exigencies of war between England and one or more of the continental powers.

*Dover to Calais* was the oldest and most natural route but had many suspensions of postal services during periods of war.

*Dover to Ostend* (or Nieuport), the traditional route to the Low Countries, was favoured by postal couriers in early times in connection with the long established central European courier posts of Thurn and Taxis, and was the quickest route of communication to the Middle East.

An important route was from *Harwich* to *Hellevoetsluis*, or Brill, in Holland and to *Cuxhaven* (the foreport of Hamburg) when the theatre of war expanded. The government depended almost solely on the Harwich packet communications for European news and intelligence during several periods of war.

*The oceanwise Packet Services to Overseas Countries* began in 1688 when the Post Office operated these services from the *Falmouth Packet Station*. Sailing ships using *Falmouth* (geographically situated far to the west), often saved many days in transit time by avoiding the variable and capricious winds of the English Channel. The Falmouth Packets sailed to *Spain, Portugal,* the *Mediterranean, West Indies*, and the East coast of *North America*, later extending to *Brazil, Uruguay* and the *Argentine*.

*The provision of Post Office Packet Boats* depended upon which of the services was involved. For the short 22 mile crossing from Dover to Calais, Thomas Witherings, Master of the Posts for Foreign Parts, in the 1630s hired Dover boatmen for a sum of forty shillings, to await the mail from London and take it across to Calais in small open sailing boats. The Holyhead to Dublin passage of 60 miles called for cutters and doggers capable of beating out of Holyhead against adverse winds. From Harwich to Hellevoetsluis was a distance of 122 miles, so the first sailing packets were sloops of approximately 70 tons. Long-distance ocean packet services from Falmouth needed stout fast sailing ships of 160 tons, manned by deep sea crews capable of defending the ship in addition to sailing her with speed.

Ships were put on to packet services in one of the following ways:—The owner of a suitable vessel was paid an agreed contract figure, usually annually, to carry mails at regular intervals over a specified route. Compensation in respect of loss or damage to be borne by the owner. Suitable ships were built by syndicates of private individuals, each taking a part share. They appointed their own commander, with whom the Post Office entered into contract. This arrangement was later improved when the Post Office laid down the building specifications, and the ships were strictly surveyed before contracts were signed. Compensation or replacement in event of loss was undertaken by the Post Office. At the end of several periods of war, naval ships, usually 10 gun sailing brigs, were transferred to the Packet Services. Commanded by redundant naval officers, these ships provided employment for a modest reserve of trained naval personnel. During the whole period of our maritime postal history, ships of the Royal Navy carried mail when the need arose. It was usually the individual man-of-war returning to her home port, or outward bound to join the fleet in overseas waters, which carried such mails and in times of war mails were frequently despatched via naval ships escorting convoys of merchantmen.

In 1819 the first Post Office paddle-steamer packet was employed on the Holyhead-Kingstown service. After this, a number of paddle steamers were specifically built for the Post Office services, a few for runs as far as the Peninsula and the Mediterranean. No steamers were employed at the Harwich station which was closed in 1834. In 1837, as a result of an enquiry into the economic losses incurred by the packet mail services, the whole Packet Establishment was transferred from the Post Office to the Admiralty. For the following years the ships were officially termed 'Admiralty Packets', until control was returned to the Post Office administration in 1860. Beginning with a Cunard steamship mail contract in 1840, further contracts were soon entered into with the P. & O. Company, the Royal Mail line, and others. A few Admiralty sailing brigs continued under canvas between Falmouth and South America via Madeira until 1850, in which year the Falmouth packet station was closed. Thenceforth until the present day the Post Office has subsidized the carriage of the Royal Mail by the vessels of steamship companies.

It will be clear from the foregoing that the maritime postal historian has a wonderful field of search and collection. Many letters by packet-boats were endorsed by the senders with the name of the packet. The names, specifications and periods of service of several hundreds of Post Office and Admiralty Packets from 1688 onwards are known and are available in listed form. The historical circumstances, particularly during wars and sea-campaigns, in which many packet letters were despatched can be traced with a modicum of reading and research; and the stories which unfold are often of remarkable interest.

The postage charges on packet letters were much more complex by comparison with ship letter rates. We have seen how the ship letter rate on incoming letters was in effect a levy, and although it was increased from time to time it remained standard in that it applied regardless of the place of origin of the letter from overseas. Packet postages were governed by different considerations. They were based in relation to the costings of the services rendered to the public; for example, the basic cost in time and money of maintaining a packet service between Falmouth and Montevideo, was many times greater than that of a service from Falmouth to Cadiz. The overseas rates of packet postage were therefore scaled to the distance and duration of the voyage to the place of destination. Also as time progressed, reciprocal arrangements between the postal authorities of other countries and the British government resulted in various modifications of packet rates in the light of advantages gained. And so by comparison with the relatively simple procedure of adding the standard concurrent ship letter rate plus gratuity to the inland mileage rate of an incoming ship letter; it is possible to work out the manuscript rates on a packet letter. To those with a mind for this type of mental exercise, working out the rate computations on packet letters can provide endless recreation.

In a similar manner to identifying ship letters by the use of appropriate handstamps, so packet letters were also struck with handstamps issued for the purpose. Here by comparison with ship letter handstamps, the complexity is reversed. Whereas ship letters came in by private ships at ports all and sundry, the Post Office Packets were based on a few ports only; in number and variety therefore packet letter handstamps were relatively limited.

Following is a summary of the use of Packet handstamps:—

The only handstruck stamps issued for "domestic' packet services, were used on the Holyhead to Kingstown service at a relatively late date. In 1860, the Post Office contracted with the City of Dublin Steam Packet company for the carriage of all mail between Holyhead and Dublin. Four large new paddle-steamers were built for this passenger service and mail rooms were installed on board the vessels to speed up the work of sorting en route. Special datestamps were introduced, and these with periodical changes of type continued in use until 1925 (Fig 134).

Fig 134

A minor 'domestic' postal service with the provision of facilities for Post Office staff, was established in 1879 on board several of the Clyde paddle-steamers on the regular passenger route from Greenock to Ardrishaig, and the small places of call en route. Handstamps were issued to the Greenock office for use in those floating post offices (Fig 135), and were in use until March 1917. At no time were British Post Office packet handstamps used on letters carried via any of the Dover or Harwich packet services.

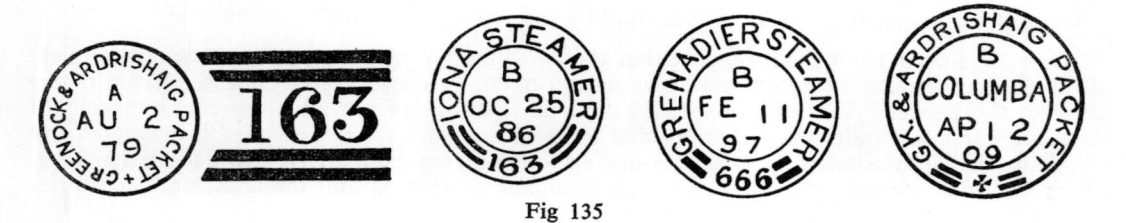

Fig 135

The first issue of packet handstamps for *Overseas packet services* was in 1802. This simple type was in use for a period of almost 60 years (Fig 136).

PACKET-LETTER          PACKET LETTER

*Packet Letter.*

Fig 136

Reference has been made to Naval vessels carrying mails in the capacity of packets when returning to their home ports in England. Such letters landed at dockyard ports were struck with packet handstamps issued for the purpose (Fig 137).

PACKET LETTER PLYMOUTH          PACKET LETTER PLYM:DOCK

Fig 137

With the establishment of steamship mail contracts, in cases where the mail was sorted at the port of entry, packet datestamps were issued to the postmasters at some of the larger ports (Fig 138).

Fig 138

Lastly we have to consider the status of letters posted on board liners, mostly by passengers, arriving at the United Kingdom and Ireland. The postal courses of these began to be indicated by the use of a particular type of handstamp soon after the Universal Postal Union Congress of

146

1891. The word "PAQUEBOT" in the official (French) language of the Universal Postal Union has from that time until the present day been used by all countries who are members of the Union. A few examples of the types used in Great Britain are shown in Fig 139.

Fig 139

The foregoing text has of necessity dealt briefly with the two main basic aspects of our maritime Postal History. It is a vast subject as yet far from fully explored, and the scope for further research along many of its by-ways is considerable. It is also an unfinished story, which is being added to not only when hitherto unrecorded handstamps and information is discovered, but as new maritime handstamps continue to be issued each year.

In conclusion here are a few brief suggestions for those who may contemplate forming a collection of Great Britain's Maritime postal history material. One can go the whole hog so to speak; that will cost time and certainly money. The subject however is so varied and has so many separate facets that it is practical and possible to build a separate semi-specialized collection by taking one or more of the ancillary aspects and developing a particular theme. Here are a few examples of by-products, under main headings:

**Historical**　　Letters carried over the pioneer sea routes in the early days of sail, and/or steam.
Seaborne letters to and from the British Isles in connection with various naval campaigns.
The effects of war and rumours of war on the routes and transmission of letters by sea.
The effects of international Postal Conventions on the rates and routes of maritime mails.
The East India Company's influence on the transmission of mails to and from the Far East.

**Geographical**　　The development of maritime mail communications over specific routes, for example:—letters to and from Great Britain by the North Atlantic routes and services to Canada and America; the development of the services to the West Indies; the ship and packet routes to Australasia, and the results of emigration from the home country; the development of the seaposts with the Cape of Good Hope and South Africa; the North Sea routes to and from the Continent and East Coast Ports, and methods of sending letters.

**Technical**　　The disinfection of maritime mail at the various quarantine stations in the United Kingdom.
The problems of the administration of matters regulating and concerning maritime mail.
The development of rates of postage and ancillary charges on G.B. Maritime mail.

**Social History**  The development and effects of Post Office seapost policies, and public practices in circumventing postal regulations.

**Specific**  Wreck letters, and mail salvaged after disasters at sea. Soldier's and Seamen's letters from overseas, and the special privilege seapost rates for Servicemen. Mail from the Royal Yachts.

**Domestic**  The Holyhead to Kingstown or Greenock and Ardrishaig handstamps on packet mail.
Mail communications by sea with the islands around the British Isles.
The considerations relating to letters carried by ships between ports in the kingdom.
The maritime postal history of a single county or section of the coast.
The maritime postal history of a specific port; for example London, Liverpool, Portsmouth, or Southampton.

**Ships and Shipping**  An enormous and almost inexhaustible subject; for example, the story of a specific ship named on the front of a letter, the various fleets of merchantmen and passenger sailing ships, and examples by each ship.
East Indiamen named on the fronts of letters from and to the East.
Letters carried by individual pioneer steamships such as *"Great Western"*, *"Great Britain"*, etc.
Letters carried by the ships of a particular steamship company, Cunard, Royal Mail, P. & O etc.

**Handstruck Stamps**  Ship Letter handstamps, Packet Letter handstamps, Naval Postal handstamps, Paquebot's.
The many supplementary Post Office instructional handstamps which appear on maritime mail.
The evolution of the rate handstamps which replaced the practice of endorsing amounts in manuscript.
Registered mail by sea and the special considerations thereof.
"India Letter" with the name of a port, indicating special inward ship letter rates.
"M.B." handstamps on letters posted in Mobile Post Boxes on board private Channel steamers.

# APPENDIX — Rural Distribution

It has been said earlier that when urban distribution was taken to court, it was found to be the responsibility of the Post Office to give free delivery within the normal limits of all post towns, but to a large extent they succeeded in dodging the issue. Uniform fourpenny and penny postage gave conveyance at a flat rate, but it was recognized as impossible for the Post Office to deliver to every hamlet without additional charges. A large number of villages had delivery by the time the penny posts were made free, of course, but many more had not: those that had a delivery were allowed to keep it. From 1840 many fresh areas received it each year, but with the increase in letter writing the problem was no nearer solution, and it was not until 1900 or later that the last few isolated areas received free delivery. To show the problem, the following Treasury Minute of 1841 is reprinted together with other papers showing the differences of opinion within the Post Office. These extracts are taken from the notes of the late W. G. Stitt Dibden.

**Note that this minute is nearly two years after the introduction of Uniform Penny Postage, and that no action resulted for at least three years after this date.**

---

**Treasury Minute of 13th August 1841**

My Lords read their Minute of the 10th November and 8th December last with regard to the extension of the Post Office distribution in the Rural Districts of the Kingdom.

My Lords have long had this important but difficult subject under consideration, and with a view to their guidance, much information has been collected under direction of the Chancellor of the Exchequer as to the extent and population of those districts which contain no Post Office, and as to the means adopted by the Inhabitants for obtaining and despatching their letters.

These enquiries have hitherto been confined to England and Wales, but even in these parts of the Kingdom in which Post Offices are more numerous in proportion to the extent of surface than those in Ireland and Scotland, My Lords find that there are districts of great extent, some measuring from 100 to 200 square miles, containing several thousand Inhabitants, which possess no Post Office whatever.

The means resorted to by the Inhabitants for obtaining and despatching their letters are, in many places, economical and well arranged, in others expensive cumbrous and inefficient. In some places a messenger is employed to carry the letters to and from the nearest Post Office (a distance occasionally of 10 or 15 miles), who is remunerated either by a subscription raised among the Inhabitants, or more frequently by a fee charged on each letter; in other places a pauper performs the Service, and thus the extra expense is reduced if not altogether avoided.

Frequently the messenger is employed by the Postmaster of the neighbouring Post Town, a circumstance which has led, in many instances, to the fee being erroneously considered by the Inhabitants as established by authority and consequently to its being submitted to even when obviously excessive; and in some cases it is stated that the Mail Guard, or other person employed in conveying the Mail through the village, leaves the letters at an appointed place and obtains a fee, generally a penny for each. But in numerous instances nothing like a systematic arrangement exists. One or two families, perhaps, have their own bags conveyed backwards and forwards at considerable expense, and the others depend on chance opportunities of calling at the Post Office (generally on market days) or send whenever they hear by accident that a letter to their address is exposed in the Office window.

The extra charge is as variable in amount as the means of collecting it. It is, perhaps, most frequently a penny, but it is in some instances only a halfpenny, in others as much as 6d a letter. In many districts the rate of a penny per mile (from the Post Town to the village) appears to be the established charge and occasionally the rate advances with the weight of the letter. In some cases these extra charges have been reduced since the reduction of postage but in others, notwithstanding the great increase of letters, they are as high as heretofore.

The unauthorised and frequently excessive charges to which a large portion of the correspondence of the Country is thus subjected, the irregularity and delay in its delivery and the risk to which it must be exposed from the employment of irresponsible messengers are circumstances which appear to My Lords to require serious attention, and the Board has anxiously considered what means are best calculated for placing the correspondence of Rural Districts on a satisfactory footing.

Some mitigation of the evil has been effected by the establishment of Guarantee Posts which has recently taken place in several parts of the Kingdom under the following arrangement.

Responsible parties enter into a written agreement with the Postmaster General to reimburse the Post Office for the full expense of establishing and maintaining the Post, and on this condition it is set on foot, the responsible parties indemnifying themselves by subscriptions among all who are interested in the measure, or in such other manner as they may agree upon.

Hitherto these Guarantees have been given for daily Posts only, but My Lords see no objection to their being taken for Posts on the alternate days or even less frequently should the parties, with a view to economy, desire it.

Still, though several Guarantee Posts have recently been established, the difficulties attending the arrangement are such that My Lords cannot regard it as affording a practicable means of complicating the system of Post Office distribution, and even if it were practicable, inasmuch as many places which now enjoy the advantage of a Post Office without any extra expense to the Inhabitants, are of inferior importance to others which have no such privilege, to rely entirely on the Guarantee Posts as a mode of completing the sytem of Post Office distribution, would manifestly be unfair.

It appears then to My Lords to be important, in the first instance, to lay down, if possible, some intelligible well defined principle by which to regulate the extent to which the official conveyance of letters, without extra charge, shall be carried.

That such conveyance cannot be extended to every place in the Kingdom, however remote and however small its correspondence, appears to My Lords to be obvious. Any attempt of the kind would certainly entail an enormous expense on the Post Office, which could only be met by the Legislature increasing the general rate of postage, and thus pressing unnecessarily and unfairly on the large Towns and restoring, as between them, the contraband conveyance of letters which My Lords have reason to hope is now effectually suppressed.

Considering, however, that the Law has for public purposes given to the Post Office alone, under ordinary circumstances, the right of conveying letters, and bearing in mind the great importance of promoting communication as far as practicable between all parts of the Kingdom, My Lords are not prepared to lay it down as a principle that the general system of Mail conveyance, meaning thereby the official conveyance without extra charge, shall include those places only where correspondence is sufficient to defray the expense. Such a principle would not only exclude many places now comprehended in the general system but would, in the opinion of My Lords, operate unfairly towards the thinly peopled districts generally. As the cost of admitting any place to the general system must depend in some degree on its distance from any existing Post Office, it is clear that the operation of the principle in question might exclude a village of considerable correspondence in which, from its being situated in a thinly peopled district and consequently remote from any Post Towns, a Post Office was much wanted, while it admitted another village of inferior correspondence in which, from its being situated in a densely peopled district and, therefore, in the immediate neighbourhood of one or more Post Towns, a Post Office was but little wanted. If however, instead of the actual, the average expense of connecting a place with the general system were compared with the amount of correspondence, perhaps this principle would be fair; but there is a manifest difficulty in ascertaining the amount of correspondence of any place which has no Post Office and, in the present state of their information on the subject, My Lords find it quite impossible to form any estimate of the additional expense to which the adoption of such a principle would lead.

Under existing circumstances, therefore, My Lords are pleased to lay down, for their present guidance, a rule which, while it is perfectly fair in itself, and while it will greatly extend the general system of Mail conveyance, will increase the expenses of the Department to an extent which when compared with the additional convenience to the public, is not very large.

The rule which My Lords propose to establish is founded on the principle that the number of Post Offices in every district should be somewhat in proportion to the amount of population and extent of surface combined, that is to say that they should be near to one another where the population is dense, but more numerous as compared with the Inhabitants, where the population is scattered.

The adoption of this rule has been much facilitated by the recent division of England and Wales into Registered Districts. The principle on which these Districts have been formed will be best shown by the following extract from the Registrar General's instructions.

"In determining the proper extent of a Registrar's District it is desirable that *Area* and "*Population* should be considered conjointly and each with reference to the other; that when "the population is *dense* the Area should be proportionately contracted; that when it is "thinly scattered over the Country the territorial extent should be proportionately increased. "With respect to the amount of *population* which a Registrar's District may comprise, I am "not disposed to require a very strict attention to numbers, but I may state that when the "population is of *average density*, that District may be regarded as well adapted to the "purposes of registration which contains about five thousand persons."

It appears from communications with the Registrar General, and from answers to queries addressed by the direction of the Chancellor of the Exchequer to certain of the Registrars of Births and Deaths, that out of about 2,100 Registrars Districts in England and Wales about 400, containing a million and a half of Inhabitants, possess no official Post Office of any description.

Returns to Parliament show that the average cost of the old Penny Posts was about £.20 per annum each; if this average could be relied on for indicating the cost of the Posts now under consideration, it would appear that the establishment of a Post Office in each of the 400 Registrar's Districts, and its connection with the general system of Mail conveyance, would cost probably about £.8,000 per annum, a sum which, in the opinion of My Lords, would be well expended in effecting so important an extension of the benefits of cheap, rapid and secure communication by Post.

In each of the 400 Registrar's Districts which have no Post Offices, My Lords are of opinion that a Post Office of some description or another, to form part of the system of Mail conveyance, should be forthwith established except, perhaps, as regards some few Districts which, although not containing Post Offices within their own limits, form parts of large Towns already included in the general system, and even as regards such districts, My Lords are of opinion that it may be expedient to conform to the general rule by the establishment of Receiving Houses.

The division into Registrar's Districts extends only to England and Wales, the proposed plan of Post Office extension is, therefore, unavoidably confined to those parts of the Kingdom, but it is the intention of My Lords, at an early period, to take into consideration means for extending the Post Office distribution of Ireland and Scotland.

As nearly every Registrar's District in which it is proposed now, for the first time, to establish a Post Office includes several villages, it of course becomes important to consider in what part of the District the Post Office shall be placed. As a general rule My Lords are of opinion that it should be placed in that village of the District which, from population and circumstances may be assumed to have the largest correspondence; but this rule My Lords are aware is open to many exceptions. For instance, if the village with the largest correspondence be very near to an existing Post Office, or inconveniently situated for communication with other parts of the District, or for connection with the general system of Mail conveyance, it may become necessary to place the Post Office in some place of inferior correspondence.

With regard to the selection of Postmasters for the new Offices, My Lords refer to a former Minute in which, with a view to public convenience and economy, the Board has been pleased to direct, with the concurrence of the Postmaster General and the Commissioners of Stamps and Taxes, that every opportunity be taken for uniting in small Towns the Offices of Postmaster and Subdistributor of Stamps.

Having laid down the principles which My Lords are of opinion should regulate the proposed extension in the general system of Mail conveyance, their Lordships are pleased to direct the Postmaster General to carry these views into effect as completely, as early and as economically as practicable. My Lords do not attempt to form any exact estimate of the additional expenditure which it may be necessary to incur, but they will rely on the Postmaster General carefully to avoid every unnecessary expense, and it is their Lordships desire that, should the cost of any single Post exceed £50 per annum, a special Report as regards such Post may be made to the Board before the expense is incurred.

Although My Lords have laid it down as a rule that, except perhaps under very peculiar circumstances, some place or other in every Registrars District shall henceforward contain a Post Office, to and from which the Mail shall be carried without extra charge to the Inhabitants, their Lordships wish it to be distinctly understood that they do not direct that in every such case and under all circumstances there shall be a delivery of letters at the houses of Inhabitants. Whether there shall or shall not be any delivery of letters, as well as the extent of such delivery in those places in which it may be established, My Lords are of opinion must depend on the number of letters, the density of the population in the neighbourhood of each Post Office and other matters which can only be ascertained by experience and by a careful examination of the circumstances of each particular place. My Lords will, therefore, leave these questions to be decided by the Postmaster General, merely expressing their opinion that a delivery of letters should take place wherever it can be established with due regard to the interests of the Revenue.

With a view of facilitating the proposed extension of Mail conveyance, My Lords have prepared, from the information supplied by the Registrars, a Table showing the Districts which are reported to have no Post Offices, their population and extent, together with the name of the chief place in each district, its population and distance from the nearest Post Office as well as some other particulars.

From this table it would appear that the average extent of the Registrar's Districts in question is nearly 20 square miles, and the population about 4,000. Also, that the average population of the chief place of the District (that of the whole Parish appears in most cases to be given) is about 4,000, and the average distance of such places from the nearest Post Office, between 4 and 5 miles. Judging from the pains which the Registrars appear to have taken, My Lords are of opinion that this table will be found to be tolerably accurate. Still My Lords would suggest to the Postmaster General the expediency of checking it, as regards the more important points, by reference to the Post Office Surveyors. The table is incomplete as regards a few places where the Registrars have, as yet, supplied part of the information only.

Transmit a copy of this Minute and of the table to the Postmaster General for his information and guidance; and direct His Lordship to report from time to time, for the information of My Lords, the progress made in carrying these instructions into effect. Add that My Lords will supply the information required to complete the Table as early as possible.

**Reference Treasury Minutes Vol. 52 f. 296.**

From The Postmaster General to The Lords Commissioners of Her Majesty's Treasury

---

My Lords,                                                                                                    31st May 1843.

In conformity with Your Lordships instructions with reference to the Treasury Minute of 13th August 1841, I have given my attention to the best mode of extending the accomodation of the Post Office in the Rural Districts. The results of my enquiry lead me to believe that the arrangement proposed in that Minute, of establishing Official Posts in the Country with reference to the population in each Registrar's District, would be attended with many practical difficulties, and with an expense far exceeding the assumed estimate.

I consider this arrangement also, being confined to England & Wales only, as partial in its operation and open to strong objection on that account.

After full consideration of the subject, I would submit that as a general principle, all places, the letters for which exceed 100 a week, should be deemed to be entitled to the privilege of a Receiving Office and a free delivery of their letters, and in this view I propose forthwith that Official Posts shall be established at all places which have already applied for the accomodation, the letters for which amount to 100 and upwards weekly, and that the same principle shall govern all similar applications that may hereafter be received.

I propose further, that where two or more small places can be combined *within one messenger's walk*, that the whole District thus included shall be considered but as one Post and that the calculation shall be made on the aggregate number of letters for all these places, and not those for each place individually.

I enclose a list of places and districts selected from the applications which have been received for Post accomodation from July 1840 up to the present time. In each of these cases the number of letters for the place, or places to be included in one Post, exceeds 100 letters a week. The expense of establishing Official Posts at all the places within this list is estimated by the Surveyors at about £3,251:15:6 per annum. It is possible, when it is generally understood throughout the Country that a measure of this nature is in operation, a very considerable number of additional applications for the same privilege of a free delivery of letters will be made immediately, all which, I submit, must be treated on the principle above laid down. I am, therefore, not prepared to say what may be the total cost of carrying out the measure throughout the United Kingdom.

In some few cases, where the letters received amount to the stipulated number, Post Towns have already been established under a guarantee from the parties interested, to defray the full expense of maintaining the Post. I propose, in such cases, that the guarantees shall be cancelled from the date of the new measure coming into operation, but where guarantees have been given in the case of places, the letters for which are under 100 per week, I submit the guarantees should be continued, and that it shall still be required in all instances where applications shall be made for Official Posts by places, the letters for which are below the rates now laid down.

If your Lordships approve the principle I now submit, I presume you will at the same time direct, in accordance with the Treasury Minute of the 13th. August 1841, that the expense of setting up any one Post shall be limited to £50, the sum specified in the Minute, with the understanding that every case where the expense will exceed that sum, shall be reported to you for special consideration.

LOWTHER.

---

**From Anthony Trollope,[*] who had been engaged on a Survey of Rural Posts**

Cheltenham.<br>19th. January 1853.

Sir,

I have found that the Fairford and Castle Eaton messenger has been in the habit of charging for the delivery of letters at houses which he has considered off his walk, and which I conceive actually to have been so, but which he reached while on his route, and in the performance of his official duties. I enclose his written explanation.

This evil is so widely spread that I think some measure should be adopted to put an end to it. Rural messengers, when put on their duties, are desired not to deliver at houses lying more than 50 yards off their walk and are also very generally told that they may employ their spare time, after completion of their duties in delivering letters, at a certain rate of payment, provided the

---

[*] Anthony Trollope, the novelist (1815-1882), spent his working life in the Post Office. He was appointed Surveyor in Ireland, and then spent two years inspecting rural delivery in England, which gave him much of the background for his novels.

parties so served are willing to receive the accomodation on those terms. The men, perhaps imperfectly understanding their instructions, but at any rate strongly interested in misinterpreting them, do very generally deliver on their route beyond the distance specified, and make absolute and specific charges for doing so. The general impression of the recipients of the letters being that they have no alternative but to comply with the demand.

Such charges, I presume, are illegal, the official delivery is delayed and the practice will, I think, be considered to be in every way objectionable.

When the usual revision has been completed, it may become a question whether it will not be expedient to require all persons, whose residences it has been found impracticable to include in a free delivery, to provide for the receipt of their own letters from the nearest office, and to prohibit any charge from being made by the servants of the department. I would, in the meantime, beg to suggest that all rural messengers should at once be instructed to confine themselves to the official free delivery of letters, and that they should in no way be allowed to make any charge for delivery out of their prescribed route, or beyond its limit. In most cases, the walk of a messenger ends at a sub office, and the delivery of letters not officially provided for is effected by the sub Postmaster at a certain charge per letter. This system at any rate, is preferable to the practice of charges made by a messenger whose special duty it is to effect a free delivery.

Should the suggestion now made be approved, I would propose that every Rural messenger should be required to sign a printed form containing instructions forbidding him to make any charge on the delivery of letters under any circumstances other than the unpaid rates of postage, and that any messenger discovered making such charges, shall be dismissed.

I am, Sir, Your obedient servant,

ANTHONY TROLLOPE.

---

In 1862, it was suggested that the ban on Rural Messengers delivering Letters beyond the limits of their walks should be removed.

---

Report from Mr Godby, the Surveyor stationed at Shrewsbury, to the Secretary.

3rd. January 1862.

The Secretary,

I beg to return the enclosed papers relating to the question of the delivery of Letters by Rural Messengers beyond their appointed walks, and to submit the following cases which have been mentioned to me by the Postmaster of Chester.

A messenger goes from Chester to Great and Little Barrow, he generally completes his delivery at 8.45 a.m., and starts on return at 4.40 p.m.; he has, therefore, nearly 8 hours of unemployed time, excepting when some little job is given to him.

There are several Farm Houses and three scattered Hamlets "Hallow Green", "Broomhill" and "Long Green", all within two miles of Barrow, which now have no delivery, and the letters for which are too few to pay for official distribution.

Several Residents at these places have offered to pay the messenger if he would deliver their letters, but he has declined because the Rule forbids him so to employ himself.

The Chester and Huxley messenger completes his walk about 9.0 a.m., and starts on return at 4.15 p.m., an interval of 7 hours, during which time he is unemployed; About a mile from Huxley are two Hamlets, "Hoofield" and "Brassey Green", whose Letters being too few for official delivery, are left at Huxley until called for. A Cheese Factor at Huxley has repeatedly applied for permission for the messenger to deliver his Letters, and offered to pay him, but the Rule has prevented his application from being complied with.

The Chester and Handley messenger reaches Handley at 8.10 a.m. and returns at 4.35 p.m., being unemployed for more than 8 hours. There are several Farm Houses and scattered cottages about 1½ miles from Handley, which have no delivery, and several persons have asked the messenger to bring their Letters, and offered to pay him, but he has refused in consequence of the Rule. I have made enquiries at other Towns in my district, as have my Clerks also when making a confidential Survey, but these are the only cases I am, at present, able to bring forward in which the alteration of the Rule, which I advocate, would afford the benefit which the change is intended to convey to the Public.

## FREE DELIVERY TO EVERY HOUSE IN THE UNITED KINGDOM

Extract from the Budget Speech of the Chancellor of the Exchequer (Sir Michael Hicks Beach). 29th. April 1897.

My noble friend the Postmaster General desires to make certain postal reforms with a view to the development of the rural districts by a more generous treatment in postal matters, and to simplify regulations and benefit trade by removing unnecessary restrictions, and to some extent benefitting the writers of foreign and colonial as well as inland letters. He has placed before me proposals which I shall shortly state to the Committee, as to which I wish to say that the credit is entirely due to him; that I have but accepted his recommendations and ask Parliament to provide the funds to meet them. In the first place, he proposes an important reform with regard to the delivery of letters in the United Kingdom. I dare say the Committee will hardly believe that at the present moment there are 16 millions of letters sent annually by the Post in the United Kingdom which are not delivered by the Post Office to the persons to whom they are addressed, but are left at the Post Office or some other house of call until they are called for. Even if we allow, as we may allow, for circulars and certain other communications which no one is anxious to receive — yet the Post Office calculates that there are 10 millions of real letters in that position every year — a number equal, I believe, to threequarters of our total foreign correspondence. It does not require much thought to see what a hardship that must be upon persons living in rural districts, and especially upon the poor. I do not think myself it should have lasted so long. It has not lasted so long in France or Belgium. In both these Countries they have, I think, a regular delivery to every house. Our Post Office intend to bring about the same. It will take a considerable time, for they will first have to commence, no doubt, with a delivery in every little hamlet, but as fast as possible they will take steps to secure that there shall be a delivery — not necessarily every day, but a regular delivery at every house in the United Kingdom. That will lead also to multiplication of rural post offices and of pillar letter boxes in order to provide for the same kind of services. . . .

**Minute 6342/97.**            5th. May 1897.

To The Treasury.

My Lords,

I have the honour to ask for the formal consent of Your Lordships to the Postal and Telegraph Reforms announced in the Budget speech by the Chancellor of the Exchequer.

(1) Alteration of the Letter Rates to 1d for 4 ozs and ½d for each additional 2 oz.
(2) Reduction of Parcel Post Rates.
(3) The extension of Rural deliveries and the establishment of additional Post Offices and Letter Boxes in connection thereinafter.
(4) Extension of Free delivery of Telegrams and reduction of porterage charges.

**RURAL DELIVERIES.**

My scheme is to make a serious effort to give a delivery to every house in the Kingdom, if not in every case a daily delivery, then a delivery as often as may be practicable.

The realisation of this scheme will not be the work of a single year but will require long sustained effort. The various items of cost will come before Your Lordships from time to time as Postmen's walks are reorganised, walking postmen are mounted, and new offices are opened. I estimate the cost at £100,000 a year.

# GENERAL POST RATES OF POSTAGE

ALTHOUGH postage rates up to 1660 have been given earlier in the book with explanatory notes, they are repeated here for ease of reference. From 1635 to 1839 charges for inland letters varied according to how many miles the letter was carried, this charge being for one sheet of paper irrespective of size. In 1637 a rate per ounce for larger letters came in, and it is probable that from 1657 the English scale was always four times the single letter for each ounce. From 1657, only exceptions to the above rules are given. Many problems remain to be solved.

## ENGLISH RATES

1635   2d per sheet below 80 miles, 4d 80-140, 6d above 140 miles within England; Scotland 8d, Ireland 9d.

1637   Unchanged, but one ounce was 6d, 9d and 1/- respectively inside England.

1653   On the reopening of the post, 2d below 80 miles, 3d above 80 miles, the details unknown of ounce rates, Scotland or Ireland.

1657   2d to 80 miles, 3d above, ounce rates 8d and 1/; Scotland 4d (1/6 ounce), Ireland 6d (2/- ounce).

1660   England and Dublin unchanged, Scotland charged from Berwick.

1711   3d to 80 miles, 4d above, London to Edinburgh or Dublin 6d.

1765   One post stage 1d, two stages 2d, other rates unchanged.

1784   One stage 2d, two stages 3d, 4d to 80 miles, 5d to 150, 6d above 150.

1796   3d to 15 miles, 4d to 30, 5d to 60, 6d to 100, 7d to 150, above 150 8d.

1801   3d to 15 miles, 4d to 30, 5d to 50, 6d to 80, 7d to 120, 8d to 170, 9d to 230, 10d to 300, 1d for each additional 100.

1805   One penny was added to all 1801 rates, so minimum 4d.

1812   4d to 15 miles, 5d to 20, 6d to 30, 7d to 50, 8d to 80, 9d to 120, 10d to 170, 11d to 230, 12d to 300, 1d for each additional 100 miles (above 700 17d).

1838   A lower minimum of 2d up to 8 miles authorized; no other change.

1839   (5 Dec.) to 1840 (9 Jan.) irrespective of the distance $\frac{1}{2}$ oz 4d, 1 oz 8d, 8d for each additional ounce up to 16 oz maximum.

1840   (10 Jan.) $\frac{1}{2}$ oz 1d, 1 oz 2d, each additional ounce 2d up to 16 oz maximum, irrespective of distance. In 1865 the ounce steps were divided, so for the first time $1\frac{1}{2}$ oz was 3d, $2\frac{1}{2}$ oz 5d, etc.

## SCOTTISH RATES
### supplied by A. Bruce Auckland

Internal rates were laid down in the Scottish act of 6 July 1695, and before that date they had been left to the individual farmers. After the Act of Union they were controlled by the London acts. Although the 1660 act decreed 2d up to 40 miles, 4d above 40 miles, it is uncertain how far this was observed, and generally many early letters seem to differ quite considerably. As 1d English equalled 12d Scots, the two are given for the 1695 act.

1695   From Edinburgh up to 50 miles (including Berwick) 2d (2/-), up to 100 miles 3d (3/-), over 100 within Scotland 4d (4/-). The double letters were double rate, etc.

1711   Up to 50 miles 2d, to 80 miles 3d, over 80 miles 4d.
1765   One stage 1d, then as 1711.
1784   One stage 2d, up to 50 miles 3d, to 80 4d, to 150 5d, above 150 6d.
1796   One penny was added to the 1784 rates.

In the 1801 act and onwards no special mention of Scotland is made, so it must be assumed that rates were the same as already listed. From 1813 all letters carried by four-wheeled conveyances in Scotland were surcharged one halfpenny for toll charges.

## IRISH RATES
### supplied by F. E. Dixon

Irish rates, like Scotland, are veiled in a certain amount of mystery. It is rarely certain whether English or Irish miles, or English or Irish currency are intended (see 1826). A careful study of a large number of letters is needed to lay down the rates that were charged in practice. Again, it is uncertain if some were charged the mileage via Dublin, and if so whether rates were for two separate journeys (as did London). Packet rates from Ireland need more study. Holyhead-Kingstown and Portpatrick-Donaghadee for most of the time were 2d, but the latter was raised to 4d in 1827 to compensate for two extra pence for crossing the new Menai and Conway bridges. Liverpool to Dublin was 8d, but there was a clause that no letter sent on this route should pay more than via Holyhead. In the south Milford-Waterford was never popular and was 6d until reduced to 2d in 1801; from 1836 it became $2\frac{1}{2}$d to pay for the improved roads in Wales. All these packet rates were for single letters and multiplied up.

1657   Up to 40 miles from Dublin 2d (8d oz), above 40 miles 4d (1/- oz).
1711?  1 oz rate above 40 miles increased to 1/4. Watson's Almanack of 1742 indicates that this 40 mile limit was not adhered to strictly, listing Loughlinbridge (41) as 2d but Arklow (36) as 4d.
1765   One stage 1d, letters via Donaghadee charged the direct distance to that port, and not via Dublin, except Belfast 1d.
1768   This principle extended, the 2d and 4d measured direct.
1773   Dublin Penny Post began 11 October. Weight limit 4 oz.
1774   1d post now 4 mile radius, outer zone 2d. 1d charged for delivering G.P. letters, or for P.P. into G.P.
1784   Up to 15 miles 2d, to 30 miles 3d, over 30 4d. Over 1 oz letters charged multiples per $\frac{1}{4}$ oz still, not per ounce at four rates.
1797   Up to 15 miles 2d, to 30 miles 3d, to 50 4d, to 80 5d, over 80 6d.
1805   1d added to 1797 rates.
1810   2d added to 1797 rates.
1813   To 10 miles 2d, to 20 miles 3d, to 30 4d, to 40 5d, to 50 6d, to 70 7d, to 80 8d, to 100 9d, above 100 10d.
1814   To 7 miles 2d, 15 miles 3d, 25 4d, 35 5d, 45 6d, 55 7d, 65 8d, 95 9d, 120 10d, to 150 11d, to 200 12d, to 250 13d, to 300 14d, for every additional 100 miles 1d. Irish currency is stressed in this act (13 pence to 1/- sterling).
1826   (5 Jan.) imperial standards were introduced, but Irish miles continued in use. Letters show that all charges were simply reduced by 1d.
1827   Dublin Almanack (printed 1827 for 1828) shows this 1d was restored, as the 1814 rates were now charged in sterling, using Irish miles.
1832   Provincial local penny posts began.
1839 and 1840   4d and 1d post as England.

# PERPETUAL CALENDAR
## or Tables for finding the day of the week for any date A.D.
(Copyright by A. F. L. Wilkinson.)

To Use the Calendar:—Look up the Index Numbers corresponding to the Century, the Year (last two figures) and the Month, respectively, in the first three tables; add these three numbers together and add also the Day of the Month: in the fourth table, *opposite the sum obtained*, read the Day of the Week.

### (1)

| Century | | | | | Index No. |
|---|---|---|---|---|---|
| 001–099 | 700– 799 | 1400–1499 | 1752‡–1799 | 2100–2199, &c. | 5 |
| 100–199 | 800– 899 | 1500–1599 | ... | ... | 4 |
| 200–299 | 900– 999 | 1600–1699 | 1800 –1899 | 2200–2299, &c. | 3 |
| 300–399 | 1000–1099 | 1700–1752† | ... | ... | 2 |
| 400–499 | 1100–1199 | ... | 1900 –1999 | 2300–2399, &c. | 1 |
| 500–599 | 1200–1299 | ... | 2000 –2099 | 2400–2499, &c. | 0 |
| 600–699 | 1300–1399 | ... | ... | ... | 6 |

† Up to September 2nd inclusive.   ‡ From September 14th inclusive. (*See* footnote.)

### (2)

§ Use column A for January and February, and column B for March to December.
\* For years up to 1700 inclusive, and also for 2000; 2400, etc.
\*\* For the years 1800, 1900, 2100, 2200, 2300, 2500, etc

| Year (last two figures) | | | | Index No. § A | B |
|---|---|---|---|---|---|
| 00\* | | | | 6 | 0 |
| 00\*\* | | | | 0 | 0 |
| 01 | 29 | 57 | 85 | 1 | 1 |
| 02 | 30 | 58 | 86 | 2 | 2 |
| 03 | 31 | 59 | 87 | 3 | 3 |
| 04 | 32 | 60 | 88 | 4 | 5 |
| 05 | 33 | 61 | 89 | 6 | 6 |
| 06 | 34 | 62 | 90 | 0 | 0 |
| 07 | 35 | 63 | 91 | 1 | 1 |
| 08 | 36 | 64 | 92 | 2 | 3 |
| 09 | 37 | 65 | 93 | 4 | 4 |
| 10 | 38 | 66 | 94 | 5 | 5 |
| 11 | 39 | 67 | 95 | 6 | 6 |
| 12 | 40 | 68 | 96 | 0 | 1 |
| 13 | 41 | 69 | 97 | 2 | 2 |
| 14 | 42 | 70 | 98 | 3 | 3 |
| 15 | 43 | 71 | 99 | 4 | 4 |
| 16 | 44 | 72 | — | 5 | 6 |
| 17 | 45 | 73 | — | 0 | 0 |
| 18 | 46 | 74 | — | 1 | 1 |
| 19 | 47 | 75 | — | 2 | 2 |
| 20 | 48 | 76 | — | 3 | 4 |
| 21 | 49 | 77 | — | 5 | 5 |
| 22 | 50 | 78 | — | 6 | 6 |
| 23 | 51 | 79 | — | 0 | 0 |
| 24 | 52 | 80 | — | 1 | 2 |
| 25 | 53 | 81 | — | 3 | 3 |
| 26 | 54 | 82 | — | 4 | 4 |
| 27 | 55 | 83 | — | 5 | 5 |
| 28 | 56 | 84 | — | 6 | 0 |

### (3)

| Month | Index No. | Month | Index No. |
|---|---|---|---|
| January ...... | 0 | July ............ | 6 |
| February ... | 3 | August ...... | 2 |
| March ...... | 3 | September ... | 5 |
| April ......... | 6 | October ...... | 0 |
| May ......... | 1 | November ... | 3 |
| June ......... | 4 | December ... | 5 |

### (4)

| Sum of Index Number | | | | | | Day |
|---|---|---|---|---|---|---|
| 1 | 8 | 15 | 22 | 29 | 36 | 43 | Sunday |
| 2 | 9 | 16 | 23 | 30 | 37 | 44 | Monday |
| 3 | 10 | 17 | 24 | 31 | 38 | 45 | Tuesday |
| 4 | 11 | 18 | 25 | 32 | 39 | 46 | Wednesday |
| 5 | 12 | 19 | 26 | 33 | 40 | 47 | Thursday |
| 6 | 13 | 20 | 27 | 34 | 41 | 48 | Friday |
| 7 | 14 | 21 | 28 | 35 | 42 | 49 | Saturday |

### Examples

1914, *August* 4th Index No.
Table 1......1900–1999...... 1
Table 2......14 (B)   ...... 3
Table 3......August   ...... 2
                  4th...... 4
                  Sum 10
Table 4......10 = Tuesday.

1215, *June* 19th   Index No.
Table 1......1200–1299...... 0
Table 2......15 (B)   ...... 4
Table 3......June   ...... 4
                  19th......19
                  Sum 27
Table 4......27 = Friday.

Note.—In England the change from the Julian System or Old Style to the Gregorian System or New Style, was made in September, 1752, when the 11 days 3rd to 13th inclusive were omitted, and Wednesday Sept. 2 was immediately followed by Thursday Sept. 14. Other countries made the change at dates varying from 1582 to 1923. (*See* p. 177).

If it is desired to look up a date after 1752 in Old Style, or before 1752 in New Style it can be done by taking a date 700 years earlier in the first case or 400 years later in the second case; *e.g.* **1923** in Old Style is the same as **1223**, and 1582 in New Style is the same as **1982**.

*Reprinted by permission of the proprietors of* **Whitakers Almanack**.

# INDEX

**Pages in heavy type are the important ones.**

## A

Abuses of Franking 55
Additional ½d Tax 114
Allen, Ralph 32, 38, **39**, 63
Althorp, Lord 79, 119
America, 16, 134
Andover (1665 Crosspost) **22**, 33
Anson, Viscount 60
Arlington, Lord (Sir Henry Bennet) 19, 24
Ashurst, W. H. 118, 125

## B

Babylon 1
Barnstaple 7
Bath 30, **40**, 52, **64**
Beaufort House Essays 132, 134
Bedford 4
Bellmen Letters 75
Belgium 111, 144
Bigg, Stephen & Richard **34**
Birmingham 84, **87**
Bishop Mark **16**, 24, 46
Bishop, Sir Henry **16**, 55
Blank Post Days 108
Bonnor, Charles 66
Boxes, Open 92, Private 104
Brighton 50
Bristol 14, 35, 39, 46, 64, 84, **86**
Bristol Road 10, 22, 29, 30, 50
Bruce Castle 122
Buckingham, see Farms
Burlamachi, Philip 11
By-Posts 7, 10, 22, 24, 25, **32**, 77

## C

Calendar, Julian and Gregorian 8
— Perpetual 158
Campaign Letters 110
Canada 16
Cancellations (of Adhesives) 79, 137
Carteret, Lord 65
Carriers **3**, 63
Carlisle 14
Cary, John 50
Chalmers, James 133
Charing 93, **95**
Charity Letters 57, 121
Charing Cross 7, 12, 29
Charges 10, 15, **20**, 27, 32, 64, 73, 76, 91, 100, 102 (Handstamps), 114, 117, 122, 156
Chelsea Hospital 57
Chester (see Holyhead Road) 10, 35, 46, **63**, 120
Chesterfield, Countess of 19
Chichester see Farms
City Posts 6
Clay Tablets 1
Clerks of the Road **22**, 24, 25, 39, 56 (Newspapers), 120
Clowes, William 119, 133
Coaches, Mail and Post **63**, 114, Parcels 70
Coffee Houses 27, 48, **67**, 69
Coggeshall (Essex) 49, 89, **96**
Coke, Sir John 9, 10
Cole, Sir Henry 118, 125, 133
Collins, Mrs (of Bath) 40
Corbould, Henry 136
Cornwall 32 **39**, 45
Country Letters 32, 42
Crewkerne 6
Cross Post 14, **32**, 46, 65, London 77
Crowns 103
Croydon 77
Cuneiform Writing **1**

159

## D

Darlot, Henry 112
Delivery, Local 80, 87, 99, 124, **149, 155**
— London 119
Dering, Sir Edward 13
Dockwra, William 26, **27**, 73, 75
Dover Road 3, 9, 10, 21, 29, 78, 144
Dublin (see Holyhead Road) 25, 58, 103, 115, 120
— Bishop 16, Penny Post 81

## E

Edinburgh 16, 57, 82, 103
Edinburgh (North) Road 10, 13, **22**, 29, 50
Envelopes, use of 132
Essex Road 10, **21**, 29, 50
Examiners Marks 105
Exeter 7, 33, **35**, 39, 46, 53, 63, 69, 87, 97

## F

Falmouth 113, 144
Farms Chichester 33, 46
      Plymouth 34
      Rye and Hastings 34
      Bedford 34
      Thetford 34
      Ferrybridge 34
      Wellingborough 34
      Lancashire 34
      Buckingham 34
      Exeter-Bristol-Chester-Oxford 35
      St Neots 36
      Walden 36
      Tonbridge 36
      Whitechapel 37
Farming the Post 14, 15, 18, 19, **20**, **25**, 33, 35, 39, 54
Fifth Clause Post 89, 121
Fire of London 22
Fleuron Stamps 51, 89
Foreign Branch 9, 14, 34, 59, **109**
Forces Letters 110
Fourpenny Postage, Uniform **129**
France 144
Free Franked Letters **54**, 124
Freeling, Sir Francis 48, **66, 70**, 79, 84, **117**, 121
Frowde, Col. Sir Philip 19, 22

## G

Gardiner, Thomas 24, **25**, 29
General Post Re-organization 76
Glasgow 88
Gloucester Coffee House 69
Goldsmiths Company 69
Greenwich Hospital 57
Grover, Jason 4
Guards, Mail 64, 69
Guaranteed Posts 89, 93, **99**, 121, 150
Guildhall, London, 14, 22, 23

## H

Harwich 21, 119, 144
Hasker, Thomas 50
Haste Post Haste 4
Hatherleigh (Devon) 49
Heath, Charles and James 134
Heath Family, smuggled letters 13
Hickes, James 15, 19, **22**
Highwaymen 67
Hill, Sir Rowland 4, 118, **122**, 125, 128
Hollar, Wenceslaus 23
Holland 111
Holyhead Road 10, 22, 29, 34, 50, 120, **144**
Honiton 97
Horses, Post 6
Hoskyns, Oswald 36, 41
Hounslow 19, 77
Houses of Parliament **54**, 57, **105**
Hull 10
Hutchins, Edward 7, 12, 29
Hutchins, Thomas 6

## I

Imprimatur Sheets 135
'In All' 102
India 16, 113
Inns 65, **67**
Ireland 25, 52, 105, 110, 119, 157
— Townstamps 47, Franking 55, Penny Post 82, 121
Ipswich 4

## J

Jersey 46
Johnson, Edward 72
Jude, Samuel 6

## K

Kent Road, see Dover Road
Kelvedon 89, 97
Kingston 77
Knight, Charles 118, 123, 125

## L

Lancaster 14
Lancashire 34
Late Fee 104
Launceston (no post at) 80
Lees, John and Edward 119
Levellers, The 17
Lichfield, Earl of 60, **121**, 124, 127
Lincoln 10
Lisbon 113
Liverpool 65, 84, 88
Lloyds Coffee House 48, 69
London Penny Post 26, **27**, 66, **72**
London Cross Post 77

## M

Maberley, Col. 98, 124, 127
Maidstone 93
Mailcoaches 50, **63**, **68**, 124
Maltese Cross Cancellation 137
Manchester 3, 65, **84**
Manley, John 14, 54
Menai and Conway Bridges 120
Merchant Posts and Marks **2**, 3, 9
Mercantile Committee 118, 125
Milford Haven 12, 50, 116, 120
Mileage Stamps 49
Moffatt, George 118, 125
Money Letters 109
Money Order Office 124
More To Pay 102
Morland, Sir Samuel 10
Mulready, Sir William 133
Mullingar 47
Murray, William 27

## N

Newbury 18
Newspapers 24, 25, 56, 118, **119**, **120**
Newport Pagnel 95
Nicholas, Sir Edward 18
North Road, see Edinburgh
Norwich 3, 4, 10, 50, 65

## O

O'Neale, Daniel 18
Open Boxes in 5th Clause 92
Ottery St Mary 97
Oulney 95
Oxford 10, 22, 33, 35

## P

Packet Ships and Letters 69, 119, 140, **143**
Paid Stamps, Early 21
Palmer, John **63**, 72
Paper, Early 2
Papyrus 2
Paquebot 147
Parchment 2
Parliamentary Mail, **54**, 57, **105**, 137
Passengers on Coaches 67
Penny Posts, Provincial 52, 72, 78, **80**, 151
Penny Posts, London **27**, 66, 72
Penny Magazine 119
'Penny Black' adhesive stamp 136
Penny Postage, Uniform 131
Peninsular War 113
Perkins Bacon & Petch 134
Pine, Henry, of Bristol 35
Pitt, William 64
Plague of London, 22
Plymouth 6, 12, 33, 40, 100
Plymouth Road — see West Road
Portsmouth 50
Post Boys 6, 67
Postmasters Petitions 6, 22
Postmasters, Condition of Service 6, 7, 20
— Monopoly of Horses 6, 80
Postmasters General, Joint 119
Post Offices, Distribution 150
Povey, Charles 31
Prideaux, Sir Edmond 11, 13, 15

161

L

Private Posts 80, 84, 90, **Boxes** 104
Prisoners of War 113
Public Post, Revival in 1653 14, 22

### Q

Quarterly Review 128
Quash, Joseph, of Exeter **32, 35, 39**, 45, 63
De Quester 9

### R

Railway, Mail by 70
Receivers (General Post) 14, 25, **29**
— (Penny Post) 27, 29, 75
Registration 109
Reynell, Thomas, of Chester 35
Richmond, Duke of 119
Rides, London 79
Roads 67
Rochester 93

### S

Scotland 31, 55, 57, 104, 114, 156
Shifnal 96
Ship Letters 3, 26, 48, 69, 113, **139**
Shooters Hill 77
Six-Day Post 21, 24, 43
Skeleton or Travelling Handstamps 53
Soldiers and Sailors Letters 110, 113
Stacey Wise, 135
Stanhope, Lord 6, 10, 11
Stanley, Francis 38
St Columb 39
Stow, Daniel 124
Stockport 49
Strabane 47
Sumer 1
Sunday Mail 106
Surveyors (Postal) **24**, 41, 42, 48, 64, 66

### T

Tankerville, Lord 65
Taunton 92
Thetford, see Farms
Three Day Post 22, 43

Thurloe, John 15, 18
Time Bills 24
Todd, Anthony 67, 84
Tokens, Tradesmens 70
Too Late 103
Tolls 64, 114
Towcester (1665 Crosspost) 22, 33
Town Cancellation on Adhesive Stamps 53
Town Sub-Offices 52
Transport Office 113
Treasury Competition 132
Trollope, Anthony 153
Tuke, Sir Brian 4, 9
Turnpike Trusts 50, 63, 114
Twopenny Post, Illegal 97

### V

Venetian Posts 2
V. R. Adhesive Stamp 135

### W

Wales 12, 15, 34, 36, 47, 55, 116, **120**
Walsingham, Lord 65, 72
Wallace, Robert 101, **118**, 125
Waltham Cross 77
Warwick, Earl of 9, 11
Warrington 39
Waterford 47, 116, 120
West Indies 16, 48
West Road **6**, 10, 19, 22, 29, 50, 69
Weymouth 15
Whitley, Col. Roger 20, 46
Whiting, Charles 132, 134
Wildman, Sir John 11, **17**
Williamson, Sir Joseph 20, 24
Williamson, Peter 82
Witherings, Thomas 4, 7, **9**, 22, 63
Witherings (Map of Post Routes) 11
Wyon, William 135

### X

X (Cross Post) Stamps 46

### Y

York 63

# BIBLIOGRAPHY

## GENERAL BOOKS

Alcock, R. C. and Holland, F. C. *The Postmarks of Great Britain and Ireland.* (Alcock, 1940). With supplements. The best book on the postal markings to 1940, detailed, well illustrated, and sometimes available in auctions.

―――― *British Postmarks, a short history and guide* (R. C. Alcock, Cheltenham, 1960). A good summary of basic types, 1660-1960 available from the publishers.

Robinson, H. *The British Post Office, a History* (Princeton University Press, 1948). Excellent on the historical side in a studious form, but much is omitted which a collector needs. Used in combination with other books written for collectors, it is most helpful. Available occasionally in auction.

―――― *Britain's Post Office.* (Oxford University Press, 1953). A good summary of the above, with some new material.

―――― *Carrying British Mails Overseas.* (George Allen and Unwin, 1964). The best history of carriage by sea and air. Should be available.

Joyce, H. *A History of the Post Office to 1836* (Richard Bentley, 1893). Of the early books this has been found the most reliable, balanced, and helpful, and it is reasonably available in auction.

*Penny Postage Centenary*, a collection of papers published in 1940 by the Postal History Society, with general and specialised articles: Witherings, Rowland Hill, the 1840 reforms, and particularly the detailed study of 1839 Treasury Competition Essays by Robson Lowe are excellent. Difficult to find but does turn up.

Crofts, J. *Packhorse, Wagon, and Post* (Routledge, Kegal Paul, 1967). A refreshingly different study of the conditions under which letters were carried, and people have travelled through the ages. Carriers, roads, stages, postboys, and coaches are all studied. Available from Vale Stamps.

## PRICED CATALOGUES

Lowe, Robson. *The Encyclopaedia of British Empire Postage Stamps:* This remarkable work was the pioneer catalogue. Recently Vol 5 was published, a very fine work dealing with British North America, but Vol. 1 (Great Britain) was last revised in 1952. It is still the only listing of Uniform 1d handstamps. Recently reprinted and available from Robson Lowe Ltd at Bournemouth Stamp Auctions.

Willcocks, R. M. *The Postal History of Great Britain and Ireland* 1972. A summarized priced catalogue up to 1840; everything but Ireland is rewritten and all the pricing is new. Available from Vale Stamps.

# SPECIALISED BOOKS

### Letters in Antiquity

Most specialised books would be too advanced, but the author found *Ancient Iraq* by Georges Roux (Pelican Books A828), *The Babylonian Legend of the Flood* by Edmond Sollberger (British Museum), and *Egyptian Papyri and Papyrus Hunting* by James Baikie (Religious Tract Society 1925) very helpful.

### Rates and Charges

*The Development of Rates of Postage* by A. D. Smith (George Allen and Unwin 1917) is the most detailed book, but is difficult to obtain and covering a vast field is notably sketchy on any one subject. The Post Office publication H.S. 10 gives a good summary of the bare rates, and is a good starting point.

### Early Post

*The Post in Grant and Farm* by J. W. Hyde (Black 1894) is very good, the best of Hyde's books, although chatty and only up to 1677.

### Penny Post

*The Penny Post 1680-1918* by Frank Staff (Lutterworth Press 1964) studies all forms of penny postage, inland and overseas. A good book with much new material, the international second half is excellent. Available in auctions.

*William Dockwra and the Rest of the Undertakers* by T. Todd (Cousland 1952) is an outstanding study of this small field, but does not go into the Government Post from 1683. Very difficult to obtain.

*English Provincial Local Post* by G. F. Oxley (Postal History Society 1973) is the detailed listing of offices and handstamps of the 5th Clause and Penny Posts. A rarity guide also serves as an index and cross reference: a very fine book, available from the P.H.S.

### Mail Coaches

*John Palmer, Mail Coach Pioneer* by Charles Clear (Postal History Society 1955) is another similar study of the work of one man. Well written and turns up in auction.

### Free Franks

*The Franking System* by George Brumell, 1936 is still excellent, detailed, and very accurate; a wonderful pamphlet for its date.

### London

*Local Posts of London* by George Brumell (Philatelic Adviser 1938) deserves the same praise: a reprint is available published by R. C. Alcock Ltd.

### Ship Letters

*A History of Ship Letters of the British Isles* by Alan W. Robertson. A complete listing of maritime handstamps, with a rarity guide and much other information, by the author of the maritime section of this book: the pioneer specialised study and not likely to be equalled. Recently republished and available from Hayes.

*Transatlantic Mail* by Frank Staff (Adlard Coles 1956) goes into the development of transatlantic communication in great detail: it is the standard work, and very helpful from the shipping angle, but the opportunity to study the large number of handstamps used on this run was missed. Turns up in auction.

### Road Books
The early itineraries of Cary and Paterson are by far the best guides to the roads along which mail was carried in the early nineteenth century, and the mileages. Fortunately they are fairly available. Both men also published books of road and county maps, 1795-1825.

### Studies of a City or Area
Studies of a City or Area are useful to show beginners the way to collect and what is available, in addition to the information they contain. Two good examples are *The Post Office at Nottingham* by Arthur W. G. Hall (1947) and a *History of the Manchester Post Office 1625-1900* by Charles Calvert (1967, available from J. E. Lea Ltd., 62 King Street, Manchester 2). Others are also very helpful.

### Scotland
Here the publications of the Scottish Postmark Group are very fine detailed studies, particularly in our period (the Mileage Marks and Edinburgh Penny Posts): details from D. C. Jefferies, 11 Craigcrook Avenue, Edinburgh EH4 3QE.

*Three Centuries of Scottish Posts* by A. R. B. Haldane (Edinburgh University Press 1971) is a new detailed historical survey which should be very helpful.

---

## The Postal History Society
The Postal History Society has published, over nearly forty years, more excellent 'meat' than anyone else. The journal is *Postal History* (formerly the *Bulletin*), back numbers are invaluable and the majority are available from the Business Manager (at present K. Hodgson, Todwick Grange, Aston, Sheffield S31 ODL) including requests by subject. Few of the Special Series books are in print, but it is hoped that some will be reprinted.

The G.B. GROUP of the P.H.S. has now started *The British Mail Coach*. REGIONAL STUDY GROUPS now cover much of England and Wales, and many have very good Journals with excellent articles. These are listed below.

---

## Source of Supply
Books in print are available in the normal way; addresses of the postal history publishers not detailed above are:

R. C. ALCOCK Ltd., 11 Regent Street, Cheltenham Glos.

ROBSON LOWE Ltd., 50 Pall Mall, London SW1Y 5JZ.

R. M. WILLCOCKS: agents VALE STAMPS, 21 Tranquil Vale, Blackheath, London SE3 OBU.

---

H. Hayes, 48 Trafalgar St., Batley, Yorks, has recently done a number of reprints of books, and has a stock of second hand books. He also runs postal auctions of literature.

Bournemouth Stamp Auctions, 39 Poole Hill, Bournemouth BH2 5PX have monthly sales containing postal history books.

---

New postal history books are handled by:
HARRIS PUBLICATIONS, 42 Maiden Lane, London W.C. 2.
G. BARRINGTON SMITH, 3 Cross Street, Oadby, Leicester.
VERA TRINDER, 38 Bedford Street, Strand, London WC2.,
and by most dealers and booksellers.

# JOIN AND LEARN FROM A SOCIETY

### THE POSTAL HISTORY SOCIETY

Interests worldwide; excellent printed Journal bi-monthly, exchange packet; monthly meetings at the National Liberal Club, London; a wide range of publications; annual conference all over the country and overseas; Subscription £3, Secretary:

**Mrs. J. Farrugia, Greenwood, Parsonage Lane, North Cray, Sidcup, Kent.**

### THE GREAT BRITAIN POSTAL HISTORY GROUP

Recently formed as a section of the P.H.S., and growing well: a printed journal, regular meetings at the National Liberal Club (mostly Saturday): subscription £2.50, or £4.50 for P.H.S. and G.B. Group. Secretary:

**Jeremy Greenwood, 50 Reigate Road, Reigate, Surrey.**

### SOCIETY OF POSTAL HISTORIANS

Interests worldwide; limited membership closed at present; duplicated bulletin quarterly, meetings monthly at the National Liberal Club, London; subscription £2.50; Secretary:

**E. G. Lovejoy, 24 Highfield Road, Sutton, Surrey,**

### EAST ANGLIA POSTAL HISTORY STUDY CIRCLE

Interests East Anglia in the widest sense; duplicated bulletin bi-monthly and some excellent books published; Saturday meetings all over the area at regular intervals and an exchange packet; subscription £2.10p; Secretary:

**H. D. Walton, 6 Towngreen, Wymondham, Norfolk.**

### LONDON POSTAL HISTORY GROUP

Interests London, all periods and widely interpreted; duplicated bulletin bi-monthly; Saturday meetings bi-monthly at Caxton Hall; a young Society hoping to publish and run an Exchange Packet in time; subscription £2; Secretary:

**M. M. English, 50 Somerden Road, Orpington, Kent, BR5 4HT.**

### CHANNEL ISLANDS SPECIALIST'S SOCIETY

Interests Channel Isle of all periods; duplicated bulletin bi-monthly and publishes catalogues; occasional meetings, exchange packets; subscription 50p; Secretary:

**O. W. Newport, 4 The Cottages, Les Hetres, St. Peter, Jersey, C.I.**

## YORKSHIRE POSTAL HISTORY GROUP

Interests Yorkshire all periods; Yorkshire's Post, a duplicated bulletin at intervals; various published books still available; Saturday meetings bi-monthly in various places, exchange packets; subscription £1; Secretary:

**W. A. Sedgewick, 25 Hunters Lane, Sheffield S13 8LA.**

## GREAT BRITAIN PHILATELIC SOCIETY

Though predominantly studying adhesive stamps from 1840, is doing a certain amount on cancellations; publishes a first class Journal bi-monthly, a newsletter, and some books; monthly meetings, subscription £6; Secretary:

**R. C. A. Payne, 14 Medway Crescent, Leigh on Sea, Essex SS9 2UY.**

## BRITISH POSTMARK SOCIETY

Predominently Twentieth Century interest; quarterly Journal, various published books; bi-monthly meetings in London, packets; subscription £1; Secretary:

**T. M. Richards, Portman Hotel, Ashley Road, Boscombe, Bournemouth, BH1 4LT.**

## WESSEX POSTAL HISTORY GROUP

For those living in Somerset, Gloucester or Wiltshire; monthly meetings (chiefly Bristol and Bath), subscription £1, holiday visitors welcome; Secretary:

**Ian M. Warn, 1 Knowsley Road, Fishponds, Bristol, BS16 2AD (Tel. 656920).**

## WELSH PHILATELIC SOCIETY

Studying Welsh Postal History; quarterly Journal and meetings in various parts of Wales; auctions at intervals, subscription £1; details from:

**Rev. A. W. R. Hughes, The Rectory, Machynlleth, Towyn, Montgomeryshire SY20 8HE, Wales**

## IRISH PHILATELIC CIRCLE

Studying Ireland, chiefly stamps; quarterly Journal, exchange packets at intervals; subscription £1.50; Secretary:

**H. J. Jamieson, 3 Cleeves Way, Hampton, Middx.**

## P.H.S. OF LANCASHIRE AND CHESHIRE

Studying this area; monthly meetings mostly in Manchester, subscription 50p; Secretary:

**Eric Turner, 19 Boswell Avenue, Audenshaw, Manchester.**

## KENT POSTAL HISTORY GROUP

Studying Kent in all periods, regular meetings in all parts of the county, the Kent Post is a good quarterly journal, subscription £2: secretary:

**R. G. Allen, O.B.E., 110 New Dover Road, Canterbury (Tel. 64067).**